The Clash of Ideas in World Politics

PRINCETON STUDIES IN INTERNATIONAL
HISTORY AND POLITICS

SERIES EDITORS

*G. John Ikenberry and Marc Trachtenberg*

(*List continues in back of book*)

# The Clash of Ideas in World Politics

## in World Politics

Transnational Networks, States, and Regime Change, 1510–2010

*John M. Owen IV*

PRINCETON UNIVERSITY PRESS

PRINCETON AND OXFORD

ISBN: 978-0-691-14238-8
ISBN (pbk.): 978-0-691-14239-5

Library of Congress Control Number: 2010928250

British Library Cataloging-in-Publication Data is available

This book has been composed in Sabon

Printed on acid-free paper ∞

press.princeton.edu

Printed in the United States of America

10  9  8  7  6  5  4  3  2  1

FOR TRISH

*Le Coeur se sature d'amour*
*comme d'un sel divin qui le conserve . . .*

# Contents

# Illustrations and Tables

## Figures

## Maps

## Tables

## A Note about the Cover Image

A 1944 Nazi propaganda poster by artist Leest Storm, intended to convince Europeans that the coming American troops were not liberators but decadent and barbarous destroyers of European culture. The text at the bottom, in Danish and Norwegian, is translated: "USA wants to save Europe's culture from going under. With what right?"

Credits: Peter Paret, Beth Irwin Lewis, and Paul Paret, *Persuasive Images: Posters of War and Revolution from the Hoover Institution Archives* (Princeton: Princeton University Press, 1992), 173; Hilde Restad, for English translation.

# Acknowledgments

THE NOTION OF WRITING a book on the tendency of states to spread their ideologies first occurred to me some years ago. I was converting my doctoral dissertation into a book. The topic was the liberal peace, the proposition that liberal democracies do not fight one another. I noticed that, time and again in the nineteenth century, liberal elites saw themselves as playing a part in a historical drama about the spread of liberty and wanted their country to propel that spread. I noticed also that nonliberal elites—absolute monarchists, for example—saw themselves in similar terms, and felt bound to promote monarchy abroad. Sometimes these drives resulted in the forcible promotion of domestic regimes. I began reading about other times and places and finding similar processes at work. Regime promotion was everywhere. Or actually not everywhere, which made it even more interesting.

This book took far too long to write, in part because I had to sort out what was happening in all of this history, and in part because I found I needed a great deal of help. Much of that help came from the kindness and generosity of many who will go unnamed here. But I must mention a few. The book would still lie in unconnected bits on my hard drive if not for the generous support of Earhart Foundation of Ann Arbor, Michigan, and the shepherding of Montgomery Brown; and of the Sesquicentennial Fund at the University of Virginia. I also thank the Institute for Advanced Studies in Culture at Virginia for support. Brian Job and the Centre of International Relations at the University of British Columbia have given me an intellectual home away from home each summer. Nuffield College and the Rothermere American Institute in Oxford hosted me for a highly productive half-year. I thank Andrew Hurrell for his sponsorship.

My colleagues at Virginia, in particular Dale Copeland, Herman Schwartz, David Jordan, Leonard Schoppa, and especially Jeffrey Legro, were interested in the project from early days and showed it by reading drafts and entertaining my often entangled ideas over lunch or impromptu chats. These, along with my colleague Gerard Alexander, kindly read an entire draft of the manuscript and, less kindly, subjected it to a three-hour scouring. In all sincerity I say that I look forward to returning the favor with each of them.

Other colleagues who have read all or part of previous drafts include Elizabeth Saunders, Todd Sechser (another Virginia colleague), Daniel Philpott, Mark Haas, Colin Dueck, Stephen Walt, Judd Owen, Stephen Krasner, Philip Potter, David Welch, Kenneth Schultz, Mira Sucharov,

Charles Doran, Jorge Benitez, Randall Schweller, and David Dessler. I presented portions of the book in various stages at colloquia at the Center for International Studies at Princeton; the Olin Institute for Strategic Studies at Harvard; the Mershon Center at Ohio State University; the Center on Democracy, Development, and the Rule of Law at Stanford; and the Program on International Security Policy at the University of Chicago. I am grateful to the colleagues and graduate students at each of these places for their trenchant critiques.

I had research help from Rachel Vanderhill and David Kearn. Without Chris Gist of the Scholar's Lab at the University of Virginia Library, there would be no map 7.1. For advice along the way—often disruptive, always productive—I thank Peter Katzenstein, Josef Joffe, Minxin Pei, Gregory Gause, Kenneth Schultz, Audrey Kurth Cronin, Joseph Nye, Alexander Wendt, Ted Hopf, Desmond King, James Davison Hunter, Andrew Hurrell, Charles Lipson, John Ikenberry, John Mearsheimer, Robert Pape, Charles Glaser, and Robert Keohane.

Portions of chapter 1 and the appendix appeared in "The Foreign Imposition of Domestic Institutions," *International Organization* 56 (2002), 375–409. I thank MIT Press for permission to re-use those portions. Preparing that paper for publication was crucial to the development of this book, and I thank the journal's editors at the time, Peter Gourevitch and David Lake, for combining relentless rigor with confidence in the project. Michael Barnett published in *Foreign Policy* a helpful commentary on that article. I also thank the two anonymous reviewers for Princeton University Press, one of whom has revealed himself to be Daniel Nexon. Dan brought to bear his formidable learning in social theory and history to make the book better. Chuck Myers at the Press has been endlessly patient and encouraging, and copyeditor Karen Verde provided superb editorial guidance. Needless to say, none of the aforementioned bear any responsibility for any errors of fact or reasoning in the book.

My long-suffering family members deserve my greatest thanks. My dear mother Pat Owen would be justified in thinking my laptop computer a strange bodily appendage. Tricia and Mark Palardy, Judd and Marion Owen, and Phil Hill and the Vancouver clan are doubtless relieved that now, when they ask me about what I am working on, I am able to talk about something other than this book. My children, Malloy, Frances, and Alice, have extended me the singular privilege of watching and helping them grow during the years of this project's gestation. A book may be an author's child, but this book is nothing beside these three living, running, talking, brilliant marvels who bring me such joy. My largest debt, and the one I feel most keenly, is to my wife Trish, to whom I dedicate this book. She is both anchor and breeze, a woman better than I deserve, lovely, amazing, and essential.

The Clash of Ideas in World Politics

# CHAPTER ONE

# Forcible Regime Promotion, Then and Now

> We are led, by events and common sense, to one conclusion:
> The survival of liberty in our land increasingly depends on
> the success of liberty in other lands. The best hope for peace
> in our world is the expansion of freedom in all the world.
> America's vital interests and our deepest beliefs are now one.
> —George W. Bush, *January 2005*

"Regime change": The ungainly phrase was once a technical neologism used by social scientists to signify the alteration of a country's fundamental political institutions. Now, around the world, it is a political term, and a polarizing one. For the verb "change" has come to imply the coercion of outside powers.[1] Regime change requires a regime changer, and in Afghanistan and Iraq the changer-in-chief has been the United States.

America's costly efforts to democratize these countries have continued under the presidency of Barack Obama, but President George W. Bush's Second Inaugural Address remains the most striking effort to frame and justify America as regime changer. Bush's critics, of course, were not impressed by the speech. The Iraq regime change in particular was not going well and seemed destined to end badly. The critics were legion, but they were not united. Some, the realists, thought Bush's policy of promoting democracy by force to be radical and moralistic, innocent of the essential nature of international relations, bound to bring on disaster. It can never be the case that America's "deepest beliefs" and "vital interests" are the same. A fundamental realist tenet is that states must always trade off some measure of their values for the sake of the national interest. Bush was departing dangerously from established prudent statecraft. He not only talked in idealistic language, he believed and acted upon it.

Setting aside, for the moment, the merits of these U.S-led wars—and there is much to criticize about each—are the realists correct? Are these wars really so extraordinary? Do states only rarely use force to try replace other states' domestic regimes? Figure 1.1 suggests otherwise.[2]

The figure depicts the frequency by decade of uses of force by one state to alter or preserve the domestic regime of another state over the past

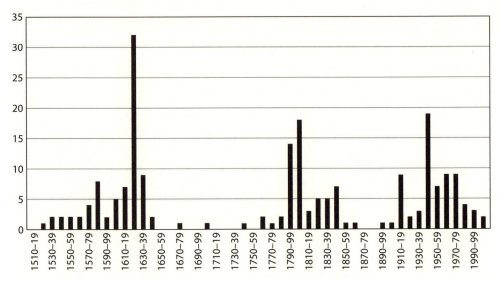

Figure 1.1 Foreign impositions of domestic institutions, 1510–2010

five hundred years. By regime I mean not simply a state's government or rulers but, following David Easton and his colleagues, its "institutions, operational rules of the game, and ideologies (goals, preferred rules, and preferred arrangements among political institutions)."[3] Some of these were what I call ex ante promotions, in which the chief object was regime promotion. Others were what I call ex post promotions, in which the initial attack was for other reasons—typically to gain strategic assets in wartime—and then, following conquest, the occupying military imposed a regime on the occupied state. Some cases are difficult to classify as exclusively ex ante or ex post. The total number of cases is 209; tables listing each promotion are below. Figure 1.1 represents raw numbers and does not control for the number of states in the international system. It also treats the estates of the Holy Roman Empire as states (see chapter 4), which affects the numbers prior to the empire's abolition in 1806. It tallies only uses of force for the purpose of altering or preserving a domestic regime; it ignores other means of promotion such as economic inducements, threats, covert action, and diplomacy. The target of regime promotion must be allowed to remain (nominally) a state; I do not include conquests that incorporate targets into empires.

Over the centuries, states have forcibly promoted domestic regimes in Europe, Asia, Latin America, and Africa. Depending upon time and place, they have promoted established Catholicism, Lutheranism, and

Calvinism; absolute monarchy, constitutional monarchy, and republicanism; communism, fascism, and liberal democracy; and secularism and Islamism. As I discuss below and throughout this book, cases of forcible regime promotion tend to cluster in time and space. The temporal and spatial patterns in the data tell us much about why states practice this particular policy. But the initial point is simply that forcible regime promotion is common enough that we can call it a normal tool of statecraft. Tables 1.1, 1.2, and 1.3, which appear later in this chapter, list each case.

President Bush faced a second set of critics, who took a less tragic view of world politics. His more liberal or idealist opponents insisted that Bush was in fact a cold and disingenuous realist. The rhetoric about freedom and tyranny masked the familiar self-aggrandizement of the American empire. The United States was replaying the old Anglo-Russian Great Game in Afghanistan and making a play in Iraq for Persian Gulf oil and the subordination of Iran. Democratization was a cover for domination.

But even if it is the case that the administration was acting out of pure self-interest in Iraq or Afghanistan, does it follow that Bush and his advisers did not care whether these countries ended up with democratic or constitutional regimes? If not, they certainly went to great lengths to continue the charade. It would have been much more efficient to set up new, more pliable dictators in place of the old ones. Figure 1.1 suggests that there have been scores of cases in which governments made calculations similar to those of Bush, spending dear resources to change a target state's regime and not simply its leadership. In fact, as I make clear in the chapters that follow, governments or rulers who use force to promote an ideology abroad nearly always believe it is in their interests to do so. They believe that they are shaping their foreign or domestic environment, or both, in their favor. Furthermore, although it is an open question whether the Bush administration was correct regarding Iraq, history shows that governments who try to impose regimes on other countries are usually right, at least in the short term. Conditions sometimes arise under which it is rational for a government to use force to change or preserve another country's domestic regime; when an intervention succeeds, the government that did the promotion is better off, the country it governs more secure.

We have here, then, something much larger than the Bush Doctrine or the war on terror or an attempt to democratize the Muslim world. We have regularity, a historically common state practice, which is surprisingly under-studied. It is a highly consequential practice, for it involves the use of force. It entails violations of sovereignty, a building block of the modern international system.[4] It is not a trivial practice or an afterthought, but a costly policy—costly not simply in its use of the promoting state's resources but in the way it can exacerbate international conflicts.

Indeed, as will become evident, forcible regime promotion can be a self-multiplying phenomenon, making great-power relations more violent and dangerous. A Habsburg invasion of Bohemia in 1618 to suppress a Protestant uprising spiraled into the Thirty Years' War. In 1830, an Anglo-French intervention on behalf of the liberal Belgian revolt alienated Prussia, Austria, and Russia, and raised the prospect of great-power war. The Soviet invasion of Afghanistan in 1979 to shore up a communist regime caused the thawing Cold War to return to a deep freeze. Forcible regime promotion can create all manner of problems in world politics even as it mitigates short-term difficulties. On the other hand, foreign regime imposition can yield benefits to the states that practice it by helping them entrench their hegemony.[5] It can also produce periods of stable relations among great powers, as in the decades following 1648, 1815, and 1945.[6] So how do we explain this regularity? What causes forcible regime promotion?

Governments tend to impose regimes in regions of the world where there is already deep disagreement as to the best form of government. They also tend to do it in moments when elites across societies in the target's region are sharply dividing along ideological lines, a condition I call *transnational ideological polarization*. Ideological polarization means that elites temporarily have unusually strong preferences for either ideology A or competing ideology B and strong preferences for aligning with states that exemplify their favored ideology. Such polarization can present governments with either or both of two incentives to use force to promote regimes. The first is what I call *external security* or a government's desire to alter or maintain the international balance of power in its favor. When elites across states are highly polarized by ideology, a government of a great power can make a target state into an ally, or keep it as one, by promoting the right ideology. The great-power ruler may also have a rival that exemplifies the competing ideology and has a parallel incentive to promote that ideology in the target; in such cases, each great power has an incentive to pre-empt the other by promoting its ideology.

The second incentive I call *internal security*, or a government's desire to strengthen its power at home. Internal security is at play when transnational ideological polarization reaches into the great power itself and jeopardizes the government's hold on power by rousing opposition to its regime. Precisely because the threat is transnational, the government can degrade it by attacking it abroad as well as at home. By suppressing an enemy ideology abroad, it can remove a source of moral and perhaps material support for enemy ideologues at home. It can make domestic ideological foes look disloyal or unpatriotic if they oppose this use of force. It can halt or reverse any impression elites may have that the enemy ideology has transnational momentum.

By no means has transnational ideological polarization been a constant feature of the past half-millennium; at many times elites cared relatively little about regime loyalties or ideologies. What triggers polarization, and hence forcible regime promotions, is either of two types of event. The first is *regime instability* in one or more states in the region. By regime instability I mean a sharp increase in the probability that one regime will be replaced by another via revolution, coup d'état, legitimate government succession, or other means; or a fresh regime change that has yet to be consolidated. Regime instability triggers transnational ideological polarization via demonstration effects, or the increasing plausibility among elites that other countries could follow suit by likewise undergoing regime instability. The second type of triggering event is a *great-power war*. A great-power war may have little to do initially with ideology, but if the belligerents exemplify competing regime types then their fighting will be seen by elites across societies as implicating the larger ideological struggle, and those elites will tend to polarize over ideology. Many of the promotions in figure 1.1 were triggered by regime instability; many others, mostly captured by the tall bars, tend to come during and after great-power wars.

The transnational nature of ideological polarization is crucial: elites across countries segregate simultaneously, and in reaction to one another, over ideology. Furthermore, they tend to polarize over a set of two or three ideologies that is fixed for many decades. Indeed, figure 1.1 depicts three long waves of forcible regime promotion, and these roughly correspond to three long transnational contests over the best regime. The first wave took place in Central and Western Europe between the 1520s and early eighteenth century, and pitted established Catholicism against various forms of established Protestantism. The second took place in Europe and the Americas between the 1770s and late nineteenth century; the regimes in question were republicanism, constitutional monarchy, and absolute monarchy. The third took place over most of the world between the late 1910s and 1980s, and the antagonists were communism, liberalism, and (until 1945) fascism. Today, a fourth struggle runs through the Muslim world, a struggle pitting secularism against various forms of Islamism. It is that struggle that helped pull the Bush administration into using force in Iraq and Afghanistan. But figure 1.1 also shows historical gaps, when no such contest over the best regime cut across states. During those gaps states used force regularly, but not to impose regimes on other states.

That forcible regime promotion occurs in such patterns—long waves over many decades, followed by long gaps—and that within each long wave the regimes being promoted are within the same fixed set, requires that we push the explanation further, to a macro-level of analysis. What explains these long waves of promotion? I argue that during each of these long waves a social structure was in place in the regions in question that heavily conditioned the preferences and actions of elites, including rulers of states. That structure was the transnational regime contest itself. Elites held a general understanding that there was such a contest stretching across their region, that it was consequential, and that at some point they might have to choose sides. It was not simply that some states had one regime and others had another, for that is typical in world politics. What made a contest was the existence across states of networks of elites who wanted to spread one regime and roll others back. These I call *transnational ideological networks* or TINs, and they were one type of agent who perpetuated the structure. Another type of agent was the rulers who ordered forcible regime promotion, because such promotion continued to energize the TINs and keep alive the general notion that there was an ongoing contest across the region over the best regime. Structure and agents were endogenous: the structure helped cause the agents to bring about forcible regime promotion, and promotion by those agents helped perpetuate the structure.

If these social structures are so consequential, but come and go (however slowly), then we must push the explanation even further: Why do these transnational regime contests arise when and where they do? Why do they persist as long as they do? Why do they fade away when they do? To complete my arguments I offer an evolutionary model analogous to Thomas Kuhn's account of scientific revolutions. A transnational contest over the best regime emerges in a region when the region's predominant regime type is beset with an accumulation of serious anomalies, but sufficient numbers of elites still adhere to it. Reformers and status quo advocates spiral into hostility and a state adopts a new regime. Over the course of a contest still other new regime types may emerge and capture states. The contest endures as long as no one regime is manifestly superior to its competitors. When one or more contending regimes encounters sufficient serious anomalies, however, elites will abandon it and affiliate with the surviving regime. This model is "ecological," appealing to the social and material environments of governments and other agents. Although ideologies can go on for some time shaping the environment, eventually exogenous material and social factors push back.

In sum, I advance arguments on a micro-level of analysis, concerning individual regime promotions, and a macro-level, concerning the transnational social structure that makes those promotions more likely. As I discuss in chapters 7 and 8, my arguments have a great deal to say about ongoing American promotions of democracy in Afghanistan and Iraq. Since the 1920s, the Muslim world—particularly in Southwest Asia and North Africa—has been going through a transnational struggle over the best regime. The antagonists are various forms of Islamism, which insists that positive law derive directly from divine law or *Shariah*, and various forms of secularism. Like the other ideological contests, this one is complex. But it does implicate the foreign alignments of Muslim states, with Islamist networks tending toward extreme anti-Americanism. The Islamism-secularism contest is by no means responsible for America's heavy presence in the Middle East—oil and Israel are the two most obvious factors—but it did help cause the two regime promotions that are the most costly aspects of that presence. One of the most grievous mistakes of the Bush administration was to think that the United States could somehow transcend the Muslims' ideological contest. Americans have found themselves regarded, at least by Islamists, as entrants into that contest, co-belligerents with the secularist enemy. The United States is not ending the struggle, but helping perpetuate it.

This book, then, is not simply about regime change. It is about grand contests over the best regime that cut across entire regions. It is, in effect, an alternative history of the past five centuries of international relations. I do not offer a teleological story in which humanity is being pulled in a particular direction. But I do claim that international history, viewed through this lens, exhibits some clear macro-patterns. A region is dominated for decades by a single regime type. Eventually that type enters a crisis and faces one or more competitors, and a long struggle ensues in the region over the best regime. That struggle both helps cause, and is sustained by, forcible regime promotion. One regime type emerges as manifestly superior, and the struggle ends with the domination of that regime. Eventually the pattern is repeated. The events that trigger these patterns are themselves unpredictable, but once a trigger is squeezed the results are, broadly speaking, predictable. Following Jon Elster, I aim at mechanistic rather than at covering-law explanation. I cannot provide a complete list of necessary and sufficient conditions for forcible regime promotion; the world is too fraught with contingency for that. I do argue that promotion tends to happen when certain conditions are present.[7]

My arguments do not explain all of the cases in figure 1.1. A number of forcible regime promotions by the United States in Latin America and the Caribbean in the first third of the twentieth century had little or nothing to do with transnational ideological movements. I discuss these briefly in chapter 6. The vast majority of cases, however, are susceptible to my arguments.

• • •

This book is the first to consider forcible regime promotion as a general international relations phenomenon. But I am certainly not the first to have argued that states fight over ideas or that those ideas have changed over time. Martin Wight observed that the past half millennium of international history could be divided into normal and revolutionary periods, with the revolutionary periods roughly corresponding to my three long waves in figure 1.1.[8] Raymond Aron contrasted homogeneous and heterogeneous international systems along similar criteria.[9] K. J. Holsti has mapped out the changes in issues over which states have fought over the past several centuries.[10] David Skidmore and his colleagues have published pathbreaking work on the importance of "contested social orders" in international relations.[11] Mark N. Katz has illumined the dynamics of revolutionary waves across societies.[12] J. H. Leurdijk has given exhaustive treatment to forcible intervention and its purposes, including the promotion of political systems.[13] And many scholars, from Richard Rosecrance[14] and George Liska[15] a generation ago to Stephen Walt,[16] Mark Haas,[17] Gregory Gause,[18] and others more recently, have written on the systematic effects of ideology on threat perception and conflict. As will be clear in chapters 2 and 3, I also borrow and build upon theoretical tools that others have fashioned, including analysis of agent-structure endogeneity, of transnational networks, and of positive feedback and path-dependence.

For all of these debts and syntheses, my arguments about forcible regime promotion do contradict various international relations theories at significant points. I emphasize two—one concerning realism and the other concerning constructivism. Realism, I argue, cannot give good reasons why states should impose regimes on other states; in fact it gives good reasons why they should not do so. Realism abstracts from states' domestic properties, apart from their military power (which is always relative). That is because realists insist that domestic properties, including regime type, have no systematic, generalizable effects on international relations. Thus, when states incur expected costs by using force to alter other states' regimes, they are doing something beyond the predictive power of realism. For some versions of realism, forcible regime promotion is anomalous. For others, it should only happen to the extent that states are externally secure and have the luxury of indulging domestic constituencies that want to export the regime.[19] Thus, it is no accident that the United States promoted democracy in Haiti in 1994, because in 1994 U.S. security was high and the country could afford to spend resources in that sort of way.

The trouble is that, as I explicate further below, forcible regime promotion tends to happen more when international security is scarce, as in hot or cold war, rather than when it is plentiful. The U.S.-Haiti case is unusual; more typical are promotions and counter-promotions by states seeking to increase their security and extend their power. Indeed, I limit my dependent variable to uses of force on sovereign states (see this book's appendix for coding rules) in part because those are anomalous for at least certain versions of realism. States use cheaper, less lethal methods to promote regimes abroad, and of course imperial powers often try to alter the political institutions of the lands they colonize, but realists are less concerned with these cheaper activities. My arguments in chapter 2 and case studies in chapters 4 through 7 explicate my differences with realism. I certainly agree that rulers seek to gain, hold, and extend their states' power; but I maintain that the ways they pursue power are constrained by ideas and the transnational networks that carry them.

My argument may be taken to be constructivist in its emphasis on the structural properties of ideological contests, but it takes issue with a strong strand within constructivism I call social-interactionist. Social interactionism takes the view that social structures, while powerful, are usually susceptible to change by creative agents. No constructivist is so naïve as to think that any agent at any time and place can change long-established mind-sets and practices. But many scholars in that school of thought argue for fairly general and common conditions for structural change. My own argument is what Paul Kowert and Jeffrey Legro call "ecological," laying out relatively rare and stringent conditions for structural change.[20] The point is not merely academic, for as I argue in chapter 8, social interactionism implies policies toward ideological adversaries, such as radical Islamists, that are at odds with my own. No doubt norms in some social realms may change without ecological changes, but I argue that transnational contests over the best regime are not among their number.

This book thus falls squarely within the large category of recent international relations scholarship insisting that "ideas matter." As several scholars recently have observed, few dispute that ideas "matter," in part because "matter" is such an imprecise verb. But disagreements endure over whether ideas are causal (external to actors) or constitutive (part of who actors are), and, if causal, which ones under what conditions. I treat ideas as causal, as structures that heavily condition actors' options, but as consequences as well of large, dimly understood social and material changes. In contrast to most constructivist work, which emphasizes "good" or "progressive" or "emancipatory" ideas—the ideas that modern liberal analysts like—I focus on all manner of political ideas, including many that exclude persons and groups. I am answering the call some constructivists have issued to study the effects of ideas decidedly alien to any liberal or social-democratic notion of shared human purpose or progress.[21] Indeed, it is clear that even ideas that are presented by their advocates as progressive and inclusive are taken by their foes to be hegemonic and exclusive. All of these ideas are vital to an explanation of crucial aspects of international politics. If scholars are truly to take ideas seriously, they must include ideas of which they disapprove, and recognize that those of which they do approve are not necessarily as universal as they think.[22]

Patterns in the Data

Tables 1.1, 1.2, and 1.3 list the universe of cases of forcible regime promotion since 1500 in the Western states system, which became global in the twentieth century. (See this book's appendix for criteria of inclusion.) A number of significant patterns emerge from the data.

### Forcible Regime Promotion Is Common

The most obvious fact is that forcible regime promotion is a fairly common practice of statecraft in the modern international system. In each case at least one state used force in order to alter or preserve another's domestic regime, either by direct invasion or by occupying the target state following victory in a war. Cases in which multiple states intervened on the same side are counted once; cases in which two or more states intervened on opposite sides are counted as two cases. It is worth noting that forcible regime promotions have been common in times and places that I do not cover in this book. Thucydides describes cases in Greece in the fifth century B.C. During the Corcyræan civil war, the Athenians intervened on behalf of the commoners, the Spartans on behalf of the oligarchs.[23] In medieval Italy, the Guelphs promoted commercial republicanism, the Ghibellines oligarchy, often in one another's cities.[24]

### Three Waves, Three Ideological Struggles

Forcible regime promotion has been especially common in three long periods: between 1520 and 1650, 1770 and 1850, and 1917 and the present day. Non-forcible regime promotion, which is more difficult to trace over the centuries, has probably been even more common. During the Cold War, for example, the Americans and Soviets commonly used economic incentives and subversion to alter foreign states' regimes; these attempts do not appear in the data. These three long periods are generally regarded as ideologically charged. Indeed, part of what we mean by "ideologically charged" is that relatively more forcible regime promotion took place during these times.

The types of regime promoted over time have varied considerably, but in a given period the types were usually two or three. During the first wave (1520–1650), Catholic and Protestant princes struggled to establish or maintain regimes of their own type in other polities. A monarch would often send troops or ships to a polity torn by a civil war between Catholics and Protestants and fight on behalf of one side. Typical were promotions by Elizabeth I of England on behalf of Protestantism in Scotland (1559–60), France (1562–63, 1585, and 1590–91), and the Netherlands

TABLE 1.1
Forcible Regime Promotion, 1510–1700

| Case | Promoter | Great Power? | Close Neighbor? | Promoter's institutions? | Target(s) | Target unrest?* | Year(s) | Counter-Promotion? |
|------|----------|--------------|-----------------|--------------------------|-----------|-----------------|---------|--------------------|
| 1 | Hesse | | x | x | Mainz & Würzburg | | 1528 | |
| 2 | Hesse et al. | | x | x | Württemberg | | 1534 | |
| 3 | Hesse, Saxony, et al. | | x | x | Münster | x | 1535 | |
| 4 | Hesse, Saxony, et al. | | x | x | Brunswick-Wolfenbüttel | | 1542 | |
| 5 | HRE et al. | x | x | x | Lutheran estates | | 1546 | |
| 6 | France | x | | x | Scotland | x | 1559–60 | |
| 7 | England | | x | x | Scotland | x | 1559–60 | x |
| 8 | England | | x | x | France | x | 1562–63 | |
| 9 | Palatinate | | x | x | France | x | 1568 | |
| 10 | France, | x | x | | Netherlands | x | 1572 | |
| | England, | | x | x | | | | |
| | Scotland, | | | x | | | | |
| | Nassau | | x | x | | | | |
| 11 | Palatinate | | x | x | France | x | 1576 | |
| 12 | Palatinate | | x | x | Netherlands | x | 1578 | |
| 13 | Spain, | x | | x | Ireland | x | 1578–80 | |
| | Papal States | | | x | (England) | | | |
| 14 | HRE | x | x | x | Aachen | x | 1581 | |
| 15 | Spain, | x | x | x | Cologne | x | 1583–89 | |
| | Bavaria | | | x | | | | |
| 16 | Palatinate, | | x | x | Cologne | x | 1583-89 | x |
| | Netherlands | | | x | | | | |
| 17 | England | | x | x | France | x | 1585 | |
| 18 | Palatinate | | x | x | France | x | 1587 | |
| 19 | Spain | x | x | x | England | | 1588 | |
| 20 | Spain | x | x | x | France | x | 1589–98 | x |
| 21 | England | x | x | x | Netherlands | x | 1585–1611 | |

TABLE 1.1 *(continued)*

| Case | Promoter | Great Power? | Close Neighbor? | Promoter's institutions? | Target(s) | Target unrest?* | Year(s) | Counter-Promotion? |
|------|----------|--------------|-----------------|--------------------------|-----------|-----------------|---------|--------------------|
| 22 | England | x | x | x | France | x | 1590–91 | |
| 23 | HRE | x | | x | Aachen | | 1598 | |
| 24 | HRE | x | x | x | Transylvania | | 1604–6 | |
| 25 | HRE, Bavaria | x | x | x | Donauwörth | x | 1606–10 | |
| 26 | Passau/Strassburg | | | x | Cleves-Jülich | | 1609–10 | |
| 27 | Nassau, | | | x | Cleves-Jülich | | 1609–10 | x |
| | England, | x | | x | | | | |
| | France | x | | | | | | |
| 28 | Prot. Union | | x | x | Strassburg | | 1609 | |
| 29 | Cath. League | | x | x | Strassburg | | 1610 | x |
| 30 | HRE | x | x | x | Transylvania | | 1611–13 | |
| 31 | Netherlands | | x | | France | x | 1616 | |
| 32 | Spain, Bavaria | x | | x | Bohemia, Moravia | x | 1618–22 | |
| 33 | Prot. Union | | x | x | Bohemia, Moravia | x | 1618–22 | x |
| 34 | Transylvania | | x | x | Habsburg Hungary | x | 1619 | x |
| 35 | Poland | | x | x | Habsburg Hungary | x | 1619 | x |
| 36 | Transylvania | | x | x | Lower Austria | x | 1620 | |
| 37 | HRE | x | x | x | Upper Austria | x | 1620 | |
| 38 | HRE | x | x | x | Palatinate | | 1623 | |
| 39 | Cath. Lg. | | x | x | Upper Austria | | 1620–25 | x |
| 40 | Cath. Lg. | | x | x | Upper Palatinate | | 1621 | x |
| 41 | Spain, | x | | x | Valtellina | x | 1620–26 | |
| | HRE, | x | | x | | | | |
| | Genoa | | | x | | | | |
| 42 | Gray Leagues, | | x | x | Valtellina | x | 1621 | x |
| | Bern, Zürich, | | | x | | | | |
| | Venice | | | | | | | |
| 43 | Baden | | x | x | Lower Palatinate | | 1622 | x |
| 44 | Spain | x | x | x | Jülich | | 1622 | |

Table 1.1 *(continued)*

| Case | Promoter | Great Power? | Close Neighbor? | Promoter's institutions? | Target(s) | Target unrest?* | Year(s) | Counter-Promotion? |
|------|----------|--------------|-----------------|--------------------------|-----------|-----------------|---------|--------------------|
| 45 | Transylvania | | x | x | Habsburg Hungary | | 1623 | |
| 46 | Spain | x | x | x | Netherlands | | 1624–29 | |
| 47 | Denmark | | | x | Lower Saxony | | 1625–29 | |
| 48 | England | x | | x | Palatinate | | 1625 | x |
| 49 | France | x | | x | Valtellina | | 1624–25 | x |
| 50 | Transylvania | | x | x | Moravia | | 1626 | |
| 51 | Bavaria | | x | x | Moravia | | 1626 | x |
| 52 | Spain | x | x | x | France | x | 1627 | |
| 53 | England | x | x | x | France | x | 1627–29 | x |
| 54 | France | x | x | x | England | | 1627–29 | |
| 55 | HRE | x | x | x | Lübeck | | 1629 | |
| 56 | HRE | x | x | x | Ratzeburg | x | 1629 | |
| 57 | HRE | x | x | x | Schwerin | x | 1629 | |
| 58 | HRE | x | x | x | Mecklenburg | | 1629 | |
| 59 | HRE | x | x | x | Brandenburg | | 1629 | |
| 60 | HRE | x | x | x | Magdeburg | | 1629 | |
| 61 | HRE | x | x | x | Halberstadt | | 1629 | x |
| 62 | HRE | x | x | x | Verden | | 1629 | |
| 63 | HRE | x | x | x | Bremen | | 1629 | |
| 64 | HRE | x | x | x | Merseburg | | 1629 | |
| 65 | HRE | x | x | x | Naumburg | | 1629 | |
| 66 | HRE | x | x | x | Meissen | | 1629 | |
| 67 | HRE | x | x | x | Minden | | 1629 | |
| 68 | Sweden | x | | x | Magdeburg | | 1630 | x |
| 69 | Cath. Lg. | | x | x | Saxony | | 1630 | |
| 70 | Sweden | x | | x | Frankfurt | | 1631 | |
| 71 | Sweden | x | | x | Mainz | | 1631 | |
| 72 | Saxony | | x | x | Habsburg lands | | 1631 | |
| 73 | Sweden | x | | x | Bavaria | | 1633 | |
| 74 | HRE, | x | | x | Württemberg | | 1634–38 | |
| | Bavaria | | x | x | | | | |

TABLE 1.1 *(continued)*

| Case | Promoter | Great Power? | Close Neighbor? | Promoter's institutions? | Target(s) | Target unrest?* | Year(s) | Counter-Promotion? |
|------|----------|--------------|-----------------|--------------------------|-----------|-----------------|---------|---------------------|
| 75 | France | x | | x | Valtellina | | 1635 | x |
| 76 | Sweden | x | | x | Habsburg lands | | 1639–45 | |
| 77 | Transylvania | | x | x | Habsburg lands | | 1644–45 | |
| 78 | HRE | x | x | x | Transylvania | | 1644–45 | |
| 79 | France | x | | x | Netherlands | | 1672–78 | |

* During the Thirty Years' War, central Europe experienced general war; cases only count here if violence was clearly used to promote a regime.

Habsburg lands denotes areas directly ruled by the Habsburgs.

The Catholic League and Protestant Union each comprised various German princes.

HRE refers to the troops of the Holy Roman Emperor.

Netherlands refers to the United Provinces, the Protestant state independent of Habsburg rule as of 1572.

*Sources*: Ronald Asch, *The Thirty Years' War: The Holy Roman Empire and Europe* (New York: Macmillan, 1997); Karl Brandi, *The Emperor Charles V: The Growth and Destiny of a Man and of a World-Empire*, trans. C. V. Wedgwood (London: Jonathan Cape, 1939); Claus-Peter Clasen, *The Palatinate in European History 1555–1618* (Oxford: Basil Blackwell, 1966); J. H. Elliott, *Imperial Spain 1469–1716* (London: Penguin, 2002); Hajo Holborn, *A History of Modern Germany*, vol. 1, *The Reformation* (London: Eyre & Spottiswoode, 1965); Robert A. Kann, *A History of the Habsburg Empire 1526–1918* (Berkeley: University of California Press, 1974); Evan Luard, *War in International Society* (London: I. B. Tauris, 1986); David Maland, *Europe at War 1600–1650* (London: Macmillan, 1980); Geoffrey Parker, *The Grand Strategy of Philip II* (New Haven, CT: Yale University Press, 1998); idem, ed., *The Thirty Years' War*, 2nd ed. (New York: Routledge, 1997); D. H. Pennington, *Europe in the Seventeenth Century*, 2nd ed. (London: Longman, 1989); N. M. Sutherland, *Princes, Politics, and Religion, 1574–1589* (London: Hambledon, 1984); R. B. Wernham, *Before the Armada: The Emergence of the English Nation, 1485–1588* (New York: Norton, 1966).

(1572–1603); and by Philip II of Spain on behalf of Catholicism in Cologne (1583–89), England (1588), and France (1589–94).

During the second wave (1770–1850), governments imposed republican (non-monarchical), constitutional-monarchical, and absolute-monarchical regimes. In the 1790s, French governments forcibly installed republican regimes in a number of small neighbors. Napoleon (r. 1799–1815) tried to impose his particular type of bureaucratic-rational institutions, and at various times his enemies tried to reverse his promotions. In 1814–15, the victorious anti-French coalition reestablished monarchy in France. In the following three decades, the typical international intervention consisted of an absolute monarchy (Austrian, Russian, Prussian, and sometimes French) invading a weaker state in Germany, Italy, or Iberia and defeating or overturning a republican or constitutional revolution. In

TABLE 1.2
Forcible Regime Promotion, 1701–1879

| Case | Promoter | Great Power? | Close Neighbor? | Promoter's institutions? | Target(s) | Target unrest? | Year(s) | Counter-Promotion? |
|---|---|---|---|---|---|---|---|---|
| 1 | France | x | x | x | England | x | 1702 | |
| 2 | Prussia | x | x | x | Austria | | 1740 | |
| 3 | Russia | x | x | | Poland | x | 1768 | |
| 4 | France, Turkey | x x | | | Poland | x | 1768 | x |
| 5 | France | x | | | United States | x | 1778 | |
| 6 | France, Sardinia, Bern | x | x x | | Geneva | x | 1782 | |
| 7 | Prussia | x | | x | Netherlands | x | 1787 | |
| 8 | Prussia | x | | | Liège | x | 1790 | |
| 9 | Russia, Prussia | x | x | x | Poland | x | 1792-93 | |
| 10 | France | x | | x | Austria | | 1792-97 | |
| 11 | France | x | | x | Prussia | | 1792-97 | |
| 12 | France | x | x | x | Britain | | 1793-97 | |
| 13 | Britain | x | | x | Corsica | x | 1794 | |
| 14 | France | x | x | x | Netherlands | | 1795 | |
| 15 | France | x | x | x | Bologna, etc. | x | 1796 | |
| 16 | France | x | | x | Lombardy, etc. | | 1797 | |
| 17 | France | x | x | x | Genoa | | 1797 | |
| 18 | France | x | | x | Rome | | 1798 | |
| 19 | France | x | x | x | Switzerland | | 1798 | |
| 20 | France | x | | x | Naples | | 1798 | |
| 21 | Britain | x | | x | Naples | | 1799 | x |
| 22 | France | x | | x | Tuscany | | 1801 | |
| 23 | France | x | | x | Cisalpine Rep. | | 1803 | |
| 24 | France | x | x | x | Helvetic Rep. | | 1803 | |
| 25 | France | x | x | x | Italian Rep. | | 1804 | |
| 26 | France | x | x | x | NW Germany | | 1804 | |
| 27 | France | x | x | x | Lucca | | 1805 | |
| 28 | France | x | | x | Tyrol | | 1805 | |
| 29 | France | x | x | x | Spain | | 1806 | |

TABLE 1.2 *(continued)*

| Case | Promoter | Great Power? | Close Neighbor? | Promoter's institutions? | Target(s) | Target unrest? | Year(s) | Counter-Promotion? |
|---|---|---|---|---|---|---|---|---|
| 30 | France | x | x | x | Batavian Rep. | | 1806 | |
| 31 | France | x | x | x | Neuchâtel | | 1806 | |
| 32 | France | x | x | x | Württemberg | | 1806 | |
| 33 | France | x | x | x | Baden | | 1806 | |
| 34 | France | x | | x | Bavaria | | 1806 | |
| 35 | France | x | | x | Frankfurt | | 1806 | |
| 36 | France | x | x | x | Naples | | 1806 | |
| 37 | France | x | x | x | Nassau | | 1806 | |
| 38 | France | x | | x | Hesse-Cassel, | | 1807 | |
| | | | | x | Brunswick, et al. | | | |
| 39 | France | x | | x | Poland | | 1807 | |
| 40 | Britain | x | | x | Sicily | | 1811 | |
| 41 | Austria, | x | | x | France | | 1814 | |
| | Prussia, | x | | x | | | | |
| | Russia, | x | | x | | | | |
| | Britain | x | x | x | | | | |
| 42 | Austria, | x | x | | Switzerland | | 1815 | x |
| | Prussia, | | | | | | | |
| | Russia, | | | | | | | |
| | Britain | | | | | | | |
| 43 | Austria | x | | x | Naples | x | 1821 | |
| 44 | Austria | x | x | x | Piedmont | x | 1821 | |
| 45 | France | x | x | x | Spain | x | 1823 | |
| 46 | Britain | x | | x | Portugal | x | 1826 | |
| 47 | Spain | x | | x | Portugal | x | 1826 | |
| 48 | Austria | x | x | x | Modena | x | 1831 | |
| 49 | Austria | x | x | x | Parma | x | 1831 | |
| 50 | Austria | x | x | x | Papal States | x | 1831-32 | |
| 51 | Britain, | x | | x | Spain | x | 1833-39 | |
| | France | x | x | x | | | | |
| 52 | Britain, | | | x | Portugal | x | 1834 | |
| | Spain | x | x | x | | | | |

TABLE 1.2 *(continued)*

| Case | Promoter | Great Power? | Close Neighbor? | Promoter's institutions? | Target(s) | Target unrest? | Year(s) | Counter-Promotion? |
|------|----------|--------------|-----------------|--------------------------|-----------|----------------|---------|--------------------|
| 53 | Britain, | x | | x | Portugal | x | 1846-47 | |
| | Spain | | x | x | | | | |
| 54 | France, | x | | x | Papal States | x | 1849 | |
| | Austria, | x | x | x | | | | |
| | Two Sicilies, | | x | x | | | | |
| | Spain | | | x | | | | |
| 55 | Prussia | x | x | x | Saxony | x | 1849 | |
| 56 | Austria | x | | x | Tuscany | x | 1849 | |
| 57 | Prussia | x | | x | Bavaria | x | 1849 | |
| 58 | Prussia | x | | x | Baden | x | 1849 | |
| 59 | Russia | x | x | x | Transylvania | x | 1849 | |
| 60 | Austria | x | | x | Sardinia | x | 1859 | |
| 61 | France | x | | x | Mexico | | 1862-67 | |

*Sources:* Jeremy Black, *Eighteenth-Century Europe* (New York: St. Martin's Press, 1999); T.C.W. Blanning, *The French Revolutionary Wars* (New York: Arnold, 1996); Michael Broers, *Europe under Napoleon 1799–1815* (London: Arnold, 1996); idem, *Europe after Napoleon: Revolution, Reaction and Romanticism, 1814–1848* (New York: Manchester University Press, 1996); Charles J. Esdaile, *The Wars of Napoleon* (London: Longman, 1995); George Childs Kohn, *Dictionary of Wars*, rev. ed. (New York: Facts on File, 1999); J. H. Leurdijk, *Intervention in International Politics* (Leeuwarden, The Netherlands: B.V. Eisma, 1986); Evan Luard, *War in International Society* (London: I. B. Tauris, 1986); R. R. Palmer, *The Age of the Democratic Revolution: A Political History of Europe and America 1760–1800*, vol. 2, *The Struggle* (Princeton, NJ: Princeton University Press, 1962).

a few cases, however, constitutional monarchies—usually Britain, sometimes joined by France during its constitutional periods—used force to promote their regime and block the spread of absolutism.

During the third wave (1919–today), governments forcibly exported liberal democracy, communism, or fascism. The wave began when various allies from the First World War tried to overturn Bolshevism in Russia; there quickly followed Soviet attempts to spread Bolshevism to neighboring Finland, Poland, and Iran. In the 1930s, Spain was a target for the Italian, German, and Soviet governments. The aftermath of the Second World War saw a cascade of forcible promotions by the governments of both superpowers on weaker states in Europe and Asia. In subsequent decades, the Soviets intervened on several occasions to uphold commu-

TABLE 1.3
Forcible Regime Promotion, 1880–Present

| Case | Promoter | Great Power? | Close Neighbor? | Promoter's institutions? | Target(s) | Target unrest? | Year(s) | Counter-Promotion? |
|---|---|---|---|---|---|---|---|---|
| 1 | U.S. | x | x | x | Cuba | x | 1899-1901 | |
| 2 | U.S. | x | x | x | Cuba | | 1899 | |
| 3 | U.S. | x | x | | Cuba | x | 1906 | |
| 4 | Britain, | x | | x | Albania | x | 1912 | |
| | Russia, | x | | | | | | |
| | Germany, | x | | x | | | | |
| | France, | x | | | | | | |
| | Austria-Hungary, | x | x | x | | | | |
| | Italy | | x | x | | | | |
| 5 | U.S. | x | x | x | Mexico | x | 1914 | |
| 6 | U.S. | x | x | x | Haiti | x | 1915 | |
| 7 | U.S. | x | x | x | Dom. Rep. | x | 1916 | |
| 8 | U.S. | x | x | x | Cuba | x | 1917 | |
| 9 | U.S.S.R. | | x | x | Finland | x | 1918 | |
| 10 | Germany | x | x | x | Finland | x | 1918 | x |
| 11 | Britain, | x | | x | U.S.S.R. | x | 1918 | |
| | U.S., | x | | x | | | | |
| | France, | x | | x | | | | |
| | Japan, | x | x | | | | | |
| | Italy | | | x | | | | |
| 12 | France, | x | x | x | Hungary | x | 1919 | |
| | Romania | | | x | | | | |
| 13 | U.S.S.R. | | x | x | Poland | | 1920 | |
| 14 | U.S.S.R | | x | x | Iran | x | 1920 | |
| 15 | Germany, | x | | x | Spain | x | 1936 | |
| | Italy | | | x | | | | |
| 16 | U.S.S.R. | | | | Spain | x | 1936 | x |
| 17 | Germany | x | x | x | Slovakia | | 1939 | |
| 18 | Germany | x | x | x | France (Vichy) | | 1940 | |

TABLE 1.3 *(continued)*

| Case | Promoter | Great Power? | Close Neighbor? | Promoter's institutions? | Target(s) | Target unrest? | Year(s) | Counter-Promotion? |
|------|----------|-------------|-----------------|--------------------------|-----------|----------------|---------|--------------------|
| 19 | Germany | x | x | x | Croatia | | 1941 | |
| 20 | U.S., Britain | x | | x | Italy | | 1943 | |
| 21 | Britain | x | | x | Greece | x | 1944 | x |
| 22 | U.S., | x | | x | France | | 1944 | x |
| | Britain, | | x | x | | | | |
| | Canada | | | x | | | | |
| 23 | U.S.S.R. | x | x | x | Bulgaria | x | 1944 | |
| 24 | U.S., | x | x | x | W. Germany | | 1944 | |
| | Britain | x | | x | | | | |
| 25 | U.S.S.R. | x | x | x | Poland | | 1944 | |
| 26 | U.S.S.R. | x | x | x | Romania | | 1944 | |
| 27 | U.S.S.R. | x | | x | Albania | | 1944 | |
| 28 | U.S.S.R. | x | x | x | E. Germany | | 1945 | |
| 29 | U.S.S.R. | x | x | x | Yugoslavia | x | 1945 | x |
| 30 | U.S.S.R. | x | x | x | Czechoslo. | | 1945 | |
| 31 | U.S.S.R. | x | x | x | Hungary | | 1945 | |
| 32 | U.S. | x | | x | Japan | | 1945 | |
| 33 | U.S.S.R. | x | x | x | Iran | x | 1945 | |
| 34 | U.S. | x | | | South Korea | | 1945 | |
| 35 | U.S.S.R. | x | x | x | North Korea | | 1945 | |
| 36 | North Korea | | x | x | China | | 1947 | |
| 37 | U.S. et al. | x | | | South Korea | | 1950 | |
| 38 | China, | | x | x | South Korea | | 1950 | x |
| | U.S.S.R. | x | x | x | | | 1950 | |
| 39 | U.S.S.R. | x | x | x | E. Germany | x | 1953 | |
| 40 | U.S.S.R. | x | x | x | Hungary | x | 1956 | |
| 41 | U.S. | x | | | Lebanon | x | 1958 | |
| 42 | Britain | | | x | Jordan | x | 1958 | |
| 43 | Egypt | | x | x | North Yemen | x | 1962 | |
| 44 | N. Vietnam | | x | x | Laos | x | 1964 | |
| 45 | U.S., | | | | Laos | x | 1964 | x |
| | Thailand | | x | | | | | |

TABLE 1.3 *(continued)*

| Case | Promoter | Great Power? | Close Neighbor? | Promoter's institutions? | Target(s) | Target unrest? | Year(s) | Counter-Promotion? |
|------|----------|--------------|-----------------|--------------------------|-----------|----------------|---------|--------------------|
| 46 | France | x | | | Gabon | x | 1964 | |
| 47 | U.S., | x | | | S. Vietnam | x | 1965 | x |
| | S. Korea, | | | x | | | | |
| | Thailand, | | x | x | | | | |
| | Philippines, | | x | x | | | | |
| | Australia, | | | | | | | |
| | New Zealand | | | | | | | |
| 48 | U.S. | x | x | | Dom. Rep. | x | 1965 | |
| 49 | U.S.S.R, | x | x | x | Czechoslo. | x | 1968 | |
| | Poland, | | x | x | | | | |
| | Hungary, | | x | x | | | | |
| | Bulgaria, | | x | x | | | | |
| | E. Germany | | x | x | | | | |
| 50 | South Yemen | | x | x | Oman | x | 1968 | |
| 51 | Britain, | x | | | Oman | x | 1968 | x |
| | Iran, | | | | | | | |
| | Jordan | | | | | | | |
| 52 | N. Vietnam | | x | | Cambodia | x | 1970 | |
| 53 | U.S., | x | | | Cambodia | x | 1970 | x |
| | S. Vietnam | | | x | | | | |
| 54 | Cuba | | | x | Angola | x | 1975 | |
| 55 | South Africa | | x | | Angola | x | 1975 | x |
| 56 | Israel | | x | | Lebanon | x | 1975 | |
| 57 | Syria | | x | | Lebanon | x | 1976 | |
| 58 | Vietnam | | x | x | Cambodia | x | 1978 | |
| 59 | Tanzania | | x | x | Uganda | | 1979 | |
| 60 | U.S.S.R. | x | x | x | Afghanistan | x | 1979 | |
| 61 | Iraq | | x | x | Iran | | 1980 | |
| 62 | Iran | | x | x | Iraq | | 1980 | |
| 63 | U.S. & Jamaica | x | x | x | Grenada | x | 1983 | |
| 64 | U.S. | x | | x | Panama | x | 1989 | |

TABLE 1.3 *(continued)*

| Case | Promoter | Great Power? | Close Neighbor? | Promoter's institutions? | Target(s) | Target unrest? | Year(s) | Counter-Promotion? |
|---|---|---|---|---|---|---|---|---|
| 65 | U.S. et al. | x | | | Somalia | x | 1993 | |
| 66 | U.S. | x | x | x | Haiti | x | 1994 | |
| 67 | Nigeria | | x | | Sierra Leone | x | 1997 | |
| 68 | U.S. et al. | x | | x | Afghanistan | x | 2001 | |
| 69 | U.S. et al. | x | | x | Iraq | | 2003 | |

*Sources*: George Childs Kohn, *Dictionary of Wars*, rev. ed. (New York: Facts on File, 1999); Raphaël Lemkin, *Axis Rule in Occupied Europe* (Washington, DC: Carnegie Endowment for International Peace, 1944); J. H. Leurdijk, *Intervention in International Politics* (Leeuwarden, The Netherlands: B.V. Eisma, 1986); Evan Luard, *War in International Society* (London: I. B. Tauris, 1986); Martin McCauley, *The Khrushchev Era, 1953–1964* (New York: Longman, 1995); On War Internet site, http://www.onwar.com/; Ronald E. Powaski, *The Cold War: The United States and the Soviet Union, 1917–1991* (New York: Oxford University Press, 1998); William Stueck, *The Korean War: An International History* (Princeton, NJ: Princeton University Press, 1995); Miranda Vickers, *The Albanians: A Modern History* (London: I. B. Tauris, 2001).

nist regimes. Both superpowers also extended the practice to the Third World. The leaders of weaker states, often at the behest of a superpower, also promoted domestic regimes by force; most striking is perhaps Cuban intervention in far-away Angola. Since the demise of the Soviet Union, American governments have continued to promote liberal-democratic regimes by force.

### Whose Regime Type?

In most cases interveners promoted their own institutions.[25] In the first wave, Catholic rulers generally sought to establish Catholicism, Protestant rulers Protestantism. France was officially Catholic, but under the Edict of Nantes (in effect from 1598 to 1685) it tolerated Protestants; in Valtellina, its rulers promoted toleration.[26] In the seventeenth century, absolute monarchies occasionally promoted their institutions against oligarchy and republicanism; then France's republican government imposed republicanism upon small border states, and the monarchies at war with France tried to reestablish monarchy there. Napoleon imposed his hybrid Bonapartist regime on conquered states. From the 1820s through 1849, absolute monarchs imposed their institutions in Italy and Germany, while the constitutional monarchies of Britain and France promoted their system. In the twentieth century, communist, fascist, and liberal-democratic governments typically promoted their own institutions.

Exceptions do occur, however. French monarchs intervened on behalf of the Lutheran Germans and Calvinist Dutch in the late sixteenth century, and joined the Thirty Years' War on the side of the Protestants in 1635. In Liège in 1790, the King of Prussia intervened ostensibly to restore the prince-bishop, but in the event preserved the liberal revolution.[27] Louis-Napoleon of France, a secular republican (at that point), restored the papal monarchy in the Papal States in 1849 (see the case study at the beginning of chapter 5). In South Korea, South Vietnam, the Dominican Republic, Laos, and Cambodia, U.S. governments forcibly promoted authoritarian institutions. (As is well known, America used various other means to support anti-communist dictators in many other states during the Cold War, a point discussed in chapter 6.)

*Great-Power Promoters*

Most promoters are governments of great powers, or states with significant relative military capability. Those that are not tend to govern regional powers. From 1555 through 1648, Spain was Europe's leading military power; its kings forcibly promoted institutions nine times. The kings of France, which regained its status at or near the top of Europe after its civil wars ended in 1598, forcibly promoted institutions seven times. The monarchs of England, a minor power until the late 1580s, at which time it joined the great powers, did so in nine cases. The most prolific promoter was the Holy Roman Emperor, who used troops twenty-four times to restore Catholicism in Protestant imperial estates.[28]

In the second wave, France's rulers were promoters in thirty-six of the sixty-two cases. In most years prior to 1815, France was Europe's leading power; between 1799 and 1814, when seventeen of its promotions took place, it came close to conquering Europe. Most of the remaining promotions were carried out by the rulers of Prussia, Russia, Austria, and Britain, the other four great powers. Occasionally an Iberian or Italian ruler would participate in a forcible promotion as an accomplice to a great power.

In the third wave of forcible promotion (1910 to the present) also, great powers participated in a majority of the seventy-one promotions. The United States has been a great power throughout the period, and its governments promoted institutions in twenty-five cases. The leaders of the Soviet Union, a great power from 1917 until its disintegration in 1991, promoted institutions in nineteen cases. The rulers of Germany, a great power until 1945, promoted institutions in six cases. Governments of Great Britain, a great power until 1945, promoted regimes in eight cases. In contrast to the eighteenth and nineteenth centuries, however, the rulers of minor states such as North Korea, North Vietnam, Cuba, and

Syria promoted institutions by themselves (although with Soviet support in the case of the first three). A related point that comes as little surprise is that promoting states tend to be much stronger militarily than targets.[29] This is especially true during the second and third waves of institutional promotion. France was the predominant intervener between 1790 and 1815, a period when it was Europe's most powerful state. During the Concert period, when the five powers were roughly equal, each promoted institutions only in states much weaker than itself. In the twentieth century, almost all promoters chose weaker targets.

Measuring power differentials during the first period is difficult, although in many cases, such as when the rulers of the Empire, Spain, France, or the confessional leagues intervened in a small German state, it is beyond doubt that promoter was more powerful than target. One strikingly determined small German promoter was the Electoral Palatinate, whose rulers in the late sixteenth and early seventeenth centuries were militantly anti-Catholic Calvinists skilled at cobbling together Protestant coalitions. In a few cases it is probable that the target had more aggregate power than the promoter, for example, when in 1562–63 England's Elizabeth I sent troops to aid the Huguenots in the French civil war. What made France weak at this time was that same civil war.

### Target Instability

In at least thirty-one out of the seventy-nine cases in the first wave, intervention was preceded by an uprising, revolution, civil war, or coup d'état in the target.[30] English and French rulers intervened in Scotland in 1559 after the heavily Calvinistic lower Scottish nobility declared a Protestant kingdom.[31] Spanish and English monarchs intervened in the French and Dutch civil wars. In Donauwörth, a free town near Bavaria, the Emperor and dukes of Bavaria invaded after Catholics began rioting against the Protestant town council.[32] During the Thirty Years' War itself, targets were almost always internally divided between Catholics and Protestants, often violently so.

In the second wave in figure 1.1, twenty-eight out of the sixty-one cases were preceded by civil unrest in the targets. Strikingly, between 1815 and 1849, all twenty promotions were carried out following rebellions in the targets. In the third wave, thirty-one of the sixty-nine targets were already experiencing civil strife. Early in the twentieth century, targets in Latin America and Europe were all torn by domestic wars or insurrections. During the Cold War, the Soviets invaded East Germany following an insurrection there. In most Southeast Asian, Middle Eastern, African, and Latin American cases, targets were undergoing civil wars, often exacerbated and encouraged by outside financial and logistical support.

By no means did all forcible institutional promotions follow high civil unrest in the target. In the tallest spike in promotion, the Habsburg re-Catholicizations of many German states in 1629–30, the targets were mostly fairly settled Protestant states. Napoleonic France usually invaded states with no violent internal conflict. Nazi Germany's forcible promotions were similar, as were many of those of the Soviet Union and United States in the 1940s. No Iraqi unrest preceded the U.S.-led attack in 2003. The Soviets invaded Hungary and Czechoslovakia after reformers peacefully began altering institutions. Even in a majority of these cases, however, target states had a cohort of elites who desired the institutions that the intervener was promoting. The promoters did not simply march in unless some important elites wanted them there.

### When Security Is Scarce

The incidence of forcible institutional promotion tends to rise steeply during periods of great-power struggle, either hot or cold wars. In figure 1.1, the three tallest spikes come in the Thirty Years' War, the French Revolutionary and Napoleonic Wars, and the Second World War and early Cold War; in each of these, forcible institutional promotion averaged more than ten cases per decade. The middle and late Cold War featured five or more cases per decade. Periods of relative international security, such as 1815–1914, feature moderate or low amounts of forcible institutional promotion (with the exception of 1848–49). The correlation with high systemic insecurity is far from perfect. Most notably, the late seventeenth and early eighteenth centuries, when Louis XIV's bid for mastery of Europe was opposed by a coalition of states, featured very little forcible institutional promotion. No forcible regime promotion took place in the First World War until the aftermath of the Russian Revolution. Clusters of forcible promotion are not identical to great-power wars.

Still, the correlation of promotion and great-power conflict raises the question of whether many of these promotions are truly puzzling. If a great power is at war and it occupies a smaller state for strategic or tactical reasons, then is it surprising that it would impose its regime on the occupied state? Setting aside the possibility that regime promotion or ideological conflict helped cause the larger war, the target is already subdued, and perhaps regime promotion is an afterthought or default policy for the occupying military. In that case, dozens of promotions in the dataset—including the dramatic spikes in the 1620s, 1790s and 1800s, and 1940s—would be epiphenomenal of power politics and should drop out of the data or be classified separately. In other words, perhaps some of the data—promotions that are triggered by domestic unrest in the target—are apples, while other—promotions that follow a wartime occupation—are oranges, and the oranges are easily subsumed under a realist explanation.

The distinction is significant, and I recognize it by noting in chapters 4 through 7 which cases are ex ante (following domestic unrest) and which ex post (following a wartime occupation). But it is wrong to assume that wartime or postwar regime promotions are costless or epiphenomenal. Any option concerning post-occupation order in a conquered or liberated state bears opportunity costs. Hence we see much variation across history in how occupying powers handle the regime question. Machiavelli, who knew something about conquest and state power, lays out three options for a prince who occupies a city or principality: ruin it; live there personally; or "let them live by their own laws" while "taking tribute from them and creating within them an oligarchic state which keeps them friendly to you." Machiavelli does not even consider foreign regime promotion except oligarchy, and that not for any ideological purpose.[33] So the assertion that promoting one's own regime is a default policy or an afterthought encounters trouble from a founding father of realism. Forcible regime promotion is not an uninteresting artifact of great-power conflict; it is costly and begs for an explanation.

Why do states not always pursue one of Machiavelli's three options, and instead promote their own regime or a regime opposed to their ideological enemies? The Holy Roman Emperor Ferdinand II in the 1620s, the French Directory and Napoleon in the 1790s and 1800s, the Americans and Soviets in the 1940s: all could have simply let the states they occupied retain their own regimes. The same is true for the Bush and Obama administrations in Iraq and Afghanistan: why do these U.S. leaders not simply assume that these states have learned their lesson, let Iraqis and Afghans work out their own regimes, and strike bargains with those regimes? In each case, the occupying government must judge that the benefits from spending resources in imposing a regime outweigh the costs. At the time of this writing, at least, the Obama administration judges that a Taliban-ruled Afghanistan would be bad enough to justify the expenditure of still more American blood and treasure; Afghanistan must have a new regime. We must inquire, then, into the variables that enter these cost-benefit calculations. I argue that in each case the rulers of the occupier judged that their own security, internal or external or both, was at stake.

## In Their Own Backyards

In the first wave, sixty-four out of the seventy-nine promotions were in states either bordering the promoter or across a narrow body of water from it; in the second wave, thirty-six out of sixty-one; in the third, fifty-nine out of sixty-nine. In the first wave the King of Sweden promoted Protestantism in German lands across the Baltic Sea. In all three waves English or British monarchs promoted institutions in France; in the first and third, in the Low Countries as well. The United States has done a majority of its promotions in the Caribbean and Central America.

Distant promotions are relatively rare. In the first wave they include kings of England and Spain in the Palatinate in 1620 and 1621 and the Swedish king's promotions in southern Germany in the 1630s. In the second wave they include French and Turkish rulers in Poland in 1768–72; the King of Prussia in the Low Countries in the late 1780s; the monarchs of Austria, Prussia, and Russia in France, and vice versa, through most of the 1790–1814 period; the British government in Naples in 1799; France's Napoleon in Poland in 1807; the British government again in Sicily in 1811, and in Portugal in 1826, 1834, and 1846–47; and Napoleon III of France in Mexico 1862–67. In the third wave, distant promotions include the Allied governments in Russia in 1918–22; the French in Hungary in 1919; the Germans and the Soviets in Spain in 1936–39; Britain in Greece in 1944–45; the various American promotions of liberal democracy in Europe and Japan after the Second World War; U.S. promotion of anti-communist authoritarianism in South Korea, South Vietnam, Laos, and Cambodia in the 1950s, 1960s, and 1970s; France in Gabon in 1964; Britain in Oman in 1968–75; Cuba in Angola during 1975–91; the United States and others in Afghanistan in 2001 and Iraq in 2003.

### Strategic Targets

Across time, many targets stand out as having geopolitical consequence. Some targets contained or bordered vital military, naval, or trading routes. Valtellina, a valley of the Adda River in Lombardy (now in Italy) that was a target several times during the Thirty Years' War, was of consequence to Spain, France, and the Emperor because it provided an east-west pass through the Alps. Britain and France intervened in Spain in the Concert period, as did Italy, Germany, and the Soviet Union in the late 1930s; Spain's significance to Mediterranean naval traffic is obvious. Territories also gain strategic importance from their natural resources. A number of twentieth-century promotions were carried out in the oil-rich Middle East. One should recall too that the strategic importance variable has an endogeneity problem: state B may acquire strategic importance for state A when A's rival state C treats B as if it already has such importance.[34] Thus, the aggregate data may not capture the strategic importance of

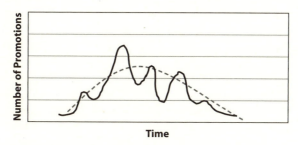

Figure 1.2  A stylized long wave

many targets. Of course, the strong association between the propinquity of two states and the probability that one will promote institutions in the other may also be attributed to strategic interest.

Toward an Explanation

These patterns suggest a number of things. Governments, it seems, care about the ideologies or regimes of other states, sometimes enough to use force and risk wider war; but they only do so under some conditions. They are more likely to do so when insecure, in territory of strategic significance, when the expected costs are relatively low, and often in reaction to rivals' actions. That they tend to do so in clusters in time and space suggests that sometimes, far from being socialized out of the practice, states find the practice fruitful and worth repeating and imitating. The evidence of five centuries makes it difficult to maintain that rulers who spread ideologies are simply irrational or possessed by ideological zeal. We seem to have a phenomenon in which ideas and material power interact.

Another conclusion warranted by figure 1.1 is that foreign regime promotion occurs in micro- and macro-cycles. On the macro-level it occurs in three long waves. On the micro-level, within each wave its incidence varies. Figure 1.2 is a stylized depiction of these two types of cycle, a long wave that contains several short waves.

The solid curve represents the actual (stylized) frequency of forcible regime promotion. The dotted curve is a rough average of the height of the solid curve and represents a long wave. The two curves are obviously related—the dotted is a simple function of the solid—but because they occupy different levels of analysis, I shall give them separate analytical treatment. Chapter 2 concerns the micro-level, the changes in slope in the solid curve. Chapter 3 concerns the macro-level, the changes in slope in the dotted curve.

As the summary of my arguments earlier in this chapter suggested, both curves take their shapes in part because of *feedback loops* connecting agents and their environments. Forcible regime promotion is sometimes self-perpetuating, and so is the absence of such promotion. Sociologists have long trafficked in arguments about feedback loops and path dependency. More recently, economists and political scientists have come to use them. The essential insight is that the social outcomes or equilibria are not always optimal, even taking into account agents' coordination problems. Instead, actions taken at time $t$ can restrict the options available at time $t+1$, resulting in a suboptimal equilibrium. What actors did in the past constrains what actors can do now.[35] On the micro-level (the solid curve), transnational ideological polarization is an example of a feedback loop at work: elites adhering to one ideology find that they must coalesce more tightly in response to the tighter coalescence of elites adhering to a rival ideology. A feedback loop also connects forcible regime promotion with the very transnational ideological polarization that causes it: promotion exacerbates polarization, making more promotion more likely. On the macro-level (the dotted curve), a transnational ideological struggle both causes and is caused by the agitations of ideological networks and governments that impose regimes abroad. On both levels I pay a great deal of attention to exogenous events that can trigger these action-reaction cycles.

Plan of the Book

In chapters 2 and 3, then, I explicate my arguments about the causes of forcible regime promotion. In chapter 4 I examine the period between 1510 and 1700 in Europe. For most of these years, the struggle between Catholicism and various forms of Protestantism was prominent. The contest emerged when the medieval political system, a complex overlapping set of political loyalties that granted a great deal of power to the Papacy and Catholic clergy, began to encounter a series of serious anomalies in northern Europe. With the emergence of Lutheran regimes in Germany in the mid-1520s there began many decades of on-again, off-again forcible regime promotion as transnational networks labored to spread their regimes and princes were implicated in the struggle. In the 1540s emerged Calvinism, a more militant type of Protestantism. The ideological contest had its miserable zenith in the Thirty Years' War. The struggle over the best regime finally faded in the latter half of the seventeenth century as it became clear that a new type of regime, religious toleration—practiced to great profit by the Dutch Republic—was superior to an intolerant Catholic or Protestant one. Princes gradually ceased to fear the advance of a rival form of Christianity. Neither peace nor religious skepticism came to Europe, but religion ceased to be a *casus belli.*

Chapter 5 treats the years between 1700 and 1900 in Europe and the Americas. Although England (Great Britain after 1707) was a constitutional monarchy, and the Netherlands remained a nominal republic, the predominant regime was absolute monarchy as exemplified by Louis XIV. "Enlightened Absolutism" began encountering serious anomalies in the middle of the century, as it seemed to impoverish its subjects and bankrupt the state. A constitutionalist movement gained momentum, and then republicanism emerged as a contending regime as well when the United States and then France adopted it. Regime instability, particularly in France, gave rulers powerful incentives at various times to march troops abroad to spread their regime type. Following the defeat of Napoleon in 1814–15, republican and constitutionalist networks remained in Europe and triggered several waves of revolution and regime promotion. The spectacular revolutions of 1848 disrupted the decades-old regime contest by raising the specter of a more radical, socialist republicanism. By the 1870s, elites in most European great powers had negotiated new regimes that were, broadly speaking, reformist conservative, and for several decades almost no forcible regime promotion took place.

In chapter 6, I examine the twentieth-century struggles over individual, class, and state. The predominant reforming conservative regime that took hold in the 1870s was increasingly beset by anomalies in the eyes of the increasingly important labor organizations. The 1917 revolution in Russia produced the world's first communist state, and a small wave of forcible regime promotion ensued. Within a few years fascism, an anti-Bolshevik, anti-constitutionalist regime, had taken over Italy. Communist and fascist transnational networks threaded through much of the world, with Nazi Germany becoming the fascist exemplar by the mid-1930s; Spain soon became a site of dueling promotions. The vanquishing of fascism in 1945 left communism and liberal democracy, and both the Soviets and the Americans carried out many forcible regime promotions in nearly every part of the world. The long contest over the best regime ended in the late 1980s, as communism had clearly proven unable to compete with liberal democracy.

Chapter 7 examines the contemporary struggle within the Muslim world—particularly in North Africa and Southwest Asia—between Islamism and secularism. In the early twentieth century the manifest decline of the Ottoman Empire, generally seen as the caliphate or empire established by the Prophet Muhammad, had produced a legitimacy crisis.

Elites in Turkey began to reject traditional Islamic institutions in favor of secular Western ones, and following the trauma of the First World War the caliphate was abolished and the Turkish Republic was established. The Turkish example inspired Iran in the 1920s; in the early 1950s secularism took hold in much of the Arab world. Saudi Arabia emerged as the exemplar of traditional Islam, which evolved into a more assertive ideology of Islamism; the Iranian Revolution of 1979 established that country as an Islamist rival to the Saudi monarchy. Forcible regime promotions have taken place in Lebanon, North Yemen, Iran, and Iraq. A schism within Sunni Islamism between pro- and anti-Westerners led the latter to launch a series of terrorist attacks on the United States and other Western countries, and U.S.-led regime promotions followed.

In chapter 8, I offer conclusions from these cases and my arguments. I contend that my arguments are more consistent with the cases than are key claims of realism and of certain varieties of constructivism. I follow with implications for the general study of international relations. I discuss emerging ideological struggles in Latin America and the republics of the former Soviet Union. I close by returning to the struggle within Islam and how it might end.

# CHAPTER TWO

# The Agents: Transnational Networks and Governments

> So savage was the factional strife that broke out [in Corcyræa]—and it seemed all the worse in that it was the first to occur. Later on, indeed, all of Hellas (so to speak) was thrown into turmoil, there being discord everywhere, with the representatives of the demos (i.e., the extreme democratic factions) wanting to bring in the Athenians to support their cause, while the oligarchic factions looked to the Spartans. In peacetime they would have had no excuse nor would they have been prepared to summon them for help, but in the midst of a war, the summoning of outside aid readily offered those on both sides who desired a change in the status quo alliances that promised harm for their opponents and, at the same time, benefit for themselves.
>
> —Thucydides, c. *411* B.C..

IN THIS CHAPTER AND THE NEXT I flesh out my explanation for forcible regime promotion outlined in chapter 1. We observe two types of variation in the incidence of such promotions. They occur in three long temporal waves and, within each of those long waves, they vary in frequency across time and space. Most of us agree that there was something called the Cold War from roughly 1946 until roughly 1989, and yet within that four-decade-plus period the incidence of forcible regime promotion varied enormously. Sometimes the Americans and Soviets did quite a bit of it, and sometimes they did very little. The same is true of the other long waves: in some times and places governments resorted to arms frequently to alter or preserve another state's domestic regime, while at other times they did not. The long waves and the short-term variation are logically related, in that a long wave is an aggregation of forcible regime promotions. But we have here two different levels of analysis, a macro- and a micro-level. The macro-phenomenon is depicted by the dotted curve in figure 1.2; the micro-phenomenon, by the solid curve. In chapter 3, I focus on the dotted curve, the long waves. In this chapter I focus on the solid curve, the variation in forcible regime promotion during the three long waves.

## Why Do Governments Use Force to
## Promote Domestic Regimes?

Governments use force to promote domestic regimes when they believe that doing so will make their international or domestic environment more favorable to their interests. They do it when they think it will gain or keep a foreign ally, or suppress a domestic enemy. That, in turn, is more likely when elites across their region are highly polarized along an ideological axis: they identify unusually strongly with one regime type and against a rival regime type. High polarization often follows two types of event: a regime crisis in a state somewhere in the region; or a great-power war. I call promotions that follow the first type of event ex ante because the decision to use force to impose a regime clearly came *before* the attack and was provoked by events in the target. I call promotions that follow the second type of event, a great-power war, ex post because the decision to impose a regime may not have been made until *after* the attack, and the attack itself was likely made for strategic (material) reasons.

But why do these two types of event tend to spur transnational ideological polarization? The ultimate answer, presented in chapter 3, is that these events take place during a long, sometimes dormant, transnational ideological struggle. That struggle, however, does not float in the ether. It is carried on by actual agents.[1] The two types of agent that are most important are the governments or state rulers who carry out regime promotions, and transnational ideological networks or TINs. Such networks, organized around a common deep commitment to a particular political regime, labor to bring about regime changes within and across states; when they appear likely to succeed somewhere, they can trigger in reaction a foreign regime promotion by a government. Under some conditions, TINs can even trigger a wave of promotions and counter-promotions. During and after large wars, when conquering armies occupy subjugated states, TINs give incentives for the governments of those armies to impose one regime rather than another. TINs endure for many decades across many countries, perpetually retaining the potential to trigger these short waves.

TINs are neither sufficient nor necessary for forcible regime promotion to take place. There have been several promotions in which TINs appear to have been absent or weak at best. Most of those cases involved the U.S. Marines preserving or installing a stable regime on a Central American or Caribbean country in the first half of the twentieth century. In chapter 6, I discuss those cases separately. The great majority of forcible regime promotions, however, are caused in part by the interactions of TINs.

## Networks in General

A vast social-scientific literature exists on networks. Walter W. Powell defines a *network* as a form of organization qualitatively distinct from either a *hierarchy* or a *market*. Networks are characterized by "lateral or horizontal patterns of exchange, interdependent flows of resources, and reciprocal lines of communication." In market-based orders, actors are independent and prices convey information; in hierarchical orders, lower actors are dependent upon higher and routines carry information. In a network, actors are interdependent and established relationships carry information. Networks arise through various mechanisms, but in general they emerge when expertise, speed, or trust is vital.[2] The social realm about which Powell originally wrote was economics, or the distribution of scarce resources. But political scientists increasingly have attended to network-like forms of *political* organization—that is, organized around a common vision for public order. Network analysis seems especially appropriate in political analysis because so often the value of the good sought—particular policies or institutions—is not readily quantified.

## Transnational Networks

International relations scholarship has analyzed various types of networks that span national boundaries. Robert Keohane and Joseph Nye name the presence of transnational networks as one of four conditions constituting complex interdependence, and argue that such networks can limit governments' abilities to control outcomes.[3] Peter Haas and others have studied epistemic communities, networks of professionals with special competence in some issue area such as environmental protection or nuclear weapons.[4] Thomas Risse-Kappen,[5] Matthew Evangelista,[6] Daniel Thomas,[7] and others have argued that transnational networks helped end the Cold War by developing and propagating ideas about national defense, human rights, and so forth. Prominent in recent international relations literature are what Margaret Keck and Kathryn Sikkink term transnational advocacy networks (TANs). TANs are networks that span state boundaries and "plead the causes of others or defend a cause or proposition." The core of a TAN is one or more nongovernmental organizations (NGOs), but TANs may include other groups such as "local social movements ... foundations ... the media ... churches, trade unions, consumer organizations, and intellectuals ... parts of regional and international intergovernmental organizations ... and ... parts of the executive and/or parliamentary branches of governments."[8] For political scientists who study international relations, TANs are noteworthy in part for their ability to alter the foreign and domestic behavior of governments, not-withstanding their own lack of direct coercive capacity.[9]

## Transnational Ideological Networks

For the entire history of the modern international system, a class of trans-national networks has existed that is not precisely covered by the work of these scholars. These are networks organized around an ideology or plan for ordering public life. Amnesty International, the International Justice Mission, and similar groups seek to alter laws and practices within states, but do not present themselves as ideological. Other transnational groups do so present themselves. Threading their way across liberal democracies today are networks seeking to increase or decrease the scope of the state in the distribution of material resources. Some of these are relatively in-stitutionalized: on the Left, the Socialist International is a consortium of 170 political parties from around the world.[10] Others are loose: on the Right, the Web site of Canada's free-market-advocating Fraser Institute lists twenty-one entities around the world "with a similar focus."[11] The concerns of these transnational networks are by no means trivial, but they do not challenge the legitimacy of liberal democracy itself. Social democrats and free-market advocates agree that a marriage of the rule of law and popular sovereignty is the best regime. Indeed, far from being radical, one effect of their work is the reinforcement of liberal democracy itself. Social democrats and free marketeers alike see their preferred poli-cies as refining or improving liberal democracy; their goal is to fulfill the regime's promise as they see it, not to overturn it.

The transnational networks on which I focus in this book have more fundamental political goals. They are constituted by common normative principles, but take those principles to be the roots of public order. TINs aim not simply to change policies or laws but to replace, in country after country, one *regime* with another or to preserve a regime against replace-ment. I borrow the definition of regime advanced by David Easton and his colleagues: regimes are constituted by "institutions, operational rules of the game, and ideologies (goals, preferred rules, and preferred arrange-ments among political institutions)."[12] Being in favor of one regime, TINs are necessarily against at least one alternative regime. They engage in what Doug McAdam, Sidney Tarrow, and Charles Tilly term *contentious politics*, and of an especially fraught kind.[13]

All TINs are by my definition radical—aiming at the roots of public order—but not all are violent or even revolutionary: some may prefer to work for regime change via reform or lawful governmental succes-sion. TINs have included the so-called Calvinist International and the Society of Jesus (Jesuits) in early modern Europe (chapter 4),[14] the liberal *carbonari* and Freemasons in nineteenth-century Europe (chapter 5), the Communist International and fascist networks in the twentieth century (chapter 6), and the Muslim Brotherhood since 1928 (chapter 7). At various times each of these, or at least some of their local chapters, have advocated the violent overthrow of the regimes they oppose; at other times, each has professed to favor peaceful change.

TINs strive perpetually to alter domestic regimes across states. They may seek regime change because they believe it coincides with their nation's interests (a more democratic world helps America) or because they are internationalists (democracy is good for all persons everywhere).[15] Regardless, members of these networks recognize their common interests and interdependence across states, and hence try to help one another through various means, including the sharing of information, strategies, and tactics, and the clarification of principles and goals. Inasmuch as their opponents may try to co-opt or coerce their members into defecting, networks also serve as mechanisms to keep a movement alive by encouragement or sanction. TINs also help their members recruit new affiliates and sympathizers.

## Governments, States, and Transnational Ideologies

Rulers or governments—I use the terms interchangeably—are the other type of agent chiefly responsible for forcible regime promotion. Rulers require far less explication than TINs. Rulers control the coercive apparatus of the state and hence, under broad conditions, have more power than other elites. I accept the common rationalist assumption that a ruler's primary goal is to retain power.[16] He may also wish to implement his vision of the good society, but to do that he must govern the state. Thus, a ruler's interests and those of a TIN with which he shares an ideology are not identical. Rulers try to exploit and dominate TINs, and TINs do the same vis-à-vis governments. In the case of the Communist International, Stalin's domination was nearly complete. Today some analysts believe that transnational Islamist networks have great influence over the Pakistani secret service (ISI). In any case, the relation of governments, and hence states, to TINs is complex and one of the most interesting aspects of clashes of ideas in world politics. Sidney Tarrow is right to complain that many studies of transnational networks do not attend adequately to the ways in which governments or states can use transnational networks for their own purposes.[17]

The relation of TINs to governments is complex in part because the two are often interpenetrated. Members of an ideological group may simultaneously be members of a government. In 1558, Elizabeth I acceded to the English throne and English Protestants—and, in a sense,

Protestants elsewhere in Europe—found one of their own ruling a rising second-tier European power. In 1830, France's Charles X, an absolutist, was overthrown and replaced by Louis-Philippe, a constitutionalist, and French liberals were suddenly responsible for governing France. In 1917, certain leaders of a radical rump group from the moribund Socialist International—the Bolsheviks—seized power in Russia. When ideologues become responsible for a state's welfare, they find themselves in a new situation with new incentives. No longer concerned simply to implement the regime at home and abroad, they are also responsible to protect the state. Their hold on power depends upon their doing so.

State rulers who are members of an ideological movement will tend to see the interests of the ideology and of their particular state as complementary, such that in protecting the state they are advancing the ideology, and vice versa. Inevitably, however, there will be times when rulers appear to foreign co-ideologues to have compromised or sold out the cause for the sake of their own power or the aggrandizement of their state. Aware of the conflicts of interest facing those in government, ideologues outside of government perpetually work to lure those in power into putting state power in service of the cause: Why hold power, they argue, if not to put it to this moral purpose? Those within government, meanwhile, will work perpetually to lure their co-ideologues outside of government to put the network's power in service of the state they govern: How can we put our power to the right purpose, they note, if we do not hold onto that power?

This tug of war between the interests of state and of ideology is perpetual. And chapters 4 through 7 make clear that rulers often betray the ideological networks that help sustain their power. In 1635, during the Thirty Years' War (chapter 4), the archetypical religious war, Catholic France joined the Protestants against the Catholic Habsburgs. Various monarchical powers treated with republican France in the 1790s (chapter 5). Josef Stalin frequently abandoned communists abroad, most notoriously Mao Zedong at certain points in the Chinese civil war of the 1940s (chapter 6). Yet, rulers often act just as their foreign co-ideologues would wish by promoting the "good" regime and combating the "bad" one abroad. The empirical chapters that follow confirm that when they do so, they are not necessarily suspending self-interest or national security for the sake of ideology. Rather, *sometimes they find it in their interests to promote their ideology, because their hold on power depends on the progress of their ideology abroad.* Insofar as they have publicly committed to a particular regime type at home, their notion of the national interest entails not simply external security but also a particular internal order or regime.[18] They sometimes find themselves compelled to defend that regime elsewhere. In a related way, they find that they are seen at home and abroad as defenders of the ideology they espouse, as warriors in its international cause.

In the 1560s, Elizabeth I of England was convinced that a Protestant Scotland, France, and Netherlands were good for Protestantism in England and hence for her own security and power (chapter 4). In the 1830s, Louis-Philippe of France believed it in his interests to join Britain in advancing constitutionalism in Spain and Portugal (chapter 5). In 1918–21, Lenin believed that the survival of Bolshevism in Russia depended upon its spread into Germany and elsewhere (chapter 6). All three rulers were seen at home and abroad as champions of their ideology as well as of their state. For them, Nigel Gould-Davies's statement about ideology in the Cold War is true: "A threat to [a state's] security is . . . by extension a threat to its ideology; and the stronger the state is, the more effectively it can spread its values and prosecute its mission."[19]

What happened to put these and other rulers in this position, in which they felt compelled to promote their ideology abroad? More generally, what leads governments to use force to promote a regime in a foreign country? The condition to which governments are responding is what I call *transnational ideological polarization*: the progressive segregation of elites and mass publics across states along an ideological axis, so that political preferences among elites across states are simplified and intensified. Such polarization entails the swelling of the ranks of TINs and their enemies. In 1620, European Lutherans and Calvinists, the two leading branches of Protestantism, were divided owing to doctrinal disputes and worked at cross-purposes; in 1629, Catholics and Protestants were more polarized and the latter—Lutherans and Calvinists— set aside their differences (chapter 4). When elites are more ideologically polarized, their rulers have incentives to follow suit. From 1629 through 1635, the rulers of Lutheran and Calvinist states cooperated to roll back Catholicism in the Holy Roman Empire. In the next section I discuss transnational ideological polarization and its effects on rulers as I analyze two classes of event that can trigger it: a *domestic regime crisis*, and a *war involving a great power*.

Forcible Regime Promotion: Triggers and Feedback

Transnational ideological networks work across states perpetually to change regimes they hate and to preserve the regimes they like. By themselves, they cannot trigger short waves of forcible regime promotion. They can capitalize on exogenous events, however, to help do so.

Suppose a region comprises five states. States A and B are great powers, and C, D, and E are lesser powers. A, C, and E are democracies, while B and D are oligarchies. Democratic and oligarchic TINs thread across all five states, working on behalf of their favored regime and against the opposing regime. The rulers of A and B regard one another's state as a rival, and attempt to undercut each other by competing for influence in C, D, and E. But, concerned not to trigger a great-power war or otherwise incur high costs, the rulers of A and B do not use force to promote democracy or oligarchy in these states. The TINs try to manipulate the governments of their respective ideological patrons, A and B, into granting them more help in states C, D, and E, but with little success; most elites in A and B care too little for the democratic-oligarchic struggle to press their rulers to fight for the ideology.

*First Type of Exogenous Event: Regime Crisis in State C*

The first type of event that can trigger a forcible regime promotion by A is a regime-threatening crisis in one of the lesser states C, D, or E. Such a crisis, by threatening to alter the lesser state's regime, tends to have demonstration effects throughout the region, increasing the influence and leverage of TINs by polarizing elites and mass publics across states according to ideology. More and more elites across states begin to identify their interests with co-ideologues across states.

Because TINs run through this region, any regime crisis in democratic C is not simply domestic, as if C's inhabitants were hermetically sealed off from foreigners. Oligarchs in C are members of a transnational network that provides them with moral and material support. TINs are insufficient to bring about a regime crisis; events outside of their control, such as fiscal collapse, defeat in war, death of a ruler, or rigged election are also necessary to bring one about. I do not offer a theory of revolution, coup d'état, or other type of domestically generated regime change; I leave triggering events exogenous.[20] But TINs make such regime crises more likely by exploiting such dire events, whatever their causes. An oligarchic international tries to bring about the overthrow of democracy in C not simply out of altruistic concern for the citizens of C: they also know that if C becomes oligarchic, oligarchy will be strengthened in all states.[21]

DEMONSTRATION EFFECTS AND TRANSNATIONAL POLARIZATION.

Suppose then that C, a democracy, is undergoing a deep fiscal crisis; C's democratic government must levy high taxes on an already impoverished population. Sensing an opportunity, oligarchs within C begin to agitate for change. C's democratic rulers choose to stand fast rather than invite oligarchs to help govern. A hostile spiral ensues and civil war begins.

This ideological conflict within C will tend to have demonstration effects across other states in the region. By *demonstration effects* I mean the *increasing plausibility of regime change in neighboring societies, among supporters, opponents, and the undecided alike*. Demonstration effects wear a positive and a negative aspect. On the positive side, as C appears more likely to become an oligarchy, oligarchy becomes increasingly plausible in A and E, both currently democracies. Previously soft supporters of oligarchy become firmer; moderates who once favored oligarchic reform come to embrace oligarchic revolution, as radical oligarchs once seen as romantics or lunatics suddenly appear competent statesmen riding the wave of the future. The discontented in democratic states A and E, even those whose problems and prescriptions are quite different from those that oligarchy is designed to redress, latch onto oligarchic ideology nonetheless.[22] Endogenous to these changes are increasing interactions among oligarchs within and across states, including the rebels in C. The plausibility of oligarchy will be supported by a heightened sense of the moral stakes. Across states, advocates of oligarchy will propagate stories of chicanery and brutality by democrats and heroism by oligarchs. Within C itself, ideologues on both sides will try to induce foreign sympathy by provoking the other side to violence. The net effect is that, for any given elite in any given state, neutrality will be progressively more difficult to sustain.

Demonstration effects simultaneously wear a negative aspect. Except in the unusual circumstances in which all democratic elites, including rulers, decide to defect to oligarchy themselves—a "pooling equilibrium" I explore in chapter 3—advocates of democracy across states will respond with alarm to the civil war in C.[23] The very developments that encourage oligarchs across countries will frighten and galvanize democrats and produce a "separating equilibrium." Those who favored accommodating oligarchs will become hard-liners. They will focus their ideological fire on the rebellion in C and its advocates across countries. That the revolutionary network is transnational enables them to depict revolution as a foreign conspiracy and to suppress dissent on that basis.

Social science has offered various mechanisms for demonstration effects. Sociologists tend to regard them as entailing conversions or changes in preference and emphasize the roles of example, identity, and authority: the more people adopt a position, the more plausible and good it seems to others, and the more others' self-esteem depends on adopting it and identifying with its group as well.[24] Economists tend to see demonstration effects as entailing changes in strategy or tactics rather than in preferences, and posit a threshold model. One may have a preference for the new ideology but keep it secret out of fear of persecution; when the marginal social cost of revealing the preference becomes low enough, as when those around one begin to admit holding that preference, one will likewise reveal the preference.[25] Whatever mechanisms operate, the net demonstration effect is that, across states in the region, neutrality becomes progressively less feasible or plausible; elites and non-elites have growing incentives to declare themselves for or against oligarchy in C. Each person reacts not simply to those with whom he sympathizes but those with whom he does not. Across all five states, the ranks of revolution and reaction both swell.

Typically, then, demonstration effects involve not the gravitation of everyone to the side of the rebels, but rather the polarization of elites into those who favor and those who oppose the rebels. By *polarization* I mean *the progressive segregation of a population into two or more sets, each of which cooperates internally and excludes externally.* In the abstract, persons belonging to multiple, overlapping social groups may segregate along any number of potential axes.[26] People in a given society may be capital or labor, male or female, black or white, and democratic or oligarchic, with each axis intersecting but distinct from the others. Charles Tilly refers to the divide along each axis as a *social boundary.* Ideological polarization *activates*, makes more salient, the democratic-oligarchic boundary in each society.[27] Prior to polarization, most democrats and oligarchs (apart from those who belong to TINs) interact normally with one another. With polarization, democrats progressively increase cooperation with one another and exclusion of oligarchs, and oligarchs do the same vis-à-vis democrats.

Along with these behavioral markers of cooperation and exclusion, ideological polarization involves the progressive identification of one's individual interests with those of one's ideological group and against the interests of competing ideological groups.[28] The more polarized a population, the more do members of one group define the other as the source of society's problems, the elimination of their ideas as the solution; and the less defensible are moderation and neutrality. Thus, polarization limits agents' range of action by altering their preferences: the more ideologically polarized a population, the more do members desire gains for their own ideological group and losses for the other. Actors' choices are path-dependent, limited by previous choices made by other actors.[29]

A crucial feature of transnational ideological polarization is that it is progressive or self-reinforcing. It is fed by what systems theorists call a feedback loop. Robert Jervis's explanation of feedback loops bears quoting at length:

> Feedbacks are central to the way systems behave. A change in an element or relationship often alters others, which in turn affect the original one. We then are dealing with cycles in which causation is mutual

or circular rather than one-way, as it is in most of our theories. . . . [I]t is difficult for observers to assign responsibility and for actors to break out of reinforcing patterns that seem to come from everywhere and nowhere. The actors' behavior collectively causes and explains itself.

Feedback is positive or self-amplifying (and destabilizing) when a change in one direction sets in motion reinforcing pressures that produce further change in the same direction; negative or dampening (and stabilizing) when the change triggers forces that counteract the initial change and return the system to something like its original position.[30]

The journalist Christopher Hitchens analyzes polarization and positive feedback in today's transnational struggle between secularism and Islamism (chapter 7) even as he participates in it:

It is often said that resistance to jihadism only increases the recruitment to it. For all I know, this commonplace observation could be true. But, if so, it must cut both ways. How about reminding the Islamists that, by their mad policy in Kashmir and elsewhere, they have made deadly enemies of a billion Indian Hindus? Is there no danger that the massacre of Iraqi and Lebanese Christians, or the threatened murder of all Jews, will cause an equal and opposite response? Most important of all, what will be said and done by those of us who take no side in filthy religious wars? The enemies of intolerance cannot be tolerant, or neutral, without inviting their own suicide. And the advocates and apologists of bigotry and censorship and suicide-assassination cannot be permitted to take shelter any longer under the umbrella of a pluralism that they openly seek to destroy.[31]

Social or group polarization involves, among other things, greater interaction with those in one's group and less with those in the opposite group.[32] Evidently something about the publicness of interactions tends to exacerbate polarization.[33]

The concept of demonstration effects or contagion across states still suffers from its association with the domino theory and the related American war in Vietnam in the 1960s. But U.S. failure in Indochina does not mean demonstration effects do not exist, and indeed the domino-like fall of communism in Central Europe in 1989 suggests that international demonstration effects happen and are consequential.[34] Mark Beissinger argues that the liberal-democratic "color revolutions" across several former communist countries in the early 2000s exhibit "modular" dynamics, that is, of example and emulation.[35] Chapters 4 through 7 below show that demonstration effects account for much of the transnational spread of Lutheranism and Calvinism in Europe at the expense of Roman Catholicism in the sixteenth century; of republicanism throughout

Europe and the New World at the expense of the *ancien régime* in the late eighteenth and nineteenth centuries; of Marxism-Leninism through most of the world at the expense of democratic and authoritarian capitalism and traditional societal forms from the 1910s through 1970s; and of secularism in the Muslim world from the 1920s through 1960s, and of Islamism since the 1970s.

*Second Type of Exogenous Event: A Great Power War*

In an ideologically heterogeneous region, war involving a great power can likewise trigger transnational ideological polarization. The war may have little to do with ideology (although ideological differences can help cause international conflict).[36] The great power may be fighting over territory or hegemony or an expected shift in the balance of power. What matters is that observers throughout the region believe that domestic political order across the region is at stake in the war. In the Second World War, it was not only the case that Germans and Russians were killing each other; it was equally the case that Nazis and communists were killing each other; Nazism and communism were contending. Today the United States is seen by Islamists as fighting for its own imperial power but also for the secular order on which they believe American power rests (chapter 7). These wars' outcomes are generally seen as implicating the ideological as well as the international struggle.

Suppose, in our hypothetical above, democratic A and oligarchic B, both great powers, fall into war over some development unrelated to ideology; for example, A attacks B because A's rulers fear that B is otherwise soon going to be more powerful than A.[37] In order to generate domestic and foreign sympathy for their respective causes, the governments of A and B both will present the war as being over the grand moral struggle that cuts across all of the societies, that between democracy and oligarchy. Elites and publics in all societies will tend to interpret the war in those terms as well. Democratic and oligarchic TINs, the ideological activists, will realize that the future of the struggle is implicated in which great-power patron, A or B, wins; they too will propagate the ideological interpretation of the war. As the war continues, the militaries of A and B will commit the usual dreary accidents and brutalities, on the one hand, and display the usual stirring heroism, on the other. Stories of brutality and heroism will be interpreted through an ideological lens: democrats will note B's brutality and A's heroism, while oligarchs will do the opposite. Less ideologically committed elites and publics will find neutrality in the war progressively more difficult to sustain. "How can you remain neutral in the face of what they're doing?" will be a question that becomes more and more difficult to answer.

Such transnational polarization took place during the Thirty Years' War, as Catholics and Protestants throughout Central and Western Europe saw the Habsburgs as fighting for Catholicism (chapter 4). In the Napoleonic Wars, many saw France's armies as bearers of republicanism and enlightenment (chapter 5). During the Second World War, the Soviet Union was seen as struggling on behalf of communism (chapter 6). At certain points since 1979, Iran has been seen as fighting on behalf of Islam (chapter 7). These interpretations were self-fulfilling, as the rulers of the belligerent powers saw that they were drawing intense ideological sympathy abroad and chose to exploit it.

It is important to note that most of the time most elites are not ideologically polarized. They are aware of a larger ideological struggle and loosely identify with one ideology or another, but are involved in other political and social matters as well and typically cooperate with elites across ideological lines on matters of common interest. Only those elites belonging to TINs are perpetually polarized, refusing cooperation with ideological opposites. It is when either of the two triggering events—regime instability somewhere in the region, or a war involving a great power—occurs that "normal" elites polarize along an ideological axis. The mechanism is similar to that which James Davison Hunter identifies at work in the "culture wars" within the United States. Most Americans most of the time hold moderate or middling views on the deeply divisive issues of the day such as abortion or gay marriage. But elites at either end of the policy spectrum, committed to cultural warfare, sometimes mobilize and polarize them with help from provocative events such as elections or acts of violence.[38] Just so, during quiet periods or "troughs" in figure 1.2, most elites and masses will not be ideologically polarized and little forcible regime promotion will take place. Such does not mean that the long ideological contest is over.

### Rulers' Responses to Transnational Polarization

Transnational ideological polarization—whether triggered by a regime crisis or a great-power war—presents governments of great powers with incentives to promote regimes in other states. In heightening actors' affinity for foreign and domestic co-ideologues and fear of foreign and domestic ideological opponents, polarization can give rulers either of two incentives to do forcible regime promotion: to protect their domestic or *internal security*, and to protect their foreign or *external security*.

These incentives result when rulers choose to continue to adhere to the suddenly besieged ideology. They do have a choice in the matter, but typically many choose not to convert to the new advancing ideology. Consider A's democratic rulers facing a newly energized transnational oligarchic threat owing to the oligarchic uprising in C. The rulers of A have three basic options. They may *convert* to oligarchy in hopes that A's oligarchs will be appeased. The risks of conversion include that oligarchs will not accept the rulers' conversion as genuine and that the democrats, whom they have betrayed, will punish them—say, if the military does not rally to them. Conversions of this sort were not unusual early in the Reformation (chapter 4). In late 1789, France's absolute monarch Louis XVI became a constitutional monarch in an attempt to mollify the revolutionaries in Paris (chapter 5). A number of statesmen claimed to convert to fascism in the 1930s or communism in the 1950s, believing they were riding the wave of the future (chapter 6). Such conversions and semi-conversions can add to the momentum of an ideology and trigger further regime changes and transnational polarizations.

Second, the rulers of A may staunchly and openly *oppose* oligarchy and pitilessly suppress domestic oligarchs. Democrats in A (now stauncher than ever) will applaud their rulers. The risk of suppression is that persecution will only increase the commitment of domestic oligarchs and provoke them into an uprising; should the military side with them, the country would have its own revolution and its democratic government would pay dearly. History also offers cases of such hard-line tactics. In the sixteenth century many Catholic rulers—the Habsburgs in Austria and Spain, the Wittelsbachs in Bavaria—responded to Lutheran revolutions in Germany by outlawing all Lutheran preaching, and many Protestant rulers prohibited the Catholic mass (chapter 4). Gustavus III of Sweden, Catherine II of Russia, and other monarchs responded similarly to demonstration effects of the French Revolution (chapter 5). In late 1918, the ruling Social Democratic Party of Germany responded to the demonstration effects of the Russian Revolution by ruthlessly suppressing German communists (chapter 6).

Third, the rulers of A may try a middle path, adopting some oligarchic reforms and co-opting "moderate" oligarchs via patronage, while mercilessly suppressing any oligarchs who refuse co-optation.[39] Such an *accommodationist* strategy might allow the government to hew to its principles while also being open to reform, and thereby avoid seriously alienating too many oligarchs and democrats. Chapters 4 through 7 offer many such cases. Francis I of France (r. 1515–47) remained a Catholic but until 1534 responded to the diffusion of Lutheranism by allowing its propagation in France (chapter 4). The wave of European revolutions in the early 1830s stirred up the liberal Chartist movement in Britain, and the British government responded with the Great Reform Act of 1832 (chapter 5). The potency of communism in the Third World after the Second World War led many nationalist leaders to cooperate with reform communists and to increase the state's share of the national economy while imprisoning those communists who remained revolutionary (chapter 6). The Iranian Revolution of 1979 led many secular rulers of Muslim countries to accelerate the Islamization of their societies that they had begun in the 1970s, even as they continued to try to crush revolutionary Islamists (chapter 7).

Which of these three options the rulers of A choose is contingent upon many exogenous factors, including the strength of their personal commitment to democracy, the decisions of other elites such as military officer corps, and their own judgments about future trends in the transnational democracy-*versus*-oligarchy contest. If they pursue either opposition or accommodation, then they have either or both of two incentives to consider promoting democracy and rolling back oligarchy in other states. The first incentive I call *internal security*. The democratic rulers of A, who face oligarchic opposition within A itself, can enhance their internal security in three ways by promoting democracy in C. First, they can make domestic and foreign audiences believe that democracy is stronger and oligarchy weaker than they initially appeared. Second, they can deprive their domestic oligarchic enemies of a measure of moral and material support from foreign confreres. Third, they can give their domestic oligarchic enemies an incentive to abandon their foreign oligarchic brethren so as not to appear unpatriotic.[40] Internal-security promotions typically occur following the outbreak of a revolution, as in Western Europe after 1789 or Eastern and Central Europe after 1917 (see further discussion in chapter 4). But they may occur in any international system in which domestic revolutions appear likely to take place, as in Europe in the 1820s or Latin America in the 1960s.

The second incentive, *external security*—the goal that realist theory emphasizes—may face even those rulers secure from domestic enemies. Such rulers can keep foreign states friendly, or turn enemies into friends, by intervening in other states to defeat ideological enemies.[41] By intervening in C to preserve democracy and defeat the oligarchs, A's rulers can increase the likelihood that A's future policies will serve A's interests.[42] C's democratic rulers may ally with A, allow A military or naval privileges, trade more with A, allow A to invest in C, and so on. State C's having a democratic regime means that pro-A actors are likely to govern C in the future.[43] Furthermore, C's democratic government is likely to perpetuate material interests in continuing close relations with A, such as economic interests that depend on such relations.[44] At the same time, were A to allow C to become oligarchic, those same benefits would accrue instead to A's rival, oligarchic B. These external-security enhancements may be short-term. Governments that share an ideology do not always remain allied; indeed, the empirical chapters in this book show that Catholic, monarchical, communist, and other supposedly fraternal groups of rulers can betray one another. Even so, during times of transnational ideological polarization, rulers may be desperate for even short-term ideological affinity. Examples of external-security promotions include Habsburg promotions of Catholicism in Germany during the Thirty Years' War (chapter 4), French promotions of Bonapartism between 1800 and 1810 (chapter 5), and American promotions of liberal democracy in the 1940s (chapter 6). Many foreign regime promotions, such as those common during the Wars of Religion or the Concert of Europe, were intended by power-seekers to secure both internal and external security. Forcible regime promotions, then, are wars intended to alter the preferences of the target state.[45]

These two incentives do not eliminate all of A's countervailing incentives *not* to intervene in C. Those incentives include the absolute costs of intervention, seldom trivial; the risk that oligarchic resistance within C will be greater than anticipated, increasing the costs; and the risk that B or other oligarchic powers—who face similar incentives regarding the outcome of C's civil war—will counter-intervene in C, or intervene on behalf of oligarchy in democratic state E, possibly leading to a more general war.[46] Indeed, as discussed later in this chapter, governments that share an ideology in highly polarized times sometimes form alliances precisely to increase these expected costs and deter forcible regime promotions. If the incentives to forgo forcible regime promotion are sufficiently high, the rulers of A will tend to rely on suppressing oligarchy within A and offering non-lethal aid to democrats in C.

## Short Waves of Forcible Regime Promotion

Many forcible regime promotions are isolated events, in which the promoter uses force in a target state in response to domestic unrest there and no further such promotions follow. When a group of Lutheran princes invaded Württemberg in 1534 to impose Lutheranism, no Catholic or other Lutheran interventions followed in the region (chapter 4). When Britain and Spain intervened in Portugal in 1826 to shore up the constitutional monarchy against an absolutist revolt, no absolutist counter-interventions followed (chapter 5). When the U.S. Marines invaded Haiti in 1994 to restore democracy, no other U.S. interventions in the Caribbean followed (chapter 6). As figure 1.1 shows, however, forcible regime promotions tend to cluster in time or to occur in short waves; often one is followed by another, sometimes by another country, which is followed by another, and so on.

Short waves of foreign regime promotion happen via two types of feedback loop. First, as I allude to above, promotion can alter the distribution of power among states by increasing the promoting state's foreign influence. Should A succeed in preserving democracy in C, oligarchic B has lost a potential ally. Thus, B's rulers have an incentive to counter-intervene in C or to promote oligarchy in democratic E. The opportunity costs of B's not doing so may be significant. Should B's rulers follow these incentives, they will likewise threaten to shift the distribution of power in B's favor, giving A's rulers incentives to carry out still more promotions.

Second, forcible regime promotion and transnational ideological polarization are endogenous. Just as polarization is self-reinforcing (see above), forcible regime promotion tends to intensify polarization and can thereby lead to still more promotions. When democratic A's rulers use force to preserve democracy in C, killing oligarchs and saving democrats in the process, they exacerbate the polarization between oligarchs and democrats all across the region.[47] TINs capitalize on the violence to recruit new members. Indeed, democrats and oligarchs throughout the system will have a growing incentive to launch a revolution or coup d'état, thinking that their great-power patron will come to their aid. That transnational ideological polarization, in turn, intensifies the incentives facing governments to carry out more forcible regime promotions. If democrats in D were pro-A and anti-B before A promoted democracy in C, they are even more so once A's intervention in C begins; A's government has all the more reason to promote democracy in D, and B's government all the more reason to promote oligarchy in D.

As suggested above, the possibility of a short wave of interventions, which can be highly costly and risk a general war, can deter a government from carrying out a forcible regime promotion to begin with. A's government, knowing that imposing democracy on C might draw B's government into a long and costly conflict, might stop short of intervening in C. But short waves of promotion, like other types of unintended violent conflict in international relations, nonetheless sometimes break out. Short waves followed a regime crisis in one state in the 1550s and 1620s in Central Europe (chapter 4); in the early 1820s, early 1830s, and 1848–49 in Central and Southern Europe (chapter 5); and in the 1930s in Europe and various parts of the Third World in the 1960s and 1970s (chapter 6). Short waves happened during a great-power war during the Thirty Years' War (chapter 4), the Wars of the French Revolution and Napoleon (chapter 5), and the Second World War (chapter 6).

Short waves of promotion decay—they are, after all, waves—and their decay is likewise a process of positive feedback. The less one government does it, the less incentive do its counterparts have to engage in it. Three types of event can trigger a waning of promotion. The first is an exogenous shift in the distribution of power among states, in particular the rise or decline of an extra-regional power. Rulers facing transnational ideological polarization do not cease to be concerned about the balance of power; indeed, as argued above, affecting that balance may be one goal of forcible regime promotion. Rulers who share an ideological enemy in a polarized system fear one another's relative gains that much less, but even they must deal with the consequences of international anarchy. Such happened several times during the Counter-Reformation, when the Catholic Holy Roman Emperor would face a renewed Ottoman threat and stop trying to overthrow German Lutherans (chapter 4). The rise of China in the 1960s helped to reduce the importance of ideology in the Cold War, leading to Soviet-American and Sino-American détente and a temporary lull in foreign regime promotion (chapter 6).

A second type of change that can suppress forcible regime promotion is *an increase in internal security or domestic stability in one or more states*.[48] Rulers by definition possess the apparatus of the state, and all else being equal we would expect them to use it to consolidate their power over time by reducing domestic ideological opposition. The Calvinist-Catholic wars in France and the Netherlands in the late sixteenth century, which attracted much foreign intervention, finally ended as Catholics triumphed in France and Calvinists won in the Netherlands (chapter 4). By the 1960s, communism ceased to be a domestic threat in Western European countries, as communist parties in these countries had distanced themselves from the Kremlin. In contrast to the early 1950s, when U.S. allies in Europe had contributed to turning back communism in South Korea, West European governments were uninterested in helping the United States in Vietnam (chapter 6).

A third type of event that can bring on the end of a short wave is endogenous: international polarization may become so costly that rulers agree to begin depolarizing the international system. Ideological wars and foreign interventions can become so destructive that rulers, notwithstanding the commitment problems in international politics, manage to agree to reduce their cooperation with foreign co-ideologues and their hostility toward ideological foes. Often they agree also to stop persecuting ideological enemies within their own borders. In 1555, following two religious wars, the princes of the Holy Roman Empire achieved the Religious Peace of Augsburg, in which each prince agreed to a rule of *cujus regio, ejus religio* (whose the realm, his the religion)—that is, to cease aiding co-religionists in other princes' territories. A similar agreement was reached in 1648 in the Peace of Westphalia, which followed a much more destructive continental war (chapter 4). The 1801 Treaty of Lunéville between France and Austria required the latter not to interfere in the constitutions of France's satellite republics (chapter 5). Soviet-American détente in the late 1960s and early 1970s was provoked not only by the rise of China but by a mutual perception that superpower competition had become too costly. Détente involved an implicit understanding on both sides that each would cease ideological interventions in smaller states (chapter 6).

Governments are typically ambivalent about these changes. Transnational ideological depolarization loosens alliances, and so rulers of great powers have some incentive to forestall it by keeping alive the fear of transnational ideological subversion in other states. Machiavelli notes that a prince might even be tempted secretly to nourish enemy factions in other states so as to perpetuate the domestic threat that keeps them dependent upon him. Such underhandedness seems rare in history, but governments do try to perpetuate fear of ideological subversion in allies.[49] The papacy often exaggerated the Protestant threat in the Counter-Reformation (chapter 4); in the 1790s, exiled French nobles (émigrés) exaggerated the republican threat to the rest of Europe (chapter 5); today many suspect that the Saudis, Egyptians, Jordanians, and others exaggerate the threat from radical Islamism in order to sustain U.S. support (chapter 7). Exaggerations by powerful actors are designed to be self-fulfilling statements.

Often, of course, the threats are not exaggerated, and indeed some actors have an interest in downplaying them. Early in his reign Francis I of France, a staunch Catholic, was blithe concerning transnational Lutheranism because he wanted to cultivate the German Lutheran princes so as to weaken his arch-rivals, the Habsburgs. Anti-Catholic demonstrations in Paris and elsewhere in 1534 changed Francis's mind and he began to persecute Lutherans, in turn damaging his relations with the Germans (chapter 4). In the 1790s, Charles James Fox and other British liberals dismissed the threat of revolutionary contagion from France in part because they so favored liberal reform in Britain (chapter 5). During the Cold War, governments wishing to distance their countries from their superpower patron sometimes deprecated the ideological threat emanating from the other bloc.

## Repolarization and More Promotions

During periods of low foreign regime promotion and transnational ideological agitation, actors often conclude that politics has returned to "normal" after a temporary spasm of ideological irrationality. In the terms of my argument, they come to believe that the grand ideological struggle is over and that *Realpolitik* has been restored, freeing countries to cooperate according to common material interest regardless of ideology. Events prove them mistaken. As long as TINs exist and retain the potential to threaten regime change somewhere in the region, the potential for transnational ideological repolarization and another round of forcible regime promotion persists. Should a domestic regime crisis erupt somewhere in the region, or a great-power war break out, governments may find themselves facing the familiar incentives to use force to alter or preserve the regimes of other states. Catholic and Protestant rulers in Central Europe got along well enough in the half-century after the Peace of Augsburg (1555), but then Protestant uprisings in Central Europe in the early seventeenth century triggered another spiral and eventually provoked the Thirty Years' War (chapter 4). The restoration of monarchism and a great-power concert in Europe after 1815 was already damaged in 1820 by a wave of liberal unrest throughout Europe, and was shattered by the wave of revolution that broke over Europe in 1830 (chapter 5). Soviet-American détente in the 1970s was damaged by ideological civil wars in Africa and finally destroyed by regime instability in Afghanistan in 1979 (chapter 6). Cooperation between Shia Iran and Sunni Pakistan and Saudi Arabia in Afghanistan in the early 1990s was broken by the rise of the militantly Sunni-Islamist Taliban (chapter 7).

### Anticipations and International Ideological Alliances

Sometimes transnational ideological polarization can lead not to forcible regime promotion but to the formation or solidification of international ideological blocs to deter such promotion. Such blocs form when rulers who adhere to a given regime type anticipate that great powers are likely to use force to overturn their regimes. Like international alliances in general, ideological alliances among states can indeed deter foreign attack. Thus, as seen in chapter 4, in the 1520s and 1530s Lutheran estates in the Holy Roman Empire sometimes formed ideological alliances to ward off feared Catholic crusading; Catholic estates would follow suit, out of fear of Protestant crusading; and relatively little forcible regime promotion actually took place.[50] Sometimes, however, alliances do not prevent wars and may indeed make them more likely.[51] In the late 1540s and early 1550s, ideological alliances did not prevent, and may have helped trigger, Catholic-Protestant wars among these same estates; at the very least, the alliances broadened the wars by obligating more states to fight them.[52]

Like forcible regime promotion, international ideological alliances "have to do with" ideology, but governments engage in them for what appear to them self-interested, *Realpolitik* reasons: they want to deter foreign attack. But foreign attack is likely under these conditions precisely because of transnational ideological polarization. Rulers who choose to continue ruling under their familiar regime make themselves enemies of rulers who adhere to a rival regime.[53] Tight ideological blocs may form even if no actor initially intended to roll back the opposing ideology or otherwise harm its adherents.[54]

### The Recurrence of Forcible Regime Promotion:
### From Agents to Structures

Our attention to agents and polarization only partly answers our central question: What causes forcible regime promotion? Figure 1.1 depicts not simply individual promotions and short waves, but three long waves, from the early sixteenth to the late seventeenth century, from the late eighteenth to the middle nineteenth, and from the early to the late twentieth. Furthermore, within each of these long waves the regimes being promoted, and hence the contending ideologies, were fairly fixed. In the first long wave the ideologies were established Catholicism and established Protestantism; in the second, absolutism, constitutionalism, and republicanism; in the third, communism, fascism, and liberal democracy.

In each of these long waves, TINs endured across time and space. The Calvinists in revolt in Bohemia in 1618 were generally regarded by friend and enemy alike as continuing or renewing the struggle of the Huguenots in France in the 1560s. And in Charles Tilly's terms, these TINs did have the power to reactivate an ideological boundary, and they used it.[55] The lines of conflict within societies in Central and Western Europe in the seventeenth century were set in the 1517–1550 period (chapter 4); those in Western Europe and the Americas in the first half of the nineteenth century, in the 1790s (chapter 5); those in most of the world in the twentieth century, in the 1910s and 1920s (chapter 6); and those in the Muslim world today, in the 1920s (chapter 7). These patterns suggest that something larger is going on across international history. If ideology is a social boundary for so many decades in so many countries, where does that boundary come from, why does it last as long as it does, and why does it eventually disappear?

The "something" is an ideological contest that stretches not only across countries but also across time.[56] Powering each long wave of forcible regime promotion was one of these contests. In the language of social theory, transnational ideological struggles are structural: they condition agents' preferences and actions and interactions. These grand struggles offered narratives to individuals that included goals, methods, and group identities. In turn, the individuals located one another and formed networks that labored to bring about regime changes and their discourse and actions, sustained the grand ideological struggles.

The discipline of sociology is home to theorizing about social structures, but political scientists, including those specializing in international relations, have adopted structural approaches in recent years. The fundamental insight is that agents' options are limited by socially held ideas—

social facts—that they cannot see or control but are nonetheless real. The Victorian novelist George Eliot captures the insight at the close of *Middlemarch*, as she justifies some of the mistakes of her virtuous heroine Dorothea Brooke:

> For there is no creature whose inward being is so strong that it is not greatly determined by what lies outside it. A new Theresa will hardly have the opportunity of reforming a conventual life, any more than a new Antigone will spend her heroic piety in daring all for the sake of a brother's burial: the medium in which their ardent deeds took shape is for ever gone. But we insignificant people with our daily words and acts are preparing the lives of many Dorotheas, some of which may present a far sadder sacrifice than that of the Dorothea whose story we know.[57]

The social norms, or "the times," in which Dorothea lives heavily condition her life and actions. Eliot also articulates the other side of the structuralist insight: "we insignificant people with our daily words and acts" reproduce the structure that conditions our actions. However unwittingly, Dorothea and her contemporaries help perpetuate the norms that constrain them.

Just so, the options and actions—indeed, the beliefs and desires—of rulers and TINs are heavily conditioned by prolonged transnational ideological struggles. These struggles condition action by telling agents who they and others are and want and how they stand in relation to one another. The agents reproduce the structure, keep it alive, by continuing to agitate for and carry out regime change. But these structures are not eternal; they arise in particular times and places, persist, and finally decay. In chapter 3 I focus on the origins, duration, and demise of these transnational ideological struggles.

# CHAPTER THREE

# The Structures: Transnational
# Ideological Contests

> *La Révolution* is but so many Alphabetic letters; a thing
> nowhere to be laid hands on, to be clapped under lock and
> key: where is it? what is it? It is the madness that dwells in the
> hearts of men. In this man it is, and in that man; as a rage or
> as a terror, it is in all men. Invisible, impalpable; and yet no
> black Azrael, with wings spread over half a continent, with
> sword sweeping from sea to sea, could be a truer Reality.
> —Thomas Carlyle, *1837*

In chapter 2, I argued that the clusters or short waves of forcible
regime promotion we observe over the past half millennium are caused
by periodic bouts of transnational ideological polarization. This polarization, entailing the progressive segregation of elites across countries according to which regime type they favor, gives governments incentives
to use force to promote their regime, or topple a rival regime, in foreign
states. Two types of event—a regime change in one state, or a war involving a great power—can trigger such elite polarization. These events are
exploited by pre-existing transnational ideological networks (TINs) who
have already been waging ideological combat.

I noted in closing that we must push the explanation beyond TINs,
rulers, and exogenous events. We must explain why governments promote the same set of regimes time and again over many decades. After
all, rulers would have more flexibility were they to break free from ideological contests. Yet, often they find that they are better off perpetuating
these contests and binding themselves, at least temporarily, to foreign co-
ideologues against foreign anti-ideologues. In 1618, Lutheran princes in
Saxony were not interested in helping Calvinist rebels in Bohemia, even
though they were fellow Protestants; but by 1629, the Lutherans had
joined the Calvinists in warring against the Catholic Holy Roman Emperor (chapter 4). We also must explain why TINs, who keep ideologies
alive and capitalize on exogenous events, are so durable across time and
space. TINs have little or no coercive power, and so their persistence—
their ability to attract and motivate actors across time and space, and
their prolonged potential to polarize and re-polarize societies according

to ideology—begs for explanation. The Bohemian revolt in 1618 was largely carried out by Calvinists who were part of an enduring transnational network and who saw their cause as continuous with that of French and Dutch Calvinists in the previous generation.

These actors, in other words, were constrained by an enduring transnational social structure. Explaining the recurrences of forcible regime promotion along the same ideological axes across so many decades requires that we explain the structures that sustain those recurrences. That is the task of this chapter. The explanation is complicated because, as I mentioned at the close of chapter 2, the structure is sustained by the very words and actions that it explains. The agitations of TINs and the actions of governments—particularly forcible regime promotion itself—perpetuate the transnational ideological struggle that constrains those same TINs and governments.[1] But the struggle—the social structure doing so much causal work—was not always there, and it eventually fades away. Thus, my explanation for long waves is what Arthur Stinchcombe terms *historicist*: "an effect created by causes at some previous period *becomes a cause of that same effect* in succeeding periods."[2] Other social scientists refer to path-dependency: actions by one set of actors at time t constrain the actions of another set at time t + 1, whose actions in turn further constrain the actions of still another set at t + 2, and so on.[3]

The burden of this chapter, then, is to explain the origins, persistence, and eventual decline of these structures, these transnational contests over the best regime. I advance what Paul Kowert and Jeffrey Legro term an ecological account,[4] specifically an evolutionary explanation, following some recent constructivist scholarship.[5] New regime types may be compared to mutations; although they are not actors (any more than alleles are actors in biological evolution), we may profitably view them as struggling for reproductive advantage, where reproduction entails adoption by states. States adopt a new regime type via revolution or other mode when the social and material environment changes enough to pose anomalies to the predominant regime type. Sometimes new environmental developments can create difficulties for the predominant domestic regime type in a region and lead to the emergence of one or more new regimes.

As long as enough elites remain confident that the old regime can weather the storm, a struggle will ensue among elites over the best regime. The struggle is sustained over time and space by the absence of a clear winner. Eventually one regime type proves best able to meet the interests of elites in a stable and secure polity. The winning regime type is revealed by the superior performance of its exemplary states—that is, their manifest superiority at prospering under the new social and material environment. Elites across states converge on the winner, the transnational struggle ends, and the social structure that causes forcible regime promotion crumbles.

These struggles are usually confined to regions. By "region" I mean what Peter Katzenstein calls a "behavioral region," defined according to the number and velocity of interactions across societies, which correlates heavily to geographical proximity.[6] In the cases in this book, only communism in the latter half of the Cold War, and liberal democracy since the 1980s, have approached global status.

## Political Regimes

"Structure" is a vague term in international relations. In recent decades much scholarly energy has been devoted to arguing what belongs in a useful conception of structure: relative military power? wealth? technology? process? information? Constructivists argue that structure consists of ideas, particularly norms and culture. The ideational structure I posit consists of deep conflict, spanning a region, over the best political regime.

Regimes are fundamental to politics, analogous to Kuhn's scientific paradigms: each is necessary to normal practice in its realm.[7] Kuhn defines normal science as "research firmly based upon one or more past scientific achievements, achievements that some particular scientific community acknowledges for a time as supplying the foundation for its further practice." Those achievements compose a paradigm. When scientists practice normal science their questions and methods, and the meaning of their answers, are controlled by the paradigm. These scientists disagree, but the rules by which disagreements are identified and managed are set by the paradigm. Far from being a straitjacket that hampers scientific progress, a paradigm is essential to such progress because scientists require some common assumptions in order to have fruitful disagreements; without a paradigm they cannot agree on which facts are important. Because a paradigm has such credibility and the opportunity costs of casting it aside are high—one paradigm may be replaced only by another—scientists avoid anomalies and, when anomalies nevertheless turn up, scientists take pains to defend the paradigm. That defense, and "mopping up" work in which the paradigm is further refined, constitutes normal science. It is, in a word, conservative.

Paradigms do get replaced, however, and the moments of replacement are Kuhn's scientific revolutions. Paradigmatic status rides upon the ability to explain facts. Although a paradigm turns attention away from anomalies and scientists try to explain away those that turn up, sometimes anomalies survive these defenses. The paradigm then enters a crisis in which many scientists doubt its veracity. One or more alternative paradigms emerge and compete with the old paradigm, and a period of *extraordinary science* ensues. The competing paradigms are incommensurable: advocates of each argue for its superiority on its own terms. Competing paradigms gain adherents who develop their logics and explain new facts. Eventually a new paradigm wins the field and inaugurates another period of normal science.

As in science, so in politics: regimes emerge, endure, and eventually give way just as paradigms do. Regimes may be distinguished along various dimensions. For Aristotle, what matters is how many ruled: the one (the good being monarchy, the bad being tyranny), the few (aristocracy or oligarchy), or the many (polity or democracy).[8] During the sixteenth and seventeenth centuries in Central and Western Europe, the most salient distinction was which would be the officially established church, and this in turn implicated the power of the prince vis-à-vis the transnational Catholic hierarchy (chapter 4). For much of the nineteenth century the salient distinctions were among republics, constitutional monarchies (in which the Crown was constrained by duly constituted bodies), and absolute monarchies (chapter 5). In the industrialized world in most of the twentieth century, regimes were distinguished (in the West) by how coercive the state was vis-à-vis private groups and individuals (chapter 6). In the Muslim world today the most salient distinction is that between Islamist and secularist regimes (chapter 7). Regardless of which regime typology is dominant, those living under a regime generally agree to manage their inevitable disagreements within a set of ground rules legitimated by a justifying narrative. Although every country at all times experiences some measure of political conflict, and not all regimes are equally just, most countries most of the time have a settled regime or set of fundamental institutions accepted by most actors.

Like scientific paradigms, political regimes are sometimes replaced. In an individual polity without a settled regime, disagreement is more dangerous precisely because agreement is lacking over the ground rules. The stakes are higher because they include the rules, institutions, and justifying narrative of the polity itself. In an absolute monarchy in eighteenth-century Europe (chapter 5), a nobleman who lost his position at the royal court was typically banished to his country estate, and he or his family could later seek rehabilitation; for other nobles, life went on as before. A democratic revolution, on the other hand, was a threat to the nobility as a class. It is crucial for us to grasp the full importance of life without an established regime: by definition, there are no established ways of settling disputes; the parties fundamentally disagree over justice, fairness, reasonableness, tradition; they differ over the meanings of words and symbols and so may be unintelligible to one another. The similarity to Kuhn's extraordinary science is not coincidental, for he uses the same analogy to build his case for the existence of scientific revolutions:

> Political revolutions aim to change political institutions in ways that those institutions themselves prohibit. Their success therefore necessitates the partial relinquishment of one set of institutions in favor of another, and in the interim, society is not fully governed by institutions at all: Initially it is crisis alone that attenuates the role of political institutions as we have already seen it attenuate the role of paradigms. In increasing numbers individuals become increasingly estranged from political life and behave more and more eccentrically within it. Then, as the crisis deepens, many of these individuals commit themselves to some concrete proposal for the reconstruction of society in a new institutional framework. At that point the society is divided into competing camps or parties, one seeking to defend the old institutional constellation, the others seeking to institute some new one. And, once that polarization has occurred, political recourse fails. Because they differ about the institutional matrix within which political change is to be achieved and evaluated, because they acknowledge no supra-institutional framework for the adjudication of revolutionary difference, the parties to a revolutionary conflict must finally resort to the techniques of mass persuasion, often including force.[9]

Part of what it means to have a regime contest is that there is no regime to manage the conflict. That does not imply perpetual chaos or slaughter. Kuhn describes the formation of competing camps, which internally and collectively impose a type of predictability on the society. These camps we may call ideological networks: interdependent actors sharing a goal, communicating intensely, sustained via trust more than wealth or coercion.

## The Structure: A Transnational Struggle over the Best Regime

What goes for politics within a country may also go for politics *across countries* in a region. When elites across a set of societies differ as to the best regime, some continuing to hew to the old, others backing various forms of a new, the region itself is in transnational ideological contest (the dotted blue curve in figure 1.2). Those who contend for the old regime interact across countries and see themselves as interdependent, their struggle as international. They define the old regime over against the new regime or regimes. Those who contest for one of the new regimes see themselves in similar fashion, defined over against the old regime. We have now arrived at the ideational structure that causes the three sets of recurring waves of forcible regime promotion analyzed in chapter 2. The structure in question is *a common understanding that the old regime is in crisis and one must either support or oppose it.* Opposing the old regime entails backing an alternative; old and new are generally regarded to be in a zero-sum contest. This structure provides a plausible narrative and identity for political elites and hence a plan of action: they are Catholics, and their enemies are Lutherans; constitutional monarchists, and their enemies are absolutists; communists, and their enemies are fascists.

During a transnational regime contest some countries settle on which regime they think best. In such societies, a majority of elites may rally to the old regime or to a new one, virtually ending deep ideological strife domestically. What brings on and sustains a long wave is that, in the region as a whole, no such consensus emerges. Across societies, and within some societies, the best regime remains a matter of contention, and each contender is defined by all as mutually exclusive vis-à-vis its enemy.[10] Before the Reformation ushered in a prolonged regime struggle, Christians were generally defined as anti-Muslims, looking to the Ottoman Empire as the Other; with the onset of the Reformation, Catholic Christianity became redefined as anti-Protestant (and Protestant Christianity was anti-Catholic). Before the rise of communism, Western liberals generally opposed absolute monarchy; with communism's rise and the increasing irrelevance of absolutism, they became anti-communist.

The foregoing paragraphs provide a re-description of a long transnational ideological struggle, during which forcible regime promotion is especially likely to occur. It is not the case that all elites are perpetually polarized along ideological lines throughout such a struggle. Most elites have various other concerns and find it possible to cooperate much of the time across ideological lines. Only elites affiliated with TINs continually make the ideological struggle their top priority; they help keep the struggle going. As described in chapter 2, two types of triggering event—regime instability in a state somewhere in the region, or a great-power war—can polarize other elites according to ideology and give governments incentives to impose domestic regimes abroad.[11]

For international relations theorists concerned with norms, I offer a clarification. A transnational ideological contest alone does not entail the destruction or even weakening of international order or society in the sense meant by the English School.[12] International norms and institutions, such as the *pacta sunt servanda* (agreements must be kept) rule, may still obtain among states during a sustained contest over the best regime. During particularly intense short waves of foreign regime promotion, relations among great powers may be so degraded that international society itself is weakened. Such was the case during parts of the Thirty Years' War (chapter 4) and the aftermath of the Bolshevik coup d'état (chapter 6). But I do not explore any interaction between a grand ideological struggle and the fabric of international society itself.

International Politics before a Transnational Ideological Struggle

During "normal" times, when no transnational struggle rages over ideology, new ideas do arise and penetrate societies, but governments successfully co-opt them and do not allow them to threaten the regime. New ideas perpetually arise among elites[13] and rulers may take active steps to monitor them and the networks that advocate them, modifying and adopting ideas when they can and opposing and suppressing them when they must.[14] Even unprincipled rulers must care about ideas because ideas are part of their social environment that they must shape to their advantage. More precisely, the regime under which they hold power is constituted in part by a particular notion of legitimacy, be it theocracy, monarchy, communism, or something else. Legitimacy, as Max Weber cogently argued, is necessary to the stability of the state: "If the state is to exist, the dominated must obey the authority claimed by the powers that be."[15] Even new ideas that may seem in the abstract unrelated to politics, if not skillfully handled by rulers, may develop into principles that are the basis of a regime challenge. Thus, rulers under totalitarian regimes such as those of North Korea or Burma today avoid the risks associated with new ideas by sealing off the country and ruthlessly suppressing disagreement.

As the wretched state of those countries shows, however, totalitarianism is extremely costly in terms of both domestic security apparatus and forgone innovation and efficiency. Thus, most rulers accept some risk by allowing their societies exposure to new ideas by means of interaction with foreign societies and some ability to absorb and develop those new ideas. The task for rulers is to turn new ideas to their advantage or at least see that those ideas do not jeopardize their power by threatening their legitimacy or that of the regime. Thus, the authoritarian regimes in China and Iran both allow their citizens access to the Internet, but spend dear resources censoring that source.

Governments of liberal democracies also must worry about new ideas. But one of liberal democracy's distinctive properties is its high capacity to produce and absorb new ideas about justice, power, wealth, technology, and so forth. The Great Depression led to the emergence and prominence of economic theories throughout the industrial world that counseled an increase in the state's control over the distribution of resources. Liberal democracies adopted Keynesian and other welfare-state ideas in the 1930s and 1940s, abandoned them in the 1970s and 1980s, and are adopting them again at the time of this writing, all without ceasing to be liberal democracies.[16] Keynesianism and monetarism never threatened liberal democracy because governments were able to take on new economic ideas through virtuous interaction with the ideas' advocates.

Rulers do not always succeed in turning new ideas to their regimes' advantage. Regime-challenging ideologies emerge when dissidents enter a vicious cycle of interaction with rulers and other supporters of the status quo regime. Radical ideologies do not emerge full-blown from the minds of isolated philosophers or politicians, but rather gain definition in a dialectical movement among ideas and interacting actors. Thinkers do have an essential role in the emergence of political ideologies; Keynes's own influence demonstrated his famous aphorism that "Madmen in authority, who hear voices in the air, are distilling their frenzy from some academic scribbler of a few years back."[17] But those academic scribblers' ideas are always a product of social interaction, as are the transformations the scribblings undergo en route to becoming policy.[18] These interactions are shot through with contingency, and hence the precise form an ideology will take is impossible to predict from antecedent conditions.[19] Among French Enlightenment figures, Voltaire (1694–1778) was an absolute monarchist, Montesquieu (1689–1755) an advocate of aristocracy, and Rousseau (1712–78) a republican. In 1765, it was not at all clear that within thirty years the Enlightenment would come to be identified across societies with republicanism.

During normal international politics, transnational networks that are alienated from the predominant regime may exist, but lack any potential to disrupt foreign policy. Today monarchist societies thread across the world, loosely linked to one another;[20] their members, when noticed at all by outsiders, are regarded as harmless eccentrics precisely because monarchism has virtually no magnetic power in most non-monarchical societies today, and is a matter of indifference even in most monarchical countries (excepting those of the Persian Gulf). Maoism remains alive today in the Philippines, Nepal, India, Peru, and elsewhere (including certain university towns in the West), and some governments, national or regional, must devote dear resources to combating them.[21] But since the People's Republic of China, Maoism's birthplace and original patron, abandoned it in 1981, the ideology has little affected international politics.

But why do rulers need to be wedded to a particular regime? Why not change regimes if ideas that challenge the regime gain enough momentum? Sometimes they do so, as discussed below. But normally, as I discussed in chapter 2, rulers find the psychic, social, and material costs too high. Ideas about public order create and sustain societal actors who benefit from them and block the creation of alternative actors. Ideas associated with capitalism create and sustain (and are sustained by) certain actors who are threatened by socialism; these press their governments to reject socialism. The same was true of communism vis-à-vis capitalism; the Soviet *nomenklatura* had real interests in blocking private enterprise and any reformers who would bring it about (chapter 6).[22] The doctrine that clothing fashion is vital to public order has created a cohort of censors and fashion police in Islamist countries who would be loath to relinquish their power (chapter 7). Regimes are not ethereal phenomena, but construct, and are embodied in, interests and institutions.[23]

Furthermore, regime change can be wrenching for the masses in society. A regime provides predictability that allows normal social interaction to flourish. Notwithstanding the French revolutionaries' self-presentation as liberators of the peasantry, the peasants of the Vendée and other regions of France fought against the Revolution of 1789 out of loyalty to the ancient institution of lord and vassal, which was familiar and, as far as they were concerned, served their interests as they understood them (chapter 5).[24] Conservatism, an attachment to tradition and a skepticism toward fundamental change, is a force to be reckoned with in most societies at most times. That is one reason why Machiavelli advised the prince to appear pious: an impious prince may lose the support of his subjects.[25]

## The Coming of an Ideological Struggle

Notwithstanding successful regimes' self-perpetuating mechanisms, contests over policy reform occasionally expand into region-wide zero-sum contests over regimes. Reformers become radicals, rulers become reactionaries, and policy ideas congeal into oppositional ideas concerning fundamental domestic regimes. Elites come under pressure to affiliate with the old regime or the new. Conditions come into being that make forcible regime promotion, and all of its consequences, more likely. What accounts for the emergence of this new ideational structure? Some accounts of ideational change in world politics look to triggering events— what Daniel Philpott calls "circumstances of reflection,"[26] and Jeffrey Legro calls ideational "collapse."[27] I build upon such notions to argue that a transnational ideological struggle emerges when the status quo regime upon which the former rests is battered, across states, by a sufficient accumulation of significant anomalies or failures on its own terms.

### Transnational Regime Crisis

The first phase of a transnational ideological struggle is a crisis for the predominant regime across societies. In describing a crisis for a scientific paradigm, Kuhn compares it to a revolutionary crisis in politics, marked by "a growing sense ... often restricted to a segment of the political community, that existing institutions have ceased adequately to meet the problems posed by an environment that they have in part created."[28] Jack

Goldstone notes that recent literature on political revolutions emphasizes that a necessary (but insufficient) condition for a revolution is elite
alienation from the regime. Alienation may be produced by governmental
incompetence, or perceived unjust treatment of elites themselves, or an
interaction between these two.[29]

How do such crises emerge? As described above, during normal international politics rulers interact with advocates of new ideas who form
transnational networks. Rulers adopt new ideas and co-opt their advocates so as to enhance their efficiency and safeguard their legitimacy. Often they do not reform their practices enough to appease some advocates
of change. Effective leaders can divide and marginalize such dissidents
through suppression and indifference, but their main weapon against
them is the continued effectiveness of the regime itself. So long as the
regime continues to succeed on its own terms, it will endure. Those terms
are historically contingent, specific to a regime's own legitimating narrative. Medieval Catholic regimes presented themselves as pious; absolute
monarchies, as powerful; fascist regimes, as superior empire-builders.

Legro describes ideational collapse as happening when "societies adhere to ideational prescriptions but the actual outcome contradicts expectations with stark failure."[30] When a regime type is manifestly failing to fulfill its own promises, it enters what I shall call a crisis. By the
1510s, particularly in the estates of the Holy Roman Empire, the Catholic Church was not living up to its own self-proclaimed standards of
piety (chapter 4). By the 1770s, absolute monarchy in Europe was not
delivering the goods it had promised, instead bringing on pointless wars
and bankruptcy (chapter 5). By the 1910s, capitalism and parliamentary
government had deeply disappointed and alienated vast numbers among
the growing class of factory workers (chapter 6). By the same decade in
the Muslim world, the centuries-old Ottoman regime had clearly failed
to restore the power and majesty of the Muslim community or *ummah*
(chapter 7).

Across states, rulers find that their reforms are insufficient not only
for a containable minority of malcontents but for increasing numbers of
important actors. Mindful of their increasing numbers, these reformers
accelerate their interactions across state boundaries, sharing information
and encouragement, and begin to make more radical demands of the
rulers. Throughout the region, rulers and other defenders of the predominant regime enter a vicious cycle of interaction with dissidents. As dissidents become emboldened by signs of regime failure, regime defenders
become more ruthless in suppressing them. Rather than melting away, as
in normal times, dissidents respond to the suppression by becoming further emboldened and find their numbers increasing. They begin to con-

clude that what is needed is not simply changes in law or policy, or even of leadership, but of the fundamental institutions of society. Across states, reformers become radicals.

This is the point at which bona fide TINs emerge: institutionalized networks of radicals cooperating, however ineffectively, to bring about regime change across countries. In turn, regime defenders see that formerly pliable reformers are now their enemies, and move from conservatism to reaction. Transnational ideological agitation of this sort took place in the Holy Roman Empire from 1517 to the early 1520s, as Lutherans polarized from the Catholic authorities and increased their cooperation and coherence with one another (chapter 4). In Europe and North America in the 1760s and 1770s, liberals networked extensively and began to buttress one another's opposition to monarchy (chapter 5). In Europe in the last quarter of the nineteenth century, socialists and anarchists cooperated and planned their bid to overturn the status quo (chapter 6). In each case status quo defenders reacted by become more repressive but found that this time repression only swelled the ranks of the radicals.

What triggers this kind of vicious cycle that produces a regime crisis? Why does a predominant regime begin to encounter anomalies? Changes in the states' material and social environment occur that the regime is unable to manage to the satisfaction of at least some elites. The environment is infinitely complex, consisting of ideational variables such as beliefs concerning the good life, how knowledge is acquired, and actors' group identities such as class or ethnicity. It also consists of material variables such as technology, birth and death rates, and natural disasters. These events are themselves unpredictable in both occurrence and impact. As with evolutionary theory in biology, the exogenous environmental changes that reward certain entities and punish others are only identifiable after the fact.[31]

The crisis in the late-medieval European regime came with new developments in learning, particularly humanism, and a long schism within the Church and growing corruption that damaged its credibility (chapter 4). The crisis in absolute monarchy in the eighteenth century was produced by expensive wars and bankruptcies and the relative inferiority of agricultural production in absolutist states (chapter 5). The crisis in reforming conservative regimes in the late nineteenth century was a result of industrialization and the associated loss of power by artisans and emergence of the factory workers (chapter 6). The crisis in the traditional Islamic regime in the early twentieth century resulted from the development of new military technologies in the West and the Ottoman Empire's obvious inability to produce such innovations (chapter 7). Each of these crises alienated many elites from the predominant regime, but other elites remained convinced that that regime could reform its way out of the problem; a vicious cycle ensued and alienated elites turned against the predominant regime.

Regime crisis alone does not thrust international politics into a sustained contest over the best regime. As long as radicals have not captured a state and set up a new regime, they are weak and fragmented, with no unified counter-ideology around which to mobilize; they know what they are against but cannot agree precisely on what they are for or who should lead them. Although they may acquire lethal means and practice terrorism or guerrilla warfare, they also lack the command of a state's coercive apparatus. Regime crisis without the establishment of a new alternative regime may last for many years. Before some estates of the Holy Roman Empire began to establish Lutheranism and root out Catholic institutions, the nascent Reformation little affected relations among princes (chapter 4). From 1848 until 1917, communism was a mere specter haunting Europe, more a matter of internal security than foreign policy (chapter 6).

*Regime Change*

When radicals capture a state and establish a new regime, the transnational ideological struggle—the social structure that is so consequential to international politics—takes shape. The regime change may be by means of revolution, coup d'état, ruler's decision, lawful succession, or other means. When disputes over regimes do not implicate the institutions concerning the ruler, that ruler may remain in power and simply convert the regime. Thus, Landgrave Philip of Hesse and the Elector John of Saxony transformed their Imperial estates from Catholic to Lutheran ones in 1526, making themselves effectively head of the local church (chapter 4). When the locus of contention implicates the ruler directly, such a conversion is not possible. Thus in France, Louis XVI was overthrown in 1792 as the First French Republic was established; there was no question of making Louis a president or other elected head of state (chapter 5). In Russia, the revolution first toppled the Tsar (March 1917), then was seized in a coup by the Bolsheviks (November) (chapter 6). In the Ottoman Empire, Mustafa Kemal carried out a coup against the Sultan in 1923 and established the modern secular state of Turkey (chapter 7).

Whatever its form, regime change in one state affects relations among states via its two effects on TINs. First, by creating an actual concrete new regime, it solidifies into a single ideology transnational opposition to the old regime, giving it coherence and protecting it against divide-and-conquer tactics by defenders of the latter. Second, the new-regime state becomes an exemplar that has a strong claim on the loyalty of the members of the TINs. A clearer social boundary, corresponding to ideology, now cuts across societies.[32] Throughout the region once dominated by a single regime type, elites are under increased pressure to choose sides for or against the new regime. The international structure so consequential for decades to come is now in place.

By definition, a regime struggle requires that some states retain the old regime. There is no complete cascade of elites to the new regime, as happened in Central Europe in 1989. Rather, a critical mass of elites in such states continues to believe in the viability of the old regime. Typically, a legitimacy crisis for the predominant regime does not shake the support of all elites, and once they decide to stand fast the new regime is by definition a threat to their power. In some countries, old-regime elites succeed in suppressing the radicals. Rulers hewing to the old regime may cooperate with one another to that end, finding a new common interest against transnational subversion. By succeeding in turning back regime change within their own borders, old-regime rulers renew the transnational credibility of their domestic institutions. They may try to form their own TINs to counter the radical TINs. Thus, a region undergoing a long wave is ideologically heterogeneous. Typically it will comprise some societies under the old regime, and some under the new. Some of these societies may be relatively united, their domestic regimes facing little domestic opposition. Others will be deeply divided internally over ideology.

## A Clarification

My accounts of individual promotions (chapter 2) and transnational regime contests (this chapter) both use the concepts of social (ideological) polarization and feedback loops. The two processes are different, however, and must be kept analytically and empirically distinct. In the emergence of a transnational struggle, the very ideological categories, the social boundaries, are created and TINs established. In particular regime promotions during a transnational struggle, the social boundaries previously established are deactivated and reactivated.[33] The process of boundary creation is distinct from that of boundary reactivation.

## Continuity through a Transnational Ideological Contest

A prolonged ideological struggle constitutes a social structure that connects with agents—TINs and rulers—via feedback loops. The structure exerts downward causation upon agents, limiting the range of preferences they can plausibly adopt and actions they can carry out. In turn, the agents act so as to reproduce the structure: TINs agitate for regime change, and sometimes rulers use force to impose or preserve regimes in foreign states. TINs and rulers thereby sustain the plausibility of the structure: oligarchs say, "See what Athens is doing in Corcyra? Democrats are killing oligarchs. The democrats *are* our enemies! Our fellow oligarchs *are* our brothers!" Agents in two or more states who otherwise have little in common attach themselves to the same ideology and thus acquire a pre-existing set of transnational friends and enemies. Of course, these transnational ideas are mediated in each country by differing conditions.[34] In the 1790s, American republicanism was different from French; Islamism today in Uzbekistan is not identical to that in Algeria or Bradford, England. Analysis that ignores those differences is useless for certain purposes. But what Charles Pouthas writes of Europe in the second quarter of the nineteenth century could be said of long ideological struggles in other periods as well: "Problems which were analogous in general took different forms in each state and produced conflicting results; the same vocabulary, the same programme, concealed dissimilar situations."[35] They often make clear that their version of the ideology is specific to their country—sixteenth-century Calvinism implied different institutions in France than in England, and Mao Zedong made clear that *his* socialism had "Chinese characteristics"—but they are understood by themselves and others to be taking sides in a grand transnational contest over the best regime. The more polarized are elites across societies, the more do these differences melt away.

*Multiple Ideologies*

Extraordinary politics is not chaotic, but neither does it feature two inert ideologies competing until one triumphs. The constant feature of a long wave is not a fixed struggle between two ideologies, but the transnational crisis of the old regime. As long as no clear winner has emerged, ideologues may develop multiple variants, some of which may capture states and join the competition. Two, three, or more alternative regimes may emerge during a long wave, constitute TINs, and capture one or more states. Sometimes one ideology splits into two or more groups that come to be rivals, as when Calvinism developed from Lutheranism (chapter 4). Sometimes one ideology may produce a second in reaction, which in turn produces a third in reaction; this is roughly the story of liberalism generating communism and communism generating fascism (chapter 6). Sometimes a third ideology arises as an attempted synthesis of the first two.[36] Sometimes moderate adherents of two ideologies coalesce around the principle of toleration. Although such a coalition may be intended to transcend the ideological divide, it actually forms a third ideological group that competes with the first two. Such happened at many points during the Wars of Religion, as when some French Catholics responded to the Reformation by becoming *politiques*, elites who favored some measure of toleration of Protestants under a Catholic regime (chapter 4).

Contests among three or more ideological groups generally follow a familiar balance-of-power logic wherein enemies of enemies are friends. Two ideological groups may coalesce against a third as a tactical measure. As is typical in such coalitions, cooperation tends to be handicapped by the possibility that the common enemy may weaken and with it the common interest binding the other two ideological groups together; either or both may later want to cooperate with the current common enemy against the current ally. In the Second World War, liberal America and Britain allied with the communist Soviet Union against the fascist powers, causing much rationalization and rhetorical backpedaling from long-standing anti-communist Westerners (chapter 6). Most infamous to today's readers are the many instances of Cold War cooperation by the United States and other Western democracies with right-wing authoritarians in Latin America, Asia, Africa, and southern Europe. Democratic-authoritarian cooperation included alliances and other security cooperation and, most notoriously, foreign interventions by democracies on behalf of authoritarians. The strength of Islamism in the Middle East and Southwest Asia has perpetuated much of the same sort of cooperation between the liberal United States and authoritarian Egypt, Saudi Arabia, and Pakistan, among others (chapter 7).

## Why Prolonged Struggles Are Prolonged

During a long ideological contest there exist times and places when governments do not engage in forcible regime promotion, and even conclude that ideological foreign policies were temporary spasms or bouts of irrationality that have ended mercifully. During the superpower détente of the 1970s many, at least in the West, believed that the Soviet-American rivalry was over. But owing to the Soviet invasion of Afghanistan and U.S. responses to it, the struggle was not to end for another decade. More generally, struggles are so durable because agents shape their environment so as to perpetuate them. Great powers that exemplify a contending regime lengthen the life of a struggle by promoting their regime abroad and by nurturing TINs. The strength of Catholic Spain helped extend the life of the Catholic-Protestant struggle analyzed in chapter 4; the endurance of the Soviet Union did the same for communism, as analyzed in chapter 6. As long as elites across societies remain divided as to the best regime, the potential for ideological re-polarization and more foreign regime promotion will remain.

The Decay of a Long Wave: One Regime Type Wins

Transnational ideological struggles eventually end, and with them long waves of forcible regime promotion. The ideologies that animate TINs shift from being radical, regime-implicating programs to being reformist programs. Rulers stop promoting regimes abroad. International relations return to the norm depicted by realists, in which states intervene abroad with little regard for ideology. In the Western world, Catholic and Protestant have long ceased to be fundamental political identities except in Northern Ireland. The same is true for republicanism and monarchism: Europe comprises states of both kinds, but few Europeans care. North Korea, Cuba, and (nominally) China are still ruled by communist parties or dictators, and communist movements continue to agitate in small countries such as Colombia, Nepal, and the Philippines. But the Marxist-Leninist regime type has lost all plausibility and appeal among most elites around the world. Within the industrialized world, Left and Right compete within a regime accepted as legitimate by all.

When and how do these ideological social boundaries lose, once and for all, their fundamental political salience? When and how do political differences descend from regime-threatening, zero-sum contests to affairs of policy, matters not of revolution but of disagreement under a common regime? The same selection mechanisms dissolve the contest as began it. Across states, elites agree that, after the decades-long struggle, one regime has emerged superior to its competitors.[37] Elites cascade toward a single regime type, in a case of what Mark Beissinger calls elite defection. Triggering this cascade is a conversion by elites in one or more great powers from one ideology to another and a concomitant regime change in those great powers. Great-power regime changes are so consequential for two reasons. First, such states' superior positions in the international hierarchy make them ideological exemplars. Their changes enjoy greater demonstration effects than changes in lesser powers. Second, it is the rulers of great powers who carry out most forcible (and non-forcible) foreign regime promotion. When great powers all come to adopt regime type A, then elites who support regimes B and C throughout the region realize that they no longer have a powerful patron.

But what triggers this cascade of elite defections, after so many decades of stubborn adherence to opposing ideologies? Here again, unpredictable exogenous changes in states' social and material environment disrupt established ways of doing things, leading elites to doubt the efficacy of the struggle itself. The changes may involve technological developments, demographic changes, or social changes such as the rise of a new class. One or more contending regimes prove less able to deliver on their promises as great powers that exemplify them fall further behind. Elites convert to an alternative regime type, even if it would dilute their power, if it has proved in other societies that it grants some privileges or rights to elites. Furthermore, over the decades of a long wave, new types of elite arise, with interests better served by an alternative regime, and these gain in number and leverage.

I have been arguing that regimes and their environments are endogenous, so how can I argue that environment can kill off a regime? Agents who impose a regime on another country are indeed attempting to transform their environment so as to make it friendlier to the regime and hence to themselves. They implicitly understand that the environment selects and they want to make the selection mechanism favor their regime type. Woodrow Wilson said America must enter the Great War to "make the world safe for democracy"; other great-power leaders using force to promote their ideology might have used a similar justification. Furthermore, agents attempt to set the standards by which regimes are judged, and supporters of a regime interpret events, including lost wars and economic crises, in ways that support that regime.

But agents cannot completely manage their environments. Not only are they competing with other agents promoting rival regimes, but the environment contains social and material factors beyond their control. Eventually some of these aspects of the environment push back. As in the emergence of a regime contest, the demise of a contest is unpredictable and its cause identifiable only after the fact. Just as the Darwinian theory on which evolutionary models are based cannot predict which species or genes will triumph—in part because these too interact with their environments—no covering-law explanation is available of which regime type will triumph.

Transnational elite convergence around a clear winner took place in all three long waves in chapters 4 through 6. The first, involving contests in Europe over church and state, ended when the institutions of religious toleration proved most successful at delivering wealth and national power. It was in the Netherlands that a new regime that had emerged in the 1570s, under which most religions were permitted (if not socially equal), proved itself better able to deliver wealth, stability, and national power than intolerant regimes, Catholic and Protestant alike. When England adopted a tolerant regime after 1688, and began to flourish, toleration began to appear to most elites the best regime (chapter 4). The second long struggle, among absolute monarchy, constitutional monarchy, and republicanism, was won in Europe by a general version of constitutionalism in the 1870s. That was the regime in Great Britain, the one great power that had proved immune to the alarming wave revolutions of 1848 and that had consolidated its position as first among Europe's great powers. When France, Austria, and Prussia all became constitutional states, and even Russia began liberal reforms, absolutism lost most of its transnational momentum (chapter 5). The third long contest, among liberal democracy, communism, and fascism, ended in two separate steps. Fascism failed in 1945 with Nazi Germany's overwhelming defeat, but liberal democracy only vanquished communism forty years later when the latter's exemplars, China and the Soviet Union, found it irredeemably wanting in helping them compete with the liberal-democratic United States.[38] Around the world, the ideology lost its luster; governments and parties switched from communist to social-democratic, and communist transnational networks lost the potential in most countries to threaten regimes (chapter 6). North Korea and Cuba hew to the old ideology, but are known outside their own borders as atavistic oddities rather than riders of the wave of the future.

In each of these cases, elites backing the losing regime bargained with their counterparts; the losers did not go quietly, and gained some concessions from the winners. But the loss was clear to all: the TINs that agitated for the losing regimes fizzled, surviving where they did on crime rather than popularity.[39]

## In Sum

In chapter 2, I sketched the agents—TINs and rulers—who bring about short waves of forcible regime promotion and offered an explanation for why rulers sometimes impose regimes on foreign countries. In this chapter I have sketched the social structures that shape these agents and their incentives, and offered an account of why those structures arise, persist, and decline. My explanation for forcible regime promotion is what Mario Bunge calls "systemist," showing the interconnections between agents and structures or micro- and macro-levels of analysis. On the macro-level, the social structure of a transnational regime contest causes the outcome of waves of forcible regime promotion. But we must examine the micro-level of agents to explain the mechanism of this causal connection.[40] Figure 3.1 puts the matter in diagrammatic form.

As for the transnational regime contests themselves, their emergence, persistence, and demise are caused by the social and material environment of the states that instantiate the regimes. An exogenous environmental change can trigger a regime contest; the contest endures as long as great-power exemplars of each regime successfully shape their environment; a

**Macro-Level**      Transnational regime contest

**Micro-Level**    Events polarize elites ⟶ Rulers forcibly promote regimes

Figure 3.1 Structure and agency

contest ends when at least one regime type fails to negotiate the environment, as evinced by its great-power exemplars' failure to compete.

## Hypotheses

I have made a number of empirical claims concerning the causes of forcible regime promotion by great powers. Chapter 2 advanced micro-level claims, chapter 3, macro-level claims.

### The Micro-Level: Specific Forcible Regime Promotions

As I explicated in chapter 2, during a long wave I expect individual promotions under either of two conditions: a revolution or other regime change appears likely in one state, or a war among great powers breaks out. Following either type of event, TINs will find elites across states more receptive to their polarizing arguments. Ideological polarization will present great-power governments with incentives to use force to promote and counter-promote one regime type or another in smaller states. Thus:

1) regime instability → transnational ideological polarization
   → ex ante forcible promotion

An ex ante promotion is often an isolated event. But sometimes it sets off a short wave of promotion, as the initial promotion exacerbates transnational polarization and gives rulers incentives to do more promotions. And sometimes these events fail to trigger any forcible promotion. In the chapters that follow I note when this happens, but it appears contingent on a number of exogenous factors and hence unpredictable.

2) great-power war → transnational ideological polarization
   → ex post forcible promotion

An ex post promotion often sets off a cluster of promotions, as great powers conquer multiple smaller states and find that ideological polarization in those states makes it rational for them to carry out forcible promotions.

## The Macro-Level: Long Waves

My evolutionary argument expects a long wave to begin in a region when the predominant domestic regime begins manifestly to fail to meet its own standards; rulers and their defenders will enter a vicious cycle of interaction with reformers, such that they become reactionaries and radicals, respectively; a revolution or other regime change will occur in one state. A long wave will endure, and indeed be self-perpetuating, as long as no contending regime type has proved manifestly superior to its competitors. A long wave will decay when one regime type proves manifestly superior on terms all elites accept. Hence:

1) Predominant regime fails some elites → regime crisis →
   new regime emerges → transnational ideological contest
2) No regime type superior → transnational contest continues
3) One regime manifestly superior → end of contest

## Alternative Explanations

In chapter 1, I observed several patterns of the aggregate data on forcible regime promotion since 1500, and argued that some of these are anomalous for certain theories of international relations. But what would various IR theories say about my arguments concerning the causes of forcible regime promotion? Again, I divide my arguments into micro- and macro-claims.

## The Micro-Level: Particular Promotions

### CONSTRUCTIVISM

As should be clear by now, my explanation for forcible regime promotion is constructivist in the sense that it ascribes central importance to a social structure, namely a multinational contest over the best regime that shapes the preferences and options of agents. Some constructivist work operates at the micro-level of decisions, however, and asserts that agents act out of principle rather than self-interest. Indeed, some scholars argue that constructivism's distinct contribution is to assert that actors act according to a logic of appropriateness, as opposed to a logic of consequences.[41] A ruler acting under a logic of appropriateness would promote Catholicism or communism because he believes it right or fitting to do so.[42] My argument does not deny that rulers and other actors may act out of principle, but does not depend upon it. (In fairness, few if any constructivists would argue that all actors always act out of principle.) Although motives are impossible to divine with certainty, some behavioral markers can be helpful. Discourse, especially confidential discussions among a ruler and his advisers, may help us discern motives; a government whose private deliberations emphasize the goodness of promoting ideology per se would provide support for a logic of appropriateness. Also, if a ruler declines some opportunities for forcible regime promotion and accepts others, and those he declines appear less likely to enhance his power or wealth, then we have reason to think he is operating according to a logic of consequences.

REALISM

Like my theory, realism asserts a logic of consequences. But the actors for realism are states rather than rulers or governments (or transnational networks). Strictly speaking, then, my claims concerning why forcible regime promotion happens when it does cannot be pitted directly against those of realism because we examine different units of analysis. Still, realism expects rulers to act on behalf of their states' interests understood in terms of relative material power; rulers know that if they fail to do so by, for example, neglecting to counter-balance a rising foreign power, they will find themselves punished by the international system. Realism thus implies that a state's ruler will serve the interests of the state; as long as we keep that rule of action in view, we can use rulers as proxies for states without violating realism's logic.[43]

Thus reformulated, realism differs with my arguments about specific forcible regime promotions chiefly as concerns the ability of the rulers of great powers to control or override nonstate actors, particularly TINs. For realism, states' coercive capacities make them the supremely important entities; the best predictor of international outcomes is states' relative material power. States will not allow international interdependence to shred their autonomy, as liberals believe.[44] Some realists appeal also to the ideology of nationalism, which empowers central governments by ensuring the loyalty of their citizens or subjects against foreigners.[45] Thus, in proportion to the relative power and coherence of their states, rulers should be able to tame transnational ideological networks and contain any demonstration effects or transnational ideological polarization that might infect the international system.

More precisely, realists would expect different processes and outcomes to follow both of the two triggering events I outline, regime unrest somewhere in the region and a great-power war. On regime unrest, suppose that a region comprises states A through E; A and B are great powers, and C through E are lesser powers; A, C, and E are democracies and B and D, oligarchies. Should an oligarchic revolt erupt in C, realism expects A's ruler to be indifferent as to whether C remains democratic or becomes an oligarchy. A's ruler should not fear for his internal security, for any demonstration effects that infect A will not ultimately undermine his own power. Stephen Walt writes that governments may fear revolutionary contagion but will usually contain the damage: "A campaign to export a revolution to other countries will immediately bring it into conflict with the national loyalties of the intended recipients."[46] If there remain oligarchs in A who do not feel sufficiently nationalistic, the rulers can use the state's various levers of power to suppress or co-opt them. A's ruler should not fear for his state's external security, because regardless of whether C is a democracy or oligarchy, its rulers will pursue C's material interest—which A, as a powerful state, is able to influence to a great degree.

Realists can expect A to intervene in C, however, particularly if C is a strategically important state. The unrest in C might make it an easier mark by focusing C's military on domestic security and distracting it from border defense.[47] But even then, realism could not give a reason why A's ruler would then use its troops to support democracy and defeat oligarchy in C. A's ruler should be indifferent as to the post-intervention regime in C. One might reply that A's ruler could invade C in order to exert influence in C but justify the invasion as an effort to defend democracy against a nefarious oligarchic uprising; it would then need to follow through by actually supporting democracy in C so as not to lose credibility. But such a reply is not realist. If A's ruler is constrained to promote democracy in C by the need for credibility among some audience—within C, within A, or perhaps more broadly—then the ideology is constraining A's ruler. A's ruler is not able to coerce or bribe away a normative constraint.[48]

A consistent realist answer must present A's ruler's decision to promote democracy in C as either costless or done for the sake of efficiency. A's military and diplomats are accustomed to dealing with a democratic C, and would have to spend more resources managing relations with an oligarchic C.

Likewise with my second type of triggering event, a great-power war: if A and B fight a war and A occupies C for strategic reasons, consistent realism must insist that A's ruler promotes democracy in C either arbitrarily (regime promotion is cheap) or for the sake of efficiency. It cannot be because democrats in C are pro-A and anti-B and oligarchs in C are anti-A and pro-C. The occupying troops of A could in principle coerce and bribe oligarchs in C to become pro-A. Realism would explain the decision not to do so—to continue instead to work with C's democrats—as based upon the desire to keep C coercible or bribable at as low a cost as possible.

### The Macro-Level: Long Waves

I have already argued that realism is silent regarding the ideational structures, such as transnational ideological struggles, that exert a sustained pull on agents' beliefs and desires. Ideas about the best regime, for realism—indeed, for standard rationalist approaches to social phenomena— are nothing but tools manipulated by the powerful for their own ends; ideas do not constrain actors, and hence the origin and endurance of ideas is uninteresting. Thus, realism has no account of why actors thousands of miles apart adopt and act upon the same ideologies for decade upon decade, and then at some point no longer do so. Such a puzzle is trivial if ideas have no consequences. But I argue that at the micro-level ideologies do have consequences. Established Calvinism, constitutional monarchy, fascism, and other ideologies prescribe certain actions and proscribe others. They can constrain self-interested elites to use force to promote one regime at the expense of another. Rulers certainly try to manipulate them, but often find themselves more exploited than exploiting.

If regime ideologies are transnational social structures, then we must look to constructivism to account for them. As I argued above, many constructivists have been more concerned to demonstrate the strength of norms than their causes. Those who do theorize about structural change offer several mechanisms. Paul Kowert and Jeffrey Legro's typology is useful: accounts of ideational change are internal, social, or ecological. Internal accounts are those that appeal to individual actors' needs and beliefs. Social accounts look to social interaction itself as producing change. Ecological accounts locate the sources of change in agents' environments. For example, Leonard Schoppa argues that the norms of Japanese-U.S. relations changed in the early 1990s from a more hierarchical to a more equal relationship owing to the end of the Cold War and the completion of the GATT's Uruguay Round. These exogenous shocks disrupted the decades-old norms of interaction and allowed agents to build new ones.[49]

My account is evolutionary and hence ecological. The prevailing acceptance across societies of a domestic regime begins to break down when that regime encounters important anomalies, whatever their source. A period of transnational contestation over the best regime endures because agents shape their environment so as to reproduce it. It ends when one regime type emerges as superior on terms accepted by most elites. That

is, agents shape their environment but that environment contains elements, both material and social, exogenous to the structure that sometimes pushes back, prodding ideational change.

Internal accounts of ideational change are useful if one focuses on the
individual level of analysis. My focus is on the social level, however, and
so the chief constructivist competitor to my ecological account is social
interaction. The general claim of this approach is that social interaction
diffuses norms. The claim sounds tautological, but embedded is a claim
that changes in discourse and practice by a few actors may gradually
change general practice. A prominent account is the "life cycle" argument of Martha Finnemore and Kathryn Sikkink. In the first stage, norm
entrepreneurs attempt to persuade a critical mass of actors (states) to
adopt the new norm. In the second, those states who have adopted the
norm attempt to get others to do likewise; when they succeed, a "norm
cascade" breaks out. The mechanisms for adoption are "a combination of
pressure for conformity, desire to enhance international legitimation, and
a desire for state leaders to enhance their self-esteem." The third stage is
norm internalization, in which actors follow a norm because they believe
it is right.[50] Another social-interactionist account is in Neta Crawford's
argument about how arguments change international practice, in particular how they helped end colonialism. Crawford writes that winning
arguments tend to have credible sponsors and to fit with the pre-existing
beliefs of those who adopt them.[51] Thomas Risse writes that persuasion
sometimes helps actors reach consensus in international relations by clar-
ifying and justifying preferences.[52]

In some respects these accounts are consistent with mine. I argue
that ideas entrepreneurs (TINs) do attempt to persuade, and are more
likely to succeed the more credible actors adopt them; for example, a regime type gains credibility when a major power implements it. But these
social-interactionist accounts lack an ecological component. I argue that
an ideology and the regime it envisages emerge under special environmental conditions and persist over decades. In fairness to social-interactionist accounts, they do not address the particular social structure I
lay out here. They would imply, however, that ideologies and ideological
struggles are not so fixed as I argue. Norm entrepreneurs will not only try
to discredit an ideology or ideological struggle—by arguing that it is im-
moral or counter-productive—but should sometimes find success, particularly as they use arguments about pre-existing beliefs and win over prestigious actors. A norm cascade and subsequent internalization require no
ecological spur. By contrast, I argue that norm entrepreneurs who wish to
defeat a regime ideology or end an ideological struggle will fail until the
ideology itself has manifestly failed to deliver on its promises.

## Case Selection and Method

The four cases I examine are the long waves of forcible regime promotion, whose deep cause are the struggles in Central and Western Europe in the sixteenth and seventeenth centuries over church and state; in Europe and the Americas from the 1780s through 1860s over the location of sovereignty; in most of the world in the twentieth century over the extent of state control over society; and in the Muslim world over mosque and state, which began in the 1920s and is ongoing. Other international systems have featured forcible regime promotions against a background of transnational ideological conflict. In classical Greece, as depicted by Thucydides, cities were divided among the demos (commoners) and *aristoi* (the "best"), pulling Athens into promoting democracy and Sparta into promoting oligarchy. I confine my attention to the modern international system, however.

Within each long case I test two types of claim, on the macro- and micro-levels. As I mentioned in chapter 1, my claims on both levels concern causal mechanisms, or events connecting cause and effect, rather than covering-law explanations, or lists of antecedent conditions necessary and sufficient to produce an outcome.[53] The macro-level, explicated in this chapter, concerns the origins, persistence, and demise of the struggles themselves—struggles that structure transnational and international interactions. I describe the old regime and why it persisted as long as it did. I depict the anomalies that confronted it at the outset of the struggle. I analyze the transnational networks that formed owing to these anomalies and how they entered a vicious cycle of interaction with defenders of the old regime, so that eventually radicals and reactionaries confronted one another across states. I show how the capture of a major state in the region by radicals solidified the radicals by giving them an exemplary country. I demonstrate how the struggle was sustained chiefly by two sets of actors: TINs who propagated their favored ideology, and rulers who sometimes used state apparatus to defeat an enemy regime in other states. I show that new challenger ideologies arose and captured states, further complicating the struggle. Finally, I show that each grand ideological struggle ended when one regime type emerged as superior on terms accepted by all elites across the region—meaning that states exemplifying that regime were the most stable and powerful.

The second, micro-level set of claims I defend in chapters 4 through 7 were outlined in chapter 2. These concern the triggers of foreign regime promotion during these four grand ideological struggles. The frequency of forcible regime promotion varied significantly during these periods, with the majority taking place in short waves or clusters in time and space. I show that a short wave tended to follow either of two types of event: exogenous regime instability in a state in the region, or an exogenous great-power war. I demonstrate that, following either type of event, elites across societies became more receptive to the arguments of TINs and began to polarize according to ideology. Needless to say, no polling data are available in any of the cases, and so I use anecdotal accounts of polarization as narrated in secondary historical sources. I show that this transnational ideological polarization presented rulers of great powers with one or both of two incentives to use force to promote regimes abroad: internal security, or suppressing domestic ideological opposition, and external security, or gaining or keeping a foreign ally. Often rulers did not respond to these incentives by using force to promote regimes, presumably because countervailing incentives—such as fear of provoking a wider war—were overwhelming. When one ruler did respond to these incentives, he exacerbated transnational ideological polarization, augmenting the incentives facing other rulers to do likewise; thus I show short waves of promotion were produced by positive feedback. Here, too, not every such sequence of events led to a short wave of forcible regime promotion; often counter-incentives, such as the fear of triggering a major war, remained too strong and only one regime promotion took place.

Most of my sources are secondary histories. The events I narrate are already amply chronicled and at the level of aggregation at which I operate, secondary sources are adequate. But the past half millennium of international relations has never been shaken up and recombined in quite this way. I do not narrate every instance of forcible regime promotion in all four long cases. Instead, I narrate exemplary events that demonstrate the mechanisms at work. I note many cases where the mechanisms were present but insufficient to produce the outcomes, and speculate why that was so.

# CHAPTER FOUR

# Church and State, 1510–1700

> Today Catholic sovereigns must not follow the same policy as
> before. Formerly friends and enemies have been distinguished
> according to frontiers and states, and have been called
> Italians, Germans, French, Spaniards, English and so on. Now
> we must say Catholics and heretics; and the Catholic prince
> has to have as his allies all Catholics in all countries, just
> as the heretics have for their allies and subjects all heretics,
> whether at home or abroad.
>
> —An Italian diplomat, *1565*[1]

Prologue: The English, the French, and the
   Scottish Calvinists, 1559–1560

IN OCTOBER 1559, A FRENCH expeditionary force of 1,500 sailed north
toward Scotland to aid the embattled Mary of Guise, Scotland's Queen
Regent, against a rebellion among the Scottish nobility. The French made
clear that they would send 10,000 more troops if necessary to restore
Mary. For 245 years, since Scotland cemented its independence from
England at Bannockburn, France had been Scotland's "auld ally." As was
typical in old-regime Europe, Scotland and France in 1559 were linked by
dynastic ties that effectively subordinated Scotland to France's powerful
House of Guise. The French expedition was shipwrecked, however, and
in December, Elizabeth I of England sent a force of 4,000 north to aid
the Scottish rebels. In February 1560, Elizabeth and the rebels signed the
Treaty of Berwick, calling for the ejection of all French troops and pro-
claiming Scotland and England allies.[2] The Guises in France determined
to counter-intervene so as to keep Scotland in the French sphere, but a
rebellion in France itself in March prevented them from doing so. Elizabeth sent 8,000 more troops north, the Scottish rebels triumphed, and
the Berwick treaty went into effect. England's intervention had brought
about a diplomatic revolution in northwestern Europe and the first step
to the eventual Anglo-Scots union of 1707.

   Elizabeth, then, used force to promote Calvinism in Scotland in order
to steal an ally from France. But why this affinity between the English
monarchy and the Scottish rebels in 1559–60? A superficial answer is

that they were both anti-French. But why were the Scottish nobles anti-French, in violation of a 245-year Scottish tradition? Why did they trust England, the "auld enemy," which on geographical grounds was always more threatening to their country? For that matter, why would Elizabeth of England aid a rebellion against a fellow monarch?

The answer lies in a development earlier in the sixteenth century that had already altered political interests and sympathies across much of Europe: the transnational contest over whether society should be ordered on Catholic or Protestant principles. That grand struggle had emerged out of a sustained crisis in the authority of the Catholic Church in the early sixteenth century. The struggle was sustained for nearly two centuries by the inability of any single model or regime type, Catholic or Protestant, to fulfill its promises manifestly better than the other. It only ended in the early eighteenth century when a third model that transcended the competitors—toleration—proved superior.

Elizabeth and the Scottish rebels were Protestant, while France's rulers—Henry II of the House of Valois, and the powerful House of Guise—were Catholic. English and Scottish Protestants had many conflicting interests and reasons to mistrust one another, and in subsequent years mistrust was to confound their relations. But in 1559, actors across northwestern Europe were highly polarized according to religious confession. Catholics were highly prone to identify their interests with co-religionists in other lands and against Protestants in their own land; Protestants were highly prone to do the same. The source of the acute religious polarization of 1559 was the unstable religious situation in England itself in the late 1550s, which had demonstration effects across the region.

Since 1534, England had been a religious shuttlecock batted back and forth between Catholics and Protestants. In that year, Henry VIII (r. 1509–47) broke with the Roman Church and became head of the Church of England. His son and successor Edward VI (r. 1547–53) and his ministers tried to entrench Protestantism; Edward's half-sister and successor Mary I (r. 1553–58) forcibly restored Roman Catholicism and married the Catholic Philip II of Spain. Following Mary's death in 1558, all of Europe watched as her half-sister Elizabeth I ascended the throne. Raised as a Protestant, Elizabeth wavered on the religious question for fear of provoking the arch-Catholic Guises of France into invading and placing her cousin, the Scottish Catholic Mary Stewart, on the English throne in her place. What reassured Elizabeth that she was secure from French intervention was an exogenous event: in April 1559, Henry of France and Philip of Spain signed the Treaty of Câteau-Cambrésis, ending the long Italian wars in Spain's favor. Elizabeth concluded that Philip would restrain Henry from invading England. The Westminster Parliament made Elizabeth head of the English Church and prohibited any worship apart from that of the Book of Common Prayer.[3] England had joined the Protestant camp again.

The Protestants' recapture of their most powerful state to date encouraged Protestants and alarmed Catholics across central and western Europe. In Scotland, Calvinists (at that time the fastest-growing Protestant group) began to smash Catholic icons in churches.[4] Catholics, meanwhile, were vexed at England's apostasy. Wrote Philip of Spain, who had contemplated marrying Elizabeth:

> This is certainly the most difficult decision I have ever faced in my whole life, and it grieves me to see what is happening over there [in England] and to be unable to take the steps to stop it that I want, while the steps I can take seem far milder than such a great evil deserves ... But at the moment I lack the resources to do anything.[5]

The long Italian wars had exhausted Spain's treasury. Exacerbating matters in Scotland was that, under the Câteau-Cambrésis treaty, Philip and Henry had agreed to redouble persecution of Protestants in their respective realms. Mary of Guise, regent in Scotland, suppressed the energized Scottish Calvinists, stoking their anti-Catholicism.[6] The persecution continued following Henry's accidental death in a jousting match in July.[7]

Immediately following Elizabeth's re-establishment of Protestantism in England, a contingent of Scottish Presbyterians (Calvinists) contacted Elizabeth's agents and broached the subject of an Anglo-Scots union.[8] John Knox, a personal disciple of Calvin's, himself wrote to William Cecil, Elizabeth's most trusted adviser, in the spring of 1559: "My eie hath long looked to a perpetual concord betuix these two Realmes, the occasion wharof is now most present, yf God shall move your hartes unfeanedlie to speak the saim for humilitie of Christ Jesus crucified."[9] Soon a bona fide Calvinist rebellion broke out in Scotland; in June, the rebels captured Edinburgh Castle. The next month a Scottish Calvinist sent to Elizabeth's Privy Council the names of the leaders of the rebel movement, men "in band with them who have not yet declarit them selfis," and still others likely to "subscribe with them to keip owt the frenche men."[10] Elizabeth's "Protestant Left" advisers—Leicester, Walsingham, and Essex—urged her to form a Protestant League comprising Germans, Scandinavians, Dutch, French, and Scots. Her moderate councilors advised caution, arguing that intense cooperation with foreign Calvinists would provoke the French Guises into invading England.[11]

In August, as the Guises prepared to send 1,500 troops to Scotland to quell the Calvinist insurrection, Elizabeth's moderate advisers now joined with the Protestant Left and pressed her to intervene in Scotland on behalf of the Calvinists. Her Privy Council remained deeply divided. A successful regime promotion would make Elizabeth more secure externally and internally: it would turn Scotland from enemy into ally and weaken Catholicism in England itself. Furthermore, it appeared likely that, notwithstanding Catholic solidarity, Philip of Spain was unlikely to help the French. In contrast to the Guises, Philip seemed to have nothing to fear from transnational Protestantism; the movement barely existed in Spain and was only starting to stir in the Spanish-ruled Netherlands. Philip refused a French appeal for help and instead ordered Spanish troops to the Netherlands to help England if France invaded.[12]

Thus ensued the abortive French intervention, and the successful English one, in Scotland. Both were what I term ex ante promotions, done directly in response to events in Scotland. Both French and English rulers were acting out of a desire to enhance internal and external security alike. What set off the chain of events was Elizabeth's re-establishment of Protestantism in England itself in the spring of 1559. Regardless of how sincere a Protestant Elizabeth was, the intensification of the ongoing transnational religious struggle confronted her with irresistible incentives to engage in ideological foreign policy.

• • •

The events in northwestern Europe in 1559 and 1560 have many parallels in other parts of Europe over the two centuries between the inauguration of the Reformation in 1517 and the early eighteenth century. During these two centuries, Central and Western Europe were intermittently torn by an enduring clash among rival versions of Christianity. Polities—cities, principalities, and large states in formation—were wracked by strife among various combinations of Catholic, Lutheran, Zwinglian, Anabaptist, Calvinist, Arminian, or other confessions. When it appeared likely that a polity would change from one established religion to another—via conversion of the rulers, lawful succession, or revolution—strife in neighboring polities would intensify and actors would identify their interest more and more closely with co-religionists regardless of polity and against inhabitants of their own polity who adhered to a rival religion. Transnational ideological polarization altered the incentives facing rulers: now they found their interests in promoting in other states the establishment of their branch of Christianity began to override other interests. Rulers would intervene and counter-intervene to overturn or support their rival religion in foreign polities.

Yet religious strife across and among states was not uniformly intense during these two centuries.[13] In some times and places, rulers were far less polarized over religion, and international politics resembled the ideology-free world envisaged by realism. When domestic regimes were relatively stable, or other exogenous changes occurred—such as a sudden change in the distribution of material power among states—societies would de-polarize to an extent and rulers' incentives would change again; they would find less reason to aid foreigners with whom they shared a reli-gion. Even in those less ideologically charged times and places, however, the religious networks continued to interact and agitate across Europe and work to re-polarize societies and states, Catholic *versus* Protestant. When exogenous conditions led to a possible regime change somewhere in Europe, or great powers would fight a war and occupy smaller states, societies would re-polarize over religion, driving rulers back toward ideo-logical foreign policy.

Religio-political foreign policies were especially common in Germany in the late 1540s and early 1550s; northwestern Europe in the 1560s and 1580s; and the entire region in the 1620s and 1630s. International relations were less ideological in northwestern Europe before 1558 and in Germany between 1555 and 1600. The early years of the catastrophic Thirty Years' War (1618–48) saw the Protestant-Catholic clash at its most severe, but from 1635 de-polarization ensued as Catholic France joined the war on the side of the Protestants. The war ended in the Peace of Westphalia, a set of agreements among princes on how to manage reli-gious diversity and change. In the 1680s, the Catholic-Protestant struggle flared up once again, inflaming relations among France, the Netherlands, and England.

Thus, for nearly two hundred years international politics in Central and Western Europe was structured in part by a continuous transnational struggle for predominance between Catholicism and Protestantism. This structure shaped relations among states as certain viruses can affect an organism: active, then dormant, then active again.

The transnational contest over which religion would prevail in politics emerged from a deep crisis in the predominant political regime in Cen-tral and Western Europe during the Middle Ages. The medieval political system was complex; the component whose evident failures triggered the macro-struggle that interests us was the political or temporal authority of the Catholic Church.[14] The Church, a "transnational" organization, enjoyed enormous legitimacy and influence over medieval society, includ-ing the powerful nobility, owing to its consistency and ability to make good on its promises. A legitimacy crisis emerged in the 1510s in north-eastern Germany, with Martin Luther's movement to reform the Catholic Church. Many would-be religious reformers in preceding centuries had failed; Luther succeeded owing to the manifest failures of the social and political status quo, whose legitimacy was based upon the Church. These failures led a number of German princes to support Luther's challenge to certain Church practices. Luther's followers and status quo advocates po-larized and two mutually negating ideologies emerged: political Luther-

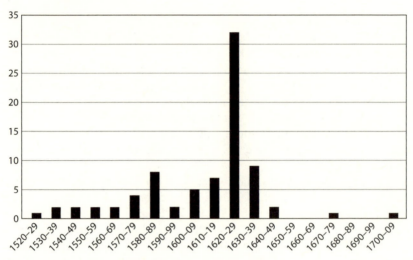

Figure 4.1 Forcible regime promotions, 1510–1710

anism and political Catholicism. In the 1540s, Calvinism emerged from Lutheranism and posed an even more potent challenge to Catholicism. The structure—transnational Catholic-*versus*-Protestant political competition—endured as long as no regime type clearly proved superior on its own terms. Only in the late seventeenth century did it become evident to most elites that a third way—a regime that tolerated religious diversity, as practiced in the Netherlands and then England—actually made for more stability and prosperity.

Figure 4.1, plotting the frequency of forcible regime promotion against time, illustrates both the macro-struggle and the micro-oscillation within that struggle.

In what follows I narrate the emergence, persistence, and demise of this long contest between ideologies of Catholicism and various Protestantisms. The narrative is complex, but a central set of dynamics is discernible, consistent with my arguments in chapters 2 and 3. The crisis of the old regime began in 1517 with Luther's initial challenges to Church teaching and practice. The ideological struggle began in the mid-1520s when several princes of the Holy Roman Empire adopted Lutheranism and disestablished Catholicism. With those official establishments, Lutheranism became tied up with the coercive power of rulers and states, making it a factor in international relations. The struggle finally decayed in the late seventeenth century as the very notion that Catholicism and Protestantism were dangerous to one another began to lose credibility among political elites.

Emergence of the Structure: Catholicism's Crisis
  and the Rise of Lutheranism

*Why Religion Was Political*

Readers today may wonder whether the religious clashes of early modern
Europe are properly classified as political. What has the process by which
God forgives sins, or the metaphysics of the priesthood, to do with the
distribution of power or institutions of governance? The general answer is
that in medieval Europe, the "religious" and "political" realms—approxi-
mated by the Christian terms "spiritual" and "temporal," respectively—
were seen by virtually everyone as intimately mingled. As Philip Gorski
writes, for civil authorities at the time "religious uniformity provided the
best foundation for political stability. In the phrase of the age, 'religion is
the bond that holds society together' (*religio vincula societatis*)."[15] "The
heretic," writes M. Searle Bates, "was a rebel and a traitor, politically and
socially as well as theologically and ecclesiastically."[16] Hence political authority, with its responsibility to maintain social order, was obligated to
monitor and enforce religious belief and practice to some extent; a ruler
who failed to fulfill this obligation cast his own legitimacy into doubt.[17]

By no means were temporal and spiritual authorities in perfect har-
mony in medieval Christendom. Indeed, the intimacy of church and state
led to countless competing assertions by princes secular and ecclesiastical
(bishops). Philip IV the Fair of France (r. 1285–1314) asserted spiritual
superiority to the Pope in France; Pope Boniface VIII (r. 1294–1303) responded by asserting supreme temporal authority over all of Christendom.[18] The poet Dante Alighieri followed in 1309 with *De Monarchia*,
an argument that it was actually the Holy Roman Emperor who held
supreme universal temporal authority.[19] But during these and other disputes, secular rulers took care not to challenge the sacerdotal priesthood,
that is, the exclusive power of the clergy to mediate between God and
man, chiefly by administering the sacraments. There were seven sacraments and, collectively, they covered the most significant aspects of medieval life: Baptism and Confirmation, entry into the Church; Eucharist,
Penance, and Extreme Unction, the individual's standing before God at
a given time; Matrimony, marriage (by definition permanent); and Holy
Orders, the priesthood itself. Put concretely, then, religious questions
were political because priests and bishops, and hence the Church as a vast
institution, monopolized authority over what were for Christians—that
is, nearly all medieval Europeans—the most important events of life. Supporting and supported by this authority was the stupendous wealth of the
Church in the form of vast landholdings, human capital, and treasures.

*Why the Reformation Happened When It Did*

So why did secular rulers tolerate for so long an order that so diluted their own power? Why not break with the Catholic Church and seize power from the clergy? Were princes in 1034 or 1234 not as rational as Henry VIII, who in 1534 *did* break with Rome and seize the Church's wealth in England?

Doubtless many, perhaps most, medieval princes were devoted sons of the Church who could not entertain such a break. But their devotion was in part a function of the Church's own successes through the preceding centuries. Notwithstanding its failings in the eyes of subsequent ages, the medieval Church generally delivered on its promises. Its doctrines, a synthesis of Christian theology and Aristotelian science, made sense of the world; the hierarchy of being it limned, stretching from the lowest rock through animals and humans to angels and God, provided a norm for order that seemed consistent with the facts;[20] its claim that Christ entrusted St. Peter and his successors with the keys to heaven was buttressed by the majesty and power of the papacy; its sacerdotalism was ratified by pious clergy. Thus the failures of various would-be reformations in the centuries before Luther are not hard to understand. Reform movements would sometimes erupt and argue that the current Church, or at least some of its leaders, contradicted its own central text, the Bible. Many of these movements enjoyed political patronage for a time, suggesting that princes were contemplating a serious challenge to the Church. The Cathars or Albigensians of the eleventh and twelfth centuries were protected for a time by nobles and even bishops in the south of France; the Waldensians of the twelfth and thirteenth centuries, by the House of Savoy; John Wycliffe and the Lollards of the fourteenth and fifteenth centuries, by the kings of England; the Hussites of the fifteenth century, by the kings of Bohemia; Girolamo Savonarola of fifteenth-century Florence, by Charles VIII of France. But none of these movements sparked a Europe-wide sustained movement.

The case of Jan Hus (1369–1415) is illustrative. Hus challenged the Church on various doctrinal points and was supported by Wenceslaus, King of Bohemia. Wenceslaus wanted to be elected Holy Roman Emperor and protected Hus so as to punish Pope Gregory XII for not supporting him. The papacy was especially vulnerable at this time because there were two claimants, one in Rome and a second in Avignon, and the Council of Pisa declared a third pope, Alexander V (eventually considered an anti-Pope). Wenceslaus supported Alexander, who soon declared Hus a heretic. Wenceslaus at first tried to mediate between Hus and Alexander. But the Council of Constance in 1415 declared Hus a heretic and Wenceslaus abandoned him to be burned at the stake.[21] This sorry story is typical:

in general, a prince supported a religious reform movement to help his political ambitions, and turned on the reformers when it became evident that his power (and perhaps his soul) was in jeopardy.

Each of these failed reform movements was "transnational" in the sense that, by means of migration and travel, each inspired at least quiet dissent in other parts of Europe. The Hussites in Bohemia were heavily influenced by the teachings and example of the Lollards in England a generation earlier. But again, none of them had a direct, lasting impact. By contrast, Martin Luther's movement quickly gained conversions across Germany among the peasantry and in the cities, which gave princes incentives to convert or at least protect Luther, which in turn encouraged more conversions.[22]

Historians agree that the prestige of the Catholic Church, and hence its claims to authority, were lower in the early sixteenth than in preceding centuries. By then the Church's actions in many realms so contradicted its teachings that many had privately come to question its authority. The Western Schism mentioned above provided one glaring anomaly: it had not been clear who occupied the Holy See. Renaissance humanism provided another in the crucial arena of the universities. The scholastic learning of the High Middle Ages had been challenged by scholars insisting that medieval glosses on ancient texts be cast aside in favor of the ancient texts themselves in their original languages. This academic return *ad fontes* (to the source) gave Luther an appeal among the learned; indeed, it is difficult to disentangle humanism from the early Reformation.[23] Steven Ozment argues as well that Catholic spirituality had become stifling and corrupt.[24]

The Church's legitimacy crisis meant that clerical abuses once tolerated were now potential flashpoints. The Church had granted indulgences, or remissions of the temporal punishments for sins, for centuries, and the doctrine had even been abused by rogue priests or "pardoners." It was only in 1517, when Pope Leo X began to expand the use of indulgences ostensibly to fight the Turks but actually to fill his own coffers and to build St. Peter's Basilica in Rome, that Church corruption finally set a spark to dry tinder. On October 31, Luther, a young Augustinian monk, posted on the door of the Wittenberg Cathedral his *Ninety-Five Theses* challenging the granting of indulgences. Luther did not intend to split the Church; indeed, the *Theses* were a disputation, an invitation to other theologians to debate the matter, following scholastic custom. The *Theses* included statements of loyalty to the Pope.[25] But the document met with loud enthusiasm among many clergy, nobles, and peasants, suggesting that many in German society had been deeply discontented with various aspects of Church authority. Simultaneously, it met with heated repudiation from Germany's leading theologians.[26] Luther, it turned out, was offering no ordinary disputation.

That the time was ripe in German-speaking Europe for sustained rejection of Church authority is seen in the parallel Zwinglian reformation in Switzerland. In 1519, a young priest in Zurich, Huldrych Zwingli, began to question openly various beliefs and practices of the Catholic Church along lines similar to those of Luther. It is difficult to trace any direct influence of Luther on Zwingli's early moves, but he was of course a product of the same time and place; Zwingli was a humanist and friend of Erasmus, and his readings of the Greek New Testament led him to reject the Church's accruals of tradition. Protected by the leaders of Zurich, Zwingli eventually became more radical than Luther, asserting that the Christian gospel had solely to do with inner faith and not at all with outward acts. Zwingli's assertion that Christ was not present in the Mass in any special way contradicted Luther's teaching and doomed efforts by German princes to unify his and Luther's movements.[27] Zurich established Zwingli's version of the Evangelical faith in 1524; Berne, Basle, Constance, and several other cantons soon followed.

### Lutheranism and Catholicism Become Mutually Negating

The anomalies that afflicted the Catholic Church may account for the enthusiasm with which many greeted Luther's *Theses*. But why did not Church authorities react with caution and try to co-opt Luther and defang his complaint, perhaps by acknowledging that indulgences were indeed being abused by rogue priests? Such an acknowledgment may have strangled the Reformation in its crib and prevented not only the great schism in Western Christendom but also much of the intermittent international warfare in the ensuing 180 years.

For many, perhaps most, clergy the Church's elaborate system still delivered on its promises. For these, Luther's disputation implied a challenge not just to the doctrine of indulgences but to clerical authority *in se*. The hierarchy reacted sharply and rapidly to Luther and the two sides began to move progressively farther apart. In early 1518, Pope Leo directed the head of the Augustinian Order to suppress him. In March, Leo asked a leading Italian theologian, Silvester Prierias, to rebut Luther's writings; Prierias produced a dialogue marked by insults and assertions of papal authority. In August, Luther published Prierias's dialogue with his own reply, calling the dialogue "sufficiently supercilious, and thoroughly Italian and Thomistic"; in November, Prierias published his own reply; Luther answered with yet another. During this exchange of polemics, Leo ordered Luther to appear in Rome to recant.[28] These interactions with Church authorities turned Luther against the papacy itself and prodded him and his circle of friends to identify more contradictions between Church teachings and the Bible, and to hold that in the event of conflict the Bible must be the final authority. Luther drew out the full implications for the reduction of the Church's authority: the Christian was saved from damnation not through the mediation of the Church, but by direct faith in the merits of Jesus Christ, faith infused directly into the believer by God.[29]

Once Luther made these moves, the Church quickly condemned him for heresy. On June 15, 1520, Leo issued the bull *Exsurge Domine*, demanding that Luther retract forty-one alleged doctrinal errors. *Exsurge Domine* concerns in large part Luther's implicit and explicit challenges to the power of the Church to mediate between God and man.[30] In August, Luther published his reply, *An Appeal to the Christian Nobility of the German Nation*, calling upon the secular princes of the Holy Roman Empire to call a Church council and found a new Church (or restore the original, ancient one) in which the clergy had no special privileges.[31] Leo excommunicated Luther on January 3, 1521. Luther responded by burning a copy of the bull of excommunication.[32] Lutheranism was now taking definite shape as anti-Catholicism; Lutherans saw themselves as retrieving pure, Biblical Christianity over against the accretions of Catholicism. Catholicism, in turn, was becoming defined in part as being anti-Lutheran; Rome's theologians increasingly emphasized clerical authority and denigrated the ability of the individual to understand scripture. Germany quickly polarized over the deepening dispute, owing in part to the use of the printing press, a technology that had not existed when previous reformers had questioned Church practices.[33]

### How the Struggle Implicated Political Regimes

The anti-clericalism of Luther's *Appeal* clearly had political implications, but in the early 1520s those implications had yet to take final shape. Catholicism was not simply a set of religious doctrines, but also a fundamental plan for ordering public life, a regime supported by an ideology. The Church was a major landholder and her princes (i.e., bishops), including the Pope, held temporal power over specified territories. The Church was not under the authority of secular princes and resisted, usually successfully, attempts by the latter to tax them. Via the power of the seven sacraments (see above), the Church controlled major events of the life of the laity. In his 1520 polemic, *A Prelude concerning the Babylonian Captivity of the Church*,[34] Luther declared that there were only three sacraments—baptism, communion, and penance—and downplayed the last, implying that the Church only had authority over purely spiritual matters.

Luther's teachings thus would empower the laity, but a struggle ensued over just how politically radical Lutheranism was. To oversimplify:

Would it simply devolve power from ecclesiastical to secular princes? After all, if the Catholic clergy were reduced or eliminated, the secular prince could distribute more patronage, increase tax revenues, own more land, and avoid having a troublesome transnational network controlled by a foreign prince—the Pope—determine the significant events and moral views of his subjects. The prince could, in other words, extend his domestic power.[35] Or, would Lutheran teaching, with its validation of individual conscience, instead lead to a leveling of the entire social order? Would Germany's peasantry and cities gain power as well from the princes?

Luther gained a hearing among a number of prominent princes. His first political patron was his own prince, the Elector Frederick "the Wise" of Saxony (r. 1486–1525). Frederick never accepted every detail of Lutheran doctrine, but nonetheless chose to protect Luther from Church authorities in August 1518 by allowing him to disobey his recall to Rome and instead arranging an interview with the papal legate at Augsburg.[36] Frederick was to continue to shelter Luther in the early 1520s, hiding him at Wartburg Castle while he translated the New Testament into German. His younger brother and successor John "the Steadfast" went farther, openly embracing the Lutheran faith.[37] Another prominent convert was Philip "the Magnanimous," Landgrave of Hesse (r. 1509–67), who was impressed with Luther's courage from the outset. In 1524, Philip began encouraging (over the objection of various relatives) the spread of Luther's teachings in Hesse, and finally began openly to profess those teachings himself.[38] Under this political sponsorship Lutheranism not only survived but spread, as Luther wrote more polemics and translated the Bible into German, thus undercutting the Catholic Church's ability to be sole interpreter of scripture.[39]

## The Peasants' War of 1525
### and the Reformation from Above

The demotion of the clergy and institutional Church was also appealing to the peasantry and cities in many parts of the Empire. In 1524, the peasants of Swabia, lately squeezed between higher prices and taxes and new restrictions on hunting, formulated their *Twelve Articles*. These called for the abolition of serfdom, the right to choose clergy, and fair tithes (church taxes), rents, and hunting rights. The *Articles* explicitly state that the test of any law or practice is the Bible rather than tradition or ecclesiastical authority. The peasants believed they were simply carrying out the principles that Luther and others were espousing.[40] In early 1525, the Peasants' War spread, particularly to areas with clerical landlords; by late

April, Franconia, Thuringia, Alsace, and Württemberg had joined the Upper Swabian and Upper Rhine regions in supporting the Twelve Articles. An estimated 300,000 peasants were under arms.[41] Many Imperial cities, hoping to get out from under the bishops' authority and powers of taxation, joined in the rebellion, seizing monasteries and cathedrals. At first the peasants were peaceful and called for leading reformers, including Luther, to arbitrate between themselves and their landlords.[42]

The question of whether Lutheranism was to be "magisterial," led by elites, or "communal," mass-based and egalitarian, was ultimately resolved by force in favor of the former. Indeed, the Reformation's first wave of forcible regime promotion—or more precisely, regime preservation—was triggered by the Peasants' War. The Swabian League of princes, with support from the ruling Habsburgs, began to suppress the movement in the spring of 1525. The peasants responded with violence, besieging monasteries and castles, and the war escalated. Luther himself, horrified at the disorder, urged the princes to put the rebellion down in violent terms, and Lutheran princes joined in the carnage. In the savagery of the summer of 1525, perhaps 100,000 peasants were killed.[43] As Peter Blickle writes, "Now the princes had to take over the Reformation. Only if they could bring it under political control could revolt be eliminated root and branch. They had to shear the Reformation of its revolutionary components, which they did by denying the communal principle as a mode of Christian life both in theory and in practice."[44]

Many Imperial princes responded to the Peasants' War by concluding that Lutheranism itself must be eliminated. In July 1525, as the war was winding down in Swabia, the Catholic princes of northern Germany gathered at Dessau to pledge to exterminate the new "sect." George of Saxony, Albert of Mainz and Magdeburg, Joachim of Brandenburg, Duke Henry of Brunswick-Wolfenbüttel, and Duke Erich of Brunswick pledged "to stand by each other in case the Lutherans attacked any one of them, in order to remain at peace from such rebellion."[45] The Lutheran princes did not immediately respond in kind to the Dessau League, but under the leadership of Philip of Hesse they agreed to stand together for the preservation of Lutheranism at the Imperial Diet at Speyer the next year. Helped by the Emperor's wish for unity against his rival Pope Clement VII, the Lutherans succeeded in blocking the Dessau League: the Speyer Resolution of 1526 declared that the ban on Lutheranism could not be enforced everywhere and that a general Church council must be summoned to settle the religious question.[46] In effect, Speyer set up the rule *cujus regio, ejus religio* ("whose the realm, his the religion"), a rule that was to wax and wane throughout Europe until the late seventeenth century, when it became permanently and generally accepted.

## The Long Wave Begins, Mid-1520s

### Lutheran States Appear

Lutheran rulers took advantage of the Speyer Resolution to establish new regimes in their estates, and thus began the long transnational struggle over whether to order society along Catholic or Protestant lines. Philip of Hesse was the first, beginning the reordering of his realm in October 1526 by reforming liturgy and teaching, seizing Church property, and establishing the University of Marburg, the world's first Protestant university.[47] In the next few years in northern Germany, the Countship of Mansfeld, the Duchy of Brunswick-Lüneburg, and Schleswig, Holstein, Brunswick-Calenberg, East Friesland, Bremen, Hamburg, and several smaller cities became officially Lutheran. In south Germany, a number of cities did likewise.[48] (Already in 1523 Sweden had separated from Denmark and its king, Gustav Vasa, declared it a Lutheran realm and seized Church property.)[49]

The new Lutheran regimes differed from their Catholic counterparts not in the question of sovereignty—Luther was indifferent as to whether a polity was monarchical or republican—but in the power of the clergy. Luther taught that the Church consists of the believers, all equal in God's sight. But he held a strong view of human sinfulness, and was convinced that many in society would never be true Christians; these doctrines, along with the Peasants' War, convinced him that robust authority was needed over society. That authority, by default, must be lodged in secular rulers. Thus the Lutheran state took shape as an *Obrigkeitsstaat*, or authoritarian state, to safeguard the preaching of the Gospel and to enforce the people's submission. The chief obstacle to true public piety was the Catholic Church, so Lutheran rulers ousted Catholic clergy and seized Church property. Lutheran princes and city councils appointed their own clergy and adjudicated theological disputes.[50]

Since breaking with Rome brought such an alluring array of princely benefits, why did not all rulers follow Frederick, John, and Philip by becoming Lutheran? Why did the cascade of conversions not end in a complete collapse of Catholicism? Why instead did Lutheranism and Catholicism reach a stalemate that thrashed Europe for so many decades? The motives of Catholics, like those of Lutherans, remain ultimately inscrutable to us. But it is clear that, for a number of powerful princes, Catholicism retained sufficient plausibility vis-à-vis the emerging Lutheran alternative. For many, the old faith, including extensive clerical authority, was still credible, and Lutheranism appeared both false and deeply subversive of all authority.

The most important Catholic stalwart was Charles V, the Holy Roman Emperor (r. 1519–56) and King of Spain. Luther had reason to hope that Charles would join his movement, if for no other reason than to drive papal influence from his vast domains.[51] Charles dithered about the religious question for decades, frustrating Lutheran and Catholic alike. In early 1521, Pope Leo asked him to put an end to Luther's agitations.[52] Charles rebuffed Leo and insisted that the wildly popular Luther receive a fair hearing. At the imperial Diet of Worms in April, Charles asked Luther to recant his writings. Luther's famous reply that his conscience required him to submit to scripture rather than Church authority outraged the Emperor.[53] Charles told the gathered princes the next day that he was bound to be true to the Habsburg heritage of defending the Catholic faith. Although he honored his commitment to give Luther safe passage from Worms, within weeks Charles changed tactics and issued an imperial edict banning Luther.[54] Charles then left Germany until 1530 and placed the Empire under the regency of his brother, the Archduke Ferdinand, hoping the Lutheran problem would somehow resolve. It does not appear that Charles ever seriously considered breaking with the Catholic Church, even when a majority of German territory was Lutheran in the 1540s; the simplest explanation is that he was a convinced Catholic who could not seriously contemplate abandoning his family's faith.

Charles's fellow Habsburgs, and the powerful House of Wittelsbach in Bavaria, all remained staunchly Catholic. For them, too, Catholicism continued to be credible and a more plausible fit with their own ambitions than the Lutheran alternative. Doubtless helpful were side payments offered by the Church. In the 1523 bull, *De Judicibus Cleri*, Adrian VI, the new Pope (r. 1522–23), granted the Bavarian dukes the right to try heretics over the heads of the Church's own bishops. Adrian also agreed to grant the Wittelsbachs one-fifth of Church revenues in Bavaria, and in the Habsburg hereditary lands he granted one-third of Church revenues to the court of Archduke Ferdinand.[55]

Whatever the motives behind the princes' decisions, by the middle of the 1520s two mutually negating plans for ordering public life had emerged in Central Europe. The two held in common the medieval insistence that societal cohesion required religious homogeneity. But Lutheranism held that the religion that bound society must be one without any mediation between the believer and God; clergy must have no special spiritual or legal privileges, and secular authorities must be supreme. Catholicism held to the older view, now sharpened by the controversy: Christ established the Church—meaning, preeminently, the hierarchical clergy—as mediator and hence its clergy do have special privileges and are unaccountable to secular rulers. The Reformation was to stimulate still more doctrinal systems and hence political regimes. Zwinglianism had developed in Switzerland, and was chiefly confined to that country; its political consequences were similar to those of Lutheranism. Anabaptism was to develop from the smoldering remains of the Peasants' War and was to spread eastward, but after the 1530s took on a political quietism that provoked little more international political turmoil. The most politically consequential Reformation movement was to be Calvinism (discussed below), which implied a regime more egalitarian than that of Lutheranism.

Over the next two centuries in Latin Christendom, Catholicism, Lutheranism, and Calvinism each had firm adherents in a number of states at once. But the salience of each varied over time and space. As seen in the following sections, Protestant and Catholic TINs, penetrating and penetrated by governments, perpetually agitated for regime change. In many times and places these TINs were ineffectual, stymied by rulers more concerned with other matters. But at other times TINs were highly effective at polarizing elites across societies and provoking rulers into imposing one regime or another on other states. As argued in chapter 2, those other times generally followed great-power wars and domestic regime crises somewhere in the region.

*Little Forcible Regime Promotion, 1520s and 1530s*

With the rapid multiplication of Lutheran regimes in the 1520s, the transnational conditions were in place for forcible regime promotions, Catholic *versus* Lutheran. For two decades, however, only a few isolated promotions took place. Instead, Catholic and Lutheran rulers responded to transnational ideological polarization by increasing suppression of the others' teaching within their own realms and forming defensive alliances to deter foreign intervention. The Catholic League of Dessau of 1525 was answered by the Lutheran League of Torgau in 1526.[56] The Torgau League, founded by Philip of Hesse and John, Elector of Saxony (r. 1525–32), grew in classic spiral-model fashion as the Catholic princes, including the Emperor Charles, appeared more menacing to the Lutherans.[57]

A second condition that contributed to the absence of short waves of forcible regime promotion during these decades was the continuing hegemony in Germany of Charles V and his Habsburg dynasty. The Holy Roman Empire, as Voltaire would later say, was neither holy, Roman, nor an empire; by the sixteenth century, power had devolved significantly to the estates; seven princes elected the Emperor.[58] Yet, Charles commanded the most troops and either he or his brother Ferdinand presided at the Imperial Diets. Lutherans hoped and Catholics feared that Charles would convert to Lutheranism. And, at various times during these years,

Charles needed help from his Lutheran vassals in combating external threats. In May 1526, a diplomatic revolution had taken place as Francis I of France, the Pope, the Duke of Milan, and the cities of Florence and Venice formed the Holy League of Cognac against the Habsburgs. It was his need for Lutheran help that prodded Charles to support the Speyer resolution of that summer, allowing the Lutherans to set up new regimes in their lands.[59] In return, the Lutherans joined the German Catholics in warring against the Cognac League.[60]

Still, the one instance of forcible regime promotion in the 1520s illustrates how high ideological tensions were running. In 1528, Otto von Pack, a bankrupt ex-adviser to the Catholic George of Saxony, forged papers documenting that the Habsburgs and other Catholic princes were preparing to launch an anti-Lutheran crusade. Philip of Hesse believed the forgery, had it printed and disseminated, and attacked the neighboring Catholic estates of Mainz and Würzburg. Sensing a hoax, Catholics exposed the papers as forgeries, and in 1529 Philip withdrew his troops, leaving the cities to remain Catholic.[61]

Philip's impetuosity further intensified ideological polarization in the Empire, and the Catholic princes banded together more tightly at the 1529 Diet of Speyer, voting to rescind the previous *cujus regio* agreement of 1526. Now Lutheranism was again officially illegal throughout the Empire. [62] The Lutheran rulers responded with an official *Protestation* (from whence the term "Protestant") and, after another rebuffing at the 1530 Diet of Augsburg, a new, more robust alliance. [63] On February 21, 1531, six Protestant princes—John of Saxony, Philip of Hesse, Ernest of Lüneburg, Wolfgang of Anhalt, Gebhard and Albert of Mansfeld, and Joachim of Brandenburg—and ten Lutheran cities entered the League of Schmalkalden.[64]

The 1530s saw more rulers break with the Catholic Church. In 1534, Henry VIII broke with the Pope and established himself as head of the Church of England. Closer to the empire, Denmark became officially Lutheran in 1536 with the accession of King Christian III. Still, in this decade the spread of Lutheranism and transnational polarization were to continue to provoke little forcible regime promotion. The most significant case came in 1534 when Philip of Hesse invaded the Catholic Duchy of Württemberg and restored the Lutheran Duke Ulrich. This promotion of Lutheranism stands out for being chiefly the work of a *Catholic* prince, Francis I of France. Desiring to pluck a strategically important land from Habsburg influence, Francis exploited transnational ideological polarization by paying Philip to promote Lutheranism in Württemberg by restoring Ulrich. It is noteworthy that although Lutheranism had won many converts in France by this time, Francis, who saw himself as a humanist, had thus far accommodated rather than persecuted the new faith. Once Ulrich was restored, Württemberg, now Lutheran, joined the Schmalkaldic League, thereby weakening Charles and the Habsburgs. (Later in 1534, Lutheran riots in Paris caused Francis to switch from accommodation to opposition; his relations with the German Lutherans suffered accordingly.)[65]

A second forcible regime promotion took place the following year in the city of Münster. At this point Anabaptism, which had arisen in the Peasants' War of 1524–25, continued to simmer and pose a transnational threat to Catholic and Lutheran rulers alike. In February 1534, Anabaptists had taken over the city and set up a sort of proto-communist utopia, complete with the abolition of family and property. In June 1535, Catholic and Protestant rulers—from Cologne, Cleves, Saxony, and Hesse—invaded together, brutally suppressed the Anabaptist leaders, and restored Catholic rule.[66]

*The First Short Wave of Forcible Regime Promotion, 1540s*

After this series of isolated forcible regime promotions, a wave of promotions finally broke in the 1540s as Lutheran growth and assertiveness at last pushed the Emperor into attempting a rollback. The first promotion came in northwestern Germany in 1542, when the arch-Catholic Duke Henry of Brunswick-Wolfenbüttel threatened the Lutheran cities of Brunswick and Goslar. Knowing that the Emperor was angry with Henry for other reasons and needed Lutheran help against the Turks, Philip of Hesse and John Frederick, now Elector of Saxony (r. 1532–-47) invaded Brunswick-Wolfenbüttel and chased Henry out. The duchy became officially Lutheran.

The Emperor had allowed this imposition of Lutheranism, but did not like the consequences. Feeling surrounded by an alliance of the French and the ever-growing German Lutherans, he decided to divide his enemies and try to destroy Lutheranism. Charles had already achieved a secret agreement with Philip of Hesse. Philip had committed bigamy and sought the Emperor's clemency; Charles granted it in return for Philip's pledge to "stand by him" in the event of a religious war.[67] Charles's first move was in Cleves-Jülich, a powerful duchy in northwest Germany. In the spring of 1543, Duke William publicized his conversion to Lutheranism and announced his intention to build a Protestant regime in Cleves-Jülich and join the Schmalkaldic League. But Philip of Hesse would not back William, and Charles's forces invaded in August. The next month William surrendered and agreed to restore Catholicism, and with it Habsburg hegemony, in the duchy.[68]

In 1544, Charles surmounted another barrier to his planned rollback of Lutheranism by signing the Treaty of Crépy with Francis of France, in which the latter agreed to no more alliances with the German Lutherans. (Francis's relations with the Lutherans had already been sour for a decade, following his own massacre of French Lutherans in October 1534.)[69]

The trigger came in January 1546: Frederick, the Elector Palatine, became a Lutheran and sought membership in the Schmalkaldic League. Under Philip's influence, the League turned him down, but Philip himself warned his fellow Lutherans to prepare for war.[70] In the spring the Imperial Diet at Regensburg was a failure, and Charles decided for war. He offered side payments to several Lutheran princes if they would remain neutral. The most consequential of these was Philip's son-in-law, the young Duke Maurice of Saxony (r. 1541–53). Evidently Lutheranism was so entrenched in his realm by this time that Maurice felt secure from any possibility of a Catholic rollback.[71]

In June the war began as Charles brought in Spanish, Italian, and Dutch troops. Charles justified the war to his son Philip (later to be Philip II of Spain): "[T]hough my goal and intention has been and still is, as you know, to make war for the sake of religion, it is considered politic to allege that the war is for the purpose of punishing rebellious subjects, especially the landgrave of Hesse and the elector of Saxony and others of similar standing. The imperial cities have been given this justification for the war."[72] With Philip fighting alongside his fellow Lutherans, the Schmalkaldic League's forces appeared stronger on paper. But the Emperor's forces won several decisive victories, with the crowning victory coming at Mühlberg in April 1547. Francis of France refused to intervene owing to his own continuing difficulties with French Protestants.[73] In the fall Charles laid down the law at the Diet of Augsburg, parading the imprisoned Lutheran rulers. The Augsburg *Interim* of May 1548 contained the Emperor's terms. The Lutherans must re-establish the Catholic Church in their realms, including most of the doctrines and practices of the old faith. Lutherans could petition the Pope for a few privileges such as married clergy, and the question of restoring Church properties was deferred. The *Interim*, however, was interpreted by most Lutherans as effectively turning back the Reformation, and it was only an "interim": they feared that the eventual general Church council would finish them off.[74] The Schmalkaldic War was the crest of the first short wave of forcible regime promotion.

The wave continued as a number of Lutheran princes, including the now sobered Maurice of Saxony, began to plan war to coerce Charles into overturning the Augsburg *Interim*. In January 1551 these allied with Henry II (r. 1547–59), who had succeeded Francis as King of France. By April 1552, the French-German alliance had defeated the Emperor's forces. After a second general war over religious ideology, the rulers of the empire called a halt. Charles abdicated, and his successor Ferdinand agreed to the Religious Peace of Augsburg (1555), which once again codified the *cujus regio, ejus religio* norm: Lutherans could do as they wished within their realms.[75] The Augsburg Peace was to hold remarkably well within the empire among Lutherans and Catholics. It did not, however, end the broad clash of ideas in Europe. Indeed, the worst was yet to come. An offshoot of Lutheranism originating in France was to become its own bona fide anti-Catholic movement and to spread within and without the empire, polarizing societies and princes and triggering, over the ensuing decades, several waves of forcible regime promotion.

The Emergence of Calvinism

Already in the 1530s a new Protestant movement had begun to emerge that was to be the most politically potent and hence helped set in motion several short waves of forcible regime promotion. John Calvin (1509–64), a French humanist and lawyer impressed with Luther's theological insights, pushed them, so he believed, to their logical conclusions. Where Luther was a rigorous and impetuous polemicist, Calvin was a comprehensive systematizer of doctrine. He stressed both that God alone elected who would be saved—in this he was like Luther—and that the elect could be distinguished from the reprobate by the righteous lives they led. Even more than Luther (but less than Zwingli), Calvin removed the physical presence of Christ from Holy Communion, hence further leveling the distinction between clergy and laity.[76] There followed an emphasis on ethical action, not simply inner faith, by all Christians. Where Lutherans had been pessimistic about the potential to have a just society on earth, and hence demanded little of their secular rulers except that they enable gospel preaching to flourish, Calvinists were driven to renew and purify society.[77]

Beginning in 1536 Calvin set up his model polity in Geneva, a city in the Swiss Confederation. His most radical reforms were within the structure of the Church. Congregations elected their officers, and synod (local church council) delegates elected one another. Congregations held regular meetings where members could voice concerns. As John Witte writes, "Implicit in this democratic process was a willingness to entertain changes in doctrine, liturgy, and polity, to accommodate new visions and insights, to remedy clerical missteps and abuses, to spurn ideas and institutions whose utility and veracity were no longer tenable." Calvin evidently did not intend to be a revolutionary in the secular realm, and indeed he insisted that Church and state had separate functions: the Church would teach and enforce spiritual norms, while the state would do the same with civil norms. But the separation was by no means complete. Secular officials' ultimate purpose was to help sustain a Christian commonwealth; they worked hand-in-glove with Church authorities. Writes Witte: "Calvin hinted that a similar combination of rule of law, democratic process, and individual liberty might serve the state equally well, though he did not work a detailed political theory." His followers Theodore Beza (1519–1605) and Johannes Althusius (1557–1638) were to formulate Calvinist political theories in subsequent generations in France and the Netherlands, respectively.[78]

In the 1550s, as Geneva flourished under Calvin's leadership, and his magisterial *Institutes of the Christian Religion* was translated, printed, and disseminated, Calvinism—often simply called Reformed Christianity—began to spread rapidly. Part of the reason for Calvinism's remarkable diffusion was the accommodation that Lutheran rulers had made with Catholicism—still suffering from a legitimacy crisis—in the 1555 Augsburg Peace. Augsburg did not cover Calvinism.[79] Lutherans came to view Calvinists as heretics, typically declaring that they would "rather turn popish than Calvinist."[80] But its illegality in the empire lent Calvinism appeal with many across Western Europe. In the Low Countries, where Charles V had brutally suppressed Lutheranism in preceding decades, leading families began adopting Calvinism from 1559.[81] In France, by the 1560s as many as half of the aristocracy were Calvinist or Huguenot.[82] In England, the arrival of a number of leading Calvinist divines from the Continent—refugees from Catholic persecution—influenced the leaders of the English Church; for their efforts to "purify" the English Church of Catholic influence, the Calvinists were called Puritans.[83] In Scotland, the movement had a sufficient following among the nobility that a Calvinist revolution broke out in 1558–59. Scottish Calvinism, called Presbyterianism for its model of church governance, developed an identity as the church (kirk) that most closely approached perfection.[84] In Germany itself Calvinism began to enjoy success when it was adopted by the Elector Frederick III (r. 1559–76) of the Rhine Palatinate; his capital of Heidelberg became a major European center of the Reformed faith.[85] Calvinism also spread eastward into Bohemia, Poland, Hungary, and Transylvania.[86] Lutheran regimes remained in place in Scandinavia and much of Germany, but by the late 1550s it was Calvinism, with its transnational momentum, that represented the more dire threat to Catholicism.

Calvinism's rapid diffusion was due also to its coherence and the deliberate strategy of the Reformers in Geneva. Calvin himself urged exiles to return to their homelands to influence developments there.[87] Demonstration effects from Geneva were powerful; a large number of pastors, theologians, and nobles visited the city in the 1550s and 1560s.[88] Calvinists drew encouragement from one another's struggles in other areas. As one Scottish Presbyterian wrote after hearing from a Huguenot, "it is not small comfort brother … to brethren of one nation to understand the state of the brethren in other nations." Calvinism, then, was a highly (although not perfectly) cohesive movement "marked," writes Menna Prestwich, "by a sense of international solidarity." When the faithful in one land suffered persecution, their brethren in other lands would offer generous financial support and take in refugees.[89] London in particular became a haven for exiled Calvinists during the rule of Elizabeth I.[90] Indeed, the success of the Huguenots in this period had palpable effects in the Spanish-ruled Netherlands. Andrew Pettegree's account bears quoting at length:

> Most of all the apparently providential success of the French churches gave evangelicals in the Netherlands courage: courage to show the same defiance to official persecution that had brought such dividends in the French kingdom. One of the most remarkable features of Calvinism in these years was its irrepressible self-confidence, often in defiance of any realistic expectations of success. And why not? In this period of almost unbelievable progress for Calvinism in northern Europe, when a tiny group of enthusiasts had converted Scotland to a Calvinist nation, and when God had obligingly carried off persecuting monarchs in both France [Henry II] and England [Mary I], why should Netherlandish Calvinists not hope for a similar providential deliverance? In the years following the outbreak of fighting in France, Dutch Calvinists therefore began to imitate the provocative and confrontational behaviour that had brought French evangelicals such success. For the first time Dutch Calvinists shrugged off the secrecy which had previously clothed their activities, and staged defiant open services; sometimes, to make the provocation more extreme, they preached in the churchyards of Catholic churches.[91]

All in all, as Garrett Mattingly writes, Calvinist cells were linked across political boundaries and "all of them, everywhere, vibrated to any impulse that stirred their connecting web."[92]

In contrast to Lutheranism, however, Calvinism appealed to few monarchs. It was chiefly a religion of the nobility and commoners; monarchs tended to suspect that its ecclesiastical structures led to republicanism. Indeed, Calvinism's implicit anti-monarchism helped make it so politically explosive. Frederick III of the Rhine Palatinate became an international champion, and Henry Navarre, vying for the French throne, did so for a time. Elizabeth of England (r. 1558–1603) was a Protestant wary of her own Calvinist (Puritan) subjects. Still, during times of high transnational religious polarization, Elizabeth supported foreign Calvinists, sometimes with troops and ships. But more typically, Calvinism would take over a

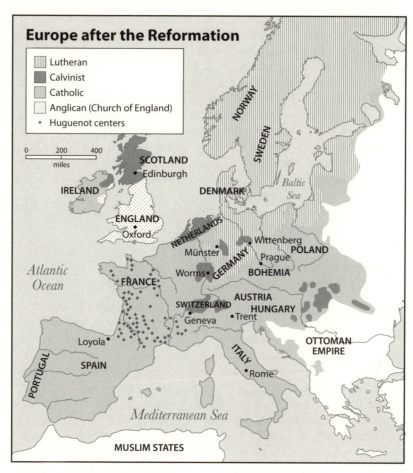

**Europe after the Reformation**

Lutheran
Calvinist
Catholic
Anglican (Church of England)
• Huguenot centers

0   200   400
miles

NORWAY
SWEDEN
SCOTLAND
• Edinburgh
Baltic Sea
IRELAND
DENMARK
ENGLAND
• Oxford
Wittenberg
NETHERLANDS
Münster •
• Prague
POLAND
GERMANY
Worms •
BOHEMIA
Atlantic Ocean
FRANCE
AUSTRIA
SWITZERLAND
HUNGARY
Geneva •
• Trent
Loyola •
OTTOMAN EMPIRE
ITALY
PORTUGAL
SPAIN
• Rome

Mediterranean Sea

MUSLIM STATES

*Source*: https://apeurope.wikispaces.com/Unit+One?f=print
MAP 4.1.  Religion in Europe, c. 1560

country via revolution, as in Scotland, the Netherlands, and Bohemia. And Catholic and Lutheran monarchs could find Calvinism terrifying, both because Calvinists sometimes went on iconoclastic rampages and because they were highly disciplined. Their branches were coordinated and represented an alternative way to organize society, one less hierarchical and more efficient than that of the old regime. Philip Gorski sees in Calvinism's discipline the origins of the modern state.[93]

During these same decades, the Catholic Church itself began to regroup and go on the offensive through various means in the so-called Counter-

Reformation. In the Council of Trent (1545–63) the Church clarified and reasserted certain doctrines and practices, attempted to purge itself of various corruptions, and concentrated more power in the Papacy.[94] Most important, the Papacy had organized a transnational network of its own, the disciplined Society of Jesus, in 1534. Jesuit missionaries spread throughout Europe (as well as the Americas and Asia), laboring to turn back the Protestant tide propeled by Lutheran and Calvinist divines. To regain influence in England, the Roman Church established an English seminary at Douai, Flanders, that produced an English translation of the Bible to rival the Protestant versions circulating in England.[95] Catholic revivals occurred in Hungary and Poland. Catholic princes regained their footing by claiming some victories against domestic Protestant rebels and suppressing Protestant practices.[96]

In the second half of the sixteenth century, then, the religio-political map of Western Europe was bewilderingly heterogeneous.

### A Wave of Forcible Regime Promotion, Northwest Europe, 1560s–1570s

At the beginning of this chapter I described how the restoration of Protestantism in England in 1559 led to a Calvinist uprising in Scotland, which in turn led to a French promotion of Catholicism, and an English counter-promotion of Calvinism, in that country in 1560. The story does not end there. French and English actions in Scotland fed back into transnational society, augmenting ideological polarization; Calvinists were emboldened in other countries and began to think of Elizabeth as their international champion.[97] The country of the most immediate consequence was France itself. Since 1555, France had been undergoing what Menna Prestwich calls "an explosion of Calvinist conversions." In May 1558, a minister in the Paris Huguenot church wrote to Calvin that "the fire is lit in all parts of the kingdom and all the water in the sea will not suffice to extinguish it." The Franco-Spanish compact to renew persecution only strengthened the movement. The Edict of Écouen of June 2, 1559, outlawed Protestantism in France; in reaction, the scattered Huguenot congregations around the country united into a single Reformed Church of France, with a single set of doctrines and polity. Historians estimate that by 1559 half of the French nobility was Huguenot; in 1560 there were 1,750 Huguenot churches and approximately 2 million believers, making up about 10 percent of France's population. Calvinism was especially strong in the Midi, the southern coast of France, which had a history of resistance to control by Paris.[98] Huguenots proved adept at organization and, under the patronage of rural lords, began to try to take over local parishes with force.[99]

Divisions among French Catholics helped the Huguenots. Catholics were divided between supporters of the ruling Valois and supporters of their challengers, the House of Guise. The Duke of Guise, the Cardinal of Lorraine, and other Catholic militants were bent on uniting France by ridding it of Protestantism, while the Valois were more willing to accommodate the Protestants in exchange for loyalty to their dynasty. Charles IX (r. 1560–74) was a Valois who effectively shared power with his formidable mother Catherine de Médici; their moderation toward the Huguenots earned them the label *politiques*. The *politiques* tolerated Protestantism so as to enlist the Huguenots against their rivals, the Guises.

In the 1560s, the *politiques* evidently did not envisage a permanent accommodation of the Huguenots. But their relative toleration of Protestants within France matched their relatively strong ties with England's Elizabeth and other foreign Protestants. By the same token, the Guises had close ties to Philip II of Spain, the Pope, and other foreign Catholics. In January 1561, Elizabeth explicitly declared England Christendom's Protestant champion. She sent an envoy to France to urge Catherine to make that country into a Protestant realm, inasmuch as "true Anglo-French friendship could only flourish if both realms adopted the same religion."[100] The advice was probably disingenuous and Catherine did not follow it, but she did sponsor an ecumenical conference at Poissy, kept the leading Reformed theologian Theodore Beza at court, and issued the Edict of Saint-Germain in January 1562 increasing the Huguenots' freedom to practice their religion.[101]

In March, the Guises reacted to Catherine's tolerant moves by massacring a group of unarmed worshiping Huguenots at Vassy. A Huguenot uprising followed and the decades-long French Wars of Religion began. Huguenot leaders, including Admiral Gaspard de Coligny and Louis, Prince of Condé, proved redoubtable in the armed struggle. Condé issued a manifesto in April and the Huguenot rebellion enjoyed wide demonstration effects across Europe; Protestant sympathy was high, and 7,000 German troops came to France to join Condé.[102] In London, Elizabeth's Privy Council pressed her to act as she had in Scotland two years earlier. As R. B. Wernham writes, the cautious Cecil "felt that Condé [the Huguenot leader] was fighting England's battle as much as the [Scottish] Lords of the Congregation had been in 1560." Robert Dudley and Nicholas Throckmorton, Elizabeth's most militant Protestant advisers, "were strenuously urging war. Might not the Huguenots be built up into an effective counterpoise to the Guises in France just as the Scots Protestants had been built up in Scotland?"[103]

Philip of Spain, meanwhile, could no longer be complacent about Protestantism: Calvinism was now spreading to the Netherlands and threatening the legitimacy of his rule there. Already in January 1561 Philip had urged the French to resume persecution of the Huguenots.[104] That same year he initiated in the Netherlands an Inquisition, a tool that had already worked well in Spain itself.[105] Philip paid subsidies to the Guises in France and warned Elizabeth not to help the Huguenots.[106]

But Elizabeth defied Philip and followed the advice of her Protestant Left councilors, sending 6,000 troops to France and lending Condé 100,000 crowns to help the Huguenots defeat the Guises. The English force arrived in October 1562. Unlike that in Scotland two years earlier, this English expedition to promote Calvinism in France went sour. The balance of power within France was held by Catherine and the *politiques*, who suspected that Elizabeth's real goal was to regain the port of Calais, which England had lost in the 1559 Treaty of Câteau-Cambrésis. Eventually Catherine and the Huguenots struck a bargain: she would tolerate them and they would help her drive the English from French shores. In July the English departed Le Havre, and by the Treaty of Troyes of April 1564 Elizabeth abandoned all claims to Calais.[107]

The Huguenot rebellion and English expedition, in turn, had demonstration effects in the Netherlands.[108] As H. G. Koenigsberger writes, "By 1565 the [Spanish] court at Brussels, undoubtedly with events in France before their eyes, began to fear open rebellion or, at least, the seizure of some important towns by the Protestants."[109] In England, the Protestant Left again urged Elizabeth to intervene on behalf of the Dutch Calvinist rebels. Elizabeth, chastened by the failure of the 1562 French expedition and fearful of pushing Philip into invading England from the Netherlands, rejected the advice.[110] Thus, Elizabeth was deterred from deepening the cycle of forcible regime promotion she had helped begin in 1560 in Scotland.

In September 1566, Dutch Calvinists rioted in several places, sacking 400 Catholic churches in west Flanders alone.[111] Early the following year Philip sent an army of 12,000 under the Duke of Alva to quell the Dutch revolt.[112] Alva's troops had to march hundreds of miles northward on the "Spanish Road," creating fear in the regions they skirted among Calvinists and *politiques* alike. The Huguenots feared a Habsburg-Valois joint action and in August entered a pact with the militantly Calvinist Frederick, Elector Palatinate. Frederick sent 9,500 troops to France to help them, under the command of his son Johann Casimir. The German troops arrived in early 1568.[113] They became irrelevant in August 1570 with the Peace of Saint-Germain, which allowed the Huguenots four secure cities for two years, and freedom of worship everywhere in France except Paris.[114] Catherine, Charles, and the *politiques* had stabilized France. Indeed, Charles drew closer to Calvinists in France, England, and the Netherlands, inviting the Huguenot Admiral Coligny to court and arranging his own sister's marriage to Henry Navarre, another Huguenot military leader who was a potential contender for the French throne. In April 1572, Charles entered the Treaty of Blois with Elizabeth of England, under which "if either party were assailed for the cause of religion or under any other privileges and advantages for the pretext, the other was bound to render assistance."[115]

Religious strife was relieved in France, but the transnational contest endured. The main theater was now the Netherlands. Some Dutch Calvinist leaders, including Louis of Nassau, had fled to French Huguenot country upon the arrival of Alva in 1567. In April 1572 the Dutch "Sea Beggars," Calvinist-led privateers, took the port of Brill, and William of Orange followed up by declaring war on Spain. Now Louis of Nassau took a Huguenot army into the Netherlands. Under the influence of Coligny, France's Charles allowed another Huguenot army to follow along. English and Scottish volunteers also fought with the Huguenots. The Calvinists took the cities of Valenciennes and Mons.[116]

The French (Huguenot) military expedition to help the Dutch Calvinists fed back into France and helped provoke the next shock, the St. Bartholomew's Day Massacre of August 1572. Catherine, concerned that her son King Charles had fallen too deeply under Coligny's influence, ordered the Huguenot admiral assassinated. The assassination attempt set off a chain of events that led to several weeks of slaughter in which an estimated 8,000 Huguenots were killed in many parts of France.[117] St. Bartholomew's Day evoked predictable reactions all over Europe. Catholic Europe rejoiced, thinking at first that the slaughter was done out of righteous zeal; thanksgiving masses were said in Rome and Madrid; Philip of Spain danced a jig and Pope Gregory sent a congratulatory note to Charles.[118] Protestant Europe was horrified and fearful. Relations with England immediately froze, as Elizabeth and most English assumed, in Wallace MacCaffrey's words, "that the massacre was premeditated, a new chapter in the unfolding conspiracy of the Catholic world—Pope, Guises, Spain—aimed at the extermination of the reformed religions throughout Europe."[119] Similar fears gripped Lutherans in Germany and Calvinists in Switzerland.[120] At first it seemed the diplomatic consequences would be dire. In England the Protestant Left advised their Queen to break relations with France and to behead Mary Stewart, the imprisoned Catholic pretender.[121] Coligny had been England's primary conduit of influence over the French court; now many English feared that nothing restrained France from re-Catholicizing Scotland and using force to place Mary Stewart on the English throne.[122]

But the St. Bartholomew's Day Massacre did not trigger more forcible regime promotion. European Protestants still regarded Philip of Spain as their chief threat, and the French *politiques* signaled them in various ways that they remained his enemy as well. They renewed a proposal that

Elizabeth marry Henry, the Duke of Anjou, another of Catherine's sons and next in line to the French throne.[123] Within France, they initiated new negotiations with the Huguenots, and in July 1573 Charles granted them toleration in certain areas.[124] They began to join forces against the Guises again.[125] In December Charles renewed negotiations with Louis of Nassau on cooperation against Spain.[126]

The Netherlands stabilized domestically after 1576. Philip's attempts to end the Dutch revolt bankrupted Spain; unpaid Spanish troops pillaged the Netherlands, driving Catholic provinces to join the Calvinists in the Pacification of Ghent, which declared a united Netherlands loyal to the Spanish Crown but free of Spanish troops. With France and the Netherlands relatively stable, the short wave of forcible regime promotion decayed.

### Another Short Wave: France's Succession Crisis and Its Consequences, 1584–1593

The lull was short-lived, however. In 1574, Charles IX died and was succeeded by Henry III. Henry remained childless throughout his reign, which elevated the importance of the Dauphin or immediate heir to the throne. In 1584 the Dauphin, Francis, Duke of Alençon, died. Now the next in line to the French throne was Henry Navarre, the Huguenot champion. Navarre's elevation significantly raised the prospects of Protestantism not only in France but also in the Netherlands and throughout Europe.[127]

In country after country Protestants were buoyant and Catholics alarmed at the news from France. Rulers and aspiring rulers began to polarize further along ideological lines. In Spain, one of Philip's ministers wrote him: "Your Majesty is obliged to make sure that no heretic succeeds [to the French throne], both because you have a duty always to defend and protect the Catholics and because any heretic must necessarily be an enemy of Your Majesty."[128] Philip agreed and in January 1585 entered the Treaty of Joinville with the Guises. The Spanish King agreed to provide 50,000 escudos monthly "for the contracting French princes, for the period they need to maintain their armies for the restoration of the Catholic religion in France, or to oppose the designs of those Frenchmen in favor of the heretics and sectaries of the Low Countries." In return, the Guises agreed to work to restore to Spain certain French-occupied cities, to cease all French aid to Dutch rebels, and to tie French Catholicism more closely to the papacy.[129] For alarmed Protestants, the Joinville treaty seemed to presage an international Catholic crusade that threatened their internal and external security.

That impression became stronger with word in late June that King Henry III, once a *politique* with whom the Protestants could do business, had switched sides by aligning with the Holy League. Now at last Catholics in France were unified with Philip against transnational Protestantism; northwest Europe approached complete ideological polarization. In England, Elizabeth's moderate advisers joined her Protestant Left to recommend that she lead an international Protestant alliance to intervene with force in France and the Netherlands. The Queen's most trusted adviser, William Cecil, now Lord Burghley, had for many years been advising her not to be too aggressive; Philip, he had counseled, was probably not crusading for Catholicism, but simply trying to suppress the Dutch revolt, as any monarch in his position would do.[130] But the Joinville treaty changed Burghley's mind.[131] His method of analyzing the Spanish threat is telling. His notes about Philip are divided into two columns, *Voluntas* (will) and *Potestas* (power). Under *Potestas* he listed Philip's acquisition of Portugal and its empire in 1581 and his treaties with the French and Turkish monarchs. Under *Voluntas*, Burghley listed a number of rebellions and plots against Elizabeth that had implicated Spain. One of these was an expedition in 1578 of Papal troops from Spain to Ireland that sought to bring about a Catholic uprising there. Burghley convinced the Queen that Philip was finally preparing to launch a Catholic crusade against England, and that she should forestall this by sending an expedition to the Netherlands to tie him down.[132]

Thus, in August 1585 Elizabeth and the Dutch Calvinists signed the Treaty of Nonsuch, declaring their mutual efforts to end Spanish tyranny in the Netherlands.[133] Elizabeth also urged Henry Navarre to go on the offensive against Spain, and sought a new alliance with Scotland.[134] In January 1586 the Earl of Leicester, a leader of England's Protestant Left, arrived in the Netherlands with 6,400 infantry and 1,000 cavalry. The Leicester Expedition met with some early successes against the Spanish but foundered against conflicting interests with the Dutch; in November 1586, the Queen recalled Leicester to England. Still, the net effect of the Leicester Expedition was to sustain ideological polarization in northwest Europe. Spanish agents began to conspire again with Mary Stewart to overthrow Elizabeth. Elizabeth had already imprisoned Mary for previous plots with English and foreign Catholics. In February 1587, Elizabeth finally had Mary beheaded.[135] That summer German troops from the Palatinate, under the Calvinist Johann Casimir, invaded eastern France to fight Holy League forces.[136]

Burghley and Elizabeth were correct that Philip of Spain had in mind invading England to restore Catholicism there. They were wrong in thinking that they could tie Philip down in the Netherlands, however.

The final provocation for Philip was a long privateering expedition by Sir Francis Drake, climaxing in a raid on Spain itself in August 1587.[137] In May 1588, Spain's Invincible Armada sailed north, determined to oust Elizabeth, place a Catholic on the English throne, and thereby "bring the Dutch to their knees."[138] All of Europe watched the Armada, understanding that the fight was not simply between England and Spain or the power of the Habsburgs: the future of the Catholic-Protestant struggle was implicated not only in England but also in the Netherlands and France. As a Huguenot leader said to Walsingham, "In saving yourselves you will save the rest of us."[139]

The storied English victory over the Armada did indeed help Protestantism in these countries, and also signaled that Spanish naval might was less formidable than it appeared. In France Henry III defected from the Holy League, realigned with Henry Navarre, and ordered the assassination of the Duke of Guise and his brother, the Cardinal of Guise.[140] But Catholic-Protestant polarization continued apace in northwest Europe, and hence so did the incentives for rulers of both ideologies to carry out still more forcible regime promotions. On August 1, 1589, a fanatical Dominican friar assassinated Henry III, making Henry Navarre, the Huguenots' military leader, King Henry IV. The horrified Guises, who controlled half of France's territory, including Paris, refused to accept Navarre's kingship and fought on.[141]

The accession of Henry IV provoked an escalation of foreign intervention in France. Philip instructed the Duke of Parma, currently fighting the Calvinists in the Netherlands, to prepare to invade France: "My principal aim [there] is to secure the well-being of the Faith, and to see that in France Catholicism survives and heresy is excluded. ... If, in order to ensure this exclusion and to aid the Catholics so that they prevail, you see that it is necessary for my troops to enter France openly [then you must lead them in]."[142] On the Protestant side, Elizabeth sent 4,000 troops to France under Lord Willoughby in September; these helped Henry's troops move on Paris in October and remained in northern France for three years.[143] In February 1590, Protestant forces blockaded Paris, creating an immediate crisis for the Holy League. In March, Philip responded by ordering Parma to invade France with 20,000 men to aid the Duke of Mayenne, now champion of the Guises. In April another 3,000 Spanish troops invaded Brittany. Philip's justification to a wealthy Spanish donor of this expensive promotion reveals the intimacy between Catholic ideology and Habsburg power:

Everybody knows about the great, continuous and unavoidable expenses that I have incurred for many years past to defend our holy

Catholic faith and to conserve my kingdoms and lordships, and how they have grown immensely through the war with England and the developments in France; but I have not been able to avoid them, both because I have such a specific obligation to God and the world to act, and also because if the heretics were to prevail (which I hope God will not allow) it might open the door to worse damage and dangers, and to war at home.

Now unable to use Parma's army to suppress the Dutch Calvinists, Philip offered them a degree of toleration in exchange for loyalty; but they refused and went on the offensive.[144]

Foreign intervention escalated still more when the most plausible Catholic pretender to the French throne, the aged Cardinal of Bourbon (who claimed to be Charles X), died in May. Now Philip considered naming himself King of France, or else his daughter Isabella Clara Eugenia as Queen, which would violate the Salic Law prohibiting a woman from ruling France. From the militantly Calvinist Palatinate Christian of Anhalt marched 6,000 cavalry and 9,000 infantry to France in August.[145] Elizabeth helped fund the German expedition and was reluctant to spend still more resources to help Henry, but in December, under urging from her close adviser Burghley, she moved one-third of her own troops in the Netherlands to Brittany. In May 1591 she sent 2,400 more troops to join them. At this point Elizabeth's chief fear was that Henry IV would re-convert to Catholicism and make peace with Spain, thereby allowing Philip to turn his attention back to invading England. In late 1592, a Spanish plot to invade England via Scotland—which still had some Catholic nobles—was exposed, and Elizabeth responded by sending another 2,000 men to Normandy.

The spiral of regime promotion and counter-promotion that had begun in 1584 was stopped only with the end of the French civil war in 1593 and de facto stability in the Netherlands. In France, Henry IV did re-convert to Catholicism in order to gain Paris without a fight. The Holy League dissolved. Elizabeth and other foreign Protestants who had spent blood and treasure aiding him were furious, and the Spanish continued to try to topple or assassinate Henry. But France stabilized as a Catholic country and in 1598 Henry issued the Edict of Nantes, ordering the toleration of Huguenots. Meanwhile, Philip of Spain had devoted so much attention to France that the Dutch Calvinists consolidated their power and achieved virtual independence in the northern Netherlands. The need for forcible regime promotion receded. But the long transnational ideological struggle continued to simmer, and the center of action was soon to shift back to Central Europe with a number of discrete promotions.

*A Series of Isolated Promotions:*
*The Holy Roman Empire, 1600–1610s*

The Peace of Augsburg of 1555, described above, was remarkably effective in halting regime promotion in Germany. With each prince and city council trusting that no one would try to change its estate's religion, forcible regime promotion and the threat of general Imperial war receded. Emperors Ferdinand I (r. 1556–64), Maximilian II (r. 1564–76), and Rudolf II (r. 1576–1612), Catholics all, were as good as their word.[146] The chief flaws of the Augsburg peace were its ambiguity over rulers who converted from one religion to another, and its omission of Calvinism.[147] These two problems combined owing to the gains Calvinism made in the Empire after the 1550s. Calvinist refugees from the Netherlands brought their religion with them and triggered two forcible regime promotions in northwest Germany in the early 1580s. In 1580, Calvinists in the city of Aachen demanded freedom of worship. The Catholic City Council refused, and the Calvinists took over the city the following year. From the Netherlands, Spanish troops invaded to try to restore Catholic control. The Diet of Augsburg in 1582 resolved nothing and the problems in Aachen dragged on for decades.[148] In December of that year in nearby Cologne, the new Archbishop, Gebhard Truchsess, announced his conversion to Lutheranism and soon after began to change the estate's regime. Condemned by Catholics, Truchsess sought outside Protestant support and received it from the stronghold of German Calvinism, Louis, the Elector Palatinate. But owing to Truchsess's friendliness toward Calvinism, Germany's Lutheran princes refused to back him. Bavarian and Spanish forces defeated him and he fled.[149]

Notwithstanding the setback in Cologne, Calvinism continued to spread in northwestern Germany, propelled to an extent by the still-militant leaders of the neighboring Palatinate. In 1598, Emperor Rudolf II ordered Spanish troops into the Rhineland to suppress Calvinism around Aachen. The Calvinists' militancy began to spread back to their fellow Protestants, the Lutherans. Protestants began to boycott the Imperial Chamber, and in 1607, in the southern city of Donauwörth, Lutherans attempted to prevent a Catholic procession. With Rudolf's blessing, Bavarian troops invaded and overturned the Lutheran government, reestablishing a Catholic regime.[150]

The following year, Protestants walked out of the Diet of Regensburg. At a conference in Anhausen in May 1609, leading Protestant princes and cities, led by the Calvinist Frederick IV, now the Elector Palatinate, formed a new Protestant Union. A Catholic League quickly formed in response, headed by Duke Maximilian of Bavaria. A succession crisis between Catholics and Protestants in Cleves-Jülich drew a Habsburg invasion in the summer of 1609; the Protestant Union answered with a counter-invasion in March 1610; in August, English, Dutch, and French troops joined the Protestants.[151] (In May a Catholic assassinated Henry IV of France for being insufficiently zealous for the faith, further raising Protestant fears.)[152] In 1612, the Protestant Union entered a defensive alliance with James I of England.[153] Again in 1613 Spanish (Catholic) troops invaded Cleves-Jülich and a Dutch Calvinist force counter-invaded. The religious alliances were intended to deter each side from widening the war, and indeed general war was averted by the Treaty of Xanten (November 1614), mediated by the English and French.[154]

In 1616, Huguenots rebelled against Louis XIII, now King of France. Helping Louis suppress the rebellion were Dutch troops under Captain-General Jan van Oldenbarneveldt. This odd Dutch intervention to help a Catholic monarch suppress a Calvinist uprising was a product of a new division within the Netherlands: Oldenbarneveldt was an Arminian, part of a Protestant movement that rejected orthodox Calvinism's strong doctrine of predestination. In the Netherlands and later in England, Arminians were to lean in foreign policy toward Catholics, whose doctrine of free will was closer to their own.[155]

### The Climactic Wave: The Thirty Years' War, 1618–1648

The major rulers of Europe did not want transnational religious conflict to lead to general war and were able to avert it for a time. They finally failed in the aftermath of a 1618 Protestant rebellion in Bohemia, at the far eastern end of the empire, owing to the ambitions of Frederick V, the latest Elector Palatinate (r. 1610–23) who followed the militantly Calvinist traditions of his predecessors. Calvinism had spread to Bohemia in the 1540s.[156] By the early seventeenth century Bohemia's population was only 10 percent Catholic, with Calvinists, Lutherans, and Anabaptists predominant. In 1609, the same year the Protestant Union formed, Emperor Rudolf tried to reassure Bohemian Protestants by guaranteeing them religious freedom so that they would stand with him against a renewed Turkish threat.[157] In 1612, Rudolf was succeeded as Emperor by Matthias (r. 1612–19), known to be more tolerant. But the Bohemian Protestants feared that Matthias would be succeeded by Archduke Ferdinand, a rigid Catholic. In 1617, Ferdinand was crowned as King-Designate of Bohemia. With Catholics and Protestants now highly polarized, their ideologies portraying one another as satanic, it took a relatively minor incident to spark conflict: Catholics destroyed some Protestant churches, and in retaliation an assembly of Protestants threw two Catholic leaders from a window in Prague Castle. The rebels intended to set up an elected

Protestant monarchy in Bohemia, and quickly elected the gratified Frederick, Elector Palatinate, as King in place of Ferdinand.

Ferdinand carried out a coup d'état against Matthias and called in 12,000 Spanish troops to Bohemia to suppress the Protestant revolt. He also enlisted the aid of John George, Elector of Saxony, a Lutheran. Like many previous Lutheran princes, John George was hostile toward Calvinism and toward Frederick in particular; he helped Ferdinand suppress the Bohemian revolt in exchange for pledges not to re-impose Catholicism on them. Protestant League troops from Transylvania and Germany counter-intervened, but could get no support from outside the empire. At the Battle of White Mountain (November 1620), Catholic forces crushed the Protestant League. Ferdinand—now Emperor—broke his promise to John George and began to suppress Protestantism in Bohemia and allied Moravia.[158] Frederick fled to the Netherlands and Catholic League armies occupied the Palatinate and began to re-impose Catholicism there.[159] In 1625, Pope Gregory XV founded the Congregation for the Propagation of the Faith, which sent Italian priests to Germany to aid in re-Catholicizing conquered estates.[160]

Simultaneously, Catholics rebelled in Valtellina, the strategic valley between northern Italy and Germany. Valtellina was part of the Grisons, an independent state that had adopted Protestantism previously. In January 1622, Spanish troops invaded and helped the rebels triumph.[161]

As had sometimes happened earlier in the century-old Catholic-Protestant struggle, forcible regime promotion and transnational ideological polarization were endogenous. The Habsburgs' forcible re-Catholicization of German lands further polarized Europeans according to ideology and made more foreign regime promotion likely. Catholic elites supported Habsburg policy, while elites in Protestant lands began to press their sovereigns to intervene on behalf of their brethren in the empire. In 1625, James I of England sent a 25,000-man expedition to join the Protestant army of Count Mansfeld. In September, the English and Dutch entered an offensive alliance, and in December Christian IV of Denmark, a Lutheran, joined. James subsidized a Danish force that attacked the Catholic League and sent an English expedition to France to support a Huguenot rebellion.[162] Gabriel Bethlen, a Hungarian Protestant prince, invaded Moravia in 1626 to try to reverse the re-Catholicization.[163]

These Protestant interventions went poorly, and in 1627 the Catholic princes felt confident enough to hold a meeting to discuss postwar plans. The result was the biggest round of forcible regime promotion in modern history. Ferdinand told the gathering at Mühlhausen that the whole object of the war was to restore to the Catholic Church the lands that had been stolen from it. In 1628 he circulated a draft document, and in March 1629, he issued the Edict of Restitution. Under the Edict the empire's religio-political situation of 1552 was restored. All Protestant advances since that time were to be reversed, and Calvinism was banned. The Edict was not enforced in every eligible estate, but in Lübeck, Ratzeburg, Schwerin, Mecklenburg, Brandenburg, Magdeburg, Halberstadt, Verden, Bremen, Merseburg, Naumburg, Meissen, and Minden re-Catholicization was either begun or completed by Imperial troops. Five hundred monasteries were seized from princes and restored to the Church. By this time, in many of these lands Protestants formed large majorities of the population, and so enforcing the edict required great coercion. The Imperial armies carried out re-Catholicization even in most Lutheran estates that had been loyal to the Emperor.[164]

The edict's redistribution of power to Catholic princes in the empire, and fear among exempted Lutheran rulers of Saxony that they would be next, intensified transnational polarization by provoking the Lutherans to rally to their Calvinist fellow Protestants. Outside powers, alarmed at the Habsburgs' consolidation of power and encouraged by the outrage among German Protestants, saw fresh opportunities to intervene. By now Louis XIII of France and his minister, Cardinal Richelieu, had suppressed the Huguenot revolt and were free to focus on foreign policy. Although Catholic, Louis entered an alliance with the Lutheran Gustavus Adolphus of Sweden. With the encouragement of the Elector Palatinate and a subsidy from Louis, Gustavus Adolphus invaded the empire in July 1630 to aid the Protestants.[165]

The Imperial army headed by the Count of Tilly took the city of Magdeburg in Northwest Germany and, perhaps inadvertently, burned it to the ground. News of the horrific deaths of 20,000 city inhabitants further polarized Europeans along religious lines. Under domestic pressure, more Lutheran princes joined the Protestant alliance, and the combined forces defeated Tilly's Catholic armies at Breitenfeld in September 1631. Over the next three years the Catholics regained momentum, and in May 1635, the princes ratified the Peace of Prague. The Prague treaty divided the Protestants by reversing the Edict of Restitution for some Protestant estates—chiefly in the northwest—but not for others. Ferdinand hoped to recruit enough Protestant support to deter an attack by Louis of France. Notwithstanding, Louis declared war on Spain (the Habsburgs' other center of power) in May 1635 and soon began fighting Imperial troops as well. War in Germany dragged on for another thirteen years, with France and Sweden battling Imperial, Spanish, and certain German forces. But with France fighting alongside Protestants, and some Protestants fighting alongside Imperial troops, the conflict had lost much of its ideological character.[166]

Still, the Peace of Westphalia of 1648 recognized the role of religion in causing the war and took steps to prevent a recurrence. As Stephen

Krasner writes, "Westphalia attempted to insulate religion from politics" by creating mechanisms to keep religious change from threatening political stability. Rulers who changed religions could not force their subjects to follow them; religious dissenters, Catholic or Protestant, must be allowed to practice their religion in private and, within limits, in public.[167] The attempt did not fully succeed. Pope Innocent X declared "null, void, invalid, iniquitous, unjust, damnable, reprobate, empty of meaning and effect for all time" those sections of the treaties he judged detrimental to Catholic interests.[168] The Pope was mostly ignored by Catholics in the empire; but in other parts of Europe the old norm of *religio vincula societatis* ("religion is the bond of society") could not be extinguished by a treaty or even by the catastrophic war that it ended.

### Two More Forcible Promotions,
### Northwest Europe, 1670s–1680s

After 1648, very few forcible promotions of religious regimes took place in Europe. Religious conflict certainly continued, but was mostly internal, and much of it intra-Protestant, as in the Netherlands in the 1610s and 1620s and England in the 1640s. International wars took place, but mainly over territory and trade.

The two cases of forcible regime promotion were by France in the Netherlands in 1672, and the Netherlands in England in 1688. France's Louis XIV (r. 1643–1715) was the exemplary absolute monarch of his time, but was also a devout and militant Catholic. In his mind—and in the minds of most western European elites at the time—Catholicism and monarchy were linked, as were Protestantism and aristocratic republicanism.[169] The Calvinist Netherlands was a republic, and England had been one while run by Puritans from 1649 through 1660. Furthermore, the Huguenots retained strong ties with the Dutch, and the latter sent aid to the former. From 1667, Louis and the Dutch Republic were in a trade war, and it is no surprise that Louis saw Calvinism within and without France as a threat to his power.[170] Thus, he attacked the Netherlands in 1672 with the object of not only coercing it but of re-establishing Catholicism there. (Louis also sought to re-Catholicize England and Scotland, and in the 1670 Treaty of Dover England's Charles II promised Louis to join in the war against the Dutch and to declare himself a Roman Catholic in exchange for financial and military aid.)[171]

Louis failed to conquer the Dutch, instead uniting them behind the militantly Calvinist William of Orange.[172] In 1674, under pressure from the Whigs—tied to the Calvinist wing of the English Church—Charles II withdrew England from the war. Now religio-political instability rose again in England. The Whig leader, the Earl of Shaftesbury, was implicated in a plot to assassinate Charles, and fled to the Netherlands. Charles died in 1685, succeeded by his brother James II, an open Catholic. James began to disestablish the Anglican Church as a way to re-empower the Catholics. Now even the High-Church Tories turned against James, and joined the Whigs in inviting William of Orange to "invade" England and occupy the throne in 1688, thus solidifying the Protestant succession and England's constitutional monarchy.[173] James II moved to France, where Louis granted him a chateau and a subsidy.[174]

## The Long Struggle Ends

After England's Glorious Revolution, wars and interventions did not cease, but rulers stopped using force in Europe to promote Catholic or Protestant regimes. The prolonged wave, which at times in the sixteenth and seventeenth centuries had seemed a permanent feature of international politics, eventually ended. How did this particular long twilight struggle end? Not in the triumph of one or another of the religious regimes: Catholic, Lutheran, Calvinist, and Anglican regimes all eventually came to coexist without trying to undermine one another. Nor did Europeans simply stop believing in revealed religion. It is true that later in the eighteenth century such religious skeptics as Voltaire, Jean-Jacques Rousseau, and Thomas Jefferson were to make powerful arguments for toleration. But in the early part of the century most Europeans, including elites, continued to be observant. Indeed, Christians of various confessions still preferred that adherents of other religions convert to theirs.

The change, rather, consisted of the fading of the medieval norm of *religio vincula societatis* (religion is the bond of society). The religious divisions, at least among Christians, came to be viewed by elites as far less relevant to politics. States retained their established religions, but what it meant to be Catholic France or Protestant England changed. Catholic no longer implied eradication of Protestants, and Protestant no longer meant eradication of Catholics. By the early eighteenth century, if Calvinism or Catholicism was gaining converts in one's own state or a neighbor, it no longer had political repercussions elsewhere. Religious heterogeneity was no longer a threat to the state or the monarch, and so the state need neither enforce religious uniformity nor fear religious changes in neighboring states. In that sense, church and state began to separate more than before, and believers no longer had to fear living under a ruler who belonged to a different branch of Christianity.

From the early days of the Reformation there were times and places in which religious toleration was already practiced as a *modus vivendi*, a tactic to achieve societal unity for the sake of some other good such as countering a foreign threat. Charles V and Francis I both allowed, at various points, the propagation of Protestant teaching within their realms. The rule of *cujus regio, ejus religio* (whose the realm, his the religion) operative at various times in the empire, amounted to an effort to bring international religious toleration by insulating polities from one another's religious turmoil. France's Henry IV and the *politiques*—French Catholics who tolerated Protestantism—had their way in 1598 with the Edict of Nantes. In Poland a *Pax dissidentium*, mandating complete toleration among Protestants (not Catholics), was agreed upon in 1573.[175] These arrangements, however, were all temporary. In France and the empire, the continuing spread of Calvinism periodically reignited persecution, polarization, and forcible regime promotion. That suggests that rulers continued to worry about competing religions' political ramifications.

All the while, as religious strife persisted, theological and philosophical arguments for religious toleration began to emerge. Sebastian Castellio published denunciations of the Calvinists' execution of the Unitarian Michael Servetus in Geneva in 1553. The historian Perez Zagorin calls Castellio the first advocate of religious toleration; he rejected the notion that one person, even John Calvin himself, had the authority to declare another a heretic deserving of death.[176] In Poland, the Socinian (Unitarian) Confession of Faith (1574) and Catechism of Rakau (1609) both mandated religious toleration based upon the headship of Christ rather than human beings.[177] In England in 1667, the Puritan divine John Owen (no known relation to the author) argued that neither scripture nor the practice of the early Church sanctioned the coercion of belief. Instead, Christians must respect the individual conscience, "God's great Vicegerent."[178] Twenty-two years later, John Locke took up the argument from conscience and added that because coerced belief is never genuine, coercion can only lead to the sin of hypocrisy.[179]

These arguments had some following among elites, particularly dissenters—Protestants in Catholic societies, Baptists in England—but little purchase among elites belonging to the religious majority in a given country. That began to change when the old religiously homogeneous regimes, Catholic and Protestant, began to encounter severe anomalies. The legitimating narrative of a uniformly Calvinist or Catholic regime maintained that God would reward the monarch and country for prohibiting heresy. But in country after country, the drive to extirpate heresy had seemed not only to fail but also to exacerbate internal divisions, subversion, and war. By contrast, societies that were pluralistic, allowing minority religions to coexist, seemed to flourish.

The chief model of national flourishing under religious toleration was the Dutch Republic. The United Provinces of the Netherlands was officially Calvinist, but its charter of 1579 prohibited anyone from being persecuted because of religious belief. At the time of its promulgation, this tolerant provision was a bid to win support among Dutch Catholics for independence from Spain; as was the case with French *politiques*, Dutch Calvinists were tolerant for instrumental reasons. And the Dutch rulers did not always follow their tolerant constitution. Nonetheless, particularly in the province of Holland, the ruling regents came to protect religious minorities from Calvinist zealots so long as the minorities' leaders took responsibility for their welfare and they were loyal to the state. Religious minorities, including Jews, began migrating to the Netherlands, and conversions from one religion to another were not uncommon. In 1672, the Swiss commander of Louis XIV's troops in Utrecht wrote that, far from comprising only Calvinists, in the Republic "there are Roman Catholics, Lutherans, Brownists, Independents, Arminians, Anabaptists, Socinians, Arians, Enthusiasts, Quakers, Borelists, Muscovites, Libertines, and many more ... I am not even speaking of the Jews, Turks, and Persians."[180]

The Dutch Republic was famous or notorious in Europe for its toleration and also for its staggering economic success. In its "Golden Age" (1620–1700) the United Provinces excelled all other European states in wealth and at least equaled them in culture. Notwithstanding its tiny size, after the Thirty Years' War (1618–48) the Netherlands stood alongside England and France as a holder of the balance of power.[181] Of course, Dutch success was not merely a function of its toleration: its prowess at international trade played an essential role and indeed helped draw the hostility of the English and French. But the model of a tolerant polity able to compete with much larger states had its effects. Writes Willem Frijhoff:

> Throughout the seventeenth and eighteenth centuries the social arrangements and political procedures, to which religious diversity based on freedom of conscience gave rise, made the Dutch Republic a testing-ground for peaceful co-existence, then for toleration. In the more or less long term, according to which contemporaries we consult, it was established in Europe as a *model* to be followed.[182]

The Anglican writer William Temple, for example, wrote in his *Observations upon the United Provinces of the Netherlands* (published in 1673, during an Anglo-Dutch war) that the Dutch government does not inquire into anyone's religious beliefs as long as he is loyal to the state. It is significant that Temple had a polemical purpose, namely to increase toleration of Catholics in his native England.[183] He was literally holding up the United Provinces as a model to be emulated. His book went through several printings, and was only one of many English tracts about the Netherlands at the time.[184]

Thus, the pragmatic case for religious toleration, based upon the common desire for security and prosperity, gained plausibility. After two centuries it was clear to adherents of each branch of Christianity that the others were not going to disappear; meanwhile, the other concerns of government—national security and prosperity—must be met. The Constitution of Carolina (1669), drafted by John Locke himself, forbade any hindrance to people's changing religious affiliation and justified this on the need for the colony to attract people. In Europe, state-building and external security may have been still more important: if France or Switzerland or the empire was bound to remain religiously diverse, then civil peace must be secured without religious uniformity.[185]

Although England itself was not to remove legal disabilities on Catholics until 1829, the state began to practice toleration in the early eighteenth century and came to be known as one of Europe's most broad-minded countries. English laws persecuting Nonconformists "largely slipped into disuse" during this period, writes M. Searle Bates. In the meantime France, which had begun to tolerate Huguenots in 1598, rescinded that toleration in 1685 under Louis XIV, who was determined to vanquish Protestantism and the Dutch Republic. By the early eighteenth century, Louis's failure cast the Sun-King's way of handling religious pluralism in a distinctly inferior light. The toleration of the Dutch and English began to appear the better way to manage religious pluralism, and pluralism itself began to appear a virtue. As Voltaire wrote: "If there were one religion in England, its despotism would be terrible; if there were only two, they would destroy each other; but there are thirty, and therefore they live in peace and happiness." In 1732, France's Louis XV (r. 1715–74) restated that the death penalty and torture would again be used against Huguenots. "But," writes Bates, "officials now tended to find public disapproval of such barbarity of more consequence than the violent enthusiasms of the Catholic clergy." Even Pope Benedict XIV intervened on behalf of French Protestants. In general, writes Bates, "The eighteenth century saw inadequate principle but relatively broad practice in England, Scotland, and the American colonies, also in Holland. Sweden began to relax, and even in France the Huguenots could hold a national synod in 1744, despite their many disabilities."[186]

Thus, the ideological struggle that structured so much of European politics in the sixteenth and seventeenth centuries began to dissolve as the ideologies—not the religions themselves, but their intimacy with the state's coercive power—so manifestly failed to deliver on their promises. Catholic and Protestant alike had long argued that religious uniformity was necessary to civil peace and hence to prosperity and security. Each group had developed an ideology that demanded the extirpation of the other within a given society and throughout Europe. During times of high ideological polarization, when these ideologies were given free rein, however, the struggle to achieve religious uniformity had been destructive, not productive. As the Netherlands and then England came to prosper under religious toleration, it appeared a more and more viable alternative elsewhere. With rulers freed from the need to enforce orthodoxy, they could become indifferent to religious movements in other countries. In the eighteenth century demonstration effects in religion continued, as when evangelical revivals broke out in Britain and the United States;[187] but these presented neither threats nor opportunities to governments. Rulers came to cooperate and confront, make peace and war, intervene or leave alone, without regard to religion.

Conclusion

From the 1520s through the late seventeenth century, princes in Central and Western Europe often did something they did not do before and have not done since: they used force to promote Catholicism or Protestantism in other polities. In most cases the promoting ruler was seeking both internal and external security; spreading or preserving the ideology abroad helped consolidate his power at home and increase his influence abroad. Elizabeth of England helped Protestants in Scotland, France, and the Netherlands because she knew that doing so would help suppress Catholicism within England and extend English influence abroad. The vast majority of these interventions entailed a great power's promoting its own ideology. In a few cases, however, the King of France would help German Protestants against the Habsburgs. He was free to do so when he felt domestically secure against the Huguenots.

Most forcible promotions followed one of two types of event. Ex ante promotions followed hard upon regime unrest in a state, usually a Protestant uprising in a Catholic state, but sometimes the reverse. Unrest often lured rulers of neighboring states to send troops to influence the outcome. Sometimes these interventions would be isolated events, with no spillover effects. Thus the Lutherans' promotion of their regime in Württemberg in 1534 was a single intervention that did not beget more. Other interventions had feedback effects and led to more such promotions. The French promotion of Catholicism in Scotland not only led to an English counter-promotion of Calvinism in 1560, but had demonstration effects back in France, leading to an English promotion of Calvinism there in 1562; events in France, in turn, had demonstration effects in the Netherlands, leading to a Spanish (Catholic) suppression and English and German counter-promotion of Calvinism. Short waves also broke out in the 1580s following the death of the Catholic heir-apparent in France, and in Central Europe in 1620 following the Habsburgs' suppression of a Calvinist revolt in Bohemia, inaugurating the miserable Thirty Years' War.

In these cases, forcible regime promotion and increases in transnational ideological polarization were endogenous.

Many episodes of regime instability did not trigger one or more forcible regime promotions. Contrary to expectations of many at the time, the St. Bartholomew's Day Massacre of 1572 did not detonate a wave of revolution and regime promotion. Rulers often reckoned that the incentives against carrying out such interventions—fear of a prolonged war, or a spreading war, of domestic opposition—were too strong. Indeed, Protestant and Catholic rulers sometimes formed defensive alliances precisely to deter forcible regime promotion.

Ex post promotions happened during or after wars involving great powers. The Thirty Years' War itself is the most obvious example: the armies of Ferdinand II, the Holy Roman Emperor, re-Catholicized a number of conquered estates in the 1620s, culminating in the dozen impositions initiated in 1629 with the Edict of Restitution. A more limited set of ex post promotions came with the 1548 Augsburg *Interim* that followed the Schmalkaldic War. Of course, the Thirty Years' War, and the Schmalkaldic War of 1546 that foreshadowed it, were partly fought over religion in any case, or at least were begun by a great power in response to religiously based defiance by subordinate princes. One can argue that every invasion that took place during these wars was a forcible regime promotion. Even if one stops short of that extreme interpretation, it is clear that war and peace during these centuries in Central and Western Europe cannot be fully explained without reference to the crisis over church and state and the contest over the best regime that grew out of that crisis.

This long wave of roughly 180 years was not one in which rulers were themselves more devout or less rational than normal. It is clear that their fears of the spread of a rival religion, and delight in the spread of their own, were based not only on religious conviction but also concern for their own power. That was because they were acting within a social structure across the region that foreclosed some possibilities for rulers and made others more attractive. The structure was an understanding common to most elites that one's own polity must be either Catholic or (some type of) Protestant, and that these branches of Christianity were struggling across Central and Western Europe for survival or supremacy. Two sets of agents perpetuated the structure: transnational networks of true believers—Lutheran, Catholic, Calvinist—who worked perpetually to spread their favored regime and roll back competitors; and the princes who sometimes used force to promote one of these established religions.

The structure emerged in the 1510s in the crisis of legitimacy in the Catholic Church and the availability of alternative ideas from previous attempts at reformation. Medieval princes had often chafed at clerical authority, but by the early sixteenth century the Church had fallen into open corruption that damaged its authority across society, particularly in Germany. When Luther publicly challenged certain Church practices in 1517, he found himself receiving much more princely support than past aspiring reformers had enjoyed. By 1522 social interactions, suffused with contingency, had yielded an anti-Catholic Lutheranism and an anti-Lutheran Catholicism; after 1525 Lutheran regimes began to appear in the Holy Roman Empire. In the subsequent generation Calvinism, still more anti-Catholic, emerged in France and became the most energetic form of Protestantism. The social structure finally disappeared in the late seventeenth century with the manifest superiority of a new regime type: religious toleration. Europeans remained religious, and their polities continued to have established religions; but elites ceased to link loyalty to prince with adherence to the established religion. Toleration had been used tactically at various times during the long wave, but it was the Dutch Republic that first made it a constitutional matter in 1579. The spectacular international success of the United Provinces demonstrated to European elites that toleration could and should be made permanent and that religious changes in neighboring states were no longer politically threatening.

# CHAPTER FIVE

# Crown, Nobility, and People, 1770–1870

> The democratic government of France is said to have
> invented a new system of foreign politics, under the names
> of *proselytism* and *fraternization*. My present letter ... will
> show that *an internal interference* with foreign states, and
> the *annexation of dominion to dominion* for purposes
> of aggrandizement are among the most inveterate and
> predominant principles of long established governments.
> These principles, therefore, only appear novel and odious
> in France because novel and despised persons there openly
> adopted them.
>
> —Benjamin Vaughan, *1793*

> It is with an armed doctrine that we are at war. It has, by
> its essence, a faction of opinion, and of interest, and of
> enthusiasm, in every country. To us it is a Colossus that
> bestrides our Channel.
>
> —Edmund Burke, *1796*

## Prologue: The Second French Republic and the Pope, 1849

IN DECEMBER 1848, LOUIS-NAPOLEON, nephew of his infamous name-sake, was elected President of France's infant Second Republic by a wide margin, a few months after France's third modern revolution had over-turned the constitutional monarchy of Louis-Philippe. Louis-Napoleon was elected by a coalition of conservatives and moderates alarmed at the radicalism of the Republic's provisional government. Judging from his writings prior to his election, Louis-Napoleon's primary goal was to restore France to pre-eminence in Europe without resorting to war.[1] Upon assuming office, the new President quickly sought a congress of the great powers to renegotiate the Vienna settlement of 1814–15, which had left France weak. Among his goals for this congress, to be held in Brus-sels, was a reduction of Austrian influence over the Italian peninsula. To Louis-Napoleon's surprise, the British government refused his invitation to join him in proposing the conference, fearing (probably correctly) that that congress also would seek to overturn the recent revolutions that had sprung up all over the continent.[2] Thus far those revolutions had weakened Britain's rivals Austria and Russia

So the Brussels Conference never occurred. Instead, Louis-Napoleon reluctantly joined a conference of Catholic powers called to address one particular revolution, that in the Papal States. Pope Pius IX, who had begun his papacy in 1846 as a liberal reformer, found that his reforms did not appease radicals in Rome and elsewhere. As the 1848 revolutions cascaded across Europe, republicans in the Papal States rebelled, demanded a lay government, and removed the Pope's guard. Imprisoned in the Vatican, Pius fled Rome in November 1848 rather than accept a republic. When Giuseppe Mazzini and other revolutionary leaders declared a Roman Republic a few months later, Pius appealed to the governments of Spain, France, Austria, and Naples to restore his temporal authority.[3] It is clear from the negotiations at the Catholic conference that two outcomes were unacceptable to the French President: continuation of the new Roman Republic, and an Austrian restoration of the Pope. Louis-Napoleon wanted Italians to restore Pius by themselves, but when it became clear at the conference that the Italians required outside help, the French Assembly in Paris quickly voted to fund a French expedition to pre-empt Austria and restore Pius.[4] Louis-Napoleon quickly sent to Rome a force of 9,000. Giuseppe Garibaldi's republican forces fought back fiercely, but French reinforcements decided the contest easily. Pius ascended his throne again as an absolute monarch.

Why both Louis-Napoleon and mainstream French opinion found Austrian restoration of the Pope unacceptable is no mystery. Virtually all French elites wanted to roll back Austria's control of Italy. But why then should France restore the Pope rather than provide diplomatic and material support to Mazzini, Garibaldi, and the other Italian republicans? The left wing in the French Assembly pushed for this policy and protested vehemently when France, now a republic again after all, betrayed a fledgling sister republic in favor of a symbol of the *ancien régime*.[5] That Pius himself preferred to be reinstated by Austria, a conservative Catholic power, suggests that France would have had a more loyal client in the Roman republicans. (And in fact, upon his restoration Pius did lean toward Austria, which he correctly believed more strongly supported the status quo in Italy.)[6]

Louis-Napoleon re-imposed the Pope's absolute monarchy in Rome out of a concern for his own domestic power. He was facing a domestic and transnational threat from the revolutionary left. As his 1839 book *Idées napoléoniennes* showed, Louis-Napoleon was, like his uncle, a man of the Enlightenment, but also a man who believed that authoritarianism was required to force Enlightenment principles of rationality and freedom upon society.[7] In 1848, as in 1793, the Enlightenment had seemed to spin out of control in France, particularly when a worker's rebellion in June raised the specter of communism and was met by brutal military suppression. Louis-Napoleon had been elected President because he promised stability and an end to destructive factionalism. The factions included the absolutists or legitimists, who sought a restoration of the Bourbons under the principle of divine right; the Orleanists, who had supported the constitutional monarchy of Louis-Philippe; the Bonapartists; the moderate republicans; and the radical republicans or "Mountain." Louis-Napoleon sat atop a coalition of absolutists, Bonapartists, and moderate republicans—groups that had in common only enmity toward the radical left.

Louis-Napoleon never considered supporting the republicans in Rome because they were part of this same transnational radical enemy. Although himself a former revolutionary who would not have come to power in France without the Revolution of 1848, he obviously was now interested in restoring France's politics to the status quo ante. Soon after his election he suppressed the radical Left by suspending constitutional guarantees of freedom of speech, assembly, and the press. He approved of bills to restore Church control over education and to add a three-year residency requirement for voters, shrinking the rolls from 9.6 million to 6.8 million.[8] It was clear to friend and foe alike in 1848–49 that the radicalism still alive in France was linked to revolution everywhere. Radicalism was a transnational movement and revolutions enjoyed demonstration effects. Thus, a victory for the radicals in Rome was a victory for the radicals in France

At the same time, the factions atop which Louis-Napoleon sat uneasily had various reasons to favor papal restoration. For the absolutists, mostly devout Catholics, Pius's overthrow was a real threat to the Church's own power in France. The moderate republicans had no particular affinity for Pius, but they shared his transnational enemy, radicalism. Louis-Napoleon thought to satisfy them by arguing that if France restored Pius he would govern as a constitutional monarch; if Austria, he would become an absolutist.[9]

Louis-Napoleon's forcible promotion of absolute monarchy makes little sense apart from the high degree of ideological polarization across the societies of Europe in 1848–49. Had populations across the Continent not identified so intensely either for or against revolution, Italian conservatives would not have been so pro-Austrian and there would not have been so many French radicals to intimidate Louis-Napoleon and his supporters.

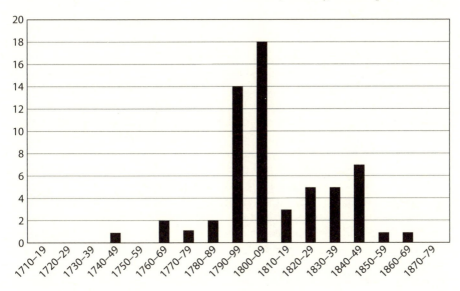

Figure 5.1  Forcible regime promotions, 1710–1879

•  •  •

Between the early eighteenth century and the 1780s, states continued to vie for position, threaten and fight wars, trade, and align and de-align in various patterns. Within and across societies, ideas about the best public order competed for allegiance. Yet, those decades were not roiled by transnational clash of ideas comparable to that which had thrashed Europe in the sixteenth and seventeenth centuries (chapter 4). No central set of ideas or common political language animated and united the discontented across states; no network of revolutionaries spanned Europe; no ideology of reaction gave governments a strong common interest. On the Continent of Europe, most rulers were bent on centralizing power in the manner of Louis XIV of France. Monarchs centralized power by subduing and co-opting nobles and continuing their traditional roles as alleged defenders of the peasantry against the nobility. With no sustained transnational contest over the right regime, monarchs were freer to act in accordance with state-centric *Realpolitik*. The eighteenth century, prior to the 1780s, was a period of classical power balancing. Indeed, in 1770, David Hume published his essay on the balance of power as a self-regulating or natural law of international relations. Wars were fought for territory, dynastic succession, and commerce, and only seldom for principles of government.[10]

From the 1790s through roughly 1850, however, the incidence of foreign imposition of domestic regimes rose sharply in Europe and even spilled over into the Americas (see figure 5.1).

The institutions being promoted and opposed had to do not with religion but with monarchical authority or sovereignty. As in the church-state struggle of the preceding centuries, the permutations were many, but in general three types of domestic regime were promoted: absolute monarchy, in which the crown was formally unconstrained by law; constitutional monarchy, in which the crown was accountable to law as interpreted by some independent body (typically comprising the nobility); and republicanism, in which there was no monarch.

Struggles over the locus of sovereignty—crown, nobility, and people—were perpetuated by networks of elites across societies. TINs during this period were seldom as coherent or centralized as were Catholicism or Calvinism in the earlier period, and they had conflicts of interest that often derived from national rivalries. Nonetheless, each showed a similar tendency to see itself, and to be seen, as continuous across time and space. Each also coalesced and swelled during polarizing events, particularly a regime crisis somewhere in the region or a great-power war. Transnational ideological polarization would present rulers with threats and opportunities. Rulers would often respond by using force to try to promote their own regime or at least block a rival regime.

The American Revolution of 1776–83 detonated the contest, and in the 1790s, the First French Republic became republicanism's great-power exemplar and carrier; after Napoleon Bonaparte's coup d'état in 1799, republicanism lacked a clear champion except for the distant and isolated United States. The paladin of constitutional monarchy throughout the period was Great Britain. Absolutism was exemplified and propelled by the three eastern monarchies of Austria, Prussia, and Russia. The 1780–1850 period was complicated by the sixteen-year rule of Napoleon (1799–1814), whose regime was a hybrid of absolutism and republicanism that itself split and polarized actors in other countries.

The threefold ideological struggle emerged in the 1770s and 1780s as a result of the manifest failures of absolute monarchy to satisfy the promises it made to nobles and commoners. At first the resistance came from constitutional monarchists; then a new and potent republicanism took the stage. The grand struggle endured as long as states that exemplified each model continued to be credible. The contest finally faded in the 1870s with new bargains across Europe between absolutists, constitutionalists, and some republicans, in the form of reforming conservative regimes. It was the radicalism of the 1848 wave of revolutions that drove elites to this new bargain which ended forcible regime promotion for a number of decades.

Emergence of the Structure: Absolute Monarchy
Reaches a Crisis

### The Old Regime: Enlightened Absolutism

In a deep sense, later illumined by Alexis de Tocqueville, the old regime whose legitimacy crisis ushered in the long wave of ideological promotion was the feudal system in which three estates—monarchy, clergy, and aristocracy—shared power.[11] But that old regime was itself a battleground for various struggles—not only that between clergy and the secular princes (chapter 4), but one between monarchs and nobles. For most of the eighteenth century on the Continent of Europe, monarchs were winning. The predominant regime type had become absolute monarchy, a set of institutions predicated on the total authority of the monarch over society owing to his legitimate (lawful) claim to the throne. When absolute monarchy began to confront serious anomalies in the 1760s and 1770s, it entered a sustained crisis throughout Europe (and the Americas) in which it contended with two competitors, constitutional monarchy and republicanism.

Absolute monarchs were unaccountable to any noble assemblies or constitutions or laws; they answered only to God. The divine accountability of absolute monarchy may obscure the regime's debt to the Enlightenment, the philosophical, scientific, and cultural movement that developed from Renaissance humanism. The Enlightenment is a term used to cover a turn in philosophy and science away from teleology to mechanism—away from the ancient and medieval emphasis on metaphysics, or learning the nature of things, and toward the modern emphasis on purposeless cause and effect. As Francis Bacon put it, natural science must abandon the "vain pursuit" of metaphysics and turn to "history mechanical," which "is of all others the most radical and fundamental towards natural philosophy; such natural philosophy shall not vanish in the fume of subtle, sublime, or delectable speculation, but such as shall be operative to the endowment and benefit of man's life."[12] The shift from Aristotelian to Newtonian physics is exemplary: Isaac Newton showed that an apple fell to earth not because it was in the apple's nature to do so, but because of the mechanical force of gravity. Newton and other new scientists relied on direct observation of matter in motion rather than on traditional authority; hence the Enlightenment stressed the overthrowing of tradition, particularly as borne by the Church.

The Enlightenment's sociopolitical project followed: if institutions were liberated from the dead hand of tradition, mankind would benefit from the true understanding of how the world works. For most Enlightenment thinkers that understanding would be mechanistic: in the social as well as the physical world, efficient causes operated and talk of final causes or the soul was mere speculation.[13] The point of knowledge was practical, "the relief of man's estate," as Bacon had put it in 1605. And man's estate would be relieved if men, in Immanuel Kant's words, would "Sapere aude!" or "Dare to know!"[14]

To many leading minds of the seventeenth and eighteenth centuries, the Enlightenment implied not democracy but the centralization of power under the rational administration of an enlightened monarch. For Thomas Hobbes, the use of right (secular) reason yielded a theory of absolutism, in which the sovereign has few meaningful limits to his power.[15] It is true that constitutionalists and republicans could also appeal to the Enlightenment. For John Locke, right reason produced a more limited sovereign in which the subjects may decide when the monarch has violated the social contract and overthrow him.[16] Jean-Jacques Rousseau, writing nearly a century after Locke, argued in favor of popular sovereignty. But historians ever since have been unsure whether to count Rousseau as an Enlightenment thinker at all.[17] And in any case, for most of the seventeenth and eighteenth centuries the Enlightenment emphasis on the new mechanistic science over against that taught by the Church sat most comfortably with monarchs desiring to seize power from Church and nobility.

The privileges of the nobility rested upon tradition, not abstract reason. Kings took it upon themselves to apply scientific principles to society by rationalizing public administration and making nobles and bishops into instruments of monarchical power. As most Europeans remained devout Christians, monarchical aggrandizement was also supported with the doctrine of the divine right of kings, which eventually was to conflict with the Enlightenment. But even divine-right theory came to be grounded not in the traditional authority of the Church, but in scripture as interpreted by the individual. Bishop Jacques-Bénigne Bossuet's robust defense of Louis XIV's absolute power, *Politics Drawn from the Very Words of Holy Scripture* (1709), invited the reader to consider the biblical data for himself, as a Protestant would, rather than to rely on clergy and bishops.[18] Religious skeptics also embraced absolutism. Voltaire, a leading anti-cleric and author of *The Age of Louis XIV* (1752), regarded Louis (r. 1643–1715) as being "responsible for the rebirth of civilization" after the "gothic and barbarous" Middle Ages.[19]

Louis, France's "Sun King," was the exemplar of enlightened absolutism. Louis owed his subjects justice tempered with mercy, but it was God's, not theirs, to judge whether he fulfilled his obligations. In concrete terms, Louis took many steps during his reign to amass power. He was to continue the practice set by his father Louis XIII (r. 1610–43) of never calling the States General, a centuries-old assembly of nobles that advised the Crown and authorized the levying of taxes. Louis XIV built a standing army and hence did not need to rely on his nobles to raise troops. He sold offices to nobles and ennobled wealthy men, appointing them to positions in his state bureaucracy. He asserted his authority over the clergy and religious orders, based upon a doctrine known as Gallicanism. By building roads and bridges and a national police force, Louis's regime created conditions for commerce to flourish as never before. Louis's power was certainly limited, and critics claimed that it was his bureaucracy, not he, that ruled France. Noble privileges remained; the *parlements*, or regional assemblies of nobles, continued to act as law courts, for example. But in Louis's France the nobility's status was far below what it had been in the Middle Ages. The influence in Europe of Louis's enlightened absolutism was enormous. In Prussia, Austria, England, Russia, Sweden, and elsewhere, monarchs imitated France's armies, administration, and arts and architecture.[20]

Enlightened absolutism, then, was a new idea in service of an old quest by monarchs to gather power. But it was not simply the eternal lust for absolute power cloaked in new words. The Enlightenment shaped absolutism by channeling it to the benefit of huge numbers of subjects. Louis XIV, Frederick the Great of Prussia, Maria Theresa of Austria, Catherine II the Great of Russia, and others used their enhanced power to advance science and technology so as to make their states and subjects prosperous.

Prior to the 1770s, the chief normative competitor to enlightened absolutism was constitutionalism, the theory that the monarch must be constrained by law as interpreted by ancient assemblies of nobles. In eighteenth-century Europe the nobility was understood not as an aggregation of individual aristocrats, but as a corporation, a body. Constitutionalism asserted that the old warrior caste had certain rights and privileges against the Crown and a crucial role as balancer between monarch and people. Constitutional polities could be quasi-republican, as in the United Provinces of the Netherlands, or monarchical, as in the case of England. Although Enlightenment thinkers such as David Hume and the Baron de Montesquieu were congenial to aristocracy, constitutionalism's main appeal was not to the new learning but to medieval practice. Indeed, the nobles' chief claim was that they had a right to their special status—as magistrates in their regions, as inheritors of government office and seats in provincial assemblies, as being exempt from taxes—because their ancestors had had those rights. To apply today's political terms anachronistically, absolute monarchy was progressive, constitutionalism conservative.

For most of the eighteenth century the contest between absolutism and constitutionalism was more domestic than transnational, and had little effect on international politics. It was mingled with transnational Catholic-Protestant struggles in northwestern Europe in the seventeenth century—Catholics tended to be absolutists, Protestants, constitutionalists (chapter 4)—and as such contributed to the dynamics among France, the Netherlands, and the British Isles that issued England's Glorious Revolution of 1688 and the Wars of the League of Augsburg (1688–97). But there are few cases of one ruler forcibly intervening in another country on behalf of absolutism or constitutionalism, and little evidence of international alignments according to ideology. It seems that during these decades, absolutism and constitutionalism were not very competitive *within* countries, once the English and Dutch regimes were safe from France. Constitutionalist rulers faced little internal threat from absolutism; absolutist rulers faced little internal threat from constitutionalism.

Thus, in striking contrast to the French Revolution a century later, England's 1688 revolution replacing a would-be absolutist with a constitutional regime did little to polarize European societies; it sparked no Continental uprising of nobles against monarchs. "Whatever its merit and shortcomings may have been," writes one historian, "there was nothing in the distinctively British social order which could tempt foreigners to imitation."[21] Why was this? Historians make clear that on the Continent at the time, absolutism was succeeding on its own terms, terms set by the Enlightenment, terms themselves accepted for many decades by sufficient numbers of nobles and commoners. The France of Louis XIV was a spectacular success; its predictions for itself—prosperity, technological advancement, victory in war, cultural superiority—usually came true. As C. B. Behrens writes, enlightened absolutism "remained unchallenged ... as long as the absolute monarchs seemed to provide more successful government than was to be had by other means." It seemed superior to alternative forms of governments "by virtue of its ability to keep the peace at home and to mobilize men and money for national defence and aggrandizement."[22] England, in rejecting absolutism for constitutionalism, was simply peculiar.

## The Constitutionalist Resurgence

As the eighteenth century progressed, however, absolutism did begin to fail on its own terms, leading to a reconfiguration of ideas, and of identities and interests, in the 1760s and 1770s. The chief difficulty with absolutism was its tendency to impoverish state and society. Already in 1748, Montesquieu's *Spirit of the Laws* cautioned that what distinguished enlightened absolutism from despotism was that the former "permitted the existence of 'intermediate powers'," namely the nobility as a corporation—something the Bourbons were not doing.[23] By 1767 Voltaire, long an apologist for absolute monarchy, was favorably comparing the liberties of constitutionalist Britain to those of absolutist France.[24] The English rejection of arbitrary power was gradually more appealing to aristocrats in France, in part owing to England's manifestly superior ability to generate wealth. While the peasantries of the Continent were increasingly impoverished, that of England was increasingly enriched owing to its application of scientific methods to farming. Constitutional monarchy now appeared more adept at applying the new Enlightenment learning to the benefit of society. François Quesnay, leader of the Physiocrats, presented an idealized picture of England's economy and argued in effect that "if France adopted the right policies, and became more like England, the French economy would grow and prosper."[25]

The Seven Years' War (1756–63) involved all the major powers of Europe and sharply increased states' debts. In France, the Paris *parlement* tried to block extension of the war tax, asserting that the King (by now Louis XV, r. 1715–74) was bound by law, a claim that would have had force in Britain but that contradicted France's absolutism. The *parlement* of Brittany tried to block the King from building a road without its permission. *Parlements* throughout the land began to coordinate, and declared that they constituted a general French *parlement* that retained the right to veto taxes or legislation. The nod to England's constitutional regime was unmistakable. In 1766, an offended Louis XV rebutted the *parlements*, and in 1770 he abolished them and set up his own law-courts in their stead.[26]

Similar events took place in the absolute monarchies of Sweden and the Austrian Empire. In Sweden the aristocracy attempted to increase its domination of the Riksdag, and in 1772, Gustavus III (r. 1771–92), an admirer of French absolutism and former student of Voltaire, intervened to suppress the nobility.[27] In the Habsburg lands of Hungary, Bohemia, Milan, and Belgium, the nobility resisted monarchical taxes; here the Empress Maria Theresa successfully suppressed aristocratic self-assertion.[28] Even in England itself, exemplar of constitutionalism, the Whig or country faction had always suspected the rival Tories of being absolutists, and under George III (r. 1760–1820) the Whigs associated with the Marquess of Rockingham began to argue that the royal court was running roughshod over Parliament.[29] Weak transnational ties are evident in these episodes. Montesquieu's arguments about the necessity for an aristocratic check on monarchs were adopted by the Hungarian nobility in its struggle against the Habsburg Empress Maria Theresa (r. 1745–80).[30]

## The Rise of Republicanism

The aristocratic resurgence of the 1760s and 1770s was constitutionalist, not republican. Republics, upholding the old Roman Republic as a model, had existed in Europe since the Middle Ages—the Venetian Re-

public was founded in A.D. 727, and the United Provinces of the Netherlands was at least nominally a republic—but the nobles in most European
lands wanted to retain a tamed monarchy. It was not until the 1770s
that commoners began to turn toward republicanism. In European monarchies, commoners traditionally identified their interests with those of
the Crown against those of the nobility. Theorists tended to justify monarchy based in part upon its ability to guard the commoners' interests
against aristocratic exploitation. As the eighteenth century wore on, tensions between commoners and aristocrats were aggravated by a decrease
in upward mobility, as the practice of ennobling wealthy commoners
(e.g., merchants) began to decrease.[31] Gustavus III's suppression of the
Swedish nobility in 1771 inspired commoners in other countries to defy
the aristocracy.[32]

But the legitimacy crisis in absolute monarchy was to produce a historical realignment in European and American politics. Starting with British North America, the upper strata of the commoners—merchants and
professionals—began to turn against monarchs and to embrace republicanism.[33] Like absolutism itself, this historic reconfiguration of identities
owes much to the principles and consequences of the Enlightenment. The
technology that enlightened monarchs put to use in public works and
finance helped create the middle class and gave it more influence and self-
consciousness. In addition, notwithstanding the early tendency toward
absolutism in Enlightenment thinkers, the principle of holding all things
up to the light of reason did not sit well, in the end, with any inherited
or traditional authority. Monarchs, after all, inherited their seats just as
aristocrats did. If all things are open to question, all institutions, especially
those that have failed, are vulnerable. The upper strata of the commoners,
and many among the nobility itself, began to question the privileges of
monarchs as well as those of Church and nobility. Indeed, democratic and
republican tendencies had begun to appear among the *lumières* in France,
notably in the writings of Jean-Jacques Rousseau. It was Rousseau who
located sovereignty not in the monarch but in the people or nation.[34]

The Long Wave Begins

*The North American Republic and French Promotion,*
  *1776–1783*

It was across the Atlantic, in British North America, that commoners first
declared themselves independent from their historic monarchical patron
and established a new republic, inspiring commoners and nobles in other
countries to become republicans and to form transnational networks.[35]

The insurrection in the thirteen colonies began, ironically, not as a republican movement but as a constitutionalist protest against what the colonial legislatures saw as a move toward absolutism in the Mother Country. Each colonial assembly, elected by the propertied classes, enjoyed "ancient" rights and privileges, including the exclusive right to tax the King's subjects within the colony.[36] A further irony was that it was Parliament, a fellow aristocratic body, that passed the Stamp Act in 1765, taxing the colonists over the heads of the colonial legislatures to pay off the Seven Years' War. Seen plainly, the dispute was among constitutionalists over which aristocratic body—a colonial one or the Parliament at Westminster—had the power to tax the Americans

Thus, the discontented Americans met with some sympathy in England. The emerging Radical faction agreed with them that Parliament was an aristocratic despotism. The Rockingham Whigs asserted that Parliament did have the right to tax the colonists but favored rescinding the tax for practical reasons. But the Tories and the other Whigs in Parliament thought the American colonists must be taught a lesson. George III, needing revenue and concerned with principles of authority, agreed; King and Parliament closed ranks.[37] The Crown-nobility coalition in Britain led to a predictable response in North America: by July 1776 the American Patriots, as they now called themselves, were blaming George himself for the injustices under which they claimed to suffer. From blaming the monarch it was a short step to blaming the institution of monarchy itself. In the hands of republicans such as Thomas Jefferson, the American Revolution pitted people against aristocracy *and* monarchy, democratizing Locke in a way that may not have pleased Locke himself.[38] The Declaration of Independence of July 4, 1776, declared the colonies "free and independent states," that is, a republic.

But the British had to be driven from the United States before the latter could secure independence. The American armies met with mixed success in 1776–77. Louis XVI of France and his foreign minister the Comte de Vergennes badly wanted to avenge France's loss to Britain in 1763 and to weaken the British Empire so that Louis could take his rightful place as, in the words of Orville Murphy, "the arbiter of Europe." French and Spanish money subsidized the Patriots; then in 1778 a Franco-American alliance was signed and large French naval and land forces joined the struggle.[39] The first forcible regime promotion of the second long wave was by an absolute monarch on behalf of republicanism. Louis and his ministers were acting out of concern for external security—to move the balance of international power in their favor—and in 1778 were not worried about any possible republican contagion into France.

Although the American Revolution was in a sense a conservative affair, intended to restore the constitutional order in the colonies, the establishment of a new republic was radical. Hence it attracted keen attention in northwestern and Central Europe and would contribute to the downfall of the French monarchy several years later. News from America was spread by returning soldiers, in Masonic lodges, and by various writers. The new U.S. state constitutions were translated and published in several European countries. Periodicals and reading groups already proliferating in the 1770s and 1780s became preoccupied with American events and tended to favor the revolution. Individuals mattered as well: Benjamin Franklin and Thomas Jefferson stimulated French enthusiasm for the Patriots, while John Adams did the same in the Netherlands; Adams even suggested that the Dutch burghers (commoners) ought to do as the Americans by reducing the power of the Stadtholder and the nobility. In effect, transnational ideological networks began to form over the republican revolution across the Atlantic. The American Revolution created an impression in many European societies, documented exhaustively by R. R. Palmer, that mankind had entered a new era of undefined liberation. A few monarchists and aristocrats began to fear that American events would inspire popular revolutions in Europe.[40]

Over the next few years, commoners in other lands began to follow the North Americans by distancing themselves from their longtime royal patrons and taking on the "patriot" label. In Spanish America creoles, or native-born elites, had become alienated from a new wave of émigré *peninsulares* or elites born in Spain; visitors and circulated documents from the young United States helped define an inchoate discontent with the Spanish monarchy.[41] Jacques Pierre Brissot, a Frenchman who later was to lead the radical Gironde faction in 1792–93 (see below), visited America in 1788 and published an account in France extolling the virtues of popular sovereignty and in particular of a new constitution created by a popular assembly.[42] Indeed, the various American state constitutions—all drafted and ratified by citizens' assemblies, not aristocratic corporations—were published at least five times in France between 1776 and 1786.[43]

*Prussia Promotes Monarchy in the Netherlands, 1787*

Demonstration effects from the American Revolution were strongest in the United Provinces of the Netherlands, a nominal republic with a Stadtholder as de facto head of state. The American constitutions also were published there and in 1787, the burghers and regents (nobility) coalesced against the Stadtholder William V, whom they accused of amassing excessive power. The progress of the Dutch revolution was strikingly parallel to that of the American: when the commoners began to demand too many concessions from the nobility, William saw his opportunity and sided with the latter. This historical realignment of (quasi-) monarch with nobility against commoners thrust the Dutch into a republican revolution. The Dutch Revolution of 1787 provoked another case of foreign regime promotion. Frederick William II, the King of Prussia (r. 1786–97) and an "enlightened" absolutist, sent 20,000 troops to help the Stadtholder (his brother-in-law) defeat the commoners.[44] Although Frederick William desired influence in northwestern Europe, this invasion would have made little sense apart from the Dutch Revolution, itself a spillover from the American.

### The French Revolution and Its Demonstration Effects, 1789–1793

Far more famous and consequential was the French Revolution that erupted in July 1789. Like the Dutch, the French Revolution was not generated entirely by domestic events. French societal contacts with Americans and others had already been extensive,[45] and the American and Dutch revolutions excited close attention in Paris. Palmer argues that Europe and the Americas during these decades were shaken by a general transnational democratic revolution that was manifest in various forms across countries. The great transnational movement cannot be reduced to class interests or material conditions. The northern British American colonies were commercial and smallholding; the southern, gentrified; France was an absolute monarchy with a subdued nobility; Poland (see below), a constitutional monarchy with an unusually strong upper nobility. Even so, revolutions in all these lands used similar language and symbols, appealed to similar sources, and were seen by friend and foe as being of a piece. The ideology itself was strong enough to obscure these differences and create common transnational bonds among very different types of elites

Like the American and Dutch revolutions, the French began as a constitutionalist revolt against absolutism. Louis XVI levied taxes to pay for a war—this time, ironically, French aid to the American patriots in the early 1780s. The *parlements* (regional noble assemblies) refused, and Louis's May Edicts of 1788 reduced the *parlements* to judicial entities. At first nobility and bourgeoisie made common cause, openly demanding a constitutional monarchy of the sort advocated by Montesquieu. Louis backed down and the Paris *parlement* announced that the States General, comprising representatives of all three estates from throughout France, would meet for the first time in 174 years. A now familiar historic realignment took place: the French commoners (Third Estate) now began to assert themselves against both King *and* nobility; the latter two in turn began to make common cause against the "mob." Advocates of popular rule, influenced by the writings of Rousseau, insisted that delegates to the States General not be segregated according to estate or rank; the nation must be one. Louis XVI rebuffed these egalitarians.[46] The commoners, led by the Abbé de Sieyès, retaliated by announcing that they constituted a National Assembly with the authority to tax. On June 20, having been expelled by Louis, they gathered on a tennis court to pledge that they would write a new constitution for France. Louis proposed a compromise, but the Assembly refused; Louis responded by mobilizing troops around Versailles and Paris. Word reached the countryside and peasants began seizing nobles' property. Commoners seized the city government in Paris on July 14 and organized a national guard.[47]

All during these weeks, and throughout the French Revolution, French elites interacted with keenly interested foreigners. Émigrés—aristocrats and clergy—fled to neighboring lands, told (often exaggerated) tales of depredations by mobs, and urged foreign intervention to halt the spread of the democratic cancer that threatened thrones and nobility alike. At the same time, thousands discontented with the status quo in their homelands flocked to France to participate in the stirring events, much as Protestants converged on Calvin's Geneva in the mid-sixteenth century (chapter 4). They founded their own societies and publications and plotted revolutions for their countries. As with the American Revolution, printing presses spread the word rapidly. The Declaration of the Rights of Man and Citizen of August 1789, itself influenced by the U.S. Declaration of 1776, was translated into a dozen languages and disseminated throughout Europe.[48]

In Poland, which had already been in the midst of a parallel movement to weaken its powerful nobility, reformers were electrified by news from Paris. As Palmer writes:

> Conscious of a revolution in their own midst, learning excitedly of the one in Paris, and remembering the one in America at the opposite extremity of Western Civilization, where Kosciusko and Pulaski and a dozen others had fought, the Poles formed an impression of revolution on a worldwide scale.[49]

In November the burghers (upper stratum of commoners) in 141 Polish towns petitioned the diet that they be allowed political representation. The diet, entirely aristocratic, was alarmed: even the reformers had not wanted the commoners to have direct power. Still, within a year it had passed reforms; the Polish Constitution of May 3, 1791, strengthened the burghers and was taken by people of all ideological stripes as an extension of the French Revolution.[50]

Even in constitutionalist England some Whigs, convinced that George III was amassing power, declared that their country needed to imitate France. The Unitarian pastor Richard Price declared his hope that Britain's parliament would follow the French example and become a national assembly:

> Be encouraged, all ye friends of freedom, and writers in its defense! The times are auspicious. ... Behold kingdoms, admonished by you, starting from sleep, breaking their fetters, and claiming justice from their oppressors! Behold, the light you have struck out, after setting AMERICA free, reflected to FRANCE, and there kindled into a blaze that lays despotism in ashes, and warms and illuminates EUROPE![51]

Thomas Paine wrote his fellow Whig Edmund Burke that, "The revolution in France is certainly a Forerunner to other Revolutions in Europe. —Politically considered it is a new Mode of forming Alliances affirmatively with Countries and negatively with Courts." But Burke, longtime defender of constitutional monarchy, saw incipient republicanism in these assertions of popular sovereignty, and responded with his *Reflections on the Revolution in France* (1790), a polemic and prophecy against the revolution.[52] So began a Herculean effort by Burke and his followers to unite Britain's constitutional monarchy to the absolute monarchies of Europe in an anti-revolutionary front.

At first most European monarchists were not as alarmed as Burke by events in France. Through the middle of 1791 it was not clear to all that the revolution threatened Europe's entire sociopolitical order, including monarchy itself. Both Joseph II (r. 1765–90) of Austria and his successor Leopold II (r. 1790–92) were enlightened absolutists, accustomed to thinking of the commoners as their allies. They blamed the hapless Louis XVI for being insufficiently enlightened.[53] The only monarch who seemed particularly frightened was Gustavus III of Sweden, who as noted above had put down his own aristocratic revolt in the previous decade. In June 1791 Gustavus, alarmed at the confinement of Louis and Marie Antoinette, helped arrange their escape from France. The royal Flight to Varennes failed and the King and Queen were returned to Paris. With the humiliation of King and Queen, monarchists—absolute and constitutional—throughout Europe began to see a broader danger and a need for cooperation.[54] In August, Leopold of Austria and Frederick William of Prussia issued the Pillnitz Declaration, calling for concerted action in France by the other great powers.[55] In Paris, the suspicion spread that an international conspiracy of nobles and monarchs was planning to overturn the revolution.

In September 1791 Louis submitted to France's new constitution. The country now joined Britain as a constitutional monarchy. Transnational ideological polarization continued between revolutionaries and absolute monarchists within and without France. Brissot, publicist of the American state constitutions, argued in the National Assembly in Paris that an international monarchical conspiracy was trying to overturn the revolution, and that France should attack Austria because patriots in Habsburg-ruled lands would rise up and help the French. In response, Leopold and Frederick William formed an offensive alliance in February 1792. In March, Gustavus of Sweden was assassinated, stoking monarchists' fears of a transnational republican conspiracy. On April 12, Vienna moved 50,000 troops to the frontier. On April 20, the Legislative Assembly in Paris declared war on Austria.[56]

A second regime change took place in France in September 1792: the National Assembly abolished the constitutional monarchy and declared France a republic. The British government of William Pitt concluded that the French could not be negotiated with and might try to "liberate" the crucial United Provinces, now a constitutional monarchy whose republicans had already asked for French intervention. The French foreign minister accused the British of stirring up counter-revolution in France, and on February 1, 1793, the Convention unanimously declared war on Britain and the United Provinces.[57]

The War of the First Coalition (1792–97) exacerbated transnational ideological polarization by making patriots more patriotic and by causing constitutional and absolute monarchists to coalesce. In Poland, England, Scotland, Ireland, Belgium, the United Provinces, Switzerland, and parts of Italy and Germany, patriots declared common cause with their counterparts in France. Jacobin and other pro-French societies appeared in England, Ireland, the Netherlands, Poland, Italy, Switzerland, Germany, and the United States. "The Masonic lodges," writes Palmer, "also provided a kind of international network of like-minded people. Their existence facilitated the circulation of ideas." In some of these lands patriots rose up and attempted revolutions of their own.[58]

### Russia and Prussia Twice Overturn Popular Sovereignty in Poland, 1792 and 1794

The 1791 Polish Constitution, inspired by events in France, was not republican. It was rather a more democratic constitutional monarchy, in which the landholding nobility lost power to the burghers and peasantry. The Polish nobility quickly revolted and asked Catherine of Russia to send troops to overturn the new regime. Catherine had two powerful reasons to intervene: the new constitution promised to strengthen Poland against foreign (Russian) influence by binding monarch and burghers; and it seemed evidence that French "*démocratisme*" was a spreading virus. As an Austrian minister wrote three years later:

One sees in [Poland] strictly the pattern of the French Revolution, and that it is from the hearth of Paris that the spark has come which had enflamed Poland and which will incinerate all of Europe ... [I]t is war to the death between sovereignty and anarchy, between legitimate government and the destruction of all order.[59]

Upon hearing that France had declared war on Austria in 1792, Catherine did indeed order an invasion of Poland to "restore the original constitution." The Polish King asked Frederick William to counter-intervene to protect Polish independence from Russia. Notwithstanding his enduring interest in containing Russian power, on June 8, Frederick William refused. Then in January 1793, he sent an army to Poland to join the Russians, declaring that Polish patriots were spreading the revolution to his domains. Within a week, Catherine and Frederick William had agreed to a second partition of Poland.[60]

The restoration of the old regime was met with a resistance movement among burghers in Warsaw; even some nobles, angry at Russo-Prussian intervention, joined. Poems and songs from the time make clear their Jacobin and Patriot inspiration. The leaders chose Kosciuszko, military leader of the 1792 resistance (and veteran of the American Revolution), then in France, as their leader. In 1794, Kosciusko returned to Poland, declared the serfs free, and led a force against the Russian and Prussian occupiers. Polish rebels composed a *Catechism of Man*:

> France is our example,
> France will be our help;
> Let cries of Liberty and Equality
> Resound everywhere.
> Let us follow in her footsteps ...
> Let the nobles and lords disappear
> Who would deny Fraternity to the people?[61]

Catherine and Frederick William were also genuinely alarmed at a Jacobin-style contagion from Poland. The King of Prussia wrote to his ambassador in Vienna, "I feel keenly how essential it is to crush in its germ this new and dangerous revolution, which touches so closely on my own states, and which is also the work of that diabolical sect against which a majority of the powers have combined their efforts." Wrote Catherine to her leading general, "for the good of Russia and the entire North she had to take arms against the wanton Warsaw horde established by French tyrants."[62] The Russians and Prussians prevailed in October 1794, and Kosciuszko was taken prisoner. Austria joined Prussia and Russia in yet another partition of hapless Poland.

Acquiring Polish territory was of course a traditional interest of Russia and Prussia; it is not necessarily the case that Tsarina and King were acting chiefly out of ideological motives.[63] But the Russian and Prussian actions make little sense without the existence of transnational republican networks. Those anti-monarchical networks gave Catherine and Frederick William, normally rivals, a common interest in overturning popular sovereignty in Poland. Had these networks not existed and been swollen by the events in France, it is likely that no foreign intervention would have happened.

### Promotions during Occupations, 1794–1799

The great-power war between France and the monarchical coalition of great powers fed back into transnational networks, further polarizing European and even American elites along ideological lines. In Latin America, creoles who had been impressed with Enlightenment writings and the formation of the United States were split by the violence and anti-clericalism of the French Revolution. A particular fear of creole slave-holders was that the Haitian revolution of 1791, which was propelled by a slave revolt and resulted in the abolition of slavery, would infect their lands.[64] In the United States, events in France aided in the polarization that eventually resulted in the formation of the two political parties, the Federalists and Republicans. The former were hostile toward the French Republic, the latter sympathetic or enthusiastic.[65]

In Europe this polarization gave the warring governments powerful incentives to carry out ex post promotions during the war. Rulers may not have invaded countries simply in order to alter their domestic regimes, but they did find in case after case that regime promotion was an efficient way to make the target into allies. Regime promotion made sense precisely because of transnational ideological polarization: elites across Europe were either intensely republican and pro-French, or intensely monarchical and anti-French. In late 1794 the British, having occupied the island of Corsica, found a sympathetic leader in Pasquale Paoli. Corsica had been annexed by France in 1770 and Paoli had fled out of hatred of the absolutist Bourbons. But the Reign of Terror of 1793 turned him against the Jacobins as well, and he sought British help in establishing the constitutional Kingdom of Corsica, a constitutional monarchy aligned with Britain.[66]

On the Continent itself the French armies did likewise, establishing republics in the lands they conquered. In 1795, they invaded the United Provinces of the Netherlands and, cheered by the Dutch patriots, ousted the Stadtholder and set up the Batavian Republic.[67] The following year in Bologna and the surrounding region, the French set up the Cispadane Republic.[68] In 1797, they established the Ligurian Republic in Genoa and the Cisalpine Republic in northern Italy.[69] The next year they made Switzerland into the Helvetic Republic and set up a Roman Republic.[70] In 1799, the French remade Naples into the Parthenopæan Republic.[71] In each of these, the revolutionary French armies were welcomed as liberators by the patriots they had inspired. But as Blanning writes, they were not simply examples of French revolutionary zeal. "One of the most inspired inventions of revolutionary politics .. .turned out to be the satellite state, a device for maximizing international control with a minimum of metropolitan effort. Puppet monarchs were nothing new in European history of course, but the satellite republic, which combined the appearance of altruism with the reality of control, was an invention with a glittering future, destined to reach its climax in post-1945 Eastern Europe."[72]

Although the conquest of these smaller countries was instrumental to the war, the imposition of constitutional monarchy by Britain or republicanism by France was no mere afterthought. These powers could have left the existing regimes in place and coerced or bribed leaders to do their bidding. Faced with such intense transnational ideological polarization, they could not afford to do so.

Bonapartism as Ambiguous Hybrid, 1799–1814

The revolutions, wars, and regime promotions of the 1790s failed to resolve the transnational struggle among absolute monarchy, constitutional monarchy, and republicanism. Each ideology retained strong advocates across several countries at once in Europe, and each retained at least one great-power exemplar. In France itself, however, republicanism was metamorphosing. It had turned from Left to Right in 1795 with the Constitution of the Year III and assumption of power by the five-man Directory. In November 1799 Napoleon Bonaparte, the country's most successful general, carried out a coup d'état and made himself First Consul. Napoleon had saved the revolution with his military victories, but he feared the revolution all the same. So began the French Republic's slide into the hybrid regime—rationalist, absolutist, imperialist—whose ambiguity complicated the ongoing transnational ideological struggle.

During his years as First Consul, Napoleon continued to enjoy the good opinion of most "enlightened" elites in Europe and the Americas. He rationalized public administration and law in France and in the lands he conquered. It was his self-coronation as Emperor of the French in 1804 that changed the opinion of many. Bonaparte deliberately designed the coronation to appeal to symbols of the *ancien régime*; it took place at Paris's Cathedral of Notre Dame, with the Pope present. Ludwig van Beethoven had so admired Napoleon that he had dedicated his path-breaking Third Symphony to him; upon hearing the news of Bonaparte's self-coronation, so goes the story, Beethoven was so infuriated that he tore up the dedication. In South America, Simón Bolívar, who had once idolized Napoleon as "the bright star of glory, the genius of liberty," turned against him.[73] Bonaparte was to go further. In 1808, he created his own nobility by endowing his generals with titles and land, just as the Bourbon monarchs had ennobled favored wealthy subjects.[74] The designation of the French state, "French Republic, Emperor Napoleon," captures the incoherence of the Bonapartist regime.[75]

Thus, Napoleon split both monarchists and republicans within France and across Europe. For some monarchists, absolutist or constitutional, his complete lack of any blood title to any throne made him forever an illegitimate ruler. These monarchists began to adopt the label *legitimist* to distinguish ancient dynasties from Bonaparte's upstart Corsican family. For other monarchists, Napoleon was acceptable: he had restored many elements of the old order in France and was doing so in the lands he conquered. Republicans, too, were divided. Some continued to insist that, for all of his flaws and betrayals, Napoleon remained preferable to his enemies, the advocates of absolutism, who sought to re-impose their regime in France and indeed in Britain.[76] In the United States, Thomas Jefferson called Napoleon a "republican emperor" and considered France a more natural friend than Britain of the American Republic.[77] In general, however, Napoleon's gradual self-aggrandizement from 1799 disillusioned and becalmed many who had identified with the French Republic.[78]

Confusion and ambiguity aside, that the First Empire was Europe's leading power for so many years, and an aggressive one at that, meant that Bonapartism was a contender in the grand ideological struggle. France's unexampled power and glory gave Bonapartism a degree of transnational appeal. Once he conquered and occupied a foreign power, Napoleon faced the usual choice as to how the target was to be governed: leave the current regime in place, let matters take their course, or install a new regime. In most cases, Napoleon did as rulers typically do in a time of transnational ideological polarization: he imposed his own institutions, in what I call ex post promotions. As Michael Broers writes, "Napoleonic rule usually entailed the introduction, in whole or in great part, of the uniform, highly centralized system of administration and justice that had evolved in France since the Revolution of 1789."[79] In 1800 in Bavaria;[80] in 1801 in Tuscany;[81] in 1803 in the Cisalpine Republic (renamed the Italian Republic, then the Kingdom of Italy in 1804) and the Helvetic Republic (renamed the Helvetic Confederation);[82] in 1804 in northwestern Germany, renamed the Duchy of Berg;[83] in 1805 in Naples, Lucca, and the Batavian Republic (renamed the Kingdom of Holland);[84] in 1806 in Neuchâtel, Baden, Württemberg, Nassau, and Spain;[85] in 1807 in more parts of Germany (renamed the Kingdom of

Westphalia) and in Poland (renamed the Grand Duchy of Warsaw);[86] in 1810 in Frankfurt:[87] Napoleon imposed various of his institutions. (Ironically, under the Franco-Austrian Treaty of Lunéville of 1801, Vienna agreed not to alter the regime of any of France's satellite states.)[88] French troops would typically divide a country into prefectures, establish modern salaried bureaucracies with responsible chiefs (rather than nobles), and rationalize the tax system. The new governments would seize lands belonging to the Catholic Church and remove all religious discrimination.[89] The Napoleonic Code and *gendarmeries* to safeguard travel in the countryside increased the well-being of the average European. They also made the French war machine more efficient, since Napoleon used the human and material resources from these lands to conquer or retain more territory.[90]

It was in many of these conquered lands that liberals felt most betrayed by Bonaparte. In Spain, where Napoleon placed his brother Joseph Bonaparte on the throne in 1808, liberals were perhaps the most difficult. Some, labeled *afrancesados*, worked with Joseph at first to craft a new constitution that reduced the power of the Church and recognized some civil liberties. Other liberals worked against the Bonapartists, and in 1812, when they dominated the Cortes or national legislature, ratified (under British protection) a liberal constitution.[91] The Constitution of 1812 became a touchstone for southern European and Latin American constitutional monarchists for decades to come.[92]

Indeed, the war on the Iberian Peninsula inspired powerful independence movements in Latin America that looked to the American and French revolutions for inspiration. The French invasion of Portugal in 1807 led the Prince Regent, later to become King John VI, to flee to Rio de Janeiro. By 1815, John had declared Brazil a kingdom co-equal with Portugal. Spain's colonies were set aflame by news that Napoleon had captured Ferdinand VII. Much like the upper strata of the commoners in Europe and the landowning and professional elites in British America, creoles had long chafed under the domination of *peninsulares*, émigrés born in Spain. Across Spanish America, creoles, usually in *cabildos* or city councils, declared self-government. Over the next two decades Spain was to fight to keep or recapture its colonies. The two outstanding military leaders of the independence movements were José de San Martín and Simón Bolívar, both of whom had spent part of the first decade of the century in Europe absorbing the new ideas.[93]

In the meantime, the British were not immune to the lure of their own fellow constitutionalists in foreign lands. Sicily was ruled by Ferdinand, a Bourbon absolutist. Sicilian barons had always resented absolutism, and as the war continued they came to admire the British constitutional model. Some began to call for a British invasion, and in 1811 the British obliged. The following year the British overthrew Ferdinand and replaced him with his son Francis, who ruled under a constitution modeled on the British.[94]

## Post-Napoleonic Promotions, 1814–1849

### The Monarchical Restorations, 1814–1815

The Congress of Vienna (October 1, 1814–June 9, 1815) was in many senses a "founding moment" for the international system, inasmuch as it created institutions for preserving order among the great powers.[95] Those institutions also involved domestic regimes. After defeating Napoleon, the rulers of the victorious powers had the usual problem of how to reconstruct order in the liberated lands. They might have left intact the Bonapartist regimes. They might have done what Alexander of Russia preferred in the case of France itself, namely to oust the rulers and let the people (however defined) decide what sort of regime they would have.[96] Or they might have imposed regimes. In the crucial French case they chose the third option, restoring the House of Bourbon and using the leverage from the occupation to set up a new regime. The powers were divided as to whether France's monarchy was to be absolute (favored by Metternich of Austria) or constitutional (favored by Castlereagh of Britain). In the end, they settled on an ambiguous compromise.[97] In 1814, the French Senate and provisional government made clear that they were inviting Louis to become King, imitating the English Parliament's invitation to William of Orange in 1688. Louis made equally clear that he was King by divine right. The Constitutional Charter of June 4 reflects the ambiguity: the King was bound to follow it, and it allowed the usual Enlightenment list of civil liberties; but he retained broad powers, including the initiation of legislation, supreme command of the armed forces, and the right to dismiss both national Chambers. French elites were divided accordingly, and for the next several decades power oscillated between the absolutists and the constitutionalists, with Bonapartists and republicans also having a presence in the legislature.[98]

In Switzerland, too, the governments of the powers imposed a constitution, essentially restoring the old regime of cantonal confederation. The Swiss constitution was included in the Final Act of Vienna and the cantons were coerced into accepting it.[99] In all other liberated states, however, the victors chose the second option, allowing the polities—meaning the elites—to set up regimes of their choosing. As Paul Schroeder writes, for the allied governments, "[m]onarchy was the unchallenged basis of constitutional doctrine and the foundation of political community."[100] Indeed, delegates to the Congress of Vienna were far from indifferent concerning domestic regimes. The consensus was that the destructive quarter century of great-power war that had just ended was caused by the revolution in France that had inevitably evolved into Napoleon's aggressive imperialism. The solution thus must include the restoration of "legitimate" monarchies, dynasties that held power owing to ancestral rights, throughout Europe. The world, so thought the delegates at Vienna, could resume its normal stable order, free of metastasizing revolutionary regimes.[101]

But the victors knew that, to their good fortune, elites in the lands the French had conquered wanted to restore monarchy. Beyond that, they left those elites to work out their institutions. In some states, such as those of southern Germany, elites chose constitutional monarchy. In others, such as Spain and most Italian states, they chose absolute monarchy. Within the latter category elites varied according to how far they retained the various institutional reforms brought by the French armies. On the whole, however, it is remarkable how tolerant the great-power governments were concerning post-Napoleonic regimes.[102] (It is also important to note that in Germany the status quo ante bellum concerning political territorial boundaries could not have been restored without great coercion. In 1806, Bonaparte had replaced the old Holy Roman Empire with the Confederation of the Rhine, reducing Germany's states from more than 300 to approximately forty; the rulers of the forty naturally preferred to keep the new arrangements.)[103]

Beneath the restorations, however, the transnational crisis over political legitimacy remained. What C. W. Crawley writes about Frenchmen was true throughout the Western world: "the 'Great Schism' .. created by the events of the 1790s was not easily healed."[104] The Revolution was not merely a memory or symbol around which to rally conservatives. It was still present as potential energy running through the societies of an exhausted Europe. Discontent with the restorations was wide, deep, and diverse. Some of the discontented were constitutionalists, others republicans of various degrees of radicalism; and in France, Bonapartism remained a force. Revolutionaries remained quietly mobilized in secret societies and Masonic lodges and worked to bring about another cataclysm. They were motivated by a strong notion of historical progress. The years 1789–94 had shown what was possible even against powerful monarchs and armies; what Geoffrey Best calls the "insurgent underground" in Europe was convinced that it could happen again, with permanent results.[105] What is sometimes broadly called the Left was divided—republicans against constitutionalists, for example—but as seen below, the Left could unite when a revolution somewhere in the system sparked demonstration effects across societies.

In similar fashion, the post-Napoleonic political Right was divided but could coalesce when faced with revolution. Conservatives favored gradual reform of traditional institutions, while reactionaries insisted on restoring what they imagined to be the old regime. What these had in common was the conviction that, having expended vast amounts of blood and treasure to defeat Bonaparte, they must not allow more revolutions. Indeed, monarchists began to turn away from the Enlightenment, now blamed for the catastrophes of the preceding decades, and toward more traditional Christian foundations for monarchy. From now on, the Enlightenment was identified not with absolutism, as in the eighteenth century, but with constitutionalism and republicanism.

Some ruling elites were perpetually terrified of revolution. The most prominent was Metternich. Knowing that the Habsburg Empire he defended was, in the words of Frederick Artz, "merely a governmental machine without any genuine national basis," Austria's Minister of State saw that "the mere introduction of democratic or nationalist ideas anywhere in Europe could easily stir up disruptive movements in [Austria]. Hence, revolutionary ideas in speeches, books, or newspapers frightened Metternich, even if they appeared as far away as Spain, Sweden, or Sicily."[106] That dynamic implicated international stability or the balance of power.[107] For example, the power of Austria, an absolute monarchy, depended in part on Habsburg influence in Italy. Should one or more states in Italy switch to a republican or constitutionalist regime, it would almost certainly become anti-Austrian, inasmuch as, in the current highly polarized atmosphere, constitutionalists and republicans abhorred Austria as an exemplar of absolutism. Revolutions in Italy would weaken Austria from within and without and would upset the delicate balance of power. Consequently, all the powers had an incentive to preserve absolute monarchy in Italy.[108] As seen below, when revolutions erupted and the Right rallied against them, the Left across states would coalesce into what Eric Hobsbawm calls "a single movement—or perhaps it would be better to say current—of subversion."[109]

The restorations accomplished, the rulers of the great powers—with the exception of Tsar Alexander—began to settle into what they thought would be normal times. In 1818, representatives of the four allies plus France conferred at Aachen (Aix-la-Chapelle) to normalize relations with France. Alexander, attending in person, had by now become even more fearful than Metternich of transnational revolution, and proposed a permanent alliance that would overturn revolutions wherever they might arise in Europe. The Prussian and Austrian delegations were sympathetic, but Castlereagh of Britain was adamantly opposed. In the end, Alexander's proposal was defeated, as Metternich was concerned about the extension of Russia's reach into Central and Western Europe.

Instead, the governments invited France to join a Quintuple Alliance and pressed its government to suppress republicanism within its own borders.[110]

### The Spanish Revolution of 1820 and a Short Wave of Promotion

An eruption of rebellion and revolution across Europe in 1820 provoked transnational ideological repolarization, and triggered a short wave of forcible promotion. First in Spain, then in Portugal, Naples, Piedmont, and Greece, subjects attempted to force kings to submit to liberal constitutions. When news of the Spanish rebellion reached Spanish America, the fledgling states of Gran Colómbia, Venezuela, Argentina, Uruguay, Peru, and Mexico all adopted constitutions patterned after the Spanish Constitution of 1812.[111] In France, the King's nephew was assassinated. Even in Britain, where the government had lately suppressed Radical dissent, attempts were made on the lives of cabinet members. The seemingly premeditated and coordinated nature of these outbreaks gave new life to Alexander's anti-revolutionary proposal from two years previous. The Troppau declaration of November included the following:

> States which have undergone a change of government, due to revolution, the results of which threaten other states, *ipso facto* cease to be members of the European Alliance, and remain excluded from it until their situation gives guarantees for legal order and stability. If, owing to such alteration, immediate danger threatens other states, the powers bind themselves, by peaceful means, or if need be by arms, to bring back the guilty state into the bosom of the Great Alliance.

In January 1821, the great-power conference moved to Laibach (Ljubljana), where the governments of Russia, Prussia, and Austria agreed that Austria would unilaterally overturn the revolutions in Naples and Piedmont. In March 1821, an Austrian army marched toward Naples and, sustaining very few casualties, overthrew the new constitutional monarchy the following month. A similar Austrian action in Piedmont had similar results.[112]

More domestic regime imposition was to come. In France the absolutist party did well in 1820 elections, and the next year the absolutist government began moving France in its ideological direction, censoring criticism of the government and suspending habeas corpus. In 1822, Spanish absolutists rebelled against their country's new constitutional regime, which by then had greatly weakened King Ferdinand, and the Russians again began calling for joint intervention to restore absolute monarchy in Spain. The French government posted an army of observation along the Pyrenees. At the Conference of Verona in November, France, Austria, Russia, and Prussia agreed to French intervention in Spain on behalf of the absolutists. In April 1823, a 100,000-man French force marched to Madrid and Cadiz and restored Ferdinand's absolute rule in a nearly bloodless counter-revolution.[113]

The one great power to abstain from all of these declarations and actions—Troppau, Laibach, and Verona—was constitutionalist Great Britain. A British delegate attended Troppau as an observer only, and back in London Castlereagh deplored the declaration, "condemn[ing] the claim that the Alliance had the right to put down revolutions anywhere."[114] In a famous Cabinet State Paper of May 5, Castlereagh condemned the very notion of external intervention in any country's domestic regime. The alliance was "never intended as a union for the government of the world or for the superintendence of the internal affairs of other States." Calling attention to Britain's distinctive constitutional nature, the Paper added: "No country having a representative system of Government could act upon [such a general principle]."[115]

Many historians have taken Castlereagh at his word: Metternich, Alexander, and the others were interventionist, but Britain was not.[116] In fact, as had been seen during the Napoleonic wars, the British had no objection to foreign ideological intervention per se; it was intervention on behalf of *absolutists* to which they objected. In the contest between absolutism and constitutionalism that continued to thread across Europe, Britain stood to lose influence from the spread of the former. Non-interventionism was a British rhetorical strategy against absolutist France, Austria, Prussia, and Russia.

Thus, what happened in 1826 in Portugal, traditionally a British ally, comes as little surprise. The 1820 Portuguese Revolution (which followed that in Spain) had produced a constitutional monarchy under King John VI. In March 1826 John died, and constitutionalists and absolutists in Iberia, Latin America, and much of Europe polarized over the succession. A concord between absolutists in Spain and Portugal led to a Spanish invasion of Portugal and the enthronement of Dom Miguel as absolute monarch. Constitutionalists in Lisbon appealed to London for help. By this time absolutists dominated French politics. Under Charles X since 1824, the French government had restored property to the émigrés of the Revolution, mandated capital punishment for sacrilege, and increased tax revenues to the Church.[117] With transnational politics so polarized, an absolutist Portugal would surely align with absolutist France. In December, a small British force easily defeated the Portuguese absolutists and restored the constitutional regime under Pedro IV.[118] Portugal was returned to the British sphere of influence.

*The French Revolution of 1830 and Another Short Wave*

As regimes stabilized in the 1820s, the incidence of forcible regime promotion decreased sharply. Yet, transnational republicanism and constitutionalism retained their potential to polarize societies and rulers. In 1830 began yet another wave of rebellions and revolutions, this one more serious than that in the early 1820s, in part because this time the first revolution was in France itself. The wave alarmed absolutists and presented opportunities to constitutionalists; both transnational groups stepped up their cooperation and hence polarization.

France's Charles X (r. 1824–30), successor to Louis XVIII, had begun to move his country further toward absolutism. Liberals began to countermobilize, and in July 1830, a coalition of liberals gained a majority in the Chamber of Deputies. The absolutist Prime Minister responded by dissolving the Chamber, reducing the electorate by 75 percent, and outlawing publications not approved by his government. A liberal revolt began in Paris and by July 30, rebels had taken the city. Charles abdicated in favor of his grandson Henry. But Henry never took the throne, and republicans and constitutionalists fought over what form the new regime would take. Republicans wanted the aged Marquis de Lafayette to be President, but constitutional monarchists wanted a new King, Louis-Philippe, the Duke of Orleans. The latter prevailed as Louis-Philippe and Lafayette embraced publicly. Louis-Philippe disavowed the divine right of kings and declared himself a "Citizen-King," a constitutional monarch on the British model. The July Monarchy abolished censorship, separated state from church, and expanded the franchise.[119]

The July Monarchy inspired liberals to rise up in Belgium, Switzerland, the German Confederation, Italy, and Poland. On August 25, Belgian nationalists, chafing against Dutch rule under the 1815 settlement and inspired by the late events in France, began demonstrating in Brussels and provincial towns. King William agreed to call the States General; in October that body declared Belgian independence. The governments of Austria, Prussia, and Russia, the three eastern absolutist monarchies, asked the government of France to support an intervention to restore the authority of the Dutch King in Belgium. But Louis-Philippe's government refused and instead joined the government of fellow-constitutionalist Britain in supporting the Belgian insurrectionists

Rumors of a great-power war spread, leading the British and French to invite the three eastern powers to join them in hammering out a Belgian settlement. The great-power talks were hampered by the very transnational polarization that propelled the crisis: the French were at pains to appease domestic liberals who sympathized with the Belgians, while the

Austrians and Prussians feared that Belgian success would exacerbate liberal fervor in the German Confederation. In the autumn of 1832, the Dutch King William invaded Belgium to re-establish control. The British and French governments responded with a joint military-naval intervention. The rulers of Austria, Prussia, and Russia did not counter-intervene, but were increasingly alarmed at this western liberal alliance; in Prussia "semi-liberal pro-Westerners" were ousted from the government for being a sort of Fifth Column.[120]

Italy was home to several liberal secret societies with contacts in France and Belgium. In February 1831, as a direct consequence of events in the latter, revolutions erupted in Modena, Parma, and the Papal States, all replacing absolute with constitutional monarchies. The liberals knew they risked provoking an Austrian intervention, since Habsburg rule in northern Italy was at stake; but they counted on their hero Louis-Philippe to rescue them. In the following month Austrian troops marched into the states, easily defeated the armies of the new governments, and restored the absolute monarchies. Louis-Philippe responded by mobilizing a force of 80,000. A five-power conference was convened in Rome in April to avert war. It failed, and the following February a French force landed in the Papal States and began to stir up liberals. In the meantime, in Piedmont a new King, Charles Albert, declared for absolutism, entered a treaty with Vienna, suppressed the secret societies, and broke relations with the constitutional regimes in Spain and Portugal.[121]

Within the German Confederation, liberals in Bavaria, Württemberg, Baden, Hesse-Darmstadt, Nassau, Brunswick, Hanover, Electoral Hesse, and Saxony responded to the French Revolution of 1830 with their own uprisings. In May 1832, at least 20,000 liberals gathered at Hambach and called for a united German democratic republic. Discontent in Germany was not simply with absolute monarchy but with the Austrian hegemony that kept it in place. Prussia, which had some reform-minded ministers, might have exploited the uprisings to weaken Austria. In the event, however, the unrest drew the two absolutist governments closer together. King Frederick William of Prussia fired his leading liberal minister and ordered cooperation with Metternich in suppressing the revolutions. Berlin and Vienna worked in concert to pressure the Diet at Frankfurt (the council of the German Confederation) to pass the Six Acts in June and July, censoring the press and handing a measure of power from parliaments to princes in the German states. Britain and France, the constitutional great powers, protested, but the absolutists prevailed.[122]

Indeed, the Prussians, Austrians, and Russians cooperated in Poland despite their *Realpolitik* rivalries. Poland was ruled by Russia at the time, and Tsar Nicholas ordered Polish troops in Warsaw to ready themselves to march westward to overturn the revolution in France. Liberal Polish officers rebelled. The Russian viceroy left for Lithuania with his garrison, and in early February 1831 the Polish diet declared Nicholas deposed. Nicholas responded with force. The Polish patriots had thought that Austria, Russia's rival, would intervene on their behalf. But Metternich, fearing liberal revolutionary contagion, advised the Poles to submit to the Tsar. The Prussians actively aided Russia by disarming Polish rebels who crossed into their territory. The French proposed to Britain a joint offer of mediation.[123]

Later in the decade more forcible regime promotions took place in Spain and Portugal. The Iberian contest between absolutists and constitutionalists had never disappeared, as transnational networks continued to agitate. In Portugal, Maria was the constitutionalist, Dom Miguel the absolutist. In Spain, Cristina was the constitutionalist, Don Carlos the absolutist. Constitutionalist Britain and France backed Maria and Cristina; the absolutist eastern powers, Miguel and Carlos. In April 1834, Palmerston of Britain and the ancient Talleyrand of France put together a Quadruple Alliance of the four constitutionalist governments. With British naval intervention and British and French volunteers fighting on the ground, constitutionalists won in Portugal in 1836 and in Spain in 1838. Palmerston asserted that the Quadruple Alliance would "serve as a powerful counterpoise to the Holy Alliance of the East," and that "the moral effect in Europe of a formal union of the four constitutional states of the West ... must be by no means inconsiderable."[124] Palmerston exaggerated the loftiness of Britain's (and others') motives, but his words illustrate how ideologically polarized was international politics in the 1830s.[125] David Thomson's summary is worth quoting at length:

> From the revolutions and other changes of 1830–33 Europe emerged divided more sharply than ever into two political regions. In Germany, Italy, and Poland the forces of conservatism triumphed over those of liberalism, and revolutions were crushed by the concerted actions of Austria, Russia, and Prussia. In France, Belgium, Switzerland, Portugal, Spain, and Great Britain liberalism triumphed, backed at times by the power of France and Britain. Europe roughly west of the Rhine was moving towards a pattern of liberal, constitutional, parliamentary government geared to the special interest of a growing commercial and industrial middle class. Europe east of the Rhine preserved all the main lines of its economic and political pattern of 1815. This remained the basic fact in international relations until 1848.[126]

Still, transnational networks remained in place—liberals in absolutist lands, conservatives in constitutionalist ones—and in 1848 they were once again to make their presence felt.

*The French Revolution of 1848 and a Final Short Wave*

The late 1830s and early 1840s saw no forcible regime promotion, as governments were relatively stable. An isolated promotion came in Portugal in 1846, as a republican (Septembrist) revolt against the constitutional monarchy of Maria II placed the regime in danger. The British Navy blockaded the mouth of a strategic river, and troops from constitutionalist Spain invaded to support Maria. By June 1847, the rebellion was over and the regime was safe.[127]

The Portuguese republican rebellion did not trigger other revolts. The story was different with the French Revolution that began in February 1848. That event set off the last great transnational ideological polarization along the lines set in the 1770s. The overthrow of Louis-Philippe's July Monarchy in Paris ran, in Hobsbawm's words, "like a brushfire across frontiers, countries, and even oceans," setting off another round of uprisings in Central Europe and Italy.[128] As usual, the conditions and sources of discontent varied from country to country; nationalists, guilds fearful of industrialization, and communists joined under a common language and set of solutions. In state after state, encouraged by one another's actions and successes, intellectuals and students demonstrated, agitated, formed assemblies, passed resolutions, toppled absolutist ministries, and pressed monarchs to adopt various liberal and democratic reforms. The revolutions of 1848 were more serious than those of 1830–31, for they infected two more great powers, Austria and Prussia. On March 13, Metternich's government in Vienna fell, and five days later the conservative ministry in Berlin likewise fell.[129] In France, the revolution threatened all property holders, middle-class as well as hereditary nobility. Socialists were granted promises of workers' rights, full employment, and greater labor representation in government. Outside of France, most of the revolutions were nationalistic—anti-imperial—as well as liberal and democratic. Hints of the Italian and German unifications that were to come in the 1860s appeared in 1848.

Just as the revolutionaries in one country drew encouragement from their confreres' successes in another, conservatives in one country drew encouragement from resistance in another. Like the revolution itself, reaction first gained a foothold in France's young Second Republic and spread from there. The radicals in Paris over-reached; the "June Days," in which factory workers fought the army and thousands were killed, led to the concentration of power in the military, which suppressed agitation. In December, French voters overwhelmingly elected Prince Louis-Napoleon Bonaparte as President of the Republic. Louis-Napoleon appointed conservative ministers, and all of Europe concluded that the revolution in France had been halted. Governments that had been knocked back on their heels rebounded and began to suppress popular agitation. By the end of 1848, the tide had begun to turn in favor of the conservative reaction.

Rulers not only drew encouragement from one another but also enhanced cooperation. In early March 1848, the new republican government of France sent a special envoy to Berlin to discuss freeing Poland from Russian rule. Progress was slow until revolution in Berlin in late March forced the Prussian King to form a liberal government, which in turn began planning a Polish revolution.[130] Absolutist governments also cooperated. Indeed, the ultimate success of the reaction all over Europe was partly due to transnational reactionary cooperation. Rulers helped ousted or embattled absolutists, sometimes by military intervention. At the beginning of this chapter I recounted the republican revolution in the Papal States and France's restoration of the Pope's absolute rule. In Tuscany, a civil war between republicans and absolutists brought an Austrian invasion to restore the rule of Archduke Leopold II in May 1849. In the same month the King of Saxony fled, and a civil war between royalists and revolutionaries was decided in favor of the former by an invading Prussian force. In the Palatinate the Prussians crushed a revolt that had set up a provisional government. In Baden, republicans forced the Grand Duke to flee and request Prussian intervention. The invading Prussians faced heavy resistance, but ultimately prevailed in July.[131] Perhaps most remarkably, in May 1849 the Austrian government requested Russian assistance against the liberal-nationalist Hungarian revolt, notwithstanding traditional Austrian fears of Russian expansion; Russia responded with three armies that successfully suppressed the Hungarians.[132]

Although Britain escaped revolution, it too was divided between supporters and opponents of the Continental revolutions. The Paris revolution had toppled the constitutional July Monarchy. Supporters of Britain's institutions feared that a republican juggernaut would storm across the Channel. The Chartists, named for the "People's Charter" they had submitted in 1838 demanding universal adult male suffrage and other reforms, were energized by the news from Paris. In March 1848, France's Second Republic enacted virtually the entire Chartist program. In April, the Chartists held a mass rally in London; the government brought in extra police to deter an uprising.[133] Still, the Palmerston government had little fear of revolution, and publicly applauded the expansion of the franchise in France. It was only when the Prussian government began moving further left in the spring of 1848 and, in the name of German nationhood, began to fight Denmark over Schleswig-Holstein, that Palmerston cooled toward the revolutions.[134]

The Long-Wave Decays, 1860s

Heterogeneity among governments in Europe and the Americas continued after 1850. Britain remained a constitutional monarchy, joined by
the Netherlands, Denmark, Sweden, Belgium, and Piedmont. Across the
Atlantic most states, including the potential great-power United States,
were republics. France had its Second Republic from 1848 until 1852,
when President Louis-Napoleon became—with voters' overwhelming approval—Emperor Napoleon III under a Bonapartist regime. The remaining great powers—Austria, Prussia, and Russia—along with a number
of smaller states remained absolute monarchies, with rulers more determined than ever to grant no concessions to legislatures. No single regime
type had triumphed in the Western world. Transnational liberal networks
continued to exist, but were decimated by the post-1848 repressions. As
Robert Binkley writes, the revolutionaries "were beginning to pass from
the scene. By 1852, all those who had led the 'people' against the 'despots'
had been given the choice of abandoning their principles or their homes."
Many went into exile in London, where they continued their hopes of
another grand revolution.[135] With the networks that once caused absolutist rulers to tremble now scattered and impotent, incapable of fomenting
serious unrest, no forcible regime promotion took place in the 1850s.

Still, absolutists remained worried about transnational radicalism. The
hero of the 1848 revolutions in Italy, Giuseppe Mazzini, retained enormous prestige and continued to work toward a revolution to oust the foreigners from Italy and create a united Italian Republic. Italy was finally
unified by war involving Piedmont, Austria, and France from 1859 until
1861. But the *Risorgimento* (resurgence), as unification was called, yielded
not a republic but a constitutional monarchy under Victor Emmanuel II
of Piedmont. The King's prime minister, Count Cavour, admired the British model of government and understood that, after 1848, Italy could
not be united under an absolute monarchy. The Italian Constitution, an
extension of the Piedmontese, featured a parliamentary assembly that
constrained the King more than the absolutists wished.[136]

Italy was a portent of what was to come elsewhere in the 1860s, which
was the compromise among liberals and conservatives and the progressive reform of most absolute monarchies into some kind of constitutional monarchy. Indeed, in all absolutist countries except Russia, and in
Bonapartist France, conservative and liberal elites struck bargains over
the course of the 1860s and a rough convergence of regime type began
to emerge. By the 1870s, the transnational contest among republicanism and the dueling forms of monarchism had lost most of its intensity because the stakes had lowered significantly. Although some liberals

remained republicans and others constitutional monarchists, absolutists had made sufficient concessions that many liberals saw little point in carrying on the struggle to topple monarchs. (As seen in chapter 6, European radicalism now came to reside in communists and anarchists.) As Michael Broers writes, "The revolutions of 1848–51 [changed] the face of European political life forever ... They shattered the existing political order in every country where serious disorder occurred. Instead of creating new radical regimes influenced by nationalism or socialism ... they gave birth to a new form of conservatism, able to absorb elements of liberalism, nationalism, and even socialism, and to transform them almost beyond recognition."[137]

In Austria, which lost a base of power when Italy unified, the Emperor Francis Joseph despised liberalism. But he loved the Habsburg Empire more, and saw clearly that if it were to be preserved he would have to reform the regime. Nationalism and republicanism among Hungarians, Slavs, and others were too powerful. In 1867, Francis Joseph named as his chancellor Count von Beust, who quickly set up the Dual Monarchy (under the Hungarian Crown was separate from the Austrian—although Francis Joseph wore both) and granted the Austrian and Hungarian assemblies more power, including in foreign affairs.[138] In Prussia, Count von Bismarck, chancellor to King William I, held a similar disdain for liberalism. Yet he, too, found that achieving his goal—the unification of Germany under the rule of the King of Prussia—required a measure of liberal reform. Following a bloody victory over Austria in 1866, Bismarck organized the North German Confederation whose constitution allowed member states to retain extensive powers. States had proportional representation in the *Bundesrat*, whose members were elected by all adult males.[139] Following the defeat of France in 1871, the Constitution of the German Empire granted the *Bundesrat* more powers. The German regime was not as liberal as the British of the time—the Emperor, not the *Bundesrat*, dismissed the government—but was several moves away from the absolute monarchy William and Bismarck would have preferred.[140]

In France the pattern was similar. As the 1850s gave way to the 1860s, Napoleon III saw that he must grant the Legislative Body more power. In 1861, he began to allow it more influence over the budget and also eased restrictions on the press. In January 1870, he had Émile Ollivier, a republican, form a government and shortly after promulgated a new constitution. The 1870 Constitution still allowed the Emperor a veto, but required him to work with the legislature and made his ministers responsible to that body.[141] In 1871, Napoleon was captured by the Prussians during the Franco-Prussian War; the Second Empire was eventually replaced by the Third Republic

The chief exception to the liberalizing trend was Russia. Tsar Alexander II believed it his duty to remain an absolute monarch, with no diminution in prerogative, no cession of power to any elected body. Even Alexander, however, felt the need to liberalize societal institutions in Russia; he freed Russia's serfs in 1861 and reformed the penal code in 1867.[142] On the whole, however, Europe was turning to constitutional government. J.A.S. Grenville sums up the trend:

> Before 1848, parliamentary assemblies worthy of the name were the exception rather than the rule. France and Britain were the leading constitutional European states. By 1878 the participation of elected parliaments was recognized virtually everywhere except in Russia as an indispensable element of good government. In Vienna, Berlin, Budapest, Rome, Paris and London, the parliamentary assemblies were acquiring increasing power; some parliaments were already elected on the basis of universal manhood suffrage.[143]

The grand ideological struggle that had begun to wrack Europe in the 1770s took a century to resolve. It began with a legitimacy crisis for absolute monarchy, which led to a resurgence of constitutionalism and then a new republican movement. The struggle consisted of a contest among these three. Its end entailed not precisely the triumph of constitutional monarchy, but the conversion of many absolutist elites—such as Cavour and Bismarck—and republican elites—such as Giuseppe Garibaldi, former partner of Mazzini—to varying constitutional compromises.

Why did the long wave decay when it did? In 1846, Cavour of Piedmont had forecast:

> If the social order were to be genuinely menaced, if the great principles on which it rests were to be at serious risk, then many of the most determined oppositionists, the most enthusiastic republicans would be, we are convinced, the first to join the ranks of the conservative party.[144]

Within two years, something very like this shift took place. Hobsbawm argues that the bargains struck in the 1870s between absolutists and liberals were a product of the sheer radicalism of the 1848 revolutions. Put simply, many liberals—constitutionalists and republicans—turned against revolution, and absolutists could then trust them for reform. In Paris, Vienna, Berlin, and other places, conservative and liberal alike caught glimpses of something terrifying: power in the hands of those who did not respect private property or the ways it had always been acquired and transferred. "From the moment the barricades went up in Paris," writes Hobsbawm, "all moderate liberals (and, as Cavour observed, a fair proportion of radicals) were political conservatives." Marx and Engels were to exaggerate the extent to which 1848 was a proletarian revolution. The leaders of the Paris Commune of 1848 were intellectuals;

most of the rank-and-file were disillusioned small shopkeepers, artisans, and peasants. Still, in effect, the radicalism of the 1848 revolutions threw into disarray the old established opposition between Enlightenment reason and traditional privilege. The year 1848 was especially jarring to the constitutional monarchists and moderate republicans who found themselves shoulder-to-shoulder with people whose solutions were sharply at odds with their own vision for a properly ordered society. The broad political left fragmented in 1848–49, with liberals and many radicals turning against other radicals and emergent socialists. The ideological boundaries that had dominated transnational politics for decades were losing their salience.[145]

For their part, absolutists had always abhorred revolution but had endured three transnational waves of it since the 1814 restorations: in the early 1820s, the early 1830s, and 1848. Now striking bargains with newly moderate constitutionalists and moderate republicans began to look more plausible. Contributing to the appeal of liberal reform was the virtuous example of Great Britain, a constitutional monarchy since 1688 and, in national mythology, since Magna Carta in 1215. Britain was the one great power to have escaped serious unrest through all three post-1814 revolutionary waves. By the second half of the nineteenth century Britain was first among the powers, with by far the world's largest empire and navy and a per capita gross national product that either doubled or nearly doubled that of each of its rivals.[146] As the Dutch Republic had shown the benefits of permanent religious toleration in the seventeenth century, Britain showed the benefits of a moderate constitutionalism in the nineteenth.

After the 1850s, the absolutists of Europe could have continued to suppress rather than accommodate liberals, and some wanted to do so. But suppression had failed many times in many countries since the restoration of the "legitimist" monarchies in 1814–15. And something in rulers' social and material environment was changing, so that the old regime no longer worked. Absolute monarchy could not handle the cocktail of changes that were manifest by the middle of the nineteenth century. In the long run absolutism was weakening dynasties and states. The path to preserving and extending monarchical power lay through accommodating some of the aspirations of at least some of the subjects. If Piedmont were to unite Italy, Prussia to unite Germany, France remain a great power, and Austria to remain an imperial power at all, they must become more like Britain.

Conclusion

For roughly seventy years, from the late 1780s through 1849, it was not unusual for rulers to use their militaries to promote absolute monarchy, constitutional monarchy, or republicanism (or, in the case of Napoleon I, his own unique Bonapartist regime) in other countries. Before the 1780s and after 1849, states fought wars and intervened in one another's domestic affairs; but rulers did not use their militaries to further one of these three regimes. This seventy-year period was different: rulers pursued their interests by trying to advance one or another of these regime types abroad

It is impossible to divine completely rulers' motives in any of these dozens of forcible regime promotions. No doubt many, even most, truly believed in the ideology they promoted and believed the alternatives were dangerous and wicked. But as in the longer 1510–1680 period analyzed in chapter 4, in which the contending ideologies concerned church and state, in none of these uses of force is it necessarily the case that the rulers were motivated primarily by ideological zeal. Each intervention makes sense if we simply assume that rulers were aiming to improve their internal or external security. In some cases, sending force abroad to overturn an enemy ideology could weaken that ideology in the ruler's own state. In other cases, it could keep the target state in the ruler's sphere of influence, or move the target into that sphere. In many cases, it could do both.

And as in the cases in chapter 4, those in this chapter vary according to whether they were ex ante, in which promoting state initially attacked the target owing more to domestic unrest in the target—a potential revolution, coup, or other regime change—or ex post, responding to the strategic or tactical need for the target's territory during a war. The many invasions of Italian and German states by absolute monarchies from the 1820s through the 1840s followed outbreaks of revolution in those targets; the great powers were not at war. By contrast, the many French impositions of republicanism on smaller states in the 1790s, and of Bonapartism in the 1800s, followed invasions and occupations of those states that were instrumental to the larger war effort: France might well have invaded its small neighbors in any case because it needed the territory to wage war. This distinction is important analytically, but in practice it is impossible to know for certain that a given invasion would have taken place had co-ideologues in the target state not encouraged it. In each of the small states the French invaded in the 1790s, patriots called for the invasion and rejoiced at the coming of their French liberators. Knowing beforehand that this would happen, the French calculated that the costs of conquest were lower than they would have been without these pro-French patriots. Indeed, Brissot, in arguing for war against Austria in 1792, asserted that victory would be easy because the people of the lands ruled by the Habsburgs would rise up and help the French.

In any case, it is important to recall that, even if we do assume that transnational cohorts of co-ideologues did not make these wartime invasions more likely, it does not follow from materialist logic that occupying armies would impose a new regime on the invaded target. Using military assets to promote a particular domestic regime bears opportunity costs; the assets could be used in other ways. The French attacked the Netherlands in 1795 because they needed Dutch territory in their war against the British. But the Directory in Paris had a choice regarding what to do about the Dutch regime once the Netherlands was conquered. The Directors could have left the current quasi-monarchical regime in place; they could have toppled the Stadtholder and let the Dutch sort things out. In the event, the French used their army to remake the country into the Batavian Republic. They repeated this type of action many more times in the 1790s and Napoleon did so many more times in the 1800s.

Occupying armies did this because in each target state there were cohorts of elites who wanted them to do so and who clearly intended to align their state with the occupier. France had friends in the Dutch, Swiss, German, and Italian patriots in the 1790s, all of whom had long been connected to French patriots via transnational networks. The same is true for those promotions triggered by unrest in the target. The British had contacts among friendly constitutional monarchists in Corsica, Sicily, Portugal, and Spain, and used its navy to help those friends gain power and set up the regime they agreed was the best. France's absolutist elites in 1823 had absolutist friends in Spain. These ideological confreres significantly lowered the costs of regime promotion and made it the rational choice. TINs typically were not the tight, ideologically disciplined entities envisaged by their enemies. They were deeply divided among liberals, who generally favored constitutional monarchy, and radicals, who favored republicanism. But they had sufficient affinity to pull together during the various waves of revolution that roiled the period. As E. J. Hobsbawm writes:

> It was now known that revolution in a single country could be a European phenomenon; that its doctrines could spread across the frontiers and, what was worse, its crusading armies could blow away the political systems of a continent. ... No country was immune from it. ... And the doctrines and institutions [the French armies] carried with them, even under Napoleon, from Spain to Illyria, were universal doctrines, as the governments knew, and as the peoples themselves were soon to know also.[147]

The same was true of their opposite numbers on the political right. As Michael Broers puts the matter, the prospect of revolution provided "the condition that fused conservatism and reaction into the Right, and liberalism and Radicalism into the Left. Only in times of stress do these wider terms gain any real relevance."[148]

In this period, moreover, the intensity and power of the TINs was endogenous with forcible regime promotion itself. Promotion in one target would exacerbate transnational ideological polarization throughout the region, increasing the incentives to rulers to do more promotions and counter-promotions.

What made these seven decades so prone to periodic explosions and ideological polarizations was the legitimacy crisis that began to afflict Europe's predominant regime, absolute monarchy, in the 1760s and 1770s. French and other elites noted that Britain, a constitutional monarchy, was more prosperous and won more wars. Old constituted bodies of nobles began to reassert themselves against "enlightened" absolute monarchs who kept raising taxes to pay for futile wars. In British North America in the 1770s, the constituted bodies were assemblies elected by commoners, and the rebellion against taxation became republican. In the Netherlands, then France, then Poland, commoners likewise began to assert themselves against Crown and nobility alike even though they had no tradition of privilege. In the hothouse that was France 1789–92, revolutionary republicanism emerged and launched Europe into a robust transnational contest over the best regime.

Absolute monarchy retained staunch support in many countries for many decades thereafter, as absolutist regimes in Eastern Europe continued to be competitive in international politics. The macro-struggle that structured transnational and international politics only ended when absolutists and many of their ideological enemies encountered a common enemy in the revolutions of 1848. Constitutionalists and many republicans began to see that their radicalism, their determination to crush absolute monarchy rather than reform it, had become dangerous. The failure of revolutionary liberalism became clear when artisans and the infant working class arose in city after city and, in some places, threatened the institution of private property itself. Socialism had appeared, and liberals came to terms with conservatives. Just as the Dutch example of permanent religious toleration had impressed European elites in the seventeenth century, the British example of reforming conservatism began to appear more attractive and plausible after 1849. Britain had become the world's most successful country in material terms. In the 1860s, in country after country, liberals and conservatives accepted one another as legitimate contenders within a lawful order, and regime change ceased to be the goal of most elites. International politics was not to become ideological again until the latter stages of the First World War.

# CHAPTER SIX

# Individual, Class, and State, 1910–1990

> This war is not as in the past; whoever occupies a territory
> also imposes his own social system. Everyone imposes his
> own system as far as his army can reach. It cannot
> be otherwise.
>
> —Josef Stalin, *April 1945*

## Prologue: America Imposes Democracy on West Germany, 1946–1949

FOLLOWING ITS UTTER DEFEAT in May 1945, Nazi Germany was occupied by Soviet, American, and British troops, all with their own geo-
graphic zones. (France was soon ceded a zone by the Americans and
British.) The Allied governments were undecided, individually and collectively, about their plans for Germany. Clearly the Nazi regime must be
dismantled and Germany disabled from aggression. But elites disagreed
over how far to punish and how far to rehabilitate the nation. Toward
the close of his life, Franklin Roosevelt had leaned toward the plan prof-
fered by Henry Morgenthau, his Treasury Secretary, that would render
Germany permanently agrarian and, Roosevelt reasoned, reassure the
Soviet Union that it could work with America in the future. But others
in the U.S. government, including former ambassador to Moscow Aver-
ell Harriman, Secretary of State Cordell Hull, and George Kennan, opposed the Morgenthau Plan because they feared already in 1945 that the
Soviets would form and dominate a communist bloc in the lands they
had liberated. Hull told Roosevelt that the Morgenthau Plan would em-
bitter and impoverish Germans so much "as to minimize the odds that
democratic institutions could take root."[1] Still, at first the Western allies
carried out a relatively harsh reconstruction plan in Germany, with no
evident plan to build democracy there. In particular the French, once
given their own occupation zone by the British and Americans, were
only interested in keeping Germany divided and weak and in annexing
the industrial Saar region.[2]

More punitive still were the Soviets, who had lost twenty million people
in the war and now set about plundering their German zone and telling
the world that they opposed German reunification. In June 1946, how-

ever, following an electoral defeat for France's Communist Party (PCF), Soviet Foreign Minister Vyacheslav Molotov began to change tactics in Germany, announcing that Moscow—unlike the Western allies—now favored a united Germany.[3] The Soviets had already merged the old German Communist Party (KPD), which had consistently attracted 15–20 percent of the vote during the German Weimar Republic,[4] with the Social Democratic Party (SPD) in their zone to form the Socialist Unity Party (SED). As General Lucius Clay, Deputy Governor in the U.S. zone, quickly saw, the Soviets thought of Germany as a prize in their increasingly competitive relations with the Western powers. Stalin wanted a united Germany that would be in the solidifying Soviet bloc. Clay urged James Byrnes, the U.S. Secretary of State, to make a counter-move that included a promise to rebuild Germany into a democracy. As Jean Edward Smith writes, Clay "was convinced that a united Germany could be attained and that liberal, democratic values would ultimately prevail. The result would be to extend Western influence to the Soviet zone and bring Poland and Czechoslovakia into direct contact with democratic ideas."[5]

In September, Byrnes finally accepted Clay's advice and announced in Stuttgart that America was going to reconstruct a Germany not only united but democratic.[6] In December, Byrnes and Ernest Bevin, the British Foreign Secretary, announced the economic merger of the British and U.S. zones into Bizonia.[7] This Anglo-American cooperation alarmed the Soviets. In March 1947, Marshal Vassili Sokolovski, Commander-in-Chief of the Soviet zone, walked out of a meeting of the Allied Control Council in Berlin.[8] In June, George Marshall, who had replaced Byrnes as U.S. Secretary of State, announced his famous plan for the reconstruction of Europe. Marshall invited Soviet participation, but Stalin refused and ordered all communist parties in Europe to do likewise. In September, Stalin formed the Communist Information Bureau (Cominform), a successor to the old Comintern (but limited to Europe), and ordered all member parties to end the wartime Popular Front strategy of cooperation with "bourgeois" parties. Stalin intended this move to intimidate the liberal governments into coming to terms over Germany. It had the opposite effect, driving them into still closer cooperation with one another and opposition to the Soviet Union.[9]

In 1949, the French merged their zone with Bizonia, and soon after was formed the Federal Republic of Germany, a democratic member of the now-solid Western bloc. During the late 1940s, the two major parties that emerged in West Germany were the Christian Democratic (in alliance with the Bavarian Christian Social Union), led by Konrad Adenauer, and the Social Democratic, led by Kurt Schumacher. Both men and their parties were adamantly anti-communist and hence Washington (which preferred the Christian Democrats) could trust them to keep West

Germany out of the Soviet bloc and indeed from declaring neutrality.[10] The Soviets, meanwhile, ended up establishing the SED-ruled German Democratic Republic or East Germany, a loyal part of the Eastern bloc. The timing of the Western decisions suggests that competition with the Soviets in the unfolding Cold War, rather than a pure desire to spread liberty, led the U.S. and British governments to promote liberal democracy in Germany. But it was no accident that the Anglo-Americans promoted that particular regime. In the late 1940s, European societies were highly polarized between communists and radical socialists, who were pro-Soviet, and Christian and social democrats, who were anti-Soviet and, over time, became pro-American.

As Soviet-American rivalry deepened, then, the incentives grew for the Americans to take advantage of the anti-Sovietism of the Christian and social democrats in Germany and to use their occupying forces to remake Germany into a liberal democracy. A parallel growing incentive faced Stalin. Not only were Soviet and American policies endogenous—the two powers were in a spiral model—but their reconstruction policies were endogenous with the polarization of German elites. The more the Americans (and the British) did to build liberal democracy, the more pro-American became German democrats and the more anti-American became German communists and radical socialists. The more the Soviets did to build communism, the more anti-Soviet became German democrats. And this ideological polarization was transnational: elites throughout Europe and elsewhere were paying attention, networking with Germans, and solidifying into ideological blocs as well. The nascent Cold War consisted in part in transnational ideological polarization precisely because that polarization helped drive the forcible regime promotions by the superpowers that divided Europe into two blocs.

•  •  •

In this chapter I offer an explanation for the long wave of forcible regime promotion that marked what Eric Hobsbawm calls the "short twentieth century."[11] As seen in figure 6.1, promotion during this long wave, as in its two predecessors, was uneven across time and space. Some decades featured isolated incidents; the largest cluster came in the years following the Second World War, when leaders of the United States and Soviet Union installed new regimes in most of the lands their militaries conquered. Tying these promotions together in a single long wave is that the regimes promoted were generally of three types: communist, fascist, and liberal-democratic. The regime whose legitimacy crisis ushered in the grand struggle was constitutional or parliamentary government, the model on which most European polities had converged in the

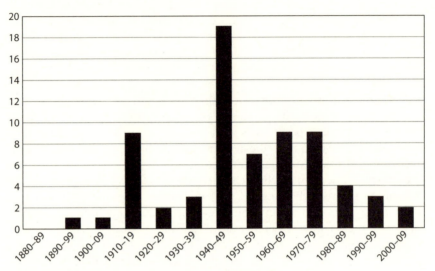

Figure 6.1 Forcible regime promotions, 1880–2010

1860s and 1870s (chapter 5). Early in the twentieth century, many elites became convinced that the predominant reforming conservative regimes that had been reconstituted in the 1860s and 1870s were not delivering on their promises. Communism developed in the 1910s as a distinct alternative with transnational appeal, and most constitutional governments reformed themselves into liberal democracies partly in reaction. Fascism appeared in the 1920s as an alternative, more militant way to combat communism. Fascism was virtually wiped out by the defeat of Nazi Germany, and communism and liberal democracy carried on their struggle until the late 1980s.

Types other than these three were promoted during the twentieth century. In the Middle East from the 1950s through 1970s, Arab nationalism was at issue. French, British, Syrian, Egyptian, and U.S. forces intervened for or against Arab socialist regimes. Arab socialists had affinities with communists and sometimes cooperated with them. But their ideological struggle was against a different foe: traditional Islamic theocracy, a regime that had been in crisis since the 1910s. I discuss this ideological struggle in chapter 7.

Another type of promotion, more infamous, was U.S. support for authoritarianism. Authoritarianism was not a transnational ideology like fascism but a pragmatic arrangement in which a dictator and cohort of elites maintained a domestic order acceptable to the U.S. government. These American promotions fall into two types. The first, comprising

U.S. interventions in Latin America and the Caribbean from the 1900s through the 1930s, involved the U.S. Marines' landing and helping one faction in a civil struggle. These cases—Cuba 1906, Nicaragua 1910, Honduras 1911, Dominican Republic 1912, Nicaragua 1912, Mexico 1914, Dominican Republic 1916, Cuba 1917, Honduras 1924, and Nicaragua 1925–33—appear in figure 6.1, but are not explained by the transnational ideological struggle among communism, fascism, and liberalism that explains most promotions in this chapter. Although transnational ideological networks existed in the Western Hemisphere, these interventions are better explained by a more conventional economic-interest hypothesis reflected in the Roosevelt Corollary to the Monroe Doctrine. President Theodore Roosevelt declared in 1904:

> If a nation shows that it knows how to act with reasonable efficiency and decency in social and political matters, if it keeps order and pays its obligations, it need fear no interference from the United States. Chronic wrongdoing, or an impotence which results in a general loosening of the ties of civilized society, may in America, as elsewhere, ultimately require intervention by some civilized nation, and in the Western Hemisphere the adherence of the United States to the Monroe Doctrine may force the United States, however reluctantly, in flagrant cases of such wrongdoing or impotence, to the exercise of an international police power.[12]

Roosevelt was referring to these countries' ability to maintain internal order so as to service their debts and protect foreigners' assets, and he had in mind in particular Colombia's refusal to allow the United States to build the Panama Canal.[13] Measured in economic terms, the Roosevelt Corollary worked as designed: U.S. economic predominance was established and the average sovereign debt price in Latin America and the Caribbean rose 74 percent after these interventions.[14]

The second class of U.S. interventions on behalf of authoritarianism took place during the Cold War in what came to be called the Third World. The majority of these interventions did not involve the direct use of American force, but rather economic and military aid and, in cases such as Iran in 1953 and Chile in 1973, covert action. Those cases do not qualify as forcible regime promotions under the coding rules used in this study. (Cases that do count include Lebanon 1958, Laos 1964–73, South Vietnam 1965–73, the Dominican Republic 1965, and Cambodia 1970–73.) But U.S. support for Third World authoritarianism is still relevant to this study for four reasons. First, such support provides numerous examples of state leaders promoting a regime type other than their own—indeed, sometimes replacing liberal democracy with authoritarianism.[15] Such promotions have precedents—Kings of France sometimes promoted

Protestantism (chapter 4), the putatively republican Louis-Napoleon promoted absolute monarchy in the Papal States in 1849 (chapter 5)—but
the Cold War featured an unusually high number of them. Second, American leaders still cared enough about the regimes of these states to spend
resources to preserve or overturn them. Completely ignoring these cases
because overt military force was not used would mislead us into thinking
that the United States was less active in the Third World than it actually
was, and to underestimate the degree to which U.S. leaders manipulated
regimes there.[16]

Third, it is important that most of these non-forcible interventions
entailed support for *anti-communist* authoritarians. Washington clearly
was not indifferent about domestic regimes in the Third World, any more
than it was in Europe or Japan. As in the German case rehearsed above,
Washington's overriding concern was keeping communists out of power
precisely because communists were pro-Soviet. In Europe and Japan,
Washington could do this by promoting liberal democracy because even
socialists in these countries ruled out working with communists (with the
temporary exception of Italy, discussed below). Conditions in the Third
World were different. In recently decolonized regions, social democrats
were often willing to cooperate with communists because they shared
some goals such as land redistribution and industrialization. Fourth, that
U.S. support for authoritarian regimes was usually practiced through
means other than direct force is significant. Direct use of military assets
entails costs and benefits not only in direct material terms, but potentially
in normative terms as well. America's global reputation would have suffered even more had it sent in the Marines to topple a democratically
elected government in a time when America presented itself as the pre-
eminent champion of liberty.[17]

This chapter will show that a majority of forcible regime promotions
in the twentieth century was part of the long transnational contest among
advocates of liberal democracy, communism, and fascism. As in past
cases, the two main types of agent perpetuating this contest were transnational ideological networks and the governments of great powers.
When a country became unstable domestically, rulers of great powers
would have the usual incentives to promote their regime or at least undermine a rival regime. The same incentives faced rulers of great powers
when they occupied countries following a war—in this case, the Second
World War, which also eliminated fascism from the competition. The long
wave that covered most of the twentieth century had its origins in the
legitimacy crisis afflicting constitutionalism in the late nineteenth century.
It was only resolved in the 1980s when communism proved decidedly
inferior to liberal democracy.

Emergence of the Structure:
The Crisis of Conservative Liberalism, 1890–1917

The latter half of the nineteenth century saw virtually no forcible regime promotion and, in the same vein, only weak ideological polarization across the states of the Westphalian system. Elites continued to speak of ideological solidarity and threats from opposing ideologies, as they had prior to 1850 (see chapter 5), but governments did little about such threats. The main exception came after the Paris Commune of the spring of 1871, the modern world's first socialist government. Many European elites saw in the Commune an international socialist-anarchist conspiracy to replicate the events of 1848. The Austrian and German chancellors called for the formation of a Capitalist International in response to the Commune. The Three Emperors' League of 1873, comprising Francis Joseph of Austria, William I of Germany, and Alexander II of Russia, was conceived as a new Holy Alliance "against European radicalism that has been threatening all thrones and institutions."[18] Each monarch had other motives as well: William, to keep France isolated; Francis Joseph, to grow closer to the newly united Germany; Alexander, to lure Germany from Austria. But their common interest was to block any chance of another transnational wave of revolution.[19] The fear, as it turns out, was needless; the Commune did not spark serious revolts elsewhere in Europe and died away after only two months. France's Third Republic proved itself a respectable moderate regime capable of suppressing revolution with public approval.

By 1907, the states of Europe were polarized, but not according to ideology. Germany, Austria, Italy, and Romania—monarchies all, constitutional to varying degrees—formed one bloc, while republican France, constitutional-monarchical Great Britain, and absolute-monarchical Russia formed the other.[20] The First World War (1914–18) was certainly portrayed by the British and French as a war for liberty, and their chief enemy Germany was indeed less liberal-democratic than they, in part because its governments were responsible to the Emperor rather than the Reichstag or electorate.[21] But that despotic Russia fought with liberal France and Britain against Germany and Austria shows that ideology was a weak factor. From 1850 through the Russian Revolution of 1917, international politics was relatively consistent with state-centric realism.

*The Rise of Transnational Socialism*

The world was certainly not free of civil strife in the latter half of the nineteenth century. In Asia there took place the Indian Mutiny against British rule in 1857 and the Taiping Rebellion against the Qing Dynasty from

1851 to 1864. The United States had its Civil War in the 1860s; Japan had its Meiji Restoration. In Northeast Africa the Mahdi Rebellion broke out against the British, Ottomans, and Egyptians in the 1880s. These and other domestic broils may have had some deep common causes, such as global demographic growth or economic recession.[22] But neither rebels nor their enemies took themselves to be part of a larger regional or global struggle. The systems in which they operated were either domestic or, in the colonial cases, connected to the colonial power. Demonstration effects and fears of wider contagion were weak.

Transnational ideological movements did exist. The political Left was active across Europe, the Americas, and parts of Asia. But in the latter half of the nineteenth century it did not proffer a coherent regime. The Left was small and its adherents were divided and ambivalent over just how radical it ought to be. Was change to come by revolution or reform? How far were existing institutions and their advocates and beneficiaries *enemies* of the Left, fit only for destruction? Historians typically divide the transnational Left in the latter half of the nineteenth century into *anarchists* and *socialists*. The two groups often made common cause, and indeed combined under Karl Marx's leadership to form the International Workingmen's Association or First International in 1864. They shared a hostility to accumulations of wealth, particularly in the bourgeoisie. They considered their roots old and deep. Radical movements to seize the property of the wealthy had surfaced during the Reformation, for example, in the Peasant's War in Germany of 1521 (chapter 4) and the Levellers in England in the 1640s. They also emerged during the 1790s, most notably in "Gracchus" Babeuf's Conspiracy of the Equals in 1796. These movements were not nearly so theoretically developed or stable over time as socialism proved to be; nor were they focused on the factory workers, whose numbers were negligible even in the 1790s.[23]

Anarchism defies precise definition, in part because anarchists rejected dogmatism, centralization, and discipline. But in general anarchists sought the elimination of the modern state. For anarchists, the state, with its coercive power, was the root of exploitation and inequality; its abolition was the route to liberation. Socialists, by contrast, saw not the state per se as the problem but its captivity to the owning classes or bourgeoisie. For socialists, the solution was for the working class to capture the state and to use it to transform society. Thus, socialists embraced elements of modern social order that anarchists did not, including, writes Albert S. Lindemann, "modern industrialism, political parties, the use of parliament, and more generally the necessity of an extended stage of bourgeois-capitalist development during which time social revolution would be impossible." Anarchists found socialists too attached to order, which implied an exercise of power.[24]

Anarchism and socialism both spread in the latter half of the nineteenth century owing to rising discontent with the liberal economics and politics associated with constitutional government. For these intellectuals, constitutionalism in its current form was failing to deliver the prosperity and security that it promised and that radicals in the eighteenth and first half of the nineteenth centuries had counted on. In Europe, the Americas, and parts of Asia, anarchism and socialism spread along with industrialization. Like transnational Lutheranism during the Peasants' War (chapter 4), anarchism and socialism developed militant, revolutionary wings well before socialism captured a state in 1917. The militancy of self-conscious socialists and anarchists probably dates to the brutal June Days in Paris in 1848 (chapter 5). It was then that the revolutionaries themselves had polarized over whether France should be liberal and *laissez-faire* or redistributionist, and liberals joined conservatives in savagely suppressing the redistributionists.[25] Thus, just as 1848–49 helped kill one clash of regimes, it conceived another—albeit one whose gestation period was to last more than half a century.

Upon the foundation of the International in 1864, labor unions formed and strikes broke out across many countries. But the International was hampered by divisions over both ideology and strategy. Following the failure of the Paris Commune, Marx let the International die off and devoted his attention to his theoretical writings—which of course would profoundly shape events in the twentieth century—but he died in 1883 a disappointed man.[26] Notwithstanding the demise of the International, socialism began to advance and gain definition in the 1870s. The growth and definition were spurred by the increase in the numbers of factory workers, the "Great Depression" that commenced in 1873, governmental exclusion and persecution, and the hegemony of Marx and Engels over the movement, which lent it a common language.

Socialism also grew as an unintended consequence of Bismarck's limited liberal reforms in Germany. In 1866, Bismarck granted universal male suffrage. The result was a spectacular growth in votes for the socialist parties: from 102,000 in 1871, to 340,000 in 1874, to 500,000 in 1877.[27] Germany's socialist parties—some revolutionary, others reformist—united in 1875 to form the Social Democratic Party of Germany (SPD). The SPD's leadership was reformist rather than revolutionary, but nonetheless in 1878, Bismarck suppressed SPD activity with his Anti-Socialist Laws. These laws strengthened the arguments of the radical Marxists in favor of revolution, but the party's leadership maintained its reformist course.[28] Similar developments were taking place in other constitutional states. Socialists were deeply disappointed that parliamentary regimes and wide suffrage were not ushering in progress as they understood it. Yet, where workers were allowed to vote and socialist parties to hold seats in legislatures—in Italy, France, Belgium, Britain, Scandinavia, and Germany—socialists typically formulated "minimum" alongside "maximum" programs. Minimum programs were designed to draw broad electoral support, and included such measures as widening suffrage, the eight-hour workday, and bettering the conditions of the workers. Maximum programs had to do with class struggle, workers' state, and other Marxist abstractions.[29] In Germany, Karl Kautsky's Erfurt Program, ostensibly revolutionary Marxist but in practice reformist, set the tone for Western Europe.[30]

It was in Russia that revolutionary socialism would come to dominate. Russia lacked any real parliamentary restraints on the Tsar's government, and so reform was not a credible strategy to achieve socialism. Indeed, tsarist repression had generated a tradition of anarchist terrorism in the nineteenth century. With the industrialization of Western Russia from the 1890s, Marxism began to take hold. The Social Democratic Labor Party formed in 1898. In 1903, the young V. I. Lenin wrenched the party toward revolution. Lenin had been radicalized by the government's execution of his brother and his own years in a Siberian prison. He was convinced that socialist revolution must be engineered by a highly disciplined organization with a small leadership clique that would not deviate from the revolutionary path or dissolve into factions. Thus was born Bolshevism.[31]

In Paris in July 1889, the centenary of the original French Revolution, the Second International formed. Unlike the First International, the Second excluded anarchists and was more consistently Marxist. It grew to include socialist parties from every European country, the United States, and Japan. Yet, the Second International was likewise hampered by visions between revolutionaries (who tended to be internationalist) and reformists (who tended to be more nationalistic or patriotic). Delegates from countries that allowed socialist participation, led by France's Jean Jaurès, argued that socialists should participate in bourgeois governments. Those from countries that kept socialists out of government, led by Germany's August Bebel, disagreed. The two sides also disagreed over whether socialists should work for or against war. Most western socialists, including Jaurès and Bebel, wanted to prevent war. Lenin and the German Rosa Luxemburg argued by contrast that war would hasten the revolution. The Second International ended up with a murky compromise.[32]

## The First World War and Transnational Communism

The First World War helped make socialism into a bona fide alternative regime type—communism or Marxism-Leninism. The war finally split the revolutionary internationalists from the reform nationalists and propelled the former into a seizure of power in Russia. The occasion for the split in the Second International was the vote in the German Reichstag on August 4, 1914, over whether to grant war credits to the government. For reasons they justified on principle—including that the threat to Germany from the east, Russia, was the most reactionary country in Europe—a majority of the SPD voted for war credits, siding with their liberal and conservative fellow Germans over foreign fellow socialists. Days later the astonished French socialists followed suit.[33] It then being obvious that, *contra* Marx, the workers had countries after all, the Second International collapsed. At a meeting in Zimmerwald, Switzerland, in 1915, Lenin pressed his fellow internationalists to push for a general strike, berating the German Luxemburg for resisting this strategy. As the war dragged on and became staggeringly bloody and futile, Lenin began to attract more followers across countries. In 1916 Lenin, now in exile in Zurich, wrote his famous essay on imperialism that held capitalism responsible for the war.[34]

At the same time, Lenin was formulating a plan for socialists to seize and perpetually grip power that amounted to a new regime type: Marxism-Leninism. The collapse of the Second International led Lenin to conclude that, although the proletariat does have a single interest across societies, its members and leaders may not always correctly discern that interest or how it is to be secured. Thus democracy, understood as the political equality of citizens, was just "bourgeois democracy," subject to manipulation by the owning classes by virtue of their ownership. "It is necessary to depose the landowners and capitalists in actual fact, to replace their management of the factories and estates by a different management, workers' management, in actual fact," Lenin writes.[35] His solution was the dictatorship of a highly disciplined party under rigid leadership. The Bolsheviks were to rule on behalf of the proletariat which could not protect itself from the wiles of capitalists and the half-heartedness of reform socialists. Marx's dictatorship of the proletariat was to take the form under Lenin of the dictatorship of their putative vanguard, the Communist Party, and within that the dictatorship of its Central Committee.[36] The communist regime, then, was one in which control of the country's physical security and economic production was in the coercive hands of a small, disciplined elite.

## The Long Wave Begins: The Bolsheviks Seize Power in Russia, 1917–1918

The revolution and abdication of the Tsar in March 1917 left Russia with divided and unstable government. In Petrograd, the capital, Alexander Kerensky headed a Provisional government recognized by Russia's allies in the Great War; the government was liberal-democratic, had good relations with Russia's liberal allies, and pledged to keep the country in the war against Germany. Over the next few months the Wilson administration in Washington offered the Kerensky government a total of $325 million in war credits. Indeed, the Russian revolution helped clear the way for the United States to join in the war against Germany by removing the American pacifists' argument that fighting would help Tsarist Russia, the most despotic of the belligerents.[37] But in various Russian cities, including Petrograd, soviets or workers' councils held effective power. In April, Lenin arrived in Petrograd from Zurich, courtesy of the German military, who knew of his plans to withdraw Russia from the war. Over the next several months the struggle for power within Russia was entangled with the actions of the Allied and German governments. The Bolsheviks, self-appointed vanguard of Russia's small cohort of factory workers, strove to win over Russia's vast peasantry by promising enlisted soldiers land if they would desert.[38] Governments in Paris, London, and Washington sent delegations of Leftist politicians and labor union leaders to the Petrograd Soviet in the summer of 1917 to try to renew enthusiasm for the war and to buttress Kerensky's government. These missions failed.[39]

Upon seizing power in November, the Bolsheviks attempted to exploit their pre-existing networks and demonstration effects to trigger socialist revolutions in Europe. Among the first acts of the Bolshevik government was to issue to the world a Decree of Peace appealing to the workers of England, France, and Germany—over the heads of their governments—to push for an end to imperialism.[40] In sharp contrast to the Kerensky government, the Bolsheviks made clear that for them France, Britain, and the United States were no better than Germany. Needing to honor promises made to Russia's peasants, and to devote resources to conquering rivals within Russia itself, Leon Trotsky, Commissar for Foreign Affairs, quickly began to negotiate a separate peace with the German government. At the same time he opened side negotiations with Allied officials who believed the Bolsheviks' rhetoric masked an underlying pragmatism. The American Raymond Robins and R.H.B. Lockhart of Great Britain reasoned that the Bolsheviks' chief need was domestic security, and that if the West could assure them that it could meet that need, they could be induced to keep Russia in the war and stop exporting their revolution. Trotsky did lead Robins and Lockhart to believe that some agreement might be reached. But Lenin never took these negotiations seriously and they came to naught.[41]

## A Short Wave of Promotion, 1918–1922

The chief decision makers in the Western governments, faced with the possibility of a Bolshevik withdrawal from the war and transnational ideological polarization reaching into their own societies, began to co-operate against the Bolsheviks. Within weeks of the Petrograd coup the Americans and French had stopped shipping foodstuffs to Russia.[42] French leaders began suggesting to the British Allied military intervention to overthrow the Bolsheviks.[43] Robert Lansing, the U.S. Secretary of State, wrote in a December 2 memorandum that the Bolsheviks displayed a "lack of any sentiment of nationality and a determination, frankly avowed, to overthrow all existing governments and establish on the ruins a despotism of the proletariat in every country."[44] A month later Lansing wrote privately to Wilson: "Lenine [sic], Trotsky and their colleagues are so bitterly hostile to the present social order in all countries that I am convinced nothing could be said which would gain their favor or render them amenable to reason."[45] When the Brest-Litovsk Treaty was announced, pulling Russia out of the war, Western governments at last agreed to invade Russia to topple the Bolshevik regime.

Thus, in May 1918 came the first forcible regime promotion of the new struggle: a Czechoslovak Corps commanded from Paris began fighting the Bolsheviks. In July, British and American troops landed at the port of Archangel in northwestern Russia; the following month, another U.S. force reached Siberia. These foreign liberal troops fought alongside the White (anti-Bolshevik) forces led by Admiral Alexander Kolchak.[46] John Lewis Gaddis concludes that behind Western intervention in Russia was "a loathing for Bolshevism so strong that it could cause honest men to put forward and possibly even believe flimsy excuses for involving themselves in the internal affairs of another nation."[47] It is not so clear that the Western governments were making "flimsy excuses," however. Germany stood to gain enormously from a Bolshevik consolidation of power, and Trotsky and the Bolsheviks redoubled their call on workers around the world to overthrow their governments and told the Russian people that "The external foe of the Russian Soviet Socialist Republic at present is British, French, American and Japanese imperialism" and that "World capital itself is now coming for us."[48] The Allies intervened for the sake of their own external security.

Demonstration effects continued. In Germany workers, inspired by events in Russia and weary of war, had struck in April 1917 and did so again in January 1918.[49] The strikes furthered transnational polarization: communists were encouraged and capitalists fearful, which in turn raised communist fears of still more capitalist attacks on the Bolshevik regime. Revolution did break out in Germany on November 9, 1918, and a replication of the Bolshevik coup appeared highly possible. Karl Liebknecht, leader of Germany's radical socialists, declared a Soviet Republic in Berlin; in Munich, Kurt Eisner declared an independent Bavarian Socialist Republic. Few in Germany doubted that a communist takeover in Germany would be met with some kind of military intervention from the Western democracies.[50] In Berlin the SPD leader Philip Scheidemann declared a parliamentary republic and the German military backed him.[51] The following month, with encouragement from Lenin, Liebknecht, Luxemburg, and others formed the German Communist Party (KPD); a month later they staged the Spartacist Uprising. Socialist revolution and Western military intervention were prevented by the SPD government's enlisting volunteer war veterans (*Freikorps*) to suppress the uprising.[52]

Much of Europe was rocked by labor unrest during the early months of 1919, and liberals and conservatives saw the "long arm of Moscow" at work. In January 1919, Lenin's friend Béla Kun proclaimed a Soviet Republic in Hungary, overturning the young liberal monarchy. Events in Hungary further raised Western fears of Bolshevism. The Hungarian Soviet Republic was to last until August, when it triggered a second forcible regime promotion. Romanian troops invaded (with Western allied support) and overthrew the Kun regime.[53]

Another promotion came in Finland, which had been part of the Russian Empire since 1809. The Russian revolution of March 1917 quickly spread to Helsinki and Finnish elites polarized over communism. The November Bolshevik coup in Russia led anti-communist Finns to declare independence from Russia, and in fact the Bolsheviks recognized independent Finland. In January 1918, civil war broke out between Finnish Red Guards, who proclaimed a socialist workers' state, and White Guards, who asked for German intervention. Russian troops still in Finland fought in support of the former. In April, German troops invaded and helped the White Guards prevail.[54]

The demonstration effects of the Bolshevik coup were not limited to Europe. In Asia and Latin America, leftists were inspired to imitate the Bolsheviks. Over the next few years communist parties were to form in China, Indochina, Turkey, and much of Latin America.[55] In January 1919 Lenin, recognizing the strength of the transnational movement but also its potential to fragment and damage Bolshevik interests, applied his own disciplinary rule and announced the formation of the Third International or Communist International (Comintern). At the first Comintern congress in March, in Moscow, the Bolsheviks made clear that they would dominate the new organization and that member parties were not to work with social democrats in their home countries.[56] The only forcible regime promotion concerning communism outside of Europe at this time took place in Iran, occupied during the war by the British. The Bolshevik renunciation of all imperial claims, Russian as well as British, sparked unrest in that country. With encouragement from Josef Stalin, who was keenly interested in revolution in Asia, Iranian communists initiated cooperation with the leading rebel, who adopted a sort of Soviet plan for

Iran. In May 1920, Red Army troops arrived to help. Disparity in goals between the Iranians and the Russians led to growing mistrust, however; Iranians came to see the Soviets as Russian imperialists, and the Soviets came to mistrust the revolutionary credentials of some of the Iranians. In 1921, the Soviets withdrew and consensus took hold among the Bolsheviks that they should carry out no more such forcible interventions under current conditions.[57]

Notwithstanding the fear among liberal European governments of communist contagion, the end of the Great War produced what David Thomson calls a "vogue for democracy" in much of Europe. In Germany, Hungary, Austria, Poland, Czechoslovakia, Romania, Yugoslavia, Finland, Estonia, Latvia, and Lithuania, liberal-democratic regimes were established in 1918–19 owing to the strength of the example of the democracies' war victory and their clear desire for such regimes.[58] Predictably, this rapid spread of "bourgeois imperialism" further alarmed communists in Russia and elsewhere, who in turn redoubled their efforts at revolution. Still, the short wave of forcible regime promotion triggered by the Bolshevik coup faded as these liberal regimes consolidated power in the 1920s. As Trotsky himself recognized in 1922, liberal governments were taking steps to prevent revolution, and those steps in turn weakened the impression of a communist juggernaut.[59] As Bolshevik hopes and liberal fears subsided, the threat of a wave of revolution faded. Under the increasing influence of Stalin, the Comintern began directing more attention to colonial areas in Asia, particularly Afghanistan, Persia, and India, and worked with "bourgeois nationalist" movements against the British Empire.[60] Some cooperation with the Western democracies began to emerge, as the British signed a trade pact with Russia and the United States extended massive food aid.[61] Stalin, who continued his gradual seizure of power following Lenin's death in 1924, decided for "socialism in one country" rather than world revolution.[62] His betrayals of international communism alienated Trotsky and others, who went on to found the Fourth International, the first of several communist splinter groups.

## The Emergence of Fascism, Early 1920s

The long wave of the twentieth century had only begun, however, and quickly became more complex with the emergence of a third regime type, fascism. Like liberalism, fascism differed across countries, but a general regime type is discernable. Common to fascists was the conviction that international communism was the chief threat to good order and that liberalism was too weak to meet that threat. In the 1930s, communism came to be virtually identified with anti-fascism.

Scholars continue to argue about what fascism was (or is). One insoluble controversy concerns whether national socialism, particularly the German variety, was fascism. The two movements had a number of common features that led their adherents to be encouraged by the other's progress. Most obviously, fascism and national socialism shared ideological enemies: liberalism, individualism, laissez-faire economics, parliamentary democracy, decadence, class-based socialism, and above all international communism. They were also in principle hostile toward capitalism and the churches—the latter they regarded as barriers to progress—although in practice both cooperated with capitalists and clergy in order to broaden their coalitions.[63] Thus, I shall follow many scholars and use "fascism" to cover national socialism.

Against socialism and communism, fascism sought to integrate the working classes into society as a whole in order to rejuvenate the nation. Fascists across countries emphasized the seizure of power, heroic leadership, violence as creative energy, the state over the individual, egalitarianism, medieval chivalry, and an organic rather than mechanistic society. Perhaps more than a specific program, fascism was an attitude: the nation could and must break free from internal and external constraints and not worry about what follows. Representative statements are from the British fascist Oswald Mosley—"No man goes very far who knows exactly where he is going"—and the Belgian fascist Léon Degrelle—"You must get going, you must let yourself be swept away by the torrent ... you must act. The rest comes by itself."[64] Fascism is often seen as a repudiation of modernity and the Enlightenment, but in fact it bundled together various strands of Enlightenment and Romantic thought: history as touchstone, idealism, the metaphysics of the will, a return to nature, a rejection of materialism.[65]

Italy was fascism's birthplace. Benito Mussolini had been editor of a socialist newspaper in Milan, but resigned over his party's opposition to Italy's joining the Allies in the First World War in 1915. When the war ended in November 1918, Italian workers, inspired by the Bolshevik revolution, struck. The earliest declaration of the *Fascio di combattimento*, in March 1919, was anti-monarchical and -parliamentarian as well as redistributionist, and supported the striking workers. But other groups— "[s]tudents, soldiers, discharged veterans unable to readjust to civilian life"—recoiled from any dictatorship of the proletariat. Mussolini, by now a man of the political Right, entered Parliament in 1921; his squads of *Fascisti* used force to intimidate socialists and break strikes. In October 1922, as unrest continued and the liberal government fell, Italy's King Victor Emmanuel III asked Mussolini to form a government.[66]

Fascist-like movements soon appeared in Germany, Austria, Hungary, Romania, Britain, Spain, Belgium, France, Finland, South Africa, and

Brazil.[67] Populist-nationalist movements also appeared in the 1920s and 1930s in much of Latin America (including Argentina, Peru, and Mexico), China, and Turkic lands. Although elites in these movements shared some affinities with fascism—for example, Peronists in Argentina—most scholars do not classify the movements as fascist.[68]

Although the groundwork for fascism had been laid in Europe prior to the Great War by cultural rejection of the materialism of liberalism and Marxism,[69] fascism emerged and spread when and where it did owing to the crisis of liberal democracy following the First World War and the Bolshevik coup in Russia. People whose countries had adopted liberal political regimes were finding that economic development lagged far behind political; liberal democracy did not deliver on its promises. The war severely disrupted societies and left in its wake millions of aimless veterans. The Versailles settlement also left Germans and Italians in particular feeling like citizens of second-class, "proletarian" nations. And the example of the Bolsheviks was inspiring factory workers to organize, strike, and agitate for revolution. As Juan Linz writes: "The obvious distortion of the idea of democracy in the reality of the early twentieth century and the incapacity of the democratic leadership to institutionalize mechanisms for conflict resolution provided the ground for the appeal of fascism."[70]

Postwar labor unrest in Germany produced a similar reaction. In the Kapp Putsch of March 1920, the *Freikorps* seized power in Berlin. Factory workers struck to oppose them, and the government restored order. But discontented German nationalists continued to agitate. From July 1921, Adolf Hitler came to control the new National Socialist German Workers' Party (NSDAP), which comprised mainly *Freikorps* men. On November 9, 1923, the NSDAP, inspired by Mussolini's rise in Italy, attempted to seize power in Bavaria. The Beer Hall Putsch failed, as most Germans recoiled from radicalism. (While Hitler was imprisoned, Hermann Göring and other Nazi leaders fled to Austria and then to Italy, where Mussolini protected them.)[71] From prison Hitler decided to try to gain control of the state through constitutional means, and the NSDAP gradually built electoral strength in the 1920s. As elsewhere, German fascists or Nazis were opportunistic concerning labor, capital, the churches, and other institutions; they were especially adept at recruiting conservatives, owing to their mutual antagonism to communism.[72] But their plan remained to overturn the Weimar Republic and establish a fascist regime.

The growth of transnational fascist networks in the 1920s alarmed communists as well as liberal democrats. Elites in countries of the industrial world became increasingly polarized among these three ideological groups. Polarization within and across countries was aggravated by Stalin's order to the Comintern in 1928 to become more militant. Stalin was initiating his first Five-Year Plan, involving rapid construction of capital goods and armaments as well as agricultural collectivization in the Soviet Union, and needed to stimulate international and transnational threats to justify the extreme measures at home.[73] Communist parties the world over were to revert to their old strategy of treating social democrats as enemies. Increasing communist militancy met with reaction on the Right, and fascist and national socialist parties gained ground.[74] The Great Depression that began in 1929 further drained support for liberal democracy toward the communist and fascist extremes, so that in the 1930s it was common for liberals to acknowledge that laissez-faire economics and even democracy itself were in retreat; the future belonged, it seemed, to statism, and the only question was whether it would be statism of the Left or Right. Stalin's Five-Year Plans were industrializing the Soviet Union at a breathtaking pace.[75]

With the Great Depression of the 1930s, fascism began to gain still more followers and fascists came to control a number of constitutional regimes. Most important was Germany. In 1930, Hitler's NSDAP had an electoral breakthrough, winning 18 percent in a national election. The NSDAP made further gains in 1932, and in January 1933, Hitler became Chancellor. In March he gained power to rule by decree, and in July all other parties were banned. In Austria, Engelbert Dollfuss began to rule by decree in 1933. (Dollfuss and the Austrian fascists became rivals to the Austrian Nazis, who sought unity with Germany and ultimately prevailed.) In Hungary the Scythe Cross formed in 1931; in October 1932, Gyula Gömbös, a fascist, became Prime Minister. In Portugal, Antonio Salazar set up his "new state" in 1933. In Spain, the Falange formed in 1933 and in 1936 began fighting to overturn the new parliamentary republic. In other states, fascists established movements but never gained power until their countries were conquered by Germany. The Dutch National Socialist Party formed in 1931. In Norway, Vidkun Quisling formed the National Union movement in 1934. In Belgium, Degrelle's Rexist movement formed in 1935. In France Jacques Doriot, a former communist, formed the French Popular Party in 1936.[76]

Mussolini made a bid to lead the international fascist networks, and ultimately a fascist bloc of states, just as Stalin led the Comintern. The Italians organized an international fascist meeting at Montreux, Switzerland, in December 1934; attending were representatives from Austria, Belgium, Denmark, Ireland, Lithuania, the Netherlands, Norway, Portugal, Spain, and Switzerland. The notion of a nationalist international sounds paradoxical, but the theorist Eugenio Coselschi laid out a general program for all fascist parties that included national revolution and the establishment of corporatist totalitarian states. The chief weakness of the Montreux conference was the absence of any representatives from Nazi Germany; in 1934, Mussolini and Hitler were at odds over the territorial questions of Austria and the South Tyrol. They also disagreed over theory: the fascists were not particularly anti-Semitic, while the Nazis were constituted by anti-Semitism and a more general racism. Mussolini lectured Hitler on at least one occasion that the Germans should emphasize nation, not race.[77] Owing in part to Nazi aloofness, the Italians never succeeded in directing the incipient Fascist International.[78]

Still, the fascist networks remained active, working for revolution and propagating their ideas. The ideas found some receptivity in states that never became fascist. Japan, Asia's first modern industrial state, departed from democratic government in the 1930s and by 1937 its leaders were consciously imitating fascist institutions.[79] Even Western liberal democracies moved in a statist direction via frequent emergency powers and "national governments" and by increasing the state's share of gross national product.[80]

### Promotions in Spain, 1936–1938

The transnational progress of fascism and communism, and resulting ideological polarization across societies, created threats and opportunities for governments in the 1930s. As already seen, Mussolini tried to help fascists and Stalin tried to help communists gain power through networking. Little forcible regime promotion took place, however. The only case in Europe in the 1930s was in Spain from 1936 to 1938. In 1934, Stalin's concern with the rising tide of fascism in the Western democracies led him to order the Comintern to revert from militant internationalism back to a "popular front" strategy, that is, to enter coalitions with social democrats and even "bourgeois" liberals in order to keep fascists out of government. Stalin made clear that the communists' goal in all countries remained a proletarian dictatorship, but that the means must now be gradual so as not to drive the liberal states, especially France and Britain, into making common cause with the fascists. Communist parties in France, Spain, Britain, and elsewhere attempted to coalesce with other anti-fascists.[81]

In February 1936, Spain's Popular Front—comprising the communists and other socialist parties and left-republicans—won an electoral victory and excluded all Rightists from government, exacerbating ideological polarization in Spain. In May, a parallel victory by the Popular Front in France, including a sharp rise in the communist vote, further polarized Spanish (as well as French) politics. In July, elements of the Spanish Army started an anti-Leftist insurgency, and Spain descended into a savage civil war. When France's Popular Front government, under pressure from its own centrists and Britain's Conservative government, refused to help its sister government in Madrid, the latter turned to Moscow for help. Meanwhile, General Francisco Franco solicited aid from Hitler and Mussolini. On September 8–9, Stalin decided to intervene on behalf of the Madrid government; a few days later, Mussolini decided to counter-intervene. All told, the Soviets sent approximately 3,000 personnel, and also created an International Brigade of between 42,000 and 51,000 (many of whom were Americans in the Abraham Lincoln Brigade); the Italians sent 70,000, the Germans 16,000, to help Franco, who ultimately prevailed.[82] The German-Italian bombing of Guernica, depicted powerfully by Pablo Picasso, has since become an iconic image of terror bombing of civilians.

The Spanish Civil War helped solidify German-Italian cooperation. In October 1936, Germany and Italy formed the Rome-Berlin Axis. The following month Germany and Japan formed the Anti-Comintern Pact; a year later, Italy joined that pact. But no further forcible regime promotion took place until the Second World War itself.

### Forcible Regime Promotion during the Second World War

The rulers of Germany, Italy, and Japan certainly intended to spread their institutions via warfare, for instrumental and, perhaps, principled reasons (even if the principles were ghastly). But most of their attacks and conquests were intended to build empires. After conquering a land they would usually either annex it or rule it directly via a military governor, governor general, or commissioner. Thus, most impositions of fascist institutions during the war do not qualify as forcible regime promotions under the coding rules I use. Such is not to say that the logic of regime promotion that I offer would not explain the sort of ideological imperialism practiced by the Axis powers. Indeed, the German and Japanese governments both understood that the more fascistic was their external environment, the friendlier it would be toward their interests.[83]

In three cases, Hitler did impose a fascist regime on a conquered land that he allowed to retain nominal sovereignty. These were Vichy France, Slovakia, and Croatia. In Vichy France, Marshal Pétain promulgated a series of constitutional acts concentrating power in the executive (under the "leadership principle") and abolishing the legislature.[84] In Slovakia, the constitution passed in July 1939 had some nominally democratic features but was modeled after fascism, particularly in its statements about national and social unity and its flexibility about the curtailment of civil liberties.[85] Croatia was ruled by the Ustase Party, an anti-Semitic labor party that disallowed any opposition.[86] Denmark was a special case: following a quick conquest in April 1940, the Nazis allowed Denmark to retain its constitutional monarchy until August 1943, when strikes and governmental recalcitrance led the Nazis to begin direct rule.[87]

As for the Allies, they clearly did intend to topple the fascist regimes of their enemies, although, as the experiences of 1944–46 show, they did not have a clear idea of what to put in the place of those regimes. Upon victory, they had the opportunity to reshape large portions of Europe and Asia politically. As the next section makes clear, transnational ideological polarization exacerbated by the war itself constrained them heavily.

## The Allies, Regime Promotion, and the Emerging Cold War, 1944–1953

Whatever the causes of the Second World War—shifts in the balance of power, ideologies of aggression, an unjust international order—one of its most profound results was the vanquishing of fascism as a transnational movement. Fascists had wanted war, or at least taken active steps that they knew would make war more likely; war for them was a proper activity of the vigorous state, and states that amassed power and asserted themselves would attract followers.[88] Belligerents and observers understood the war to be a test not only of nations but also of political and economic systems. The governments presented it in that way, in part to rally support among elites and publics within and without their states' borders. A victory for Germany meant that fascism would win, both normatively and practically; thus, communists and liberals within Germany's enemies fought hard, and fascists in those countries collaborated and welcomed German occupation. The same was true for the Soviets and communism: fascists were convinced that Soviet victory meant communism in their own countries, and fought all the harder for that reason, while communists in Europe collaborated against the Nazis. Although most of their ideological fire was directed at communists, the Nazis insisted that an American victory would mean that European civilization would give way to crass barbarism.[89] Following the total defeat of the Axis powers, fascists scattered, their leaders dead or imprisoned, their transnational links mostly severed.

The war affected the grand transnational ideological struggle in a second way: it triggered a short wave of forcible regime promotion such as had not been seen since the Napoleonic impositions in the 1800s (chapter 5). Fascists were decimated, but there remained in Europe and elsewhere liberals, conservatives, and communists who had agreed on the evils of fascism but who disagreed profoundly as to the best regime. Of these, the group with the most momentum and transnational strength were the communists. Transnational communist networks that had been mobilized and swollen by the war and their members considered their system, championed by the heroic Soviet Union, the real winner. Communists had fought alongside "bourgeois" elements in another manifestation of the "popular front" strategy against fascism. In country after country across the European theater they had fought *against* fascism, but not *for* bourgeois liberalism or capitalism. Still, good feeling ran high among communists and their non-communist allies at the end of the war, not least because Allied leaders were determined early on not to let ideology wreck their cooperation. Franklin Roosevelt in particular understood the potential for ideological strife to sunder the Grand Alliance and strove to diminish its importance. Roosevelt was relatively complacent about the possibility of Soviet "communization" of lands bordering Russia, and indeed wanted Britain and the Soviet Union to divide postwar Europe so that the United States could manage the Western Hemisphere and the Pacific.[90] Stalin, too, wanted to minimize ideological polarization, as his top priority remained building communism in the Soviet Union and doing so would be easier with Western help after the war. Hence, he ordered the communist parties in France and Italy not to start revolutions after liberation from the Nazis; did not help the communists in the Greek civil war (1944–49); and withdrew the Red Army from northern Iran in 1946.[91]

Even so, as the power of transnational fascism faded with that of Germany and Japan, elites in Europe and Asia began to polarize increasingly according to whether they sympathized with the communists or not. Complicating matters was that most liberated countries contained communist and anti-communist elites, each with a vision for its country sharply at odds with that of the other. Communists had earned prestige in their societies by fighting bravely against the fascists. Stalin proved willing to exploit their unstinting loyalty. Anti-communists included some who had collaborated with the fascists but some who were liberal or Catholic. The latter found a great deal in common with the victorious American and British governments. Transnational ties developed quickly between various European conservatives, who had traditionally been suspicious of political and economic liberalism, and the United States. In particular, Christian Democrats in Italy and Germany made common cause with the Anglo-Americans.

With so many countries teetering between communism and liberalism, it is no surprise that the fall of any country in one direction or the other would polarize others and tempt the Allied governments to promote their own regime type. Neither the Soviet nor the U.S. government seriously feared a domestic overthrow by the other's ideological movement (although some American elites did have that fear in the early 1950s). The wave of forcible regime promotion in the latter half of the 1940s was done to increase the superpowers' external rather than internal security. Promotion was a tool to extend or preserve one's sphere of influence and to arrest the spread of the other's sphere. In a classic case of endogeneity, Anglo-American and Soviet actions in occupied states exacerbated transnational ideological polarization, making still more forcible regime promotion in more states increasingly sensible for Washington and Moscow. Narrating the feedback loops across societies and between networks and governments would be exceedingly complex. The general outline is clear, however: cooperation among ideological confreres begot not only more such cooperation, but conflict between adherents of rival ideologies, and governments and their policies of forcible regime promotion were part of the process. As David Painter and Melvyn Leffler write of Europe in general:

> US policymakers worried that wherever and however Communist groups attained power they would pursue policies that served the interests of the Soviet Union. The potential international impact of internal political struggles invested the latter with strategic significance and embroiled the United States and the Soviet Union in the internal affairs of other nations.[92]

Communists in occupied countries identified increasingly not only with the Soviet Union but against the United States; that identification tempted Stalin to impose communist regimes in those countries. The same dynamic, *mutatis mutandis*, operated for liberals and other anti-communists vis-à-vis the United States in the same countries. Moscow and Washington increasingly saw opportunities to use their respective networks to expand their sphere of influence, and increasingly feared that the other was doing the same thing.

The first forcible regime imposition took place in occupied Italy over several years following the fall of Mussolini in July 1943. Communists, socialists, liberals, and other anti-fascists had fought together and indeed were still fighting the Nazis who occupied the northern part of the country. Following Mussolini's deposition, Roosevelt announced that America aimed to allow the Italian people freedom to set up their own democratic institutions.[93] What sounds to liberal ears like a natural and laudable goal sounded threatening to communists, as if the Italians were "free" so long as they chose a U.S.-style regime—a regime that would, of course, tilt toward the West. And indeed, the Americans and British began cooperating to establish a new interim regime in Italy and excluded the Soviets from the Allied Control Council there. In a September 1943 memorandum to the War Department, General Dwight Eisenhower suggested that among the conditions under which the Allies would grant co-belligerent status to the interim government of Pietro Badoglio was "a decree restoring the former [liberal] constitution and promising free elections after the war for a constitutional assembly."[94] To Soviet protests the Americans and British replied that they had troops in Italy and the Soviets did not.

Stalin retaliated by using the Red Army to impose communism in Bulgaria, where no Anglo-American troops were stationed. After the Red Army conquered Bulgaria in the autumn of 1944, the communist-led Fatherland Front seized power and executed all Nazi collaborators.[95] Stalin claimed Western actions in Italy as a precedent.[96] Churchill, Roosevelt, and Stalin were keenly aware of the need to coordinate a postwar settlement, and at the Yalta Conference in February 1945 they agreed that the Lublin Polish government, recognized by Stalin a few months earlier, would hold free elections including broad representation throughout society. The Big Three signed a "Declaration on Liberated Europe," pledging governments in central Europe "broadly representative of all democratic elements in the population" and "the earliest possible establishment through free elections of governments responsible to the will of the people." The language seemed clear to Western liberals, but was flexible enough for Stalin to impose a compliant government on occupied Romania two weeks later. Upon assuming the presidency in April, Harry Truman lectured the Soviets about violating Yalta. At the Potsdam Conference in July, the powers agreed to divide Germany into zones, but Truman and Churchill failed to persuade Stalin to follow the Yalta declaration more closely.[97]

In the meantime, back in Italy elites remained highly polarized between Left and Right. The Left—the Communists (PCI) and Socialists (PSI)—felt an intense common interest with the Soviet Union and staunchly opposed Italy's accepting Marshall aid or aligning with the West. The PCI leader, Palmiro Togliatti, had spent twenty years in exile in Soviet Russia. The Right comprised mainly the country's largest party, the Christian Democratic, which included not only democrats but also monarchists who for religious and cultural reasons mistrusted American-style institutions.[98] The U.S. authorities took steps to stack the deck in favor of the Right and to ensure that the Italian regime would be a liberal republic. Washington supported the pluralistic provisional post-fascist governments. It pressured the interim government in 1946 to reject the communist-socialist plan for an all-powerful, popularly elected *costituente* that would set up a postwar "worker's state," and to accept instead a plan that made a radical regime much less probable: local governments would be elected first, making centralization more difficult; a referendum on whether Italy would retain the monarchy would follow, simultaneously with *costituente* elections that would write the constitution; finally national elections would be held.[99]

By 1947, a liberal-democratic constitution was in place in Italy. In the crucial national election of April 1948, the United States acted covertly to degrade the odds of the PCI-PSI Popular Front victory. (The Soviets, for their part, supported the Popular Front.) The Christian Democrats won, in part because the Popular Front defended the communist coup in

Czechoslovakia in February 1948; that cast severe doubt on their claims to desire to work through parliamentary institutions.[100] Finally, Washington offered extensive economic aid to Italy, adding credibility to the U.S.-supported regime.[101] Democratic Italy ended up accepting Marshall aid and joining NATO in 1949.

The most incendiary case of forcible regime promotion was Germany itself; as recounted at the beginning of this chapter, the Truman administration only decided to promote liberal democracy in the western zones to compete with the Soviets, who had already begun "communizing" their zone. But the Soviets imposed communist regimes elsewhere as well. In keeping with Yalta, democratic Poles were allowed to join the communist-dominated government, but when elections were finally held in January 1947 the communists controlled the outcome, and a Stalinist regime was established. In Romania the Soviets saw to it that the government was dominated by communists, who, as in Poland, fixed the elections of November 1946. A "people's democracy" was established in April 1947. In Hungary and Czechoslovakia the Soviets and local communists proceeded more slowly, perhaps because a greater proportion of elites were anti-communist. What Anton DePorte calls "reasonably free elections" were held in Hungary in November 1945 and in Czechoslovakia in May 1946, producing pluralistic governments. In December 1946—the same month that the Soviet Central Committee declared that the world was dividing into "two camps"—Stalin ordered the suppression of anti-communists, and in June 1947 the Prime Minister, leader of the Smallholders Party, resigned. The communists imposed a coalition on the leftist parties in the August elections, and won a majority; they very quickly established a Stalinist regime.[102]

In Czechoslovakia, the May 1946 elections produced a communist-led coalition government under Klement Gottwald. The President, Eduard Benes, and Foreign Minister, Jan Masaryk, still believed they had sufficient freedom of action to accept Marshall aid from the United States. But the communists vetoed the acceptance. In September Stalin created the Communist Information Bureau (Cominform), a reconstitution of the old Comintern but confined to Europe, as a way to tighten his grip on communist parties. In February 1948, all non-communist ministers resigned from the Czechoslovak cabinet. Benes accepted a new cabinet that was thoroughly communist except for Masaryk, who was found dead soon after.[103] The Prague Coup completed Stalin's grip on Central Europe and, as mentioned above, helped turn enough Italians against the communists to ensure a Christian Democratic victory in the April 1948 elections there.

Rulers used other means to try to promote regimes in Europe. Most famously, Josip Broz Tito of Yugoslavia extended material aid and advice to Greek communists. Stalin supported Tito until Truman announced that the United States would help the anti-communists in Greece. Tito, who sought hegemony over the Balkans, insisted on continuing to aid the Greek communists, defying Stalin and accomplishing communism's first great schism.[104] The U.S. government also helped non-communist labor unions in France to compete with communist unions that sought to destabilize the restored Fourth Republic.

Transnational ideological polarization, and forcible regime promotion, occurred during these same years in East Asia in the aftermath of the Pacific War. Communist parties had been founded in China, Japan, Korea, Indochina, and elsewhere in the 1920s following the establishment of the Soviet Union. As in Europe, communists had supported the Soviet Union against fascism and Japanese imperialism and by the close of the war enjoyed prestige among many elites. Anti-communists, too, were mobilized as in Europe. Transnational ideological polarization in East Asia gave each superpower reasons to seek to spread its regime, or block the spread of the other's regime. In early August 1945, upon hearing that America had dropped an atomic bomb on Hiroshima, Stalin—who had promised to join the fight against Japan within three months of Germany's surrender—requested that Truman allow Soviet troops to join in the occupation. Truman refused and decided to send U.S. troops to occupy the southern part of Korea.[105] The Soviets helped establish a Stalinist regime in the North of Korea, while the Americans set up a centralized republic under Rhee Syngman; the Americans allowed Rhee and several successors to avoid democracy as long as they were anti-communist.

By the time of Japan's surrender in August 1945, U.S. occupation policy had been worked out in debates among the State, War, and Navy departments. The plan approved by Truman was to demilitarize the country and reconstruct it as a liberal constitutional monarchy, including representative government and civil liberties. Truman approved the plan and General Douglas MacArthur, who directed the occupation, implemented it. In Japan, elites were less liberal than anti-communist. MacArthur threatened to put the constitution to a referendum so as to dissuade elites from revising it in a more conservative-monarchical direction. The Americans also broke up the *zaibatsu* or wealthy industrial conglomerates that had so dominated Imperial Japan.[106]

Kim Il Sung, dictator of North Korea, sent forces to China in late 1946 or early 1947 to aid Mao Zedong's communists in their civil war against Chiang Kai-Shek's nationalists. Little is known publicly about the extent of this forcible regime promotion.[107] Stalin did not send direct military help, but did extend various types of material aid and advice to Mao. The old revisionist view that Stalin wanted Mao to lose cannot be sustained against the evidence.[108] But the Soviets never directly intervened with their own military assets.

The first such promotion—by the United States and a number of allies in South Korea in 1950—provoked a counter-promotion by China. North Korea's Kim Il Sung rejected the division of the Korean peninsula, and from early 1949 began pressing Stalin to allow him to invade the South. Once Mao's communists began to win in China in 1948, he began pulling troops back to North Korea. In the spring of 1950, Stalin began to warm to the idea, thinking that the Americans were unlikely to respond militarily and also that a Korean war would force Mao to align China more closely with the Soviet Union. Kim believed that upon hearing of the invasion, the masses in South Korea would arise and help topple Rhee's regime. U.S. leaders would have agreed that Rhee's regime was unpopular, and partly for that reason judged that the main communist threat to the South was through subversion rather than invasion.[109] Kim's invasion of South Korea in June 1950 does not qualify as a forcible regime promotion because Kim's aim was to absorb the target.

The U.S. counter-intervention that began a few weeks later, however, was certainly a forcible regime promotion. The Truman administration had already "lost China" in 1949, and its ability to "regain" it through Chiang Kai-Shek's Taiwan would be further degraded by a communist victory on the Korean peninsula.[110] Truman feared demonstration effects in Japan and beyond. In the highly polarized East Asia of 1950, communism was a carrier of Soviet influence and power. There was little possibility of separating Kim (or Mao) from Stalin at that time. The United States intervened massively in the Korean War because U.S. leaders saw in the spread of communism a threat to American national security. In September, Truman signed a directive authorizing U.S. (UN) forces to cross the 38th Parallel into North Korea so as to topple Kim's regime and reunify Korea.[111] The intervention's end now changed from simply preserving Rhee's non-communist regime to overturning Kim's communist one. The expanded goal, and the northward advance of U.S. troops toward the Yalu River, provoked Mao into counter-intervening the following month. The approach of U.S. troops to the Chinese border was threatening to Mao's regime precisely because, in such an ideologically polarized time, the United States was so thoroughly identified with anticommunism and hence against Mao's revolution.

Between 1943 and 1950, then, forcible regime promotion begot more forcible regime promotion. This vicious cycle of interaction among rival superpower governments and transnational ideological networks is part of what we mean by the emergence of the Cold War. TINs and the ongoing struggle over the best regime in Europe and Asia were by no means the only causes of the Cold War. The long Soviet-American rivalry was a complex phenomenon with a complex set of causes, including the bipolar distribution of power and the personalities of leaders. Yet, transnational polarization over communism presented Soviet and American leaders with opportunities and threats to which they felt compelled to respond. In responding—by promoting their regime and opposing that of the rival—the United States and Soviet Union became progressively more threatening to each other. Leffler describes the situation as follows:

> At the end of the war, international society was astir with demoralized peoples yearning for a better future after decades of depression, war, genocide, and force migration. In the center of Europe and in northeast Asia the defeat of Germany and Japan left huge vacuums of power. In time—and not a very long time, contemporaries assumed—the occupations would end and the Germans and Japanese would reconstitute their governments and political economies. They would then decide how they would configure themselves in the international system, but their future trajectory was a huge, unsettling question mark.[112]

The bipolar structure of the international system may have made inevitable some type of rivalry between America and the Soviet Union. But the ongoing deep transnational disputes over the best regime made that rivalry especially intense and dangerous, because it pulled the superpowers into dozens of countries where they competed for influence. Had the two superpowers been the United States and Great Britain, both liberal democracies, there is little doubt that any resulting "cold war" would have been a far less dangerous matter.[113]

### Isolated Promotions in Europe: Hungary 1956 and Czechoslovakia 1968

The remainder of the Cold War was to be marked by efforts by each superpower, and often by its allies, to promote its regime or at least block the spread of the other's regime in the Third World. Washington and Moscow used economic incentives, diplomacy, covert action, and other means to try to gain influence in these regions. As in the 1940s, neither superpower government seriously feared for its domestic stability. Rather, the promotions were done for reasons of external security—more precisely, to extend or preserve one's sphere of influence at the expense of the other's. As discussed earlier in this chapter, the United States (and sometimes its British and French allies) by no means always promoted liberal democracy. In the Third World it usually supported authoritarian regimes so long as they were anti-communist.

The Cold War after 1950 did feature a number of forcible regime promotions by the superpowers. These were one-time events in the sense that they did not lead to any short waves of promotion. Each of these was triggered by either domestic unrest or a forcible attempt at national reunification (in the case of the Korean War). Like such events in previous eras, these had demonstration effects and polarized elites in neighboring states along ideological lines, giving Soviet and American leaders incentives to carry out still more forcible promotions. But the superpowers' leaders faced overwhelming incentives not to counter-promote and risk setting off a short wave. The chief incentive was probably the need to avoid nuclear war.

In 1956 the Soviet re-imposition of communism on Hungary took place. That promotion was far along a chain of events initiated by the death of Stalin in March 1953. Stalin's demise was followed by a succession contest in the Soviet Union. Nikita Khrushchev, Georgi Malenkov, and other reformers struggled against remaining Stalinists. The reformers set out to de-Stalinize the country and the Eastern bloc, both as means and end. Khrushchev and his circle were not trying to make the Soviet Union into a free-market constitutional democracy; they were determined to maintain the communist party's monopoly of power. But they believed that the Soviet Union and communism had suffered under the rigid, closed, terrifying state that Stalin had built, and that openness to new ideas, including from abroad, would strengthen the regime and country. In good Leninist fashion they purged Stalinists from the Soviet Communist party. Thus, the reformers in the Kremlin urged East European rulers to de-Stalinize their regimes and in some cases purged Stalinists from leadership of their parties.[114]

Kremlin-directed reform from above was to have unintended consequences. In a milder version of what was to occur under the reforms of Mikhail Gorbachev in the late 1980s, the Khrushchev Thaw encouraged the dissemination of new ideas and the bottom-up formation of social groups within the Soviet Union and across the Soviet bloc. Dissenting communists were released from prison and allowed to resume their reformist activities.[115] An early indication of what was to come occurred in the form of a worker's uprising in East Germany in June, quickly suppressed by Soviet tanks. As Khrushchev consolidated his power in the Kremlin over the next few years, struggles continued among communists in Eastern Europe between Stalinists and reformers. At the 20th Party Congress in February 1956, Khrushchev made his famous speech denouncing the personality cult of Stalin. In June a workers' uprising occurred in Poznan, Poland. The Polish party, headed by Wladislaw Gomulka, sided with the workers and began acting independently of Moscow. The autonomy of Eastern European states was not what Khrushchev had in mind, and Soviet tanks moved toward the Polish border. But Gomulka told the Soviets that the Polish army would fight back. The resulting bargain was that the Polish party could practice communism in its own way but would keep Poland in the Warsaw Pact.[116]

The Polish uprising, in turn, had demonstration effects in Hungary. In October, thousands of Hungarians took to the streets of Budapest and the government called in Soviet tanks to restore order. Civil war ensued, and the reform communist Imre Nagy became Prime Minister. Nagy had briefly been Prime Minister in 1953, following de-Stalinization. In 1955, he had published *On Communism*, outlining his liberalizing plans; the book increased his following among dissidents.[117] Now, once again head of the government, Nagy became increasingly radical—that is to say, liberal-democratic—bringing reformers into his cabinet and promulgating what he called "socialism with a human face." Nagy's program included multiparty democracy and the dissolution of the communist party. In the Kremlin the Soviet leaders were nonplussed. On October 30, the Soviet Central Committee issued a statement acknowledging Soviet errors concerning Hungary and the other "people's democracies." But two days later, when Nagy announced Hungary's withdrawal from the Warsaw Pact and official neutrality, the Soviet rulers decided to move. On November 3, Nagy and other reformers were arrested and Soviet tanks rolled into Hungary, quickly restoring the communist regime under the compliant János Kádár.[118]

The events in Hungary in 1956 deterred other reform communists from trying what Nagy had tried until 1968, when Alexander Dubcek attempted a subtler and more limited set of reforms in Czechoslovakia. Dubcek, one of a group of communists looking to renew de-Stalinization, took office in January 1968. He began to weaken censorship and the power of the secret police and to allow more political action by those outside the communist party. Careful not to duplicate the most provocative moves of Nagy, Dubcek kept Czechoslovakia in the Warsaw Pact. Nonetheless he alarmed the Kremlin. As John Lewis Gaddis writes, "What the Russians feared was ...the impact of 'reform communism' on their long-range military position in Eastern Europe and, ultimately, on the security of the Soviet regime itself."[119] As in 1956, liberalism was a carrier of Western, and ultimately American, influence and hence would degrade Soviet power. Brezhnev ordered the Warsaw Pact to invade and Dubcek was overthrown. Rigid communist party rule was preserved.

### Forcible Promotions in the Third World

In the vast, heterogeneous set of less industrialized states that came to be known as the Third World, the most powerful ideology by far was nationalism. The greatest burden on Third-World elites, and the surest route to legitimacy among their peoples, was to achieve national unity, strength, and independence from their present or former colonial masters. Communist parties across regions formed transnational networks, whose nerve center was in Moscow. But except for in Southeast Asia, communists were relatively weak and usually unable to seize a state by themselves. They were helped, however, by the credibility that communism enjoyed owing to the formidable example of the Soviet Union. Stalin's successes in wrenching an agricultural society once ruled by a backward monarchy into an industrial powerhouse in the 1930s, and a superpower in the 1940s, made a deep impression on many post-colonial elites who sought national sovereignty and progress. In 1913, Russia's industrial output had been only 6.9 percent of America's. In 1932, Soviet output had risen to 27.3 percent of American, and in 1938, 45.1 percent.[120] After the war the Soviet Union was suddenly ahead of France, Germany, and even fellow victor Great Britain; it went on to develop an atomic bomb only four years after the United States (albeit with help from espionage). From 1951 to 1955, Soviet annual economic growth averaged 14 percent; from 1956 to 1960, nearly 11 percent.[121] In 1957, it was the first country to place a satellite in orbit around the planet. Nikita Khrushchev's boast in October 1961 that the Soviet economy would surpass that of the United States within twenty years appears risible today, but for several decades it was consistent with the trend in relative strength between the superpowers. At the outset of the Second World War, the Chinese Communist Party was the only strong one in non-Soviet Asia; at the end, communist parties in Japan, India, Malaya, Indochina, the Philippines, Korea, the East Indies, and Burma all were large and enjoyed much popular support by virtue of their heroics against the Imperial Japanese regime.[122]

Non-communist elites in the Third World were a diverse lot. The chief goals of a great number, beyond acquiring and keeping power, were to develop their states with public works and industry, redistribute resources from landholding elites to peasants, and secure independence from their former colonizers. Regional movements inflected with ideology—Arab Socialism, African Socialism—arose. Some countries, such as Mexico and Ghana, insisted on a unique national path to development that nonetheless involved a high degree of state control of the economy and no meaningful political competition. These socialists were not communists, but they shared many goals with the communist parties in their countries, and the Soviet Union, at various times, was prepared to help new rulers achieve them.[123]

Liberal democracy and capitalism, by contrast, were associated with the Europeans and their new patron, the United States. The European states were the very ones from which Third World elites were seeking independence. The United States, as mentioned above, had had an informal empire in much of the Caribbean and Central America earlier in the century, and many Latin American elites regarded the Americans as essentially as imperialistic as the Europeans. Decisions made early in

192 • Chapter Six

the Cold War by the Truman and Eisenhower administrations to help the French fight communist independence movements in Indochina permanently damaged in much of the world America's reputation for being an anti-imperialist power.[124] It was the traditional holders of power in the Third World—large landowners and capitalists—who tended to favor cooperation with the Americans and other Western powers. The Western governments favored the preservation of property rights and hence the hostility toward communist and socialist redistribution. The chief divide that emerged in the Third World, then, was over strategy for national development and autonomy. This meant that in many cases, the Left tended toward anti-Americanism and pro-Sovietism, and the Right—notwithstanding its political illiberalism—pro-Americanism and anti-Sovietism.

Soviet leaders eventually began to exploit these communist and socialist elites and networks in the Third World. But they did not do so immediately after the Second World War ended. Stalin had concluded from setbacks in China in the late 1920s that nationalism would hijack communism in non-industrial societies. Andrei Zhdanov included communists from Vietnam, Indonesia, India, Egypt, and Syria at a Cominform meeting in September 1947; but no Third World party was invited to join the organization. What changed Stalin's mind was the communist victory in China in 1949. The Soviet dictator began to believe that "the center of the revolutionary movement had shifted from the West to the East" and that, as Chinese communist leader Liu Shaoqi proclaimed, the Chinese revolutionary model might "become the main path toward the liberation of other people in the colonial and semicolonial countries where similar conditions exist." In turn, with Stalin's encouragement Mao Zedong began to provide military assistance—strategic advice and training and supplying troops—to Ho Chi Minh's communists (Viet Minh) in Vietnam in their struggle against the French.[125]

Following the French defeat in Indochina in 1954, the Vietnamese belligerents and French agreed at Geneva that elections would be held to decide the future of Vietnam. The Eisenhower administration deepened U.S. involvement by supporting the republic in South Vietnam, headed by the staunch anti-communist Diem Ngo Dinh. The Viet Cong, or communist insurgency in the South, grew and the Hanoi rulers began increasing their support for it in the late 1950s. (As in the Korean case, the North Vietnamese attempt to alter the South's regime does not qualify as a forcible regime promotion because Hanoi's goal was to annex the South.) Increasing unrest in the South, and related communist guerrilla activity in neighboring Laos, drew in U.S. military support in the early 1960s. The unpopular Diem was assassinated in 1963, and the South was unstable for months. Ho increased support for the Viet Cong still further. In August 1964, in the Gulf of Tonkin, a U.S. ship exchanged fire with several North Vietnamese torpedo boats. The Tonkin Gulf incident led U.S. President Lyndon Johnson to escalate U.S. military involvement the following year.[126] "America's longest war," as George Herring calls it, was an attempt to preserve South Vietnam from a communist takeover. The consensus in Washington was that a communist South Vietnam would ipso facto mean an extension of Soviet influence and a shift in the balance of power in Asia. Transnational ideological polarization made it difficult for U.S. leaders to resist forcible intervention. U.S. promotion in South Vietnam provoked no Soviet (or Chinese) counter-intervention; other communist governments were content to provide material support.

Parallel to events in Vietnam was a regime contest in neighboring Laos. French departure from Indochina in 1954 left an independent country torn by three factions: the communist Pathet Lao, right-wing forces, and "neutralists." A neutralist government was overthrown by a right-wing coup in April 1964, and civil war erupted. In the summer the North Vietnamese government began to send forces to Laos to help the Pathet Lao. The Johnson administration responded by beginning a bombing campaign to support the Laotian government. The situations in Laos and Vietnam were heavily interdependent, not least because along the border between the two ran most of the Ho Chi Minh Trail, a route of communist infiltration from North to South Vietnam. The government of Thailand, also anti-communist, sent forces to Laos as well.[127]

A third Southeastern Asian target of forcible regime promotion was Cambodia, which likewise shared a border with Vietnam and a segment of the Ho Chi Minh Trail. Neutral in the Vietnamese war, monarchical Cambodia was highly polarized by it, with the communist Khmer Rouge and conservatives increasingly hostile. The government of Prince Sihanouk knew that Hanoi's use of the Ho Chi Minh Trail was a provocation to the Americans, but could do little to stop it. In March 1970, Sihanouk was overthrown by the pro-American Lon Nol, who abolished the monarchy and declared a republic. President Richard Nixon then had U.S. forces bomb the Trail and invade Cambodia so as to cut off the Trail and to support Lon Nol's new republic against a possible North Vietnamese invasion. North Vietnamese already had troops in Cambodia on the Trail, and now these moved deeper into the country to support the Khmer Rouge in their struggle to overthrow Lon Nol and establish a communist regime. (In 1975, the Khmer Rouge succeeded, but by then had split from the Vietnamese Communists and leaned toward the Chinese Communists; Vietnam invaded Cambodia in 1978 and overthrew the Khmer Rouge, establishing a puppet regime in its place.)[128]

The consensus among Western political analysts is that American fears of falling dominoes in Southeast Asia were mistaken and tragic: dominoes seldom fall.[129] But in fact, communists in Cambodia and Laos won their civil wars after the Americans left Vietnam in 1973; Cambodia aligned with China, Laos with Vietnam and the Soviet Union. And demonstration effects from the civil unrest in Indochina were serious enough to spur the formation of the Association of Southeast Asian Nations (ASEAN) in 1967. ASEAN was originally a cooperative effort by the governments of Indonesia, Singapore, the Philippines, Thailand, and Malaysia to commit to and coordinate policies to fight communist subversion. Simply because America failed in Indochina, or ASEAN was successful (and has since outgrown its original purpose), does not mean that demonstration effects are a fiction or that dominoes cannot fall. Rather, the strength of these threats is what produced ASEAN.[130]

Outside of East and Southeast Asia, Stalin did almost nothing to aid communists and woo socialist state-builders. It was his successor Nikita Khrushchev who recognized the potential for the Soviet Union to place itself on the side of the "wars of national liberation" and weaken U.S. influence over much of the globe.[131] Rulers of newly decolonized states accepted his offers. In the late 1950s and 1960s, Soviet engineers and construction crews fanned our over the Third World, leaving public works and factories in their wake.[132]

In Latin America and the Caribbean, communism had an elite following across most states. Discontent with large landholding families and U.S. hegemony was widespread among many elites. Fidel Castro's regime in Cuba, established in 1959, inspired some of the discontented to embrace communism, and made others willing to cooperate with communists. No U.S. administration ever used direct force to topple Castro, but covert action, some of it tragic and some comical, was used. Part of the bargain that resolved the Cuban missile crisis of October 1962 was an agreement by the Kennedy administration not to invade Cuba.[133] But transnational communism in the Western Hemisphere remained a preoccupation for successive U.S. administrations. So did the openness of social democrats in Latin America and the Caribbean to working with communists and adopting some of their programs, such as state-directed import-substituting industrialization. The Kennedy administration sought to win social democrats to the U.S. side through the Alliance for Progress, which was to transfer hundreds of millions of dollars to the region in return for various liberal reforms. But in 1964, the Johnson administration was concerned that the example of Castro's state socialism was overwhelming the Alliance for Progress. Needed instead was U.S. intervention to keep out the "statists."[134]

U.S. attempts to keep communists far away from power are well known. The two occasions on which such attempts involved the direct use of American military force were in the Dominican Republic in 1965 and Grenada in 1983. In the Dominican Republic, Juan Bosch, a social democrat and the country's first elected President, was overthrown by a military junta in 1963 after promulgating a new constitution. In 1965, military officers who favored Bosch rebelled. Johnson sent 22,000 U.S. troops in April to prevent, as he said, "the establishment of another Communist government in the Western Hemisphere."[135] Bosch was not a communist, but the fear in Washington was that he would move the country in a statist direction and an alignment with Cuba would eventually result. Eighteen years later, Ronald Reagan sent 1,900 U.S. forces to Grenada to overthrow a Marxist regime that recently had toppled another Marxist regime. Three hundred troops from the Organization of East Caribbean States joined the Americans. The Americans restored the constitutional government that had been overturned in 1979.[136] (The Reagan administration used other means to undermine the Marxist Sandinista regime in Nicaragua and to buttress non-communist regimes elsewhere in Central America.)

In sub-Saharan Africa the Soviets and Americans began to compete for influence in the 1960s by aiding particular factions in various countries. The factions were seldom originally constituted by commitment to one or another ideology, but instead were tied to particular tribes or tribal coalitions seeking hegemony over their newly independent state. Still, the desire for and possibility of superpower patronage led some to adopt one or another Cold War ideology. In Angola, which gained independence from Portugal in 1975, the Popular Movement for the Liberation of Angola (MPLA) took on Marxism-Leninism. Its chief rival, the National Union for the Total Independence of Angola (UNITA), had Maoist roots but struck a bargain with the American-led bloc and began to espouse constitutional government and free markets. In August 1975, South African troops invaded to support UNITA. In October, thousands of Cuban troops invaded to support the MPLA. The following year the U.S. Congress cut off aid to UNITA, and the MPLA won the first war. UNITA regrouped and, with help from South African forces, made significant headway. By 1985, when the Reagan administration renewed aid to UNITA, 50,000 Cuban soldiers were in Angola.[137]

The Soviets offered aid to Middle Eastern Arab states, and Arab socialists—Nasser in Egypt, Assad in Syria, and others—accepted it. Several forcible regime promotions took place in the region in the 1960s and 1970s. Most of these had more to do with the intra-Muslim struggle between Islamism and secularism that I analyze in chapter 7. But British and Iranian military intervention in Oman was aimed at keeping that country from becoming communist. Communist movements gained momentum on the Arabian peninsula in the 1960s, helping force the British out of their long-time colony Aden and eventually setting up the People's Democratic Republic of Yemen (South Yemen) in 1970. The independence movement in Aden, and simultaneous Nasserist revolt in North Yemen (chapter 7), inspired a rebellion in the Dhofar region of Oman, then ruled by the conservative Sultan Said ibn Taimur. The rebels first aimed for a progressive republic, but Yemeni communists aided them and in 1967, the Dhofar rebels adopted a broad program under the name Popular Front for the Liberation of the Occupied Arabian Gulf (PFLO). The PFLO received Soviet and Chinese aid and sought to spread communist revolution throughout the Persian Gulf. A number of governments—the Saudi, Jordanian, UAE, British, Iranian, and even Egyptian rulers—wanted to halt communism and Soviet influence in the region and aided the Omani monarchy in various ways. In 1970, British troops helped the Sultan's son and successor Qabus ibn Said hold on to power; in 1973, the Shah of Iran began sending troops—eventually numbering 3,000—to help.[138]

One of the most consequential forcible regime promotions of this long wave was the Soviet invasion of the Republic of Afghanistan in December 1979. Because that intervention was also part of the intra-Muslim struggle between Islamism and secularism, I address it in chapter 7. The Soviets' prolonged failed attempt to support a communist regime in Afghanistan was a significant event in the discrediting of the Soviet model and hence of the end of the long wave.

## The Long Wave Ends: Communism Fails in the 1980s

As with previous long ideological struggles, that between communism and liberal democracy sometimes appeared to have ended, presumably in a draw, but then the struggle would reignite later. Superpower détente in the 1970s was prolonged and deep enough that elites began to refer to the struggle in the past tense. Patience, rationality, and good diplomacy (including U.S. withdrawal from Vietnam) had permanently de-polarized international politics, it was thought. In 1977, President Jimmy Carter famously proclaimed that Americans were over their "inordinate fear of communism which once led us to embrace any dictator who joined us in that fear."[139] Language used in 1978 by James Chace, then managing editor of *Foreign Affairs* magazine, is typical of elites at the time: "At a time when foreign policy is clearly vulnerable to a variety of interest groups, is it even possible to erect a broad foreign policy consensus *as was done in the cold war era*?"[140] But as long as the question of the best domestic regime remained so contentious, and the contenders mutually exclusive and enjoying huge transnational followings, the struggle could not end. Carter acknowledged the struggle had restarted when the Soviets invaded Afghanistan. It could end only when ideologies converged or one lost its credibility across states. In the event, it was the latter. The failure of communism as a strategy toward sovereignty, prosperity, and justice became manifest in the 1980s. Marx had once looked forward to the "withering away of the state." It was the Soviet state, and with it communism itself, that withered away.

Today, the old contest between the individual and the collectivity has passed from most regions of the world. Cuba and North Korea remain communist, and China and Vietnam retain ruling Leninist parties with a rhetorical commitment to the old Marxist vision. Maoist guerrillas continue to plot and fight in Nepal, the Philippines, and parts of South America. Hugo Chávez of Venezuela is trying to revive some variety of transnational state socialism, and may yet succeed in polarizing politics at least in the Americas (chapter 8). It is safe to say, however, that the long legitimacy crisis that struck constitutional government in the 1910s, that began to affect international relations directly with the Russian Revolution of 1917, and that spawned the self-destructive fascism, was ending by the mid-1980s. It ended when it became nearly incontestable that communism did not work on its own terms. The countries that tried it were falling behind, while those that tried democratic capitalism were moving ahead. Communists the world over lost credibility and support, and socialists began to abandon their traditional embrace of *dirigisme* and began to favor "neoliberal," market-based economic policies. Communist TINs lost membership and their ability to make rulers tremble; the political Left as a whole decided that reform rather than revolution was the best strategy to effect change.

The liberal economic reforms begun in China in 1979 by Deng Xiaoping were a signal that communism was not fulfilling its promise to raise standards of living and make great the nations that implemented it. In the Soviet Union itself, economic growth never again reached the impressive levels of the 1960s. The period of Leonid Brezhnev's rule was to become known in the late 1980s as the "years of stagnation," and with good reason. As Willie Thompson, a British communist, puts the matter:

> The year 1981 was supposed to have been the year when, according to Khrushchev's boast at the 22nd Congress, the USSR would overtake the USA in material consumption, not to speak of other indicators of public welfare. All that had, of course, been quietly forgotten, and the continuing dependence of the Soviet Union on US grain imports were [sic] a humiliating reminder of just how inferior in that capacity it was to a country with a much smaller agricultural sector.[141]

Daniel Patrick Moynihan adds that, as a U.S. Senator in the late 1970s, he noted Soviet statistics indicating acute manpower shortages; a ten-year and widening gap between male (64) and female (74) life expectancy; and a steep rise in the infant mortality rate from 22.9 deaths per 1,000 births in 1971 to 31.1 deaths in 1976. "In a word," Moynihan writes, "communism was dead."[142] All in all, Leonid Brezhnev had led the Soviet Union into what Western writers were to call "imperial over-extension," an overextension that was partly a function of communism's intrinsic incapacities.

In Africa, Latin America, and East Asia, countries that adopted Marxism-Leninism generally fared much worse than their counterparts that adopted economic liberalism. David Lane writes:

> Capitalism on a world scale has proved to be more successful as a system of production and consumption than anticipated by a succession of communist leaders from Lenin to Brezhnev. ...[T]he "developmental model" of state socialism had positive effects in Eastern Europe and the Third World immediately after the Second World War. But from the 1980s the rise of the capitalist South-East Asian economies such as Taiwan, Malaysia and South Korea provided an alternative for the developing societies of the Third World.[143]

Fred Halliday adds: "In the end ...it was the pressures of the West, above all the demonstration effect of capitalist economic success, which brought the Soviet system, and that of its defected allies, down."[144] Neo-Marxist dependency theory, which had prescribed socialist revolution and no economic interaction with the United States and the West in general, was likewise failing. Zbigniew Brzezinski points out that in the 1980s, Tanzania, which had adopted state socialism, was economically stagnant and actually reducing industrial output, while neighboring Kenya, which had adopted more market mechanisms, enjoyed modest overall and industrial growth.[145]

Compounding the problem for Third-World communists was the growing scarcity of Soviet aid, a scarcity itself caused by communism's stagnation. In the 1970s, Moscow had begun to target aid on strategic countries such as Angola and Ethiopia.[146] No longer was massive aid available to any Third World regime that was adopting Marxism-Leninism. Mikhail Gorbachev, who took office in 1985, further cut aid to foreign communist parties and regimes even as he moved the Soviet Union itself toward democracy and capitalism. By the mid-1980s, Moscow was telling clients in Africa and Asia, including Mozambique, Angola, Ethiopia, and Vietnam, to integrate into world markets and try to attract foreign investment, "clearly signaling thereby," as Brzezinski writes, "that the Kremlin was not about to foot their development bills."[147] Gorbachev informed the Cubans that they should improve their economic situation by conciliating the United States.

The effects in the Third World of the decline of socialism are difficult to trace directly. By the 1980s, however, the World Bank and International Monetary Fund, those international lending agencies that were gatekeepers to the international capitalist economy, began insisting that borrowers implement more monetarist policies.[148] Economic development now meant austerity to shrink state control over the economy. It was beside the point that South Korea and Taiwan were not laissez-faire economies; what mattered was that they had succeeded with capitalist openness rather than with socialist autarchy.

## Conclusion

During the twentieth century, at least sixty-eight forcible regime promotions took place. As in previous periods, governments cared enough about the domestic institutions of other states that they sometimes spent dear resources, and risked still more resources, to alter or preserve those institutions. Of these, the great majority were ordered by governments trying to exploit the opportunities, and answer the threats, that the long transnational contest among liberal democracy, communism, and (in the early decades) fascism presented them with. Some interventions—ex ante ones—followed domestic regime instability in one or more states. A short wave of promotion followed the Bolshevik takeover of Russia in 1917. The Allied intervention in Russia, which entailed capitalist and communist armies killing one another, intensified the demonstration effects from the Russian Revolution and added to the incentives facing the Bolshevik and democratic governments to promote regimes. A smaller wave hit Southeast Asia in the 1960s, as regime instability, fomented by transnational communist networks and aided by the Soviet and Chinese governments, gave the United States incentives to intervene.

The biggest wave—an ex post one—broke during and after the Second World War, when the German, Soviet, and American governments' forces found themselves with powerful incentives to use their occupying troops to install new regimes in conquered lands. These promotions were not simply afterthoughts or epiphenomenal of the war effort. The Nazi, Soviet, and American governments all had choices concerning what to do with the lands their armies occupied. The Nazis allowed Denmark to remain a constitutional monarchy; the Soviets allowed Finland to remain a constitutional democracy. Using troops to impose a regime on an occupied country cost resources and, as all sides knew, risked alienating the other powers. Had the Roosevelt and Truman administrations not made Italy a democracy after 1943, or Stalin not made Bulgaria communist in 1944–45, superpower relations may have been less hostile. But it would have been difficult indeed for them not to do those things. As in previous ideological struggles in previous centuries, transnational polarization was an exceedingly powerful magnet.

Isolated forcible regime promotions also occurred. Among these were Soviet and Italo-German interventions in Spain in 1936 and U.S. interventions in the Caribbean and Latin America in the 1980s. In all of these cases, the intervening government sought to extend or preserve influence by blocking an unfriendly regime. Throughout these decades, as in other long waves, governments also used economic and military support, covert action, and other tools to try to promote one regime or another.

The mechanisms present in previous long waves—regime instability or great-power war triggering transnational ideological polarization, in turn leading governments to use force to promote domestic regimes—were present during the so-called short twentieth century. Revolutions and coups, and the Second World War, excited ideological activism in many countries and sometimes made regime promotion almost irresistible to great powers. As in previous periods, there were also episodes of regime instability or revolution that did not produce any forcible regime promotion. The United States never invaded communist Cuba (although it did virtually everything short of that). There were also cases in which a great-power government did not impose a regime on a conquered land. Stalin did not install a communist regime in Finland in the late 1940s. In such cases, countervailing incentives were too powerful. Even so, dozens of forcible regime promotions took place, demonstrating that governments cared enough about the regime types of other states that they sometimes spent dear resources and risked more to alter or preserve those regimes.

Notwithstanding the important differences in circumstances across these decades, the forcible regime promotions are connected by a strong thread: they took place in states containing elites who were part of transnational ideological networks, and the ideologies that constituted those networks displayed remarkable continuity throughout the period. Communists in Southeast Asia in the 1970s used tropes and symbols similar to those of communists in China in the 1940s and in Russia in the 1910s. Fascists in Hungary in the 1940s were self-consciously similar to fascists in Italy in the 1920s. These continuities point us to a larger ideational structure, the legitimacy crisis facing constitutional governments that gathered steam in the early twentieth century. When the Bolsheviks seized power from a constitutional provisional government in Russia in November 1917, one leading contender for legitimacy became Marxism-Leninism. When Mussolini and his circle took power in constitutional Italy in 1922, fascism became a second contender. Communism and fascism both generated transnational networks of remarkable robustness and energy. *Qua* networks, they were not always coherent or tightly controlled. There was no centralized, effective conspiracy at any point. Governments did attempt to control and exploit them, and Soviet rulers had more success than did Mussolini. What is striking is that, as in previous cases, the ideas to which these networks appealed—their diagnoses and above all their prescriptions for societal ills—had such traction across so many countries for so long. In the communist case, elites in Third World societies far from industrialization nonetheless found the Soviet model inspiring; even those who did not become communists admired the rapid state-building that Stalin had accomplished.

Communism, fascism, and constitutional democracy—the last of which had only weak networks except in the Soviet bloc after the mid-1950s— each had its advocates and exemplars. For decades each had a plausible claim to superiority. The rise of Italy in the 1920s and the far more spectacular rise of Nazi Germany in the 1930s made fascism appear, in the words of Anne Morrow Lindbergh, "the wave of the future."[149] The Soviet Union's rapid industrialization in the 1930s and its indispensable role in crushing Nazi Germany in the early 1940s lent it formidable prestige among elites the world over. Constitutional democracy had the United States, Britain, and France as exemplars in the 1920s and 1930s, and the much more impressive U.S. example from the 1940s onward.

The grand ideological struggle endured as long as no clear winner emerged. The *Götterdämmerung* of 1945 pushed fascism off of the stage. In the 1950s and 1960s, communism appeared to have more momentum than constitutional democracy, particularly in the Third World. Even in the West a school of thought arose about the robustness of communist totalitarianism.[150] The struggle only ended in the late 1980s, when communism's failures to make good on its promises regarding growth and industrialization led the leaders of China and the Soviet Union to abandon it. Constitutional democracies, with their capitalist economies, had clearly outdone communist ones with their command economies. Transnational communism lost its Soviet patronage and its animating energy. Communist guerrillas, particularly Maoists, remained in some countries but had to fund themselves through criminal activity, further undermining their credibility. Social democrats in the Third World had little reason to cooperate with the shrinking, dispirited communists.

There is ample reason to think that constitutional democracy will face more legitimacy crises in the future. Indeed, at the time of this writing a reconstituted socialist authoritarianism, called Bolivarism or Chavism, is enjoying a powerful influence across most Latin American societies. In chapter 8 I discuss possible implications of transnational socialism for U.S. foreign policy and international relations more generally.

# CHAPTER SEVEN

# Mosque and State, 1923–

> We do not consider our principles as dogmas contained in
> books that are said to come from heaven. We derive our
> inspiration, not from heaven, or from an unseen world,
> but directly from life.
>
> —Atatürk, *1937*

> If under the present conditions we manage to create an
> acceptable type of society and set up a model of development,
> progress, evolution, and correct Islamic morals for the world,
> then we will achieve what the world has feared; that is, the
> export of the Islamic revolution.
>
> —Hashemi Rafsanjani, *1988*

## Prologue: Baathists, Khomeinists, and Dueling Regime Promotions, 1979–1980

REZA PAHLAVI, SHAH OF IRAN, and Saddam Hussein, President of Iraq,
had much to fight about. They were immediate neighbors and both
claimed the strategic Shatt al-Arab waterway on the Persian Gulf. Iraq
was Arab, Iran, Persian. Whereas the Shah supported U.S. hegemony in
the region and cooperated with Israel, Saddam leaned toward the Soviets
and sought to lead the Pan-Arab movement. Notwithstanding these serious occasions for conflict, in the 1975 Algiers Agreement Saddam had
relinquished Iraqi claims to the Shatt al-Arab waterway, and the Shah
had ceased supporting Kurdish separatists in Iraq. In September 1977,
as anti-Shah demonstrations were breaking out in various Iranian cities,
Saddam had agreed to the Shah's request to expel the Ayatollah Ruhollah
Khomeini from Najaf, Iraq, from which he was inspiring and directing
the unrest in Iran. This last bit of cooperation points to one common interest of increasing importance. Each despot ruled a country the majority
of whose population was Shia Muslim, and each was attempting to develop his country by means of state-led growth, centralization of power,
and secularization. And therefore the two rulers shared a surprisingly durable and resilient enemy: a transnational, resurgent Shia-Islamism that
insisted on the restoration of religion to its traditional position in society,
a resurgence largely propelled and symbolized by Khomeini.

From Iraq Khomeini went to Paris, from which he continued to stir up and harness political radicalism in Iran. On January 17, 1979, the besieged Shah fled Iran, and two weeks later Khomeini arrived from Paris. It was not yet clear what direction the Iranian Revolution would take, as liberals and Marxists had joined Islamists in ousting the Shah. Islamists themselves were divided between Khomeini's radicals, who sought a *faqih* or clerical regime, and moderates who did not. Mehdi Bazargan, a moderate Islamist, headed the provisional government. Like the Russian Bolsheviks in 1917 (chapter 6), the Khomeinists sought to seize control of the domestic revolution by stirring up revolution abroad. On February 11 Khomeini announced, "We export our revolution to the four corners of the world because our revolution is Islamic; and the struggle will continue until the cry of 'There is no god but Allah, and Muhammad is the messenger of Allah' prevails throughout the world."[1] Khomeini's most immediate target was his former home-in-exile, Iraq. Iraq's territory housed six Shia holy sites.[2] During his sojourn there, Khomeini had become close to Ayatollah Muhammad Baqr al-Sadr, head of the Islamic Call Society (*al-Dawa*), a movement that sought to combat Saddam's Baathist secularism. Now that Khomeini was back in Iran, Sadr sent congratulations and praised his plans to implement a *faqih* regime.

Events in Iran polarized Iraq between those who favored a similar revolution in Iraq and those who did not. Transnational coalitions strengthened and their competition intensified: Khomeini and his circle in Iran and *al Dawa* in Iraq promoted a Shia *faqih* regime in both countries, while the Baathist regime in Baghdad and moderates in Iran opposed such a regime in both. Each faction reached into the other country to try to influence events there, knowing that the outcome in one country would affect the outcome in the other. In June, as Ayatollah Sadr tried to lead a procession to Tehran to congratulate Khomeini, Saddam placed him under house arrest.[3] Shii demonstrated in several Iraqi cities in response, and, as Dilip Hiro writes, "Tehran Radio's Arabic service referred to Sadr as the 'Khomeini of Iraq' and called on the faithful to replace 'the gangsters and tyrants of Baghdad' with 'divine justice'."[4] In July, Saddam submitted to Iraq's figurehead President Ahmed Hassan al-Bakr a list of Islamists, including some in the military, for execution. When Bakr balked, Saddam placed him under arrest and named himself President. At the same time, Saddam tried to keep more Iraqi Shii from joining the Islamists by hinting that his Sunni-led Baath Party would share more power with them and declaring as a national holiday the birthday of one of the Shii's major figures. In March 1980, Saddam had scores of *al Dawa* leaders executed. In retaliation Iraqi Shia Islamists tried to assassinate Tariq Aziz, Saddam's (Christian) deputy, in April. Saddam responded by having Sadr executed. On the same day, Iran's Foreign Minister announced, "We have decided to overthrow the Baathist regime of Iraq."[5] The Khomeinists in Tehran began training Iraqi Shia guerrillas and sending them back to Iraq. Saddam hosted key officials under the deposed Shah and broadcast their propaganda into Iran. These Baghdad-sponsored officials attempted military coups against Khomeini on May 24–25 and again on July 9–10.[6]

With regime change the goal of each for the other, the stakes could rise no higher for either Khomeini or Saddam. In August, Saddam visited the rulers of Saudi Arabia and Kuwait and secured their quiet support for the toppling of Khomeini, by force if necessary. Saudi Arabia was itself an Islamist country, but the Saudi dynasty was Sunni rather than Shia and hence had two strong motives to see the world rid of Khomeinist Iran. Their country's own Eastern Province had a Shia majority, some of whose members were inspired by the Khomeini revolution. And Khomeinist Iran was denouncing the Saudi monarchy as corrupt and unfit to lead the Muslim world, thereby challenging the monarchy's chief claim to legitimacy.[7] By September, Saddam had 50,000 troops massed on the Iranian border and abrogated the 1975 Algiers Agreement: now the Shatt al-Arab, he insisted, was all Iraqi territory. Iraqi forces invaded Iran on September 22, claiming that Iranian forces had attacked first.[8]

Like most bordering states, Iraq and Iran had many conflicts of interest in 1979–80, conflicts that made war a perpetual possibility. But the two states had cooperated for four years. What ruined the cooperation and brought on the Iran-Iraq War, a war that lasted a decade and killed as many as 1.5 million people, was the stated desire of each ruler, Saddam and Khomeini, to overthrow the other's regime. The immediate cause of those mutually conflicting, zero-sum preferences was the Iranian Revolution and establishment of Khomeini's *faqih* regime in Tehran.[9] But the revolution had the effect that it did on Iranian-Iraqi relations because it was embedded within a longer transnational struggle between Islamists and secularists. Secularism was a domestic and foreign danger to Khomeini's vision for Iran. Islamism was a domestic and foreign danger to the Baathist vision for Iraq. The revolution intensified the transnational struggle by heightening the threat to Saddam's regime, which in turn began to threaten Khomeini's regime; the war, in turn, intensified the struggle still more. And the struggle extended far beyond Iran and Iraq; elites in much of the Muslim world had been participating in it for many decades.

## Who Legislates, God or Man?

On its surface, our final case study of a long wave of forcible regime promotion is less spectacular than our first three. It has produced far fewer direct uses of force to promote one regime or another. But as discussed below, there have been a number of such regime impositions, many by outside, non-Muslim powers—most recently, the United States and various allies in Afghanistan and Iraq. As in the cases in chapters 4 through 6, governments in the region have also used other means, including propaganda, economic aid, military training, and covert action, to promote one regime or another. The struggle has been most intense in North Africa and Southwest Asia, and so in this chapter I exclude Southeast Asia, home to hundreds of millions of Muslims.[10]

As with previous long waves of forcible regime promotion, one condition that has helped cause this one is a prolonged transnational ideological struggle among Muslims over the best regime. The struggle is among various types of secularist and various types of Islamist. It is perpetuated by networks of elites that span Muslim states and agitate for one or another of the ideologies. As with earlier transnational struggles, rulers and would-be rulers have attempted to harness these networks and their ideas and turn them to their own ends. At times rulers have found themselves more controlled by than controlling the networks. Rulers take sides in the struggle because their legitimacy is at stake. Like all transnational ideological struggles, that dividing the Muslim world is complex. But the core disagreement concerns the proper source of society's laws and institutions. Ought positive law—the laws of human society—to derive from Islamic law or *Shariah*, that is, divine revelation to the Prophet Muhammad (the Quran) and the sayings and practices of the Prophet (*hadith*)?[11] Or ought positive law to derive from non-religious sources such as autonomous human reason or natural law? If *Shariah*, then which version of Islam, Sunni or Shia, will set the terms? If secular, then should the regime be more like a Western, multiparty one or the single-party one exemplified by Nasser's Egypt? Map 7.1 displays majority-Muslim states according to the degree to which law derives from each source. Some states, such as Turkey, have entirely secular law; others, such as Saudi Arabia, entirely divine; others, such as Egypt and Afghanistan, mixed constitutions; still others, such as Nigeria and Pakistan, vary by province or region.[12]

Unlike the struggles analyzed in chapters 4 through 6, that cutting across the Muslim world is ongoing at the time of this writing and seriously affects relations among sovereign states, including non-Muslim states such as the United States. The intra-Muslim contest over the best regime may yet have a long life ahead. The struggle is seen in the persistent eruptions of legitimacy crises in countries and provinces whose populations contain significant proportions of Muslims. Across time and space, these crises have a common shape. Actors who have diverse discontents with diverse causes nonetheless appeal to common sets of symbols and present themselves as participating in a single battle that others past and present have waged. In the early years of the struggle, from the 1920s through

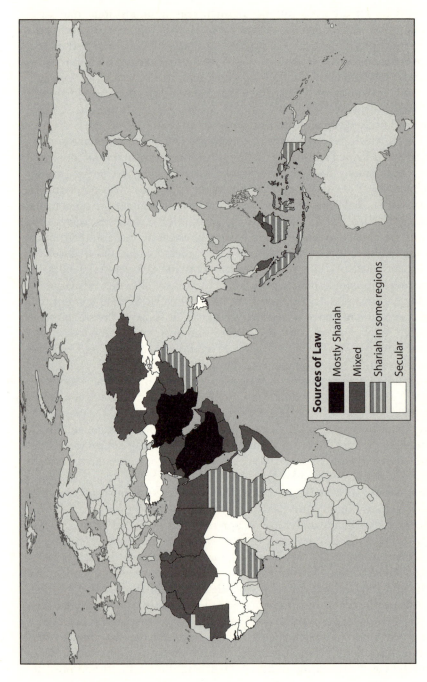

MAP 7.1. Islamism v. Secularism in heavily Muslim countries, 2009
*Source*: Central Intelligence Agency, World Factbook, https://www.cia.gov/library/publications/the-world-factbook/

the 1960s, secularism had the wind at its back and traditional Islam was in retreat. The wind reversed direction in the 1970s, as discontented intellectuals and army officers began to find in Islamism—an ideology reformulating traditional Islamic society—an articulation of their discontents and a set of prescriptions. The contest originated in the late nineteenth and early twentieth centuries as Muslim elites grappled with their societies' clear decline vis-à-vis the West. In more recent decades, a crucial test of legitimacy among many Muslim elites (and masses), particularly in the Middle East, has become which regime type is better able to damage Israel. From 1948 until 1967, secularism appeared better equipped to destroy Israel; since that time Islamism has assumed that position.

During this ongoing grand struggle, when one country appears on the verge of changing from a secular to an Islamist regime, or when there is a contest between Sunni and Shia Islamists, demonstration effects appear in other countries and actors polarize according to whether or not they favor the change. Elites then have stronger incentives to thwart ideological foes in neighboring countries. The ideological struggle has come to dominate not only majority-Muslim countries stretching from West Africa to Southeast Asia, but also affects the millions of Muslims in India and Western Europe. It also affects the United States owing to America's global power, particularly in the Middle East, and its status as an exemplar of secularism. Many Islamists consider America the "far enemy" because they believe it keeps the "near enemy"—secularist and apostate Muslims—in power in Muslim countries.

Why isolate Islamism, when other major religions also contain anti-secularist movements? What Gilles Kepel calls the "revenge of God"—the resurgence of religion in defiance of the expectations of social science—has been at work among Christians, Jews, Hindus, and others since the 1970s.[13] But thus far only Muslims have been able to activate a transnational movement that has captured states and bids to capture more. Notwithstanding the rhetorical efforts of some religious conservatives such as Dinesh D'Souza[14] and secularists such as Andrew Sullivan,[15] there is no Religious or Anti-Secular International and will almost certainly never be one. The connections among conservatives or radicals in each religion are weak; Islamists draw little or no comfort from the successes of the Christian Right in America (who, in any case, do not seek to overthrow the American regime of constitutional democracy, but simply to reform it); orthodox Jews in Israel are not dejected at the setbacks suffered by Hindutva in India.

Like all the transnational movements in this book, Islamism and secularism are complex and multiform. Islamists may be Sunni or Shia, monarchist or republican, left- or right-wing.[16] Broadly speaking, Islamists agree that for Muslims to live piously their laws and institutions must model and enforce piety; Islam, Arabic for "submission," applies to society as well as the individuals within it. Thus, Islamists cannot accept the notion that religion is a private matter or that the public realm must be secular. Nor can they accept, in the long run, life in a society constructed by some alternative religion such as Christianity or Hinduism. Secularist Muslims, for their part, vary in militancy. The aggressive atheism of communism sought to eliminate revealed religion, sometimes by direct coercion. Most Muslim secularist regimes have instead sought to tame religion by fashioning a Hobbesian state that controls religious training and regulates practice.

By no means are all Muslims Islamists; indeed, that is what I mean when I argue that the Muslim world is in a prolonged period of ideological strife. Many Muslim elites in some countries, and most in a few, are secularists who accept the legitimacy of law deriving from extra-Islamic sources. Among the Islamists, not all are radicals or terrorists. Some, such as Turkey's *Adalet ve Kalkinma Partisi* (AKP) or Justice and Development Party, have evidently embraced constitutional democracy and the European Union's list of human rights. (Indeed, it is not clear whether the AKP qualifies as Islamist.) Some Islamists, sometimes called religious nationalists, seek revolution in their own country as the only route to *Shariah*.[17] The most radical Islamists are internationalists, aiming to destroy the nation-states that divide the Muslim world and to re-establish the caliphate. For internationalist Islamists, religious nationalists satisfied with *Shariah* in their native Egypt or Lebanon are missing the point: the restoration of pristine Islam requires a united Islamic empire under the rule of the legitimate successor to the Prophet Muhammad. As with previous transnational movements, Islamism attracts people with diverse grievances, some contradictory. Especially attracted in many lands are the poor and their advocates, who see a restoration of traditional institutions as a route to greater equality.

The extremists are sustained to some extent by the latent sympathies of some of the moderates, who admire the activism if not the methods of the extremists. In times of high polarization, when middle ground is disappearing, moderates feel compelled to sympathize with the extremists against the common foe, and differences among Islamists and among secularists disappear.

## Emergence of the Structure: Traditional Islam's Crisis, 1830–1923

Islamism today is typically labeled radical, but in the Islamists' own telling it is restorationist, aiming to re-establish the old regime against the radical innovations of the secularists. From the Middle Ages through the

TABLE 7.1
Forcible Promotions of Secularism or Islamism, 1958–2005

| Year | Target | Intervener | Against | For |
|------|--------|-----------|---------|-----|
| 1958 | Lebanon | U.S. | Secular (Arabist) | Secular (pluralist) |
| 1958 | Jordan | Britain | Secular (Arabist) | Islamist (monarchy) |
| 1962 | N. Yemen | Egypt | Islamist (monarchy) | Secular (Arabist) |
| 1975 | Lebanon | Israel | Secular (Arabist) | Secular (pluralist) |
| 1976 | Lebanon | Syria | Secular (Arabist) | Secular (pluralist) |
| 1979 | Afghanistan | USSR | Islamist | Secular (communist) |
| 1980 | Iran | Iraq | Secular (Arabist) | Islamist (Shia) |
| 1980 | Iraq | Iran | Islamist (Shia) | Secular |
| 2001 | Afghanistan | U.S. et al. | Islamist (Sunni) | Secular (democratic) |
| 2003 | Iraq | U.S. et al. | Secular (Arabist) | Secular (democratic) |

nineteenth century, the Muslim world accepted that the only legitimate regime was the theocracy established by the Prophet Muhammad in the seventh century A.D. Muslims were certainly divided politically. Competition was common among ethnic groups, branches of the faith, and of course tribes, families, and individual leaders. Muslims differed over whether the ruler is the sole interpreter of the law (as the Shii held) or whether he should consult jurists (as the Sunni held). But Muslims agreed that the proper regime was a theocracy. The original Islamic regime was a unified *umma* (community) under the temporal and spiritual rule of a single man, the caliph, successor to the Prophet. As sultans, temporal monarchs, came to assume de facto power in the caliphate, Islamic jurists developed theories legitimating their rule. Al-Ghazali (1058–1111) argued that if necessary the ruler could be someone other than the legitimate caliph as long as he enforced *Shariah*. For Ibn Taymiyya (1263–1328), the ruler must consult with a council of (religious) scholars when interpreting the law. Ibn Khaldun (1333–1406) dealt with the development of states within the *umma* and argued that a pious regime of *Shariah* was possible even then.

Common to all of these theories of authority was an absence of recognition of a secular realm of life, one separate in some sense from spiritual or transcendent reality. Hence, mosque and state could not be divided. Islam, "submission" to God, was not simply a plan for the individual to achieve paradise in the afterlife, but also a plan for a community or *umma* in this life made harmonious by the obedience of all to *Shariah*. This community required enforcement of *Shariah*, however, and hence a central coercive authority—a state. As Albert Hourani writes: "in the Muslim *umma* power was a delegation by God (*wiyala*) controlled by His will and directed to the happiness of Muslims in the next world even more than in this." Thus in the eighteenth century, when some Ottoman military officers and diplomats began pushing for Western-style reforms to strengthen their empire, the political leadership was concerned not to relinquish *Shariah*. History was the divinely directed movement from the rule of ignorance (*jahiliyya*), in the form of traditional tribal and monarchical rule, to that of knowledge, in the form of this Islamic state. During the Umayyad caliphate (660–750), the *umma* regressed toward human tendencies for rulership and became internally divided. During the Abbasid caliphate that followed (750,1258), writes Hourani, "the principles of the *umma* were reasserted and embodied in the institutions of a universal empire, regulated by law, based on the equality of all believers, and enjoying the power, wealth, and culture which are the reward of obedience." Ever since, Sunni thinkers have looked to a restoration of the golden age rather than a progressive improvement in the human condition.[18]

Traditional Islamic theocracy was tolerant of the Jews and Christians who lived under its rule. Adherents of these older religions, whose sacred texts Muslims revered, were "people of the book," with valid (if incomplete) divine revelation, entitled to their own worship and the ruler's protection as long as they paid a special tax. In the mature Ottoman Empire, the Sultan invested Jewish and Christian leaders with political authority over their respective communities, granting them virtual autonomy in return for loyalty and the poll tax. But Islamic regimes were not secular in the modern sense: the ruler had the burden to enforce orthodoxy among Muslims.[19]

*Secularism and the Muslim World in the Nineteenth Century*

It was the slow but unmistakable decay of the Ottoman Empire that produced the crisis of the old theocratic order. Western ideas and institutions came to appear more attractive to Ottoman officials as imperial decline began to ensue in the seventeenth century. It was then that the economic and political effects of European colonization in Asia and the Americas came to be felt. Ottoman trade routes were disrupted and prices rose. The Turks had to import from the West military innovations such as firearms and fortification techniques. The notion began to take hold among many Turkish elites that Muslim greatness would return not with closer fidelity to the past but with the adoption of new technologies and practices of the now-predominant West. Eighteenth-century sultans tried piecemeal reforms. Selim III (r. 1789–1807) initiated a systematic reform of his military with help from French officers. Selim was overthrown by conservatives, but under his successor Mahmud II (r. 1808–39) there developed a cohort of military officers and diplomats with extensive contacts in Europe, determined to make the empire more Western in order to save it from Western domination. The empire must be centralized under rationalized administration, including a professional army officer corps and the equality of all subjects under the law.[20]

At the same time, among Arab elites ruled by the Ottomans Western ideas were taking hold following Napoleon's 1798 conquest of Egypt. Muhammad Ali, Ottoman Viceroy of Egypt (r. 1805–48), carried out modernizations similar to those of Mahmud II, including legal equality for adherents of all religions. Arabs studied in Europe and became acquainted with Voltaire, Rousseau, Montesquieu, and other Enlightenment thinkers. Many of these Arabs were Christians from the Levant, and so their immediate effect on Islamic culture was limited. But as the century progressed, many Arab intellectuals—Muslim and Christian alike—began to argue that secularization was the route to an Arab revival. They brought the Western Enlightenment and its skepticism about traditional religion to the Arab world.[21]

Ottoman decay accelerated as the nineteenth century progressed. The threat of dissolution signaled by Greek independence in 1832 led the Empire's rulers to attempt to modernize and rationalize their empire along Western lines. During the Tanzimat period (1839–76) the Sultan extended equal legal rights to all subjects regardless of religion, in hopes that the 25 percent who were not Muslim would have less reason to follow the Greeks' lead. This liberalism was gradually reversed during the Hamidian period (1876–1908), which foreshadowed the full-blown Islamism that was to come later. Resurgent Western imperialism in the 1880s generated an Islamic reaction: it must be the case, reasoned many intellectuals, that infidels rule Muslims because Muslims have strayed from the correct path.[22] These concerns, along with a desire to deflate growing Arab ethnic consciousness (itself due to Western influence), led Sultan Abdul Hamid (r. 1876–1909) to renew the traditional emphases on his role as caliph and the Islamic character of the empire.[23] In some ways Abdul Hamid reenacted the enlightened absolutism of eighteenth-century Europe (chapter 5) by attempting to centralize power and rationalize society based upon a religious claim to legitimacy. He built a railway from Damascus to Medina to facilitate pilgrims on the *hajj*.[24] Although Jews, Christians, and other religious minorities continued to enjoy legal equality with Muslims, and the Sultan enjoyed little de facto authority over much of the empire outside of the cities, the regime remained a traditional theocracy, with Sultan as caliph and *Shariah* as law.[25]

By the turn of the twentieth century, traditional Islam's political regime lay in ruins. Most of the Muslim world was divided among European empires: the French, Spanish, and Italian (North Africa), British (South Asia and Malaya and, with the Ottomans, Egypt and the Sudan), Russian (central Asia), and Dutch (the East Indies). Persia and Egypt were semi-autonomous and the Ottoman Empire itself continued its formal rule over most of the Middle East. But the empire continued to decompose. In 1878, under the Treaty of Berlin, Austria-Hungary had begun to administer Bosnia-Herzegovina; in 1881, France occupied Tunisia. Fearing dissent from Westernizing reformers, Abdul Hamid suspended the 1876 constitution, censored the press, and employed a secret police force. In response, reformers in the universities and military academies formed secret societies analogous to the old Italian *carbonari* (chapter 5).[26] From Paris and Berlin, expatriate dissenters published pamphlets denouncing the Sultan's backward autocracy.[27] Dissenters were opposed to more than simply theocracy; the old religio-political institutions were one part of a more general problem with the Ottoman Empire. Their solutions comprised more than simply secularism, or separating mosque from state. But inasmuch as secularism entailed decreasing the power of clergy and the normativity of tradition, it was integral to their program of strengthening Muslim society against Western imperialism, and it proved the most polarizing aspect of that program.

### The End of the Caliphate and the Muslim World's First Secular Regime, 1908–1923

One reformist secret society founded by Mehmet Talaat, Minister of the Interior, grew into the Young Turkey Party. A number of junior army officers, including Enver Pasha, joined the Young Turks, and in July 1908 the group seized power in Constantinople and imposed a constitutional monarchy, relegating the Sultan to a figurehead. The Young Turks were modernizers, committed to technological development, secularism, and nationalism.[28] For several years they shared power with more liberal modernizers, and then took control of the Ottoman imperial apparatus. The Young Turks found in Germany a great-power sponsor to protect their empire from foreign attack. During the First World War they fought alongside the Germans and Austrians. The British, helped by Colonel T. E. Lawrence, tried to weaken the modernizing Ottomans by encouraging Arab nationalism, but a revolt by the Emir of Mecca in June 1916 failed.

Following the defeat of the Central Powers in November 1918, General Mustafa Kemal, the Ottomans' hero of Gallipoli, assumed power over much of Anatolia. While the Allies met in London in February 1920 to decide the fate of the Ottoman Empire, Kemal consolidated power among Young Turks in the middle ranks of the army and Muslim clergy, who were unaware of his strong secularist leanings. Kemal revolted against the new Sultan and repeatedly defeated French forces fighting on the Sultan's behalf. An anti-communist, Kemal nonetheless accepted aid from the young Bolshevik regime in Russia.[29] Kemal abolished the 700-year-old Osmanli sultanate in 1922, and in October 1923 the Republic of Turkey was declared.

Kemal, later known to the world as Atatürk, not only ended the caliphate but carried earlier Westernizing reforms much further, aggressively weakening Islam's influence in Turkish society. Writes William Cleveland: "Secularism was a central element in Atatürk's platform, and the impatient Westernizer pursued it with a thoroughness unparalleled in modern Islamic history." As a Turkish nationalist, Atatürk was by definition a secularist: nation-states had no place in traditional Islam. But he also took concrete steps to shrink the role of Islam in public life. He abolished the office of sheikh al-Islam, closed all religious schools, and abolished the government's religious ministry. Sunday replaced Friday as the day of rest. Atatürk had the Quran translated into Turkish and required the calls to prayer to be in Turkish rather than traditional Arabic.[30] He replaced *Shariah* with the Swiss Civil Code, banned the fez and discouraged the veiling of women, replaced the Arabic with the Roman alphabet for the Turkish language, and constructed a secular nationalist ideology, Kemalism. Although Islam was by no means banished, it was no longer to be a pole of loyalty to compete with the state; rather, it was under the control of the secular state. The *ulema* lost prestige and influence and their numbers dwindled.[31]

Atatürk's cultural revolution enjoyed demonstration effects in much of the Muslim world, attracting admiration from intellectuals, lawyers, and military officers in country after country. It was in Iran, a country that had been relatively impervious to Western ideas in the nineteenth century, that Kemalism had its greatest immediate effects. During the First World War Iran had been occupied by British and Russian troops. The latter withdrew after the 1917 revolution but the British remained and sought to reorganize society to their advantage; much of the countryside was run by competing tribes. Reza Khan was a talented army colonel who seized power in February 1921. By 1926, he had become Shah and established the new Pahlavi dynasty.

Reza Shah (r. 1926–41), writes Cleveland, "borrowed many of his programs directly from the Kemalist experience." He reformed and expanded Iran's army and established a large state bureaucracy. Like Atatürk, Reza Shah was a thoroughgoing secularist. The scope of *Shariah* was reduced to family law, with a code modeled on the French governing civil disputes. State courts were created and their secular-trained judges given the power to decide which cases were in the jurisdiction of the *ulema*. The *ulema* themselves were now trained and licensed by the state, and the state founded the secular Tehran University to foster a non-religious intelligentsia. In the 1930s, laws were passed requiring men to dress like Westerners and forbidding women to wear the *chador* or veil. Iranian nationalism was emphasized, pan-Islamism discouraged.[32]

In the Arab world, however, such radical secularization was still decades away. The collapse of the Ottoman Empire led to the creation of the Arab states of Syria, Lebanon, Palestine, Iraq, Transjordan, Hijaz, and Yemen. Only the last two enjoyed full independence in the Middle East; the others were League of Nations "mandates," ruled by France or Britain until such time, said the League, as they could govern themselves. The typical pattern was for the British or French to strike bargains with local elites that involved some modernizing reforms but not the radical regime changes of Turkey or Iran. In the Levant, under French mandate, Lebanon was created as a "confessional" state, essentially secular but dominated by Christians (Maronite Catholics).[33] Egypt gained nominal independence from Britain in 1922 owing to the efforts of the Wafd Party, an organization of landed gentry and lawyers, many of whom had been educated in Europe. From 1924 to 1936, Egypt was a constitutional monarchy whose parliament was dominated by the Wafd Party. Cleveland writes of the "diminution of religious values and religious institutions in the regulation of legal affairs and personal relationships" under Wafd governance. A liberal Egyptian elite flourished that emphasized the country's pre-Islamic heritage ("pharaonism") and its Mediterranean aspect. A robust feminist movement was founded in 1923.[34]

*The Traditionalists' Reaction and the Emergence of Islamism*

Traditional Islam remained predominant in the Arab world through the 1950s. In Jordan and Iraq, the House of Hashemite—which traced its lineage to the Prophet Muhammad's tribe—ruled and kept in place traditional institutions. And Islamic resistance to modernization was flourishing on the Arabian peninsula. In 1902, Abd al-Aziz ibn Saud (1876–1953) had seized the city of Riyadh from the family's rivals, the Rashidis. Over the next two decades, Ibn Saud conquered much of the peninsula, establishing the Kingdom of Saudi Arabia (and erasing the Kingdom of Hijaz) in 1932. Ibn Saud's success came not only from military prowess but also from the legitimacy conferred upon him by his status as head of the Wahhabi movement within Sunni Islam. In the eighteenth century, Abd al-Wahhab and the House of Saud had become permanently joined. Founded by Muhammad ibn abd-Al Wahhab (1703–92), Wahhabism has been compared to Calvinism in Christianity (see chapter 4). Wahhabists reject various accretions of tradition in Islam that, as they would have it, detract from pure monotheism. They reject any mediating role for saints between the believer and Allah. Claiming to recapture the primitive religion as revealed to the Prophet, they call themselves Salafists, or those who return to the earlier generations.[35] Ibn Saud capitalized on this integral relationship by propagating Wahhabism to the tribes and requiring their shaikhs to attend a religious institute in Riyadh. In return he provided their tribes with farming supplies and weapons. Thus, Ibn Saud made local leaders loyal subjects with a transcendent mission: to spread the pure, rigorous Wahhabist form of Islam throughout the peninsula.[36]

At the same time, in those countries where secularism was making inroads, Islamists began quietly to mobilize in reaction. The *ulema* understood that secularization had a great deal of elite support, and so chiefly criticized its detrimental effects on Muslims' piety. In Sunni Egypt, the Muslim Brotherhood was founded in 1928 by Hassan al-Banna. Branches of the Brotherhood appeared in subsequent years in other Arab countries. The Egyptian Rashid Rida (1865–1935) founded a journal, *al-Manar* (*The Beacon*), urging the preservation of Islamic tradition. From Switzerland Amir Shakib Arslan (1869–1946), a Lebanese Druze exiled by the French, propagated the notion that freedom from imperialism would come with a return to traditional Islam. "A staunch opponent of Atatürk, Arslan wrote that the callous disregard of cultural tradition would undermine the spiritualism that made Eastern civilization superior to the shallow materialism of the West," writes Cleveland.[37] Among the Shii in Iran the young Ruhollah Khomeini and other clergy quietly taught and wrote against the Shah's effacing of the divinely ordained order of society.[38] These early Islamists proclaimed loyalty to their nation's regimes and in general worked within the system for reform; like the secularists, they sought independence from European (i.e., infidel) colonialism. But their teachings were nonetheless subversive of the secularist project. Khomeini and other Shia Islamists practiced *taqiyya*, or dissimulation, to avoid persecution.[39]

Thus, in the second quarter of the twentieth century elites in many societies of the Middle East were polarizing over whether secularism or Islamism presented the better account of what success entailed and how to achieve it. Until the 1950s, however, neither secularists nor Islamists carried out any forcible regime promotions. Although rulers had some incentives to export their regimes, those incentives were outweighed by familiar incentives not to attack neighbors. Saudi Arabia was the chief exemplar of traditional Islam, but it was militarily weak. Secular Turkey and Iran were stronger, but the hegemony of outside powers—the British and French between the world wars, the Americans and Soviets after 1945—suppressed the possibility of Atatürk's or the Shah's using force to spread secularism. Things were to change, however, with the eruption of radical secular ideology in the Arab world in the form of Gamal Abdul

Nasser's regime in Egypt. Nasserism exacerbated polarization in Arab societies between traditionalists and secularists, making both more militant. Indeed, Nasser's brutal suppression of the Muslim Brothers helped transform traditional Islamic resistance to secularism into militant Islamism. In so doing, Nasserism created threats and opportunities for the rulers of these societies.

### Nasserism's Demonstration Effects, 1950s

Decolonization in the Muslim world following the Second World War ushered more secular regimes into the Muslim world. In British India, Muhammad Ali Jinnah had been inspired by Atatürk's transformation and renewal of Turkish society.[40] Jinnah went on to found Pakistan as a secular Muslim state, in which Islam was an ethnic marker rather than the comprehensive way of life it had traditionally been. In Arab societies secularism also took hold in the form of Arab nationalism. A diverse phenomenon, Arab nationalism, like Kemalism, sought to modernize Muslim societies by rationalizing administration and centralizing power in the state, which in turn entailed reducing the independent influence of the clergy. Like European nationalisms of the nineteenth century, Arab nationalism recognized a spiritual as well as material element, and was propelled among elites by a transnational set of intellectuals, including Taha Hussein of Egypt, Sati al-Husri of Yemen, and Michel Aflaq of Syria, founder of the Baathist (Renaissance) movement (and a Christian).[41]

Arab nationalism's most important advocate was Nasser, who ruled Egypt from 1954 until 1970. Nasser had been an Egyptian army officer during Israel's 1948 war with Arab forces. Following the Arabs' defeat, Nasser and his clique of officers set out to modernize Egypt. The Muslim Brotherhood aligned with him out of common hatred of both British imperialism and Soviet communism, and cooperated in overthrowing the Egyptian monarchy in 1952 and establishing a new republic. But with the common enemy vanquished, the divergence of the secularist and Islamist visions for Egypt became difficult to ignore; each began to threaten the other. In January 1954, Nasser dissolved the Brotherhood.[42] On the surface Nasser appeared to be strengthening Islam in Egypt by building more mosques, supporting al-Azhar University in Cairo, and making religion compulsory in school examinations. But Nasser altered traditional Islam by removing it from the control of the *ulema* and bringing it under the sway of the Egyptian state. He abolished the private *Shariah* courts in 1955.[43] He successfully co-opted leading *ulema* and al-Azhar University, the ancient and prestigious center of Islamic scholarship. Following the general Muslim secularist line, Nasser recast Islam as a religion suitable for modern state-led development.[44] As Barnett Rubin writes, "the regime did not abandon the potent power of religion to its enemies [the Muslim Brotherhood], seeking instead to re-interpret and dominate Islam as a pillar for its own rule."[45]

Nasser's early program concerned Egypt primarily, but he clearly saw advantages to the spread of his regime to other societies. When the Algerian war of independence broke out in November 1954, he provided support and training for the rebels in their struggle against the French. At the 1955 Bandung Conference that launched the Nonaligned Movement, Nasser was recognized as the leader of Arab anti-colonialism.[46] His prestige rose further with his successful defiance (with American help) of the Israelis, British, and French in the 1956 Suez crisis. Nasser turned his humiliation of imperialists and Zionists to his advantage, and Nasserism became the leading form of pan-Arabism, enjoying momentum among intellectuals, military officers, and others throughout the Arab world, including within the conservative monarchies of the Arabian peninsula.[47] Propaganda broadcasts from Radio Cairo called for the overthrow of corrupt and weak monarchical regimes.[48] Nasserism was to find a kindred movement to Egypt's east in Baathism, whose program was similar. In the republic of Syria, where a majority of army officers were Baathist, the government sought political union with Egypt. Nasser granted it and the United Arab Republic (UAR) was born on February 1, 1958.[49]

## A Short Wave of Forcible Regime Promotions, 1958

The sudden spread of Nasserism into Syria implicated the interests of the United States and Soviet Union and led to two forcible regime promotions. Already in the 1950s the Cold War had spread to the Middle East, with both superpowers courting rulers and political movements. The United States had organized the Baghdad Pact in February 1955, comprising Iraq, Turkey, Iran, Pakistan, and Britain. Nasser sought to maintain a nonaligned stance, frequently consulting Tito of Yugoslavia for advice. He courted both the American and Soviet governments, seeking to extract maximum benefit by playing the two off against one another. It was a desire not to alienate Nasser and the Arab world in general that led Eisenhower to back Egypt in the Suez Crisis. Nasser also made the most of Khrushchev's desire for the Soviet Union to lead the "wars of national liberation" (chapter 6). Notwithstanding Egypt's putative nonalignment and Nasser's persecution of Egyptian communists, he was anti-British and -French; insofar as his movement eroded Western influence, its spread was a net gain for the Soviet Union. On July 14, inspired by their confreres in Syria, Baathists in Baghdad carried out a coup d'état, overthrowing the Hashemite monarchy of Faysal II. Although Nasser was not involved in the coup, Iraqis waved his picture in victory parades and the new Iraqi rulers immediately asked that Iraq be allowed to join the UAR.[50] The new Arab-nationalist Iraq quickly withdrew from the Baghdad Pact.[51] The spread of secularism was a net gain for the Soviets and a corresponding loss for the Americans.

The Syrian accession to the UAR had demonstration effects in other Arab countries as well. In Jordan and Lebanon Arab nationalists began to press for regime change and membership in the UAR as well. Lebanon was not a traditional Islamic state but rather a republic with a secular regime dominated by Christians. Although Arab nationalism was not originally Muslim per se—Michel Aflaq, the Syrian founder of Baathism, was a Christian—Lebanese Muslims discontented with their subordinate status latched onto it as a formula for empowerment. When President Camille Chamoun refused to seek membership in the UAR, rebels seized large parts of Lebanese territory and demanded Chamoun's resignation. Chamoun requested U.S. intervention, and on July 15, U.S. Marines began to land on Lebanese beaches. Around 10,000 U.S. forces eventually arrived.[52] Jordan's monarchy, being of the same Hashemite dynasty as Iraq's had been, was in deeper jeopardy. King Hussein asked for British intervention, and on July 17–18 some 2,400 British paratroopers entered the country to safeguard the regime.[53] Saïd Aburish writes that "there is little doubt that both countries would have fallen to pro-Nasser forces without the American and British presence."[54]

## Nasserism and Militant Islamism

Just as Lutheranism and Calvinism prodded Catholicism to become more mobilized and militant (chapter 4), Nasserism prodded traditional Islamists into a more assertive and precise ideology. Islamism became more militant through two overlapping pathways—one through rulers who formed and ran networks, particularly the Saudi dynasty, and another through the transnational Muslim Brotherhood.

King Saud (r. 1953–64) was quick to see the threat that Nasserism posed to his own Islamist regime. For decades the desert kingdom was famously closed to the outside world, but the discovery of oil led to its partial opening at the elite level. Requiring trained engineers and civil servants loyal to the regime, the Saudi government in the 1950s began sending young men to Europe and North America to study and young military officers to train in Egypt. These returned to Saudi Arabia not only with technical expertise but also with secularist political ideas. In 1955, a group of Egyptian-trained Saudi military officers plotted to overthrow the monarchy, just as Nasser had done in Egypt three years earlier; the plot was foiled but sent shock waves through the royal family.[55] Notwithstanding this ideological threat, for several years Saud cultivated good relations with Nasser out of common opposition to the Hashemite dynasty that ruled Iraq and Jordan (a competitor with the House of Saud for prestige among Muslims). Saudi-Egyptian relations deteriorated sharply from late 1956, as Saud began to see that Nasser's persecutions of the Muslim Brothers and socialist pan-Arab vision contradicted his dynasty's entire system. Saud began to tilt toward the Hashemites as potential allies against Nasserism, and in 1957 he visited King Faysal II in Baghdad. The following year, when Faysal was overthrown by allies of Nasser (see above), an attempt by a Syrian to assassinate Nasser was traced to the Saudis.[56]

The Saudis continued to go on the ideological offensive in the early 1960s, organizing an anti-revolutionary bloc to subvert the secularist regimes. [57] In May 1962, Saudi Prince Faysal organized a conference at Mecca to discuss how to combat secularism and socialism. The result was the Muslim World League, an international educational and cultural organization. The League ever since has promoted Wahhabism around the world. Working through Saudi embassies, the Muslim World League has supported Muslim Brothers in various Arab countries and Islamist movements in South Asia and Africa. It has combated Nasserism, Baathism, and other secular movements as well as Sufism and other forms of Islam considered heretical by Wahhabis. In 1972, the Saudis founded the World Assembly of Muslim Youth, which works among young Muslims to serve the same purposes.

Perhaps the most lasting consequence of Nasserism was its radicalization of the Muslim Brotherhood. Nasser imprisoned and tortured many Muslim Brothers. (The Saudis interceded with Nasser on behalf of many and gave asylum to those who fled Egypt.)[58] Among the imprisoned was Sayid Qutb (1906–66), the movement's leading intellectual.[59] Qutb spent most of the last twelve years of his life in prison and was ultimately hanged for treason in 1966. His time in prison, along with his earlier years of study in the United States (1948–51), led him to elaborate a deep critique of modern secular society as a version of paganism. "Our whole environment," wrote Qutb, "people's beliefs and ideas, habits and art, rules and laws—is *jahiliyah* [infidelity or ignorance] even to the extent that what we consider to be Islamic culture, Islamic sources, Islamic philosophy, and Islamic thought, are also constructs of *jahiliyah*."[60]

Required, argued Qutb, was a return to pure Islam, meaning a strict, literal application of *Shariah* to society. In turn, this return required the formation of a force capable of pushing back the secular juggernaut:

> The Muslim society cannot come into existence simply as a creed in the hearts of individual Muslims, however numerous they may be, unless they become an active, harmonious, and cooperative group, distinct by

itself, whose different elements, like the limbs of a human body, work together for its support and expansion, and for its defense against those elements that attack its system. This group must work under a leadership that is independent of the *jahiliyyah* so it can organize its various efforts in support of one harmonious purpose, and strengthen and widen the Muslims' Islamic character in order to abolish the negative influences of *jahili* life.[61]

Following Qutb's execution in 1966, the Muslim Brothers debated precisely what Qutb meant for this separate, pure entity to do: to work within existing institutions, or to overthrow and replace them? The separatism of Qutb, however, was clear. Pious Muslims could no longer continue to participate in secular, impious society.[62] The years of secularist triumph were in fact years of deep, quiet polarization within Egypt, in which Islamists and secularists became mortal enemies.

### The Saudis versus Nasser in Yemen, 1960s

With Islamism no longer simply a conservative way of life but now a vibrant competing ideology, it was to pull the Egyptians and Saudis into competing forcible interventions in North Yemen. In September 1962, Imam Ahmad died and his son Muhammad al-Badr assumed the throne. Junior army officers, aided by the Nasser government, quickly deposed al-Badr and declared a Yemeni Arab Republic. Egyptian troops began to pour into Yemen to support the republic against al-Badr's forces; by the middle of 1963, 30,000 Egyptian soldiers and advisers were in country; by the next year the number had swollen to 40,000.[63] The Saudis saw the young secular republic on their southern border as a sign that Nasserism was spreading and responded by arming the royalists. As Paul Dresch writes, "a fiery front dividing the whole Arab world now ran through Sanaa with on one side the Arab monarchies, most importantly Saudi Arabia, and on the other Egypt."[64] The Cold War and European colonialism were overlaid onto the conflict. The British, who ruled southern Yemen and were fighting an insurgency there (chapter 6), joined the Saudis in supporting the Yemeni royalists. In November, Nasser announced the formation of a National Liberation Army to liberate Yemen from al-Badr's forces. The war was to persist until 1970. (The Yemeni civil war's demonstration effects helped trigger a rebellion in the Dhofar region of neighboring Oman; the Dhofar revolt took a Marxist turn and is treated in chapter 6.)

Although the Islamists—the Saudis, the Muslim Brotherhood—were fighting back, there is no question about secularism's forward momentum during these years. Secularist governments could suppress Islamists and risk driving some of them toward radicalism because Islamist ideas had little purchase in the universities or among average people. In the words of Kepel: "At that time it was thought—mistakenly—that secularization was a straightforward, unstoppable process, in the Muslim world as elsewhere. Islam was regarded as an outmoded belief held only by rural dotards and backward reactionaries." Most dissenters from these regimes latched onto Marxism-Leninism, not Islam, and criticized the governments for betraying socialism.[65]

## Islamism Seizes the Momentum, 1967

In June 1967 Nasser finally overreached, and secularism in the Muslim world has never recovered. Intending to demonstrate his secular pan-Arabism's superiority once and for all, Nasser and the governments of Syria and Jordan determined to destroy Israel, reversing the humiliation that the weak traditional Arab regimes had suffered in 1948. Israel's stunning defeat of these three larger nations showed that the balance of power in the Middle East was not as all had supposed: under Nasser's leadership the Arabs remained weaker than tiny Israel. Waiting in the wings to articulate the crisis and prescribe a solution were the Islamists, who had been predicting Arab socialism's failure all along. The Muslim Brothers propagated their narrative that the fundamental problem was that Muslims had abandoned the true path, and the fundamental solution was Islam—not Nasser's Hobbesian version of a religion run by a secular state, but pristine Islam, untainted by ideas and institutions from the West. Writes Kepel: "A fault line—initially secular in origin—then opened up across the various societies concerned, demolishing the political consensus which had experienced no such shock since independence."[66] James Piscatori adds several other mechanisms for the supplanting of secularism by Islamism: the modernizing process itself uprooted people, chiefly by encouraging them to move from the countryside to cities such as Cairo, Damascus, and Tehran, and Islamism provided them with moral and material support; modernization simultaneously increased the ability for elites to communicate and mobilize actors, which benefited Islamists; and, in order to co-opt devout Muslims, all along the secularists had used Islamic language and symbols to legitimize their rule, thereby implicitly acknowledging the normative power of the religion in public life.[67]

The sudden weakness of the secularists is clear in their attempts to embrace certain aspects of traditional Islam. Nasser's and other Arab secularist regimes struck a new bargain with the Islamists: they would halt their secularizing efforts at home and abroad in return for Saudi aid and a united Arab front against Israel. The Arab League summit in Khartoum, August 29–September 1, 1967, ended in the famous "three noes" declaration: no peace with, recognition of, or negotiations with Israel.[68] Nasser withdrew Egypt from Yemen and ceased all efforts to destabilize Islamist regimes.[69] His protégé and successor Anwar Sadat, who took power in 1970, went further and lifted the ban on the Muslim Brotherhood, assumed the title "Upholder of the Faith," claimed that his first name was Muhammad, and supported religious instruction in the schools.[70]

Sadat also tried to vindicate Arab secularism by combining with Syrian forces in attacking Israel in October 1973. Although Israel won this war too, in the early stages Arab armies repulsed Israeli forces, restoring some measure of Arab pride. Even so, Islamism emerged from the 1973 war still stronger owing to war's role in strengthening the Saudis, who tripled the price of oil and thereby transferred massive wealth from the West to the oil-producing states. By bidding fair to end Western predominance altogether, Saudi Arabia finally supplanted Egypt as the Arab exemplar. Before the 1970s, Egypt was generally thought of as progressive, Saudi Arabia as backward. By the late 1970s, writes Kepel, the roles had reversed: "Islam, championed by the Saudis, was a synonym for victorious confrontation with Israel, America and their allies."[71] Young and disaffected Arabs across states began to turn to Islam, the Muslim Brotherhood, and writers such as Qutb. Islamic charities appeared in the urban shantytowns; Islamic educational organizations began to supply materials to distended, under-funded universities. By the late 1970s, Islamists had begun to challenge secularist regimes from within. In 1977, Sadat had to suppress an Islamist rebellion in Egypt.[72]

The momentum of Islamism was also aided by expanded Saudi promotion of Wahhabism. Sharply increased rents from oil following the OPEC embargo in 1973 allowed the Saudis to pour massive amounts of money into the World Muslim League. As David Commins writes:

> By the time of King Faysal's assassination [by a relative seeking revenge] in March 1975, he had put Saudi Arabia at the center of a robust set of pan-Islamic institutions, contributed to a new consciousness of international Muslim political issues, ranging from Jerusalem to Pakistan's troubles with India over Kashmir to the suffering of South Africa's Muslims under the apartheid regime.[73]

The bargain between the Saudi royals and the *ulema* who propagated Wahhabism worked well for both: the House of Saud relied on the *ulema* for legitimacy; the *ulema*, on the royals for money and protection.[74]

## Syrian Promotion in Lebanon, 1976

Not all Arabs agree that secularism had failed in 1967; committed secularist elites argued instead that Nasserism had not been sufficiently radical. They insisted that reviving Islamic tradition was precisely the wrong route to Arab greatness. This view predominated among one crucial group, Palestinian elites, for another two decades.[75] Palestinian nationalism, which emerged in reaction to Jewish settlements in Palestine in the early twentieth century, has too complex a history to explore here. Mehran Kamrava writes that it was eclipsed by Nasserism from 1952 to 1967, but after the Israeli war victory in June 1967, Yasser Arafat's Palestine Liberation Organization (PLO) became predominant. The PLO, itself dominated by the al-Fatah movement, is explicitly secularist owing in part to its determination to include Christian Arabs.[76] Its declarations state that the PLO aims to build a Palestinian state where Muslims, Christians, Jews, and others are equal; its stated objection to Israel is that it is a Jewish state.[77] It is difficult to divine the precise regime that Arafat intended to build in the 1970s, because ideological statements were vague owing to the need to build consensus among various Palestinian factions and to recruit Muslim and world opinion to the cause. Official PLO declarations named "secular democracy" as their favored regime. The chief in Beirut stated that the PLO had in mind "not a liberal democracy according to the one man-one vote system" but "popular democracy," meaning in the language of the time a single-party leftist regime.[78] Thus, the PLO fits within the secular, Arab nationalist category.

Because the Palestinians had no territorial state during this period (and still have none at the time of this writing), we do not count as forcible regime promotions Israeli incursions into the West Bank or Gaza. In 1975–76, however, civil war in Lebanon raised the possibility that Arab nationalism, in the form of a PLO-dominated regime, would take over that country and replace its Christian-dominated secular regime. The Lebanese were divided into a number of factions, but when Christian Phalangists killed a busload of Muslims in April 1975, the population polarized and Muslims rallied to the PLO. Outside powers quickly became involved. Israel used direct force by blockading the coast to prevent support from reaching the PLO-Shia coalition. When the latter nonetheless began to win the war in early 1976, Syrian President Hafez al-Assad—himself a Baathist—began to fear an Israeli invasion to block regime change. In a complex move, Assad sent 20,000 troops and 450 tanks into Lebanon to prop up the regime. The regime in the end survived, although a de facto partition was in place from 1976; the southern part of Lebanon was effectively ruled by Shia, Druze, and Palestinian forces.[79]

Those forces continued to harass northern Israel, and Israeli forces invaded Lebanon in 1978, 1980, and 1982, the last with a large force of 60,000. These interventions were intended not to alter or preserve Lebanon's regime but to weaken or destroy the PLO and to install a Lebanese government to take a harder line against the PLO and Shia militias and sign a peace treaty.[80]

*The Eruption of Shia-Islamism: Iran's 1979 Revolution
and Its Demonstration Effects*

Through the late 1970s the Islamist side of the transnational ideological contest was dominated by Sunnis, owing to Saudi patronage and the Muslim Brothers. With the Iranian Revolution of 1979, Shia Islamism was to bid to supplant Sunni Islamism. Shia-Islamist networks had spanned Iraq and Iran, and their victory in the latter produced a regime that contrasted with the Sunnis' chiefly in its attitude toward America's presence in the Middle East. Whereas the Sunni Islamists were more pro-American (and anti-Soviet), the Shii Islamists were decidedly anti-American.

The Sunni-Shia division has often bedeviled Islamism since its emergence in events following the death of Muhammad in A.D. 632. On the whole, Sunni and Shia Islamism are ambivalent regarding one another. Some Islamists of one branch will openly admire the other when it is fighting secularism elsewhere; thus the (Sunni) Muslim Brotherhood in Egypt praised the (Shia) Khomeini revolution in Iran in 1979. But other Islamists in each branch adamantly oppose the other. Their points of contention may seem trivial to outsiders, especially since Sunni and Shia both regard the Koran and *hadith* (sayings and actions of Muhammad) as authoritative. But these sacred sources require interpretation, and the theories of authority that divide the two branches mean they cannot agree on who is entitled to interpret or apply *Shariah*. Sunnis (from the Arabic for "tradition") assert that the Prophet Muhammad left it to his disciples to choose his successor or caliph. SunniIslam has developed a consensual model of legal interpretation: scholars designated by the ruler are authorized to say what divine law implies for society today.

Shii claim, by contrast, insist that there is an *imam*, an infallible interpreter of the divine law, and only a descendant of the Prophet Muhammad may be an imam. Muhammad named as his heir his son-in-law Ali (Shia literally means "follower," as of Ali). With the disappearance of the Prophet's lineage, Shii have had to formulate provisional accounts of authority. As a practical matter, modern Shii allow *fuqaha* (jurists) to act as the imam's surrogates, but consensus among *fuqaha* must include an imam's infallible opinion. For the sub-branch known as Twelver Shiism, the Twelfth Imam went into hiding in A.D. 874 and will reappear as the *Mahdi* or messiah to end injustice on earth.[81] The Shii's strong notion of clerical authority has made them much more reluctant than the Sunnis to accept rule by laity. For most of Muslim history, the caliphate was Sunni and the Shii had to submit to a regime they regarded as heretical. Even within Shia realms—such as the Safavid Dynasty that ruled Persia from 1501 to 1742—a secular ruler was recognized by the clergy or *ulema* as the deputy of the imam and hence legitimate.[82] Sunnis and Shii are both geographically concentrated, with Shii predominant in Iran, Azerbaijan, southeastern Iraq, Bahrain, and parts of Syria, Lebanon, Yemen, and Afghanistan. Pockets of Shii exist elsewhere in southwest and south Asia, but most of the rest of the Muslim world, including North Africa and Southeast Asia, is Sunni.

It is not entirely clear how far Sunni and Shia Islamists have influenced one another. As a young scholar, Ali Khamenei, currently Supreme Leader of Iran, translated a work of the Sayid Qutb into Persian.[83] In turn, the writings of Ruhollah Khomeini and Ali Shariati, another Iranian, have influenced Sunni Islamists in various countries. The influence of Sunni Islamism on the Iranian Revolution of 1979 is hazy and indirect.

Iran's conservative *ulema* had supported the U.S.- and British-sponsored overthrow of the secularist government of Muhammad Mosaddeq in 1953, and their relations with the Shah were cooperative in the 1950s. The Shah and the *ulema* were both anti-communist and anti-Baha'i (Bahaism is an offshoot of Islam). They had fundamentally different visions for Iran, however, and different attitudes toward the West and the United States in particular: the Shah saw aligning with America as the route to development, while the *ulema* saw America as a carrier of impiety and hence alignment with it as a road to ruin. The difference sharpened in the early 1960s. The Kennedy administration, aiming to reduce the appeal of communism throughout the Third World, began to press friendly authoritarian governments to redistribute land to their countries' peasants. In Iran, the religious establishments were among the major landowners, and the *ulema* protested. Ruhollah Khomeini began to emerge as an Islamist leader. The Shah's government, seeking to weaken the *ulema*, proposed further reforms including female suffrage and office-holding by non-Muslims. In March 1963, the Shah suppressed dissent at various mosques; in June he imprisoned Khomeini, released him, and imprisoned him again. Upon his release Khomeini denounced the Shah and his close relations to the United States. He was re-arrested and exiled.[84] From Turkey, Khomeini went to Iraq in 1965, where he continued to develop his version of Islamism:

> Islam has a system and a program for all the different affairs of society: the form of government and administration, the regulation of people's dealings with each other, the relations of state and people, relations with foreign states and all other political and economic matters. ... The mosque has always been a center of leadership and command, of examination and analysis of social problems ...

he declared in a typical sermon in Najaf.[85]

As mentioned at the outset of this chapter, Saddam Hussein, Iraq's secularist dictator, and the Shah had come to see enough common interest in suppressing Khomeini's movement that they began a rapprochement in 1975, and in 1977 Saddam agreed to the Shah's request to expel Khomeini from Iraq. The revolution against the Shah began in late 1978 as a coalition among diverse anti-Shah elements, including liberals and communists. When Khomeini arrived from Paris in January 1979, he began to seize the revolution and use it to build a *faqih* or clerical theocracy. Indeed, like the Girondists in 1792 (chapter 5) and the Bolsheviks in 1917 (chapter 6), the Khomeinists recognized the potential of foreign demonstration effects to strengthen their grip on power at home. They sought to foment Islamist insurrections in many countries and to transcend the Shia-Sunni (and Persian-Arab) divide by using nonsectarian language.[86] Proclaimed Khomeini in December 1979: "Islam is not peculiar to a country, several countries, a group [of people or countries], or even the Muslims. Islam has come for humanity. Islam addresses the people and only occasionally the believers. Islam wishes to bring all of humanity under the umbrella of its justice."[87] From Tehran was broadcast the Arabic-language "Voice of the Islamic Revolution," urging Muslims everywhere to overthrow their governments.[88]

Demonstration effects were clearest among the Shii in other lands, and most alarmed were those Arab rulers of countries with significant Shia populations, namely Iraq, Bahrain, Saudi Arabia, and Lebanon. A wave of unrest hit these countries and was met with a wave of repression. In Bahrain, a majority of whose population was Shia, the Islamic Front for the Liberation of Bahrain attempted a coup against the monarchy in December 1981; seventy-three alleged plotters were arrested.[89] Saudi Arabia's Eastern Province, whose population is roughly one-third Shia, experienced some unrest, as did Kuwait, with a similar percentage of Shii.[90] The Khomeinists saw Lebanon, whose population was approximately one-third Shia, as one of their most promising targets.[91]

The Iranian revolution's effects among Sunni Islamists were more complex. Those who operated outside of state apparatus—the Muslim Brothers—tended to support the Khomeinists. In Egypt, the Brothers declared that all Muslims were duty-bound to support Khomeini's movement. Fathi Abd al-Aziz published *Khomeini: The Islamic Alternative*, which declared that Khomeini's revolution was not an attempt at Shia predominance, but concerned the beliefs common to all Muslims.[92] The Islamic Student Association (*al-Jamaah al-Islamiyyah*) at Cairo University gave its unqualified endorsement.[93]

The Khomeini Revolution thus intimidated secularist rulers of Sunni societies. Anwar Sadat of Egypt, like Saddam Hussein, at first tried to conciliate the new Tehran regime in hopes of helping the moderates prevail in seizing the revolution back from the Khomeinists. But Sadat's warm reception of the Shah in January 1979 immediately alienated Islamists throughout the Muslim world. When Mehdi Bazargan fell in Tehran in November, writes R. K. Ramazani, it "unleashed the ideological crusade of the Khomeini regime against Egypt." The radicals in Tehran depicted Sadat's regime as un-Islamic, like that of the Shah.[94] Sadat was particularly vulnerable to Islamist criticism because in recent years he had turned on the Muslim Brothers and, in 1978, had signed a peace treaty with Israel. During these years Mohammed Adb al-Salam Faraj wrote "The Absent Duty," arguing that a Muslim's first duty was to work not to "liberate" Jerusalem but to topple his country's apostate government. Faraj helped plan the assassination of Sadat in 1981. "'The Absent Duty'," writes Fawaz Gerges, "became the operational manual of the jihadist movement in the 1980s and remained so through the first half of the 1990s."[95]

In Libya, Tunisia, and Sudan, all of which had secular regimes, society was polarized as Islamists were encouraged by the Iranian revolution. Events in Tehran also impressed millions of Muslims in Southeast Asia and Western Europe, leading to some conversions from Sunni to Shia Islam.[96] But the Khomeinists were not able to exploit these Sunni movements.[97]

Crucial to the long-term shape of the secularist-Islamist struggle was the response of the Saudis, the long-time Islamist exemplars, to the Khomeini revolution. That response was hostile. To the Saudis, Khomeini's Iran was a latecomer and a heretical usurper.[98] Iran's assertive anti-Americanism was an open challenge to the Saudis' longtime pro-U.S. foreign policy. Like the deposed Shah, the Saudis had struck a bargain with the United States after the Second World War on ensuring stable energy prices and limiting Soviet influence in the region. Because Soviet communism was atheistic and menacing to Islam, as seen by its rule of historically Muslim societies in Central Asia, the Saudis could simultaneously be Islamist and pro-Western. Indeed, the Shah and the Saudis had cooperated to contain Arab nationalism in the Persian Gulf.[99] Ramazani sums up the differences between Iranian and Saudi Islamism as follows: "clericalism versus monarchism; populism versus elitism ... Shiaism versus Suniism; and anti-Westernism versus pro-Western nonalignmentism."[100]

Hence, the Khomeini regime in Tehran was a double challenge to the Saudis. It was stirring up the Shii in Saudi Arabia's Eastern Province, and attempting to erode Saudi influence throughout the Muslim world by supplanting the House of Saud as vanguard of Islam. The Khomeinists began accusing the Saudis of degeneracy, elitism, and toadying to America and Israel. Tehran's Arabic-language radio network began broadcasting messages of this sort:

The ruling regime in Saudi Arabia wears Muslim clothing, but it actually represents a luxurious, frivolous, shameless way of life, robbing funds from the people and squandering them, and engaging in gambling, drinking parties, and orgies. Would it be surprising if people follow [*sic*] the path of revolution, resort to violence and continue their struggle to regain their rights and resources?[101]

The Saudis responded by portraying the Iranian Revolution as "outside the mainstream of Islamic culture" owing to its Shiism and disrespect for legitimate authority.[102]

Tehran's propaganda had an effect: In November 1979, Sunni militants seized the Grand Mosque at Mecca during the *hajj* or annual pilgrimage, repeating Khomeini's line that the Saudi monarchy was counterfeit Islamic.[103] The Iran-Iraq War, however, by pitting a Shia- against a Sunni-ruled (if secular) regime, reduced Sunni sympathy for the Iranian republic. Iran began to appear less an instrument of the Islamic revival and more one of Shia or Persian imperialism.[104] Most Sunni Islamists still revered the Saudi monarchy at this point and saw the Khomeinists as upstarts—admirable for their overthrow of the apostate Shah, but still heretics unfit to unite the *ummah*.[105] On the governmental level, the Gulf Cooperation Council (GCC), comprising Saudi Arabia, Bahrain, Kuwait, Oman, Qatar, and the United Arab Emirates—Sunni monarchies all—formed in May 1981 and cooperated to block Shia-Islamist subversion and Iranian predominance. The GCC's formation further polarized Sunni and Shia, and in December Khomeinists attempted a coup d'état in Bahrain. The Saudis openly condemned the Iranians for engineering the coup attempt and sent agents to Bahrain to interrogate suspects. In February 1982, two GCC ministerial meetings were held, the second declaring the "intervention by any country in the internal affairs of one of the member states is considered to be intervention in the internal affairs of the GCC states [as a whole]."[106] The GCC came to cooperate with the governments of Jordan and Egypt, as well as the United States, in aiding Iraq; Shia-ruled (secularist) Syria, on the other hand, aided the Iranians.

## The Soviets Preserve Communism in Afghanistan, 1979

At roughly the same time as the Shia-Islamist resurgence in Iran, Sunni Islamism was surging to Iran's east, in Pakistan and Afghanistan, further complicating international relations in the region and more broadly. The ideological surge followed top-down secularizing, centralizing programs from governments—a communist one in Afghanistan, and a non-communist one in Pakistan. In Pakistan the rise of Islamism involved increasing influence for a movement that originated in the nineteenth century in Deoband, a city north of Delhi in British India. The Deobandi sought to return Muslims to strict practices concerning dress, worship, and behavior; they rejected various accretions of tradition such as "what they regarded as excesses at saints' tombs, elaborate lifecycle celebrations, and practices they attributed to the influence of the Shia."[107] Most Deobandi opposed the formation of secular Pakistan in 1947, preferring instead to cultivate a pure parallel Muslim society within a secular India; some splinter groups disagreed.[108] The Deobandi were not a significant political force until the 1970s, when the transnational Islamic resurgence hit Pakistan. President Z. A. Bhutto, a secular socialist, was overthrown in 1977 by General Zia ul-Haq, a devout Muslim who proceeded to "re-Islamicize" Pakistan as a way to combat Soviet influence. Zia gave state certification to the *madrassas* (Islamic schools) and infused them with anti-communist jihadism; in 1975, only 100,000 *taliban* (students) were in these schools, but in 1977 the number grew to approximately 540,000. The resulting surfeit of mullahs contributed to the proliferation of state-supported *Shariah* courts.[109]

Early Deobandism had no evident connection to Saudi Wahhabism. But the programs of the two were similar, and the Saudi-sponsored World Muslim League poured funds into Zia's re-Islamicization project. Wahhabi-Deobandi cooperation was to accelerate and expand in Afghanistan. In April 1978, the secularist regime of Muhammad Daoud Khan was overthrown by Nur Muhammad Taraki of the People's Democratic Party of Afghanistan (PDPA), a Soviet-sponsored communist party. Taraki's efforts to remake Afghanistan rapidly into a modern communist society, including land redistribution and the education of women, generated deep resistance among the devout peasantry. Under the influence of religious elites, the resisters began to identify the problem as atheistic communism and the solution as fidelity to Islam. Burhanuddin Rabbani, a philosophy professor at Kabul University who had studied at al-Azhar in Cairo, quickly organized the National Rescue Front, comprising nine Islamic organizations.[110] As Anthony Arnold writes, "Rural resentment had already become resistance; resistance was becoming rebellion; and rebellion showed signs of becoming *jihad*, a holy war against the infidel Kabul regime."[111] By August 1979, an estimated 100,000 Afghan refugees were in Pakistan. The Zia government refused to return the refugees, and relations between Islamabad and Kabul quickly soured.[112]

Taraki's Soviet sponsors worried that the Islamist resistance was a tool of Zia's regime and, since Pakistan was aligned with the United States, linked to American and Chinese efforts to weaken the Soviet Union. Islamism was hurting the Soviets in Afghanistan and had the potential to polarize and destabilize Soviet Central Asia.[113] As the KGB Chairman for Soviet Azerbaijan put it shortly after the Soviets invaded: "In view of the situation in Iran and Afghanistan, the U.S. special services are trying to exploit the Islamic religion—especially in areas where the Moslem population lives—as one factor influencing the political situation in our country."[114] The communists suspected Khomeini of engineering a savage uprising in March 1979 in Herat, a Persian-speaking Afghan city near the Iranian border. Mobs butchered scores of communists, and as many as a hundred Soviets were killed. Khomeini vigorously denied any involvement, but did warn Taraki that he must reverse his anti-Islamic policies or suffer the Shah's fate.[115] Over the course of the 1980s, Tehran and the Pakistani and Afghan Islamists were to become increasingly hostile over the status and future of Afghanistan's sizeable Shia minority.[116]

On December 25, 1979, thousands of Soviet tanks rumbled into Afghanistan to try to preserve the PDPA regime and thereby Soviet influence in Southwest Asia. The Soviet invasion increased ideological polarization in the region, heightening Muslims' identification with one another across state borders against a common atheistic foe.[117] The Sunni Islamists of Pakistan and Saudi Arabia responded predictably. With encouragement from the Saudis, Arab Islamists from all over North Africa and the Middle East went to Afghanistan to wage jihad against the communist invaders. Pakistan's Inter-Services Intelligence (ISI) was delighted not only at Saudi financial help and propaganda but also at the demonstration effects in Kashmir, a Muslim Indian province claimed by Pakistan.[118] Indeed, the ISI was under the influence of Pakistani Islamists who saw the struggle in Afghanistan as linked to their own struggle against Pakistani secularists in the Foreign Ministry and, beyond that, to their efforts to claim Muslim Kashmir from India.[119] The ISI was in charge of distributing Saudi money to the Afghan *mujahideen* and also directed their military operations. In 1987, Islamists received more than two-thirds of the weaponry the ISI distributed.[120] Indeed, some Saudi aid ended up in the hands of Pakistani Islamists near the Afghan border.[121] General Hamid Gul, who headed the ISI in 1988 and 1989, later made clear that he favored the Islamicization of Pakistan and supported the Taliban in its fight against the United States and its allies.[122]

The conflict in Southwest Asia was overlaid with the Cold War (chapter 6). As early as the spring of 1979, prior to the Soviet invasion, U.S. intelligence did discuss aiding the *mujahideen* (Islamist "strugglers") with Pakistan's ISI, and the Saudis proposed a joint program with the CIA and the Afghan rebels.[123] Under the Reagan administration, CIA cooperation with Sunni Islamists greatly expanded. The Chinese government was also involved in the general effort to stymie the Soviets.

*Transnational Sunni Islamism Expands, 1990s*

The Soviets failed and finally withdrew from Afghanistan in 1989. Over the next decade there followed a sustained period of energy, expansion, and radicalization among Sunni Islamists. An uprising by Islamists in Algeria led to a long, savage civil war. In Sudan and Afghanistan, Sunni Islamists succeeded in setting up regimes. Events in all three countries had demonstration effects, but none led to a forcible regime promotion.

Following independence from France in 1962, Algeria had a secular, left-wing regime. The next year Islamists, influenced by the writings of Sayid Qutb, organized to propagate Islamic values. Islamism simmered and expanded in Algeria, and in October 1988 urban riots began, the rioters identifying with Islamism and the Afghan *mujahideen.* The following year the Islamic Salvation Front (FIS) was founded; in June 1990, the FIS dominated local elections, and in December 1991 it won the first round of parliamentary elections. The army cancelled the second round (to the relief of secularists throughout the Muslim world and beyond) in January 1992 and arrested thousands of FIS members. The FIS rebelled, and civil war raged with varying intensity for the rest of the decade. The FIS was divided within itself between the devout middle class and the urban poor; the latter formed the Groupe Islamique Armé (GIA) and included veterans of the Afghan wars. Kepel writes of the demonstration effects of the Algerian civil war:

> Islamist leaders and opposition parties all over the Muslim world were riveted by the unfolding of the Algerian conflict, with each camp expecting a boost from the success of whichever faction it supported. In Egypt, where a wave of terrorism was sweeping through the Upper Nile Valley and where the radical group Gamaa Islamiya was exchanging messages of sympathy with the GIA, the Algerian conflict was followed intently. In France, where a very large Algerian population resided and links formed with Algeria over 132 years of colonization were still very strong, the civil war quickly acquired a domestic dimension.[124]

The GIA exported the war to France, hijacking an Air France jet in December 1994 and carrying out terrorist attacks in 1995. Following an FIS defeat in the June 1997 parliamentary elections, the GIA began a series of civilian massacres, which provoked the devout middle class into defecting to the secularist government.[125] The civil war ended in 2000 with an amnesty offer from the regime.

Islamists had more success in Sudan. With a population 70 percent Muslim, 25 percent animist, and 5 percent Christian,[126] Sudan had a secular, Muslim-dominated regime dating from its independence from Egypt in 1955. In 1969, with civil war against the non-Muslim south raging, General Djafar Nimayri seized power with help from communists and Nasser's Egypt. Through the 1970s the Sudanese Muslim Brotherhood, led by the western-educated Hassan al-Turabi, labored to infiltrate Nimayri's secular regime. Lacking domestic legitimacy, Nimayri allowed the Islamists increasing influence. In 1977 the Saudis, always eager to help

Islamicize society, opened banks in Sudan. In 1983, Nimayri declared *Shariah* the law of the land, but Islamists were not appeased; within two years he had fallen. Sudan had a democratic regime until 1989, when the Islamist General Omar Hassan al-Bashir staged a coup d'état. The new regime brutally extirpated secularists from the state apparatus.

Hassan al-Turabi, who wielded real power in Sudan, aspired to wrest leadership of transnational Sunni Islamism from the Saudis.[127] In April 1991, capitalizing on Muslims' disillusionment over Saudi support for the United States against Saddam Hussein's regime in Iraq (see below), Turabi organized the Popular Arab Islamic Conference. The inaugural conference comprised leading Arab, Persian, and South Asian Islamists, as well as some anti-Western Arab secularists. Turabi offered Sudan as a global training ground for jihadis and made some progress in fostering cooperation between Sunni and Shia Islamists; in return, he accepted money from Iran, Iraq, and others to solidify Islamist rule in Sudan itself. Turabi was eventually to host exiled Hamas leaders and Osama bin Laden.[128]

Most consequential of all was the Taliban takeover of Afghanistan. When the Gorbachev government withdrew Soviet troops from Afghanistan in 1989, the civil war continued and became more complex, with shifting coalitions of warlords overlaid with competing versions of Sunni and Shia Islamism, monarchism, and secularism. The Saudis and Pakistani ISI continued to cooperate to bring about a strict Sunni-Islamist Afghanistan, while Iran's rulers worked for a regime that would allow the Shii to practice free of Sunni interference.[129] One Sunni faction of unusual discipline, skill, and tactical flexibility staged a spectacular rise in the 1990s. The Taliban (Pashto for "students") owed their success also to their willingness to strike bargains with a wide variety of actors. Their organic connections to the Pakistani Deobandi made them natural allies of the ISI; the influence of Wahhabism via the Arab *mujahideen* and Saudi subsidies made them natural allies of the Saudis as well.

The governments of Iran, India, and Russia cooperated in financing the interim government's fight against the Taliban.[130] The Indians opposed whatever would strengthen Islamists in Pakistan and India itself, while the Yeltsin government in Russia feared demonstration effects in Chechnya and the former Soviet republics in Central Asia. The Taliban were bent on exporting their ideology and provided bases for jihadis from Tajikistan, Uzbekistan, Kyrgyzstan, Xinjiang Province in China (home to Muslim Uighurs), and elsewhere.[131] The Fergana Valley, which spans Uzbekistan, Kyrgyzstan, and Tajikistan, became a hotbed of politico-religious conflict in the 1990s.[132] The Clinton administration, meanwhile, was concerned chiefly with blocking Iranian ambition in the region and so was content to allow the Saudis and Pakistanis to continue supporting the Taliban.

In September 1996, the Taliban took Kabul, the capital city, executed the former President Muhammad Najibullah, and began to impose their strict form of *Shariah* upon that relatively modern and secular city. The governments of Saudi Arabia and Pakistan quickly recognized the Taliban government, and Sunni Islamists in surrounding lands were energized. At a summit meeting in Kazakhstan the Russian and Central Asian governments agreed on the need to stop "Talibanism" from spreading.[133] The Taliban tried to pre-empt foreign intervention and to placate the Clinton administration by disavowing any intention to export their revolution or sponsor terrorism.[134] At the same time, Mullah Omar invited Islamists in Pakistan to send scholars to help write the new Afghan constitution.[135] The Yeltsin government brokered a pact between two anti-Taliban factions to form the Northern Alliance.[136] The Iranians reportedly set up five training camps for 8,000 Shia Afghan fighters.[137]

The Taliban's progress strengthened the Islamists' hand in secularist Pakistan.[138] Even as the ISI organized seminarians into fighting units in Afghanistan and Kashmir, the government of Benazir Bhutto arrested forty Islamists and sought to restrict admission to seminaries.[139] In March 1996, Bhutto pressed the Taliban to negotiate an end to the civil war. In November she was dismissed by President Farooq Leghari under allegations of corruption.

### Al-Qaeda Terrorism and U.S. Promotions in Afghanistan (2001) and Iraq (2003)

The expansion of Sunni Islamism was tied up with a schism within the movement. Moderates, led by the Saudis, continued to abide by the old bargain with the Americans, under which they would align with the West in exchange for stable oil prices and domestic stability. Radicals sought to oust America from the Middle East. One especially militant group of radicals, the al-Qaeda network headed by Saudi exile Osama bin Laden, executed audacious terrorist attacks against the United States on September 11, 2001, leading to two American-led forcible regime promotions that continue at the time of this writing.

The schism began in the early 1990s. Fawaz Gerges writes that the experience of thousands of "Arab Afghans" fighting the Soviets in the 1980s laid the groundwork. Islamists were fighting not apostate Muslim rulers such as those of Egypt or Syria, but a non-Muslim superpower that controlled the Afghan regime. They were directly attacking a foreign entity that had injected unbelief into the *ummah*. And, in their telling, they had won. Bin Laden, a wealthy, charismatic young Saudi who had exhibited some leadership in Afghanistan, became convinced that Muslims must no longer truck with infidels.[140] When the Iraqi army of the secularist Saddam Hussein invaded Kuwait in August 1990, endangering the Saudi dynasty, bin Laden urged his government to rebuff offers of protection by the Americans and instead to let him organize thousands of veterans of the Afghan war to repulse or deter any Iraqi invasion. The Saudi government dismissed bin Laden's offer. This stinging rebuff led bin Laden to change his view of his own government. Far from the pious guardian of the true faith, it was in thrall to the Americans, just as the communist Afghan regime had been a vassal of the Soviets. The Saudi royal family was asking the crusaders to occupy the land of Mecca and Medina, contradicting the Prophet's deathbed remark, "Let there be no two religions in Arabia."[141] Bin Laden and his al Qaeda movement were the first to break with the "near enemy" tradition and target the "far enemy." They reasoned that not only was America the root of the problem for Muslims, but that America was more vulnerable than Islamists had supposed.[142] Bin Laden began to defy the government and in April 1991 left Saudi Arabia. Turabi in Khartoum had been courting him since 1990, and now bin Laden settled in Sudan, where he provided Turabi's regime with funds in exchange for facilities for jihadi training camps for his Afghan Arabs.[143]

During bin Laden's years in Sudan, Turabi supported Islamist fighters against U.S. troops in Somalia in and the World Trade Center bombing in 1993, as well as an attempt to assassinate Hosni Mubarak, President of Egypt, in June 1995. Under increasing U.S. pressure, Turabi and Bashir decided by January 1996 that they needed to shed their terrorist reputation. Bashir offered to turn bin Laden over to the United States via Saudi Arabia, but U.S. officials did not trust him and were unsure whether bin Laden had been involved in any anti-American terrorism.[144] Turabi convinced his allies in Afghanistan to take bin Laden and his jihadi entourage, and in May they left Sudan.[145] Two months later, from Kandahar, Afghanistan, bin Laden issued his infamous "Declaration of War against the Americans Occupying the Land of the Two Holy Places." Announced bin Laden: "it is essential to hit the main enemy who divided the Ummah into small and little countries and pushed it, for the last few decades, into a state of confusion. The Zionist-Crusader alliance moves quickly to contain and abort any 'corrective movement' appearing in the Islamic countries."[146] It was time to go after what bin Laden called the "head of the snake."

A fierce struggle ensued among Sunni Islamists as to whether to follow bin Laden's strategy and aim directly at America. The conventional wisdom, exemplified by the writings of bin Laden's ally Ayman al-Zawahiri, head of Islamic Jihad in Egypt, was that it was more efficient to fight the near enemy: governments such as those of Sadat or Hosni Mubarak were unpopular and close at hand; the United States was powerful and far away. Zawahiri labored for years to penetrate the Egyptian military so as to stage an eventual coup d'état, much as Turabi had done in Sudan. Bin Laden, by contrast, saw the near enemy as more difficult to defeat and less fundamental in any case. Zawahiri began to change his mind in the late 1990s, owing to the effectiveness of Mubarak's repression of Islamism in Egypt. In 1995, hundreds of Islamists were imprisoned in Egypt and Zawahiri, low on funds, suspended attacks by his terrorist group, Islamic Jihad. Zawahiri began to encourage young jihadis to go to Afghanistan to train in bin Laden's well-funded terrorist camps. In 1998, al Qaeda executed attacks on the U.S. embassies in Kenya and Tanzania. Mullah Omar, head of the Taliban, agreed to support bin Laden's anti-American jihad, directly defying the Saudi and Pakistani governments.[147] In October 2000, al-Qaeda attacked the U.S.S. *Cole* in a Yemeni harbor. In the summer of 2001, Zawahiri and bin Laden agreed to merge the Egyptian Islamic Jihad into al-Qaeda.[148]

The September 11 attacks on the United States succeeded well beyond the expectations of bin Laden and Zawahiri, killing nearly 3,000 persons and destroying the famous, highly symbolic World Trade Center. The 9/11 attacks seemed to prove the superiority of the "far enemy" strategy: the *mujahideen* had brought down one superpower in Afghanistan, and now they were bringing down the other. The galvanizing immediate effects of 9/11 on politics in the United States are well known. In the Muslim world, demonstration effects were strong but complex. Footage of Arabs dancing in the streets and waving photographs of bin Laden was broadcast the world over, and many Muslims were indeed gleeful that America was receiving some of the violence that they maintained it had been meting out for years. At the same time, the fanciful theory became widespread that Jews, not Muslims, had carried out the horrific attacks.[149]

The Bush administration's decision to topple the Taliban regime in Afghanistan is unsurprising and a clear example of what I call an external-security promotion. The Taliban and al-Qaeda were deeply interdependent, and so defeating the former would help defeat the latter. Given the possibility of further massive terrorist attacks, America's vast military superiority, and the extreme unlikelihood that any country would do much to oppose or hamper a U.S. intervention, the Bush administration carried out a predictable regime change. In October 2001, U.S. and British forces began aiding the Northern Alliance in driving the Taliban out of the territory they held.

It is noteworthy that the United States has not imposed liberal democracy on Afghanistan. Rather, heavily constrained by traditional Afghan elites and norms, the Bush administration permitted Afghan elites to promulgate a mixed constitution that has Islamist elements. The Constitution of 2004 names the country an Islamic Republic, requires the state to oversee mosques and religious education, and ensure the "the sacred principles of Islam" govern family life. It does not mention freedom of conscience, and one Afghan, Abdul Rahman, was given the death penalty in 2006 for apostasy for his conversion to Christianity. (Under heavy foreign pressure, the sentence was commuted on a technicality.)[150] At the same time, the constitution declares recognition of the Universal Declaration on Human Rights, the legal equality of men and women, and freedom of expression and association.[151]

In some respects, the U.S.-led regime change in Iraq that began in 2003 is likewise unsurprising in light of the past five hundred years of forcible regime change. It is a matter of controversy how important regime change was to the Bush administration's decision to attack. But it is clear that, whatever the administration's chief goal—and the leading contender seems to have been stopping a nuclear weapons program that it turns out did not exist—the Bush administration intended all long to topple the Baathist regime and replace it with some sort of constitutional democracy. Indeed, regime change had been the official U.S. goal since President Clinton signed into law the Iraq Liberation Act in 1998.[152] The architect of the Bush Middle East policy, Paul Wolfowitz, made clear that he saw the Iraq invasion as a way to push over the region's most vulnerable authoritarian domino, with others to fall as a result. For Wolfowitz, the appeal of radical Islamism was especially strong in authoritarian societies, and so ridding the region of the latter would cause Islamism to wither.[153] Wolfowitz signed an open letter to President Clinton in 1998 calling for the forcible replacement of the Baathist regime in Iraq, as did future Bush officials Donald Rumsfeld and John Bolton.[154] Regime imposition was no mere afterthought or post-invasion justification; it was part of the plan from the start.

In other respects, however, the U.S.-led regime change in Iraq has been different from most historical precedents and contradicts some of my arguments. The chief difference is that there were very few pro-American liberal-democratic elites in Iraq. Muslim elites were divided by ideology—Islamist versus secularist, Sunni versus Shia—but there was only weak elite support for the Americans. The ethnic Kurds in the north favored strong relations with the West, owing to American and British protection and support since the 1990s against Saddam's forces. But most Iraqis are Arab, and Arab secularists were mostly anti-American in the traditional Baathist mode. Most Iraqi Islamists were Shia and leaned toward the Iranian regime; as narrated earlier in this chapter, Ruhollah Khomeini had built his movement in the 1960s in Najaf, Iraq.[155] Sunni Islamists were complex, with sympathies toward the Saudi monarchy but also obvious and growing ties to its enemy, al-Qaeda. Liberal-democratic

Iraqi elites did exist, and the leading faction among those was the Iraqi National Congress, led by Ahmad Chalabi. But Chalabi turned out to be a dubious ally who later was accused of distorting intelligence in order to provoke U.S. invasion.[156]

Some similar cases are in our dataset. The most obvious are Napoleonic France's promotions of Bonapartism in the 1800s (chapter 5). French Imperial troops imposed at least some of the institutions that Napoleon had set up in France—the Napoleonic Code and rational centralized bureaucracies, to name two—in places where there was no significant elite constituency for them prior to the invasion. French troops had the most difficulty in Spain from 1806. Some Spanish liberals did collaborate with the government of Joseph Bonaparte, but other liberals fought against it, as did the absolutists. The ideological ground was not adequately prepared in Spain for Bonapartism or a pro-French policy. In Iraq, it appears that liberal-democratic, pro-American ideological ground was likewise lacking. Perhaps like Napoleon, the Americans believed their overwhelming military power would make up the deficit.

If the American intention was to break the Middle East out of its destructive ideological stalemate between secular authoritarianism and Islamism, a stalemate that serves radicalism, then in the short term it has failed. In waging these wars the United States—long involved in the politics of the Middle East as patron of Israel—made itself, in the eyes of Islamists, a co-belligerent with the secularists. Thus, whatever the long-term outcomes in Afghanistan and Iraq, these wars have exacerbated ideological polarization in the Muslim world. With images of Iraqis killed by U.S. forces broadcast on television by al-Jazeera and al-Arabiya, Sunni and Shia Islamists alike in Iraq were radicalized by the war. Riyadh has tried to capitalize on Sunni-Islamist energy, while Tehran has tried to do the same with Shia-Islamism. As often happens, the transnational networks often seem more controlling than controlled. Radical Sunnis in Saudi Arabia carried out major suicide attacks in May and November 2003.[157] Thus far the U.S. interventions have not dampened Islamist radicalism in the region, but have done nearly the opposite.

## Conclusion

The U.S.-led wars in Afghanistan and Iraq were only the most recent of a set of forcible regime promotions in the Muslim world dating to the 1950s. Through all of the historical narrative, it is clear that the dynamics of forcible regime promotion in the Muslim world are remarkably similar to those in the earlier contests in the preceding chapters. All of the promotions were what I call ex ante: When one country changes from one regime to another, or appears likely to do so, elites in neighboring countries polarize according to whether they favor the change. State rulers, who want to assure their own domestic security and if possible increase their foreign influence, find themselves facing incentives to intervene.

More often than in our cases in chapters 4 through 6, rulers responded to transnational ideological polarization not by using force to promote regimes abroad, but rather by increasing suppression of domestic dissent. In the case of the Sunni monarchies of the Persian Gulf, fear of Iran-based Shia Islamism led them to form the Gulf Cooperation Council. But in ten cases, governments have used force. Half of these promotions have been by outside great powers acting out of concern for the balance of power. The Anglo-American interventions to defeat Nasserism in Lebanon and Jordan in the 1950s, the Soviet invasion of Afghanistan in 1979, and the U.S.-led wars in Afghanistan and Iraq were all external-security interventions. The government of the intervener was trying to preserve or increase its power and influence in the region, knowing that the target state's foreign policy depended in part upon its domestic regime.

There have been a few promotions by governments of Muslim countries done for the sake of internal as well as external security. "Nasser's Vietnam" came in the 1960s when the Egyptian ruler sent thousands of troops to North Yemen to aid Arab secularists there. Spreading Nasserism would help him at home and increase Egypt's influence at the expense of Saudi Arabia. (The Saudis subsidized the traditional Islamic monarchy for the sake of their own domestic security.) The most traumatic cases were the mutual promotions by Iraq and Iran from during the 1980s, when Khomeini tried to topple Iraq's Baathist regime and Saddam Hussein tried to topple Iran's new Islamist regime. Both governments wanted to weaken ideological opposition at home as well as to expand their nation's influence.

These promotions of Islamism and secularism have a deep structural cause, namely a struggle within the Muslim world over the best regime, a struggle now nearly a century old, propelled across the decades by transnational networks of elites and by governments seeking to exploit them. Divisions among Muslim elites between Islamists and secularists have their origins in the nineteenth century, when the theocratic Ottoman Empire was decaying in the face of European power and efficiency. The way to restore greatness to the Muslim world, many elites decided, was to imitate the Europeans, with their nation-states, their centralized bureaucracies, and their secularism. The authority of the *ulema* (clergy) must be reduced, and popular loyalty redirected to the state. Thus in Turkic, Persian, Arab, and other Muslim lands, traditional Islam—which shaped societies and their institutions, not simply individual behavior—went on the retreat. Yet, the *ulema* and devout laity resisted. The (Sunni) Muslim

Brotherhood formed in Egypt in 1928 and soon had affiliates in a number of Muslim countries. Parallel events took place in the Shia world. In the 1950s, in response to persecution by secularists, traditionalists became more overtly political, developing a general ideology, Islamism, capable of supplanting secularism. In the late 1960s, secularism began to lose much elite support and Islamism gained shape and energy.

Like previous transnational ideological struggles, that between Islamists and secularists is not simple. Both sides are internally divided, and intra-Islamist and intra-secular rivalries sometimes override that between Islamism and secularism. State rulers have attempted to capture and dominate the transnational networks, with varying degrees of success. Nasser held sway over Arab socialists in the 1950s and 1960s, as do Iran's rulers over Shia-Islamists in Iraq and Lebanon today. But the networks often show a strong independence, as seen in al-Qaeda's relation to the Saudi monarchy, and even an ability to influence state policy, as seen in Pakistan. The Islamist-secularist struggle also has been overlaid by great-power politics, particularly during the bipolar Cold War struggle. Each superpower tried to exploit one or another movement—the Soviets and Nasserism in the 1950s and 1960s, the Americans and Sunni-Islamism in the 1980s—and had some success but often found itself more exploited than exploiting.

International politics in the Muslim world is about much more than the struggle between Islamism and secularism. Israel, American hegemony, oil, poverty, ethnic rivalries, weak states, and authoritarianism all play significant roles. But much of the armed conflict, including by the United States and other outside great powers, has been caused in part by the struggle over whether God or man ought to make law. The contest shows no sign of fading. In chapter 8 I discuss how it might fade and what policy makers can do until it does.

# CHAPTER EIGHT

# The Future of Forcible Regime Promotion

> We, unhappily, are living in the hiatus between two dreams.
> We have waked from one and not yet started the other.
> We still have our eyes, our minds, our hearts, on the dream
> that is dying—How beautiful it was, tinting the whole sky
> crimson as it fades into the west! But there is another on
> its way in the gray dawn.
> —Anne Morrow Lindbergh, *1940*

WHY DO GOVERNMENTS USE FORCE to promote domestic regimes in other countries? In a deep sense, it is because they decide that rival regimes are not the wave of the future but are only temporary, misguided attempts to organize society that will eventually exhaust themselves. Anne Morrow Lindbergh was not willing to fight to advance liberal democracy and turn back fascism because she believed that fascism was the wave of the future. As King Canute showed, it is folly to fight a wave. Morrow Lindbergh's government, the Roosevelt administration, disagreed with her about fascism, and fought. So did Winston Churchill, and Stalin as well, once forced to choose. It was not at all clear to these leaders that their respective regimes had lost the transnational ideological competition that had been raging for nearly two decades.

Once elites decide that their own regime has a future, it becomes in their interests to defend it. And sometimes—as the American, British, and Soviet governments did during and after the war—they believe that doing so requires that they go on the ideological offensive by promoting their regime abroad. I have argued that in the great majority of cases over the past half millennium, rulers believe this when political elites across states are highly polarized over ideology. High transnational ideological polarization means that, by promoting a particular regime in a foreign state, a ruler can make that state into a friend or keep it from becoming an enemy. Foreign regime promotion sometimes can also weaken ideological opposition within the ruler's own state. Transnational ideological polarization tends to take place against a background condition of a prolonged regional struggle over the oldest question in the study of politics: What is the best regime? The past five hundred years featured several such long struggles. Each featured some periods of relatively low transnational elite polarization, but also times of high polarization. It was in the latter periods that forcible regime promotion tended to take place.

I arrived at this answer through several steps. I first noted the variation across time and space of forcible regime promotion over the past half millennium. In some times and places the practice has not been unusual, while in others it has been virtually unheard of. The variation in the incidence of forcible regime promotion is complex: it has occurred in three long waves—from 1520 through 1690 in Central and Western Europe, from 1770 through 1850 in Europe and the Americas, and from 1918 through 1990. Within each long wave there has been micro-variation. In some years no forcible promotion has taken place; in some, one or two cases have occurred; and very occasionally, states have done multiple forcible promotions.

On the macro-level, each long wave coincided with a protracted transnational and international contest over the best domestic regime. Each protracted contest emerged when enough elites across states decided that the status quo regime was not fulfilling its promises. Intellectual ferment across states led to a spiral of hostile interaction with defenders of the status quo, and elite networks began to decide that institutional reform was not sufficient; the regime itself must be replaced. When one major state threw off the old regime and installed a new one, that new one became a standard around which rallied the discontented across the region, regardless of the source of their discontent. Sixteenth-century elites with diverse complaints against late-medieval institutions became Protestants; in the twentieth century elites discontented with capitalism, wealth disparity, or colonialism became communists. Meanwhile, some elites would continue to uphold the old regime, convinced of its continuing viability and their own interests in its perpetuation. These contests over the best regime were not just short revolutionary spasms that abruptly affected international politics and then receded, allowing states to return to their normal ways. They would subsist for many decades across societies in diverse circumstances, carried forward by rulers and transnational networks of elites, and erupt again and again. Third and fourth alternative regimes would emerge and join the contest.

On a micro-level, even during a prolonged transnational ideological contest, most rulers were usually at pains to eschew forcible regime promotion owing to its expected costs. Two types of event tended to set off dynamics that could (but did not always) raise rulers' expected benefits enough to lead them to carry out such promotions: intense *regime instability* in at least one state in the region, or a *great-power war*. Both types of event could trigger transnational ideological polarization, or the progressive segregation of elites into ideological camps across states. Regime instability tended to have demonstration effects and raise the specter of ideological contagion; this followed not only the great revolutions such as the French of 1789 and Russian of 1917, but also less spectacular unrest such as that in France in the 1550s, Spain in the early 1820s, and North Yemen in the early 1960s. These all set off ex ante promotions. Great-power wars polarized elites because elites tended to see the war as partly about ideology. The Habsburg suppression of the Bohemian revolt in 1618 was not just about Habsburg power but about the fate of Protestantism; the Second World War was not simply about the balance of power but the fates of communism and constitutional democracy. These were ex post promotions. Thus, the tendency for forcible regime promotions to cluster in time: belligerent great powers had strong incentives to carry out such promotions when they occupied countries during and after wars because elites in such countries tended to be so ideologically polarized.

These processes were shot through with endogeneity, such that cause and effect were in a recursive relationship. Transnational ideological polarization was self-reinforcing: the more elites observed adherents of a rival ideology coalescing tightly, the more they would do the same. Forcible regime promotion exacerbated the transnational polarization that caused it: when state A overthrew oligarchy in state C and replaced it with democracy, oligarchs throughout the region were that much more ideologically agitated. Declines in the incidence of forcible regime promotion also involved positive feedback. When one ruler would cease promoting regimes, he could trigger transnational ideological de-polarization and reduce the incentives to other rulers to do such promotions.

In Thomas Risse-Kappen's phrase, the contending ideas did "not float freely," but were carried and reproduced chiefly by two types of agents: transnational ideological networks (TINs) and rulers or governments. TINs, true believers in one particular regime type, labored to spread the ideas and bring about revolutions, coups d'état, and other types of regime change. They kept adherents of rival regimes alarmed and maintained the conviction on all sides that there was a long-term contest over the best regime. Rulers kept the ideological contests going by promoting one regime at the expense of others. The relation of governments and TINs was often intimate and complex. Each tried to penetrate and exploit the other, with varying success.

Each protracted ideological contest persisted as long as at least two contending regime types maintained plausibility in the region. Each contest ended when consensus emerged among elites across states that one contestant regime was manifestly superior on terms that all agreed upon. In the late seventeenth and early eighteenth centuries, the remarkable example of the Dutch Republic helped cause religious toleration to be seen by European elites as not merely a regrettable temporary tactic to quiet unrest but a superior permanent route to national greatness. In the late nineteenth century, Britain's conservative reforming constitutionalism began to appear superior to rigid absolutism or radical republicanism. By the 1980s, constitutional democracy and capitalism were manifestly superior to communism. In all these cases rulers under the old regimes loosened their rigid commitments to a losing ideology and began to reform their regimes; those who failed to do this paid the price by losing power or relegating their states to inferiority.

In chapter 7, I presented the ongoing struggle within the Muslim world over whether the best regime was that laid out by the teachings and example of the Prophet Muhammad, as claimed by Islamists; or one in which the laws and sovereignty come from mundane sources. This contest, which began emerging in the nineteenth century and solidified in 1923 with the establishment of modern Turkey, has produced relatively few forcible regime promotions, but those it has produced have followed the same patterns as those in the earlier cases. Until the late 1960s, secularism had the momentum and was destabilizing traditional regimes and occasionally pulling in outside intervention. Since the 1970s the momentum has shifted to Islamism, with similar results. Most recently, the contest has pulled the United States to deepen its already heavy involvement in the Muslim world by promoting democracy in Afghanistan and Iraq.

In this concluding chapter I carry out four tasks, the first two academic and the latter two practical. First, I return to the two main alternative explanations laid out at the end of chapter 3, realism and a particular version of constructivism, and argue that the historical evidence is more consistent with my predictions than with theirs. Second, I consider how my theory relates to broader understandings within IR concerning ideas and preferences, states and transnational networks, and agents and structures. Third, I briefly consider the claims some have made that new ideological struggles are starting to infect international relations. Some analysts see in Latin America a resurgent socialism that could throw the Western Hemisphere back into a sort of Cold War–style zero-sum ideological contest. Others have seen in the rise of China and Russia an emerging authoritarian-capitalist ideology bidding to compete with liberal democracy. Finally, I close by returning to the ongoing ideological struggle in the Muslim world analyzed in chapter 7, considering how the struggle might finally end.

## Alternative Explanations

In chapter 1, I noted that certain features in the aggregate data appear in tension with typical realist claims about international relations. One of these was the sheer fact of forcible regime promotion itself. Structural realism asserts that states' domestic properties have no general effects on international outcomes—all types of state, regardless of regime type, are socialized into balancing behavior—and so cannot supply a rational account of why one state would ever spend dear resources promoting a regime in another state. In particular, forcible regime promotion—ceteris paribus, the most costly type—should not happen, or should at most happen only occasionally as states learn how pointless it is. That I have assembled 209 cases over the past five hundred years suggests that forcible regime promotion is not as rare—it takes place in four years out of ten, on average—as this straightforward structural realist account would predict. Some versions of realism would allow that when external security is plentiful, states are more able to indulge domestic ideologues who want to promote their favorite regime. Such may have been the case, for example, in the U.S. restoration of democracy in Haiti in 1994. But the majority of forcible regime promotions have taken place during wars, when international security was scarce. Indeed, such promotions tend to cluster when rivalries are especially intense: during the Thirty Years' War (especially in 1629), the wars of the French Revolution and Napoleon (1790s and 1800s), and the early Cold War (1944–50).

I noted also that a purely ideological theory—one that says states promote regimes out of a logic of appropriateness—would have trouble with the evident purposive, strategic behavior of states that promote regimes abroad. Governments tend to choose targets already undergoing domestic unrest and strategic targets such as neighbors or states that control valuable assets. That suggests, in turn, that governments tend to use expected-utility calculations, at least implicitly, when deciding when and where to promote regimes, and the utility they seek to enhance is their own or that of their state.

Beyond these inferences from the descriptive statistics, what do the case studies tell us? Following the general structure of my argument in chapters 2 and 3, I divide my explanation into the micro-level of individual promotions, and the macro-level of the social structure that makes such promotions generally more likely.

## Realism

MICRO-LEVEL: INDIVIDUAL PROMOTIONS.

Realists may still protest that forcible regime promotion is cheap and hence not a puzzle but a straightforward consequence of war. For realism, state A uses force on state C not to alter or preserve C's domestic regime, but to coerce C into becoming or remaining friendly to A's interests. And C's regime type has nothing to do with its friendliness or enmity with A. After subjugating C, A promotes its own regime in C because A's military and diplomatic corps know better how to deal with that regime. There is no constraint on A from any ideational structure, but simply instrumental knowledge. My argument, by contrast, is that A will promote a regime in C because A is constrained to do so: adherents of that regime in C are pro-A and adherents of alternative regimes are anti-A. Discerning the motives of A's government is difficult, but what do the case studies suggest?

In the regime promotions with which I open chapters 4 through 7, the discourse and actions of the promoting governments are more consistent with my argument. Elizabeth I's decision to promote Protestantism in Scotland in 1560 (chapter 4) was clearly based on an understanding— shared by Catholics—that the Scottish Calvinists were pro-English and anti-French, and Scottish Catholics pro-French and anti-English. Scotland's external alignments were at stake, and the Guises in France knew it as well. Elizabeth also was concerned to remove Scotland as one possible route of Catholic invasion into England to overthrow her and place her Catholic half-sister Mary Stuart on the throne. In 1849, Louis-Napoleon sent a French expeditionary force to Rome to re-establish the papal monarchy (chapter 5), not because he thought it more efficient to deal with, but because he wanted to take the wind out of the sails of radical republicanism in France itself.

The Truman administration started promoting liberal democracy in Western Germany (chapter 6) in 1946 because the Soviets had already begun promoting communism in their German zone and communists were anti-American and pro-Soviet. Statements and actions of U.S. officials betray no thought that regime symmetry between Germany and the United States would make relations more efficient. Indeed, the Americans were not sure what sort of regime to impose on Germany until the Soviets began doing their own imposition to the east. The Khomeini government in Iran and Saddam Hussein in Iraq each promoted its regime in the other state because it wanted to suppress ideological opposition within its own borders. Shii in Iraq tended to want a Khomeini-style revolution in Iraq; "moderates" in Iran wanted for their country not the clerical theocracy (*faqih*) of Khomeini but a regime led by laity.

The U.S.-German case of 1946–49 was an *external-security* promotion. The U.S. government knew that a communist Germany would be hostile and a democratic one friendly. The France-Rome case of 1849 was an *internal-security* promotion. Louis-Napoleon knew that suppressing radical republicanism in southern Italy would damage its prospects in France in a time of turmoil. The English-Scottish case of 1559–60 and Iran-Iraq case of 1980 were both internal- and external-security promotions. In both cases the promoting rulers knew that helping ideological confreres abroad would simultaneously damage ideological enemies at home and make the target state friendlier. All of these ideological conflicts were transnational, and the fortunes of each in one country implicated its fortunes everywhere.

These are only a few cases out of more than two hundred, and a full test would involve similar studies of the motives of all promoting governments. The historical narratives that form the bulk of chapters 4 through 7 suggest the same dynamics: promoting governments recognize that elites in target states are ideologically polarized and that their own interests are at stake in which ideology prevails in those targets. These are not simply stories of regime promotions done as afterthoughts or for the sake of technical efficiency.

MACRO-LEVEL: IDEATIONAL STRUCTURES

In chapter 3, I noted that realism generally treats ideas as instrumental to the needs of powerful actors. Ideologies are nothing more than sets of tools that elites use to mobilize masses to serve their interests. Norms concerning the best regime do not constrain elites. One regularity across the past half millennium that is at least unanticipated by this realist account of ideas is the staying power of certain ideas across time and space. If an ideology is just a way of talking or a set of symbols manipulated by power-seeking rulers to mobilize the masses, as realists maintain, then it seems odd that rulers resort to the same symbols time and again, in lands far from one another. If the Bohemian revolt of 1618 (chapter 4) was nothing but an effort by some elites to throw off Habsburg rule, then at the very least those elites felt constrained to present themselves as devout Protestants and their struggle as continuous with that of Protestants in Western Europe one and two generations earlier. In so doing, the rebels closed off any possibility of aligning with Catholics in the empire—and there were many—discontented with Habsburg rule. If Habsburg resistance to that revolt was nothing but status quo rulers seeking to protect their power, then it is puzzling that those rulers portrayed their effort as continuous with faraway Catholic struggles against Protestantism by people long dead. In so doing, they made it difficult for themselves to recruit Calvinists and even Lutherans to their side. The simplest explanation is that the Habsburgs were constrained to adopt the ideological framework that they did.

In like fashion, rulers in Europe from the 1770s through 1850 often professed allegiance to an extant ideology that made certain possible strategies and tactics much harder to follow. In appealing to the norms of the *ancien régime*, absolutists alienated republicans and many constitutionalists and left themselves little choice after 1815 but to promote absolutism (chapter 5). Republicans after 1815 appealed to the symbols and language of the First French Republic (1793–99) and the Spanish Constitution of 1812. Doing so helped them mobilize followers across states, but also made cooperation with absolutists and constitutional monarchists much harder. In the twentieth century (chapter 6), fascist governments found it in their interests not simply to intervene in the Spanish Civil War but, in doing so, to help their Nationalist co-ideologues and hence to fight against communists. Stalin was more flexible, professing to be the paladin of communism yet compromising principle routinely, but he paid a price in doing so, losing a measure of credibility among many communists, who (under Leon Trotsky) formed the Fourth International. It is difficult to sustain the realist proposition that ideologies reduce to tools controlled by rulers. Surely rulers would have retained far more flexibility had they invented ideologies out of whole cloth. Time and again, however, rulers knew that the ideologies that could effectively mobilize people were already fashioned in previous generations. They knew that these ideologies would constrain them, sometimes to the point of making it rational for them to use dear resources to promote those ideologies abroad, but they appealed to them nonetheless. They were, in other words, constrained by an ideational or social structure.

### Constructivism

#### MICRO-LEVEL: INDIVIDUAL PROMOTIONS

As discussed at the end of chapter 3, on the micro-level of analysis—individual regime promotions—one version of constructivism expects actors to operate under a logic of appropriateness. Rulers will promote their regime abroad out of principle; they believe in Lutheranism or constitutional monarchy or fascism to the point that they feel compelled to spread it by force without regard to their personal or their state's interest. They promote because it is fitting or right to do so. My own argument does not rule out such ideologically committed action, but does not require it of rulers.[1] What does the evidence say?

In general, we find a great deal of discourse and behavior consistent with a logic of consequences. In sixteenth- and seventeenth-century Europe (chapter 4), most Catholic and Protestant rulers do seem to have been devout believers. But they were also princes concerned to keep and expand their power, and were loath to follow without question the wishes of clergy who, they supposed, had interests of their own. To the consternation of popes and prince-bishops, the Holy Roman Emperor Charles V passed up many opportunities to turn back Lutheranism because he needed Lutheran help against the Ottomans and, sometimes, against the Pope himself. Elizabeth I of England, Henry Navarre (later

Henry IV of France), and many German Lutheran princes displayed a similar prudence concerning religious solidarity. As one German prince wrote to another about their Lutheran League of Schmalkalden: "Our league is villainously built and full of holes."[2] Elizabeth, the Protestants' champion, was notorious for betraying her co-religionists when her coffers were low or she needed French help against Spain or vice versa. Between 1555 and the early seventeenth century Catholics and Protestants lived in relative peace in the empire. In the 1580s, English, Dutch, and German Protestants joined with some French Catholics (the *politiques*) against other French Catholics and the Spanish. Particularly prone to help the other side were France's monarchs, from Francis I to Henry III to Louis XIII.

The French republicans of the 1790s who declared all monarchists their mortal enemies, practiced divide-and-conquer politics with some skill, making separate peaces with those same enemies when it suited them (chapter 5). As early as 1794, France's republican rulers and the absolutist rulers of Prussia, the Netherlands, and Spain made peace. The French Directory (r. 1795–99) imposed republicanism on conquered lands but treated these republics as satellites and suppliers of food and manpower to their war machine. The same was true of Bonapartist France (1799–1814). The arch-conservative Metternich certainly desired to promote absolutism, but that he reined in Tsar Alexander's plans to go on an extended crusade suggests that Metternich was thinking primarily of Habsburg power. In 1839–40, Britain cooperated with Russia to help preserve the absolutist Ottoman Empire from collapse, infuriating the government of France, by then a constitutional monarchy whose leaders had invested in ideological solidarity with the British. Louis-Napoleon, as already noted, promoted absolute monarchy in Rome in 1849 even though he was not himself an absolutist.

The most familiar cases of ideological compromise and betrayal come from the twentieth-century contest among constitutional democracy, communism, and fascism (chapter 6). As Soviet dictator, Josef Stalin would support or undermine communists in other lands—Iran, China, and elsewhere—depending upon whether the Soviet Union needed the cooperation of the governments they sought to undermine. Indeed, the 1970s saw the United States cooperate with both communist giants even as the latter were bitter enemies. Most infamously, U.S. administrations used force in South Korea, South Vietnam, Laos, and Cambodia to promote authoritarian regimes. (Washington also used covert action and other means to overthrow democratic regimes in the Third World on several occasions.) It is significant that these forcible regime promotions were aimed to keep communists out of power, and so may be seen as principled in that sense.[3] But surely they evince a willingness to compromise commitment to liberal democracy, at least in the short term, for the sake of some other goal.

The case for a logic of appropriateness is stronger for some rulers. Several of the Electors Palatine in the sixteenth and seventeenth centuries do appear to have set aside prudence for the sake of spreading Calvinism, or at least to have so closely identified their good with the spread of their faith that they subordinated the former to the latter. The outcome at the end of the Thirty Years' War was the devastation of the Palatinate and its rulers' loss of the Imperial Electorship (chapter 4).[4] In 1792, the Brissotins seemed to set aside prudence in urging the French Assembly to go to war against Austria to spread republicanism and roll back monarchy. Tsar Alexander I of Russia wanted the Concert of Europe to make the defense of absolute monarchy its top priority in 1818, well before Austria's Metternich and other absolutists thought it sensible to do so (chapter 5). Among the Bolsheviks, Leon Trotsky may have been a completely principled promoter of communism, without regard for his own power or that of Russia (chapter 6). These rulers, however, stand out precisely because they seem so reckless. Far more typical are the prudent rulers who are committed to an ideology but realize that, in order to promote it, they must husband their states' power. For these prudent rulers, ideological foreign policy was conditional. They promoted regimes abroad when elites across states were highly polarized by ideology. Otherwise they usually preferred not to.

MACRO-LEVEL: IDEATIONAL STRUCTURES

If the struggle over the best regime is so consequential, then how do such struggles arise, why do they endure as long as they do, and why do they fade when they do? Following Kowert and Legro, I posed my ecological account of ideational change and stasis against a broad class of social-interactionist accounts. Both accounts are constructivist, but ecological accounts locate the sources of change in the environment; they expect structures to remain stable until some exogenous environmental change, such as a technological development or a war, disrupts the agent-structure dynamic. Social-interactive accounts look to interaction itself as the source of change. Structures evolve gradually as particular agents—norms entrepreneurs—come up with new ideas, propagate them, and win converts.

The cases themselves suggest that ideas entrepreneurs, persuasion, and social interaction are indeed necessary to the emergence and persistence of our four prolonged ideological struggles and the demise of the first three. When proposals for reforming the predominant regime become radical proposals to replace it, amounting to the emergence of a new ideological struggle, the process is one of social interaction; likewise with the process through which elites form a consensus that one regime type is superior to its competitors, which signals the demise of an ideological struggle. But ideational changes of this sort are not as gradual or frequent as envisaged by a purely social-interactionist account. Agents are perpetually formulating new ideas or modifying old ones to fit new circumstances. They are perpetually trying to persuade others to adopt their ideas. But in the realm of ideologies, they usually fail.

As noted in chapter 4, Martin Luther was by no means the first medieval European to propose something like a Reformation, and it is easy to argue that princes in preceding centuries would have been better off had they sponsored a Wycliffe or a Hus. Yet only Luther was able to attract and sustain sufficient princely sponsorship to allow his movement to survive. Historians argue that the Reformation emerged in northern Europe in the early sixteenth century because the predominant medieval regime was finally failing to fulfill its promises to crucial elites. Clerical corruption, Renaissance humanism, the Western Schism, and other failures of the Catholic Church created dry tinder for Luther to ignite. Yet, even after the Reformation gained traction, the old regime worked well enough for other elites that many defended it to the death. All through these many decades of religious strife, some elites proposed and propagated religious toleration as a solution. Many princes tried toleration, but only as a temporary truce. Elite consensus over toleration as a permanent institution only came when intolerance proved so destructive in Germany and France in the seventeenth century and the Dutch example of toleration proved so successful at strengthening the state.

In chapter 5 we saw that ideas entrepreneurs challenged the predominant regime of absolute monarchy in the early and middle eighteenth century, but it was only when France's exemplary regime began to totter near bankruptcy that challengers gained many elite converts. The three-way contest that took hold—among absolutism, constitutional monarchism, and republicanism—lasted for many decades notwithstanding the emergence of new and synthetic ideas, the most prominent of which was Bonapartism, Napoleon's hybrid of absolutism and republicanism. The struggle finally faded after 1848 with the rise of radical socialism. In the 1870s, enough absolutist and constitutional and republican elites concluded that defeating this common ideological foe required their cooperating under a new bargain, some type of conservative reforming regime roughly based on the successful British model. Social interaction among elites, both rulers and others, is certainly part of the story, but both the emergence and decline of this long ideological struggle were caused partly by exogenous changes in agents' environments.

The same is true of the twentieth-century struggle among constitutional democracy, communism, and fascism. As foreshadowed in 1848, constitutionalism appeared a failure to many elites, who began to develop radical socialist and anarchist alternatives. It required the traumas of the First World War to crystallize some of the radicals into the Bolshevik movement and to usher in the first communist regime, the Soviet Union. During the transnational ideological struggle of the following seven decades, norms entrepreneurs were hard at work proposing reforms that would soften or end the conflict, yet the conflict endured as long as each regime type had a successful exemplar. It took utter military defeat in 1945 to discredit fascism among its elite followers, and the unmistakable decline of the Soviet Union in the 1970s and 1980s vis-à-vis the United States, to discredit communism.

Thus, the evolution of regime ideologies is not the gradual, incremental, cumulative change envisaged by purely social-interactionist models. It is rather more like punctuated equilibrium,[5] except that the equilibrium takes many decades to come into being. Between equilibria—periods when a region has a predominant regime—two, three, or more regime types struggle for predominance, each defended by an exemplar that attempts to shape the environment in its favor.

## International Relations Theory

The arguments in this book touch on several bodies of international relations literature, challenging certain prominent propositions and affirming others.

### The Importance of Ideas

IR scholarship is now at a point where virtually all scholars acknowledge that "ideas matter."[6] That consensus is due in part to the hazy verb "matter." I have argued that certain types of ideas—namely ideologies, or principles of public order that imply particular domestic political regimes—are causal under certain conditions. When elites across states are polarized over ideology, governments' foreign policy choices are limited. Rulers can be constrained to promote their ideology, or block a rival ideology, in other countries, even to the point of using force. Rulers have many reasons to avoid using force. The mainstream academic rationalist position has become that the use of force is by definition a failure, because the belligerents could have arrived at the same bargain short of fighting and avoided the dead-weight loss of war.[7] As discussed above, the case studies in this book make clear that rulers use force, in spite of the expected costs, to alter or preserve regimes in other states because their domestic or foreign security can depend upon it.

At the root of this constraint is the ruler's need to commit publicly to his state's regime type. Rulers may have power as their primary goal, but many also have normative commitments—particular notions of the best regime—that lead them to seek power to begin with. What about rulers with weak or no commitments except to their own power? A strong strand within realist thought insists that successful rulers must be weakly committed and ready to betray principles for the sake of power. Hence, we should observe that rulers shed ideologies as a snake sheds its skin. But it was Machiavelli himself who counseled the prince to "appear pious," for the sake of his power. Appearing faithful to his regime, in practice, can bind him to it and give him strong incentives to defend it abroad. Put in social-scientific language, rulers may bear high audience costs when they betray the ideology upon which their legitimacy is based.[8]

But the cases in this book show not only that ideas constrain rulers, hence states, to do what they otherwise would not. They also show that rulers perpetuate those same ideas by their self-interested actions. Rulers use foreign regime promotion to make their domestic and international environments friendlier. In so doing, they reinforce the social structure, the transnational ideological struggle, that gives them incentives to carry out those same promotions. Far from being above the ideological fray, Machiavellian princes are belligerents in it. Thus, forcible regime promotion is a vivid illustration of the agent-structure problem in international relations.[9]

### Ideology, Alliances, and War

My arguments have implications for phenomena beyond forcible regime promotion. Much recent literature has reopened the old debate about how much ideology affects states' perceptions of foreign threat, alliance patterns, and wars. Quantitative studies show robust correlations between states' regime types and their alliances. Since 1945, democracies have been more likely to be allies than random chance would predict.[10] Some extend the same relationship to all regime types,[11] and others further extend the relationship back to 1816.[12] More directly relevant here, Randolph Siverson and Harvey Starr find that changes in alliance portfolios between 1816 and 1965 correlate strongly to changes in domestic regimes.[13] Other studies contradict these findings.[14] Process-tracing case studies which try to identify mechanisms connecting ideology and alliances likewise yield mixed results. Stephen Walt and Steven David both find little causal connection between common ideology and alignment choice.[15] Mark Haas and Gregory Gause both find the opposite.[16]

It is worth exploring whether the relationships between ideology and these dependent variables—threat perception, alliances, and war—depend on a condition I have stressed throughout this book: transnational ideological polarization. I have argued that such polarization can prod governments that share an ideology to try to deter forcible regime promotion by forming an alliance. Such happened several times among Protestant and Catholic estates in the Holy Roman Empire in the sixteenth and seventeenth centuries (chapter 4). In more recent times, ASEAN and the Gulf Cooperation Council—not military alliances but international organizations whose members cooperate on security affairs—both formed in response to a transnational ideological threat.[17] Perhaps transnational polarization is a common mechanism that heightens foreign threats and generates alliances.[18]

As to war, I have not claimed that most of the major conflicts covered in the case studies were caused solely by ideology. Other variables—anticipated changes in the balance of power, misperception, and aggressive leadership, to name three—were no doubt involved in the outbreak of the Napoleonic Wars, the Second World War, and the Cold War. But if my arguments are correct that forcible regime promotion can alter (or preserve) the balance of power among states, then balance-of-power arguments about war ought not to be separated from my arguments. If the Cold War happened because, in an anarchical international system, the two superpowers feared one another's gains in power, we must ask why the balance of power was so volatile in the latter half of the 1940s. The answer that emerges from chapter 6 is that elites across Europe were polarized over communism, which in turn was linked to Soviet influence. Had communism and anti-communism not been so strong in Germany, France, Italy, Poland, Czechoslovakia, and so on, both superpowers would have found it less urgent to compete for influence in these countries. Foreign regime imposition by both superpowers in the late 1940s helped cause the Cold War even as they were part of what we mean by the Cold War. In sum, it also is worth exploring whether great-power conflict is made more severe by transnational ideological struggles.[19]

*Transnational Networks*

As discussed in chapter 2, international relations scholars are paying considerable attention to transnational networks. My arguments certainly justify this attention. Transnational ideological networks (TINs) exist, display remarkable robustness over time and space, and help create conditions that make it more rational for governments to impose domestic regimes in other countries. Unlike the networks studied by most constructivists, however, TINs are about conflict as well as cooperation. They build cooperation with co-ideologues, but conflict with actors of rival ideologies. They are all about ideological boundaries: they clarify so as to exclude as well as to include; they are at pains to say what they are not so as to define what they are. Such is obviously true of a network such as al-Qaeda, or its grandfather the Muslim Brotherhood. But as I discuss briefly below, it is also arguably so with transnational networks that we normally associate simply with justice or human progress. Networks have played a crucial role in democratization in former communist lands in Eastern Europe and South Central Asia. Such groups as Amnesty International and the Soros Foundation see themselves as simply promoting human freedom. But because they threaten the power of authoritarian rulers, they are necessarily political actors. The literature on transnational networks would profit from attending more to the political ramifications of such entities.

Indeed, as Sidney Tarrow has urged, the entanglement of transnational networks and states or governments needs more scholarly treatment.[20] Inasmuch as networks can create conditions that alter or preserve the distribution of power among states, it would be astonishing if states and their rulers were indifferent to their activities. The cases in this book make clear that governments and networks are typically interpenetrated, each trying to exploit and capture the other. The U.S. government helps fund some of the networks that promote democracy and human rights today. Ties between the Saudi and Pakistani governments and transnational Sunni-Islamist networks are extensive, as are those between the Iranian government and Shia-Islamist networks. Although realism teaches that states always predominate, the cases in chapters 4 through 7 show that networks sometimes gain the upper hand and lead governments to do what they otherwise would not. More research is needed on conditions under which a network will have more leverage over a government and vice versa.

### Positive Feedback and System Effects

My arguments bolster claims that systemic concepts such as positive feedback, path dependence, and social polarization are useful in IR scholarship. Polarization is useful to understanding how preferences form, at least preferences over strategies. Polarization has long been present in IR theory in the spiral model and associated security dilemma.[21] Robert Jervis has recently extended it into other questions in international relations.[22] The historical cases in chapters 4 through 7 show that, on a microlevel, elites can polarize over ideology across states, leading governments to polarize as well by promoting regimes and trying to deter others from doing so. The decision by a ruler to promote a domestic regime abroad is heavily conditioned by earlier actions by elites across societies. In turn, forcible regime promotion feeds back into transnational society, further polarizing elites according to ideological affiliation.

On a macro-level of analysis, my arguments support claims that institutions or structures can be sticky or resistant to change. John Ikenberry makes path-dependent arguments about international institutions.[23] I argue that transnational contests over the best regime are also structural and show remarkable staying power. They are reproduced by governments that promote one domestic regime type and undermine competing types, and by transnational ideological networks laboring to foment revolutions, coups d'états, and so on. Both of these types of agent find it difficult to cease regime promotion. At the same time, I offer an explanation for those extraordinary times when such social structures emerge and disappear. At certain points exogenous forces—technological or social developments—push back and disrupt established ways of doing things, causing the structure to decay.

*International History*

History may be interpreted in any number of ways. The states system has spread throughout the globe; great powers have risen and fallen; globalization has gradually increased. Starting with figure 1.1 and running through my theoretical claims and case studies, I have implied that international history is, among other things, a cyclical story of a series of ideological struggles. The skeleton of the struggle may be read right off of the data on forcible regime promotion, which show that for five hundred years hard-headed statesmen have sometimes found it in their interests to act like ideologues. But underneath those actions were the structures I have been arguing for: zero-sum disputes over ideology that told actors who they were and what they should want. International history may plausibly be read as a recurring contest over a question asked by Aristotle 2,500 years ago: what is the best regime?

Furthermore, although one can attempt to divine a teleological unfolding of the answer, in the manner of Kant, Hegel, Kojève, and Fukuyama—after all, individual liberty and limited government do seem to emerge as the winners over time—what is most striking may be the regular patterns evident in the cases. Transnational ideological struggles happen across time and space and follow a recognizable life cycle. Exogenous changes in the environment, both social and material, disrupt a predominant regime type and set off a chain of events that produce alternative regimes. Struggles over regimes continue to interact with the environment in the form of forcible regime promotion. In the end, one regime emerges as superior. Forcible regime promotion, then, points us toward ways in which states and ideas regularly interact with the larger material and social environment. It is not at all clear that these patterns have ceased with the end of the Cold War, and indeed it may be that the post-1989 lull was unusually brief.

## Ideological Contests Today: History Is Back

Some thinkers have argued in recent decades that the contest is finally over and its winner is liberal democracy.[24] My treatment of the triumph of liberal or constitution democracy in the late 1980s (chapter 6) may be taken to imply that I agree. In fact, my argument, which is about unpredictable environmental changes and their effects on ideas and regimes, cannot make such pronouncements. Which brings us to current events. Some analysts see alternative regime types contesting liberal democracy in Latin America, in the form of Hugo Chávez's Bolivarism, and in Eurasia, in the form of the authoritarian capitalism of Vladimir Putin and the Chinese Communist Party. Full treatments of these questions are well beyond the scope of a section of a final chapter of a book, but I do venture a few propositions about each based upon the arguments and history I presented in the preceding chapters.

### Bolivarism

Hugo Chávez, President of Venezuela, is the main figure in a rejuvenated socialist movement that currently spans Latin America. Called Chavism or Bolivarism after the nineteenth-century revolutionary Simón Bolívar (chapter 5), the movement follows the classical pattern seen in past ideological movements of taking power away from propertied elites by concentrating it in the head of state, who ostensibly uses it to benefit the masses. A longtime socialist revolutionary who, as an army colonel, attempted to overthrow Venezuela's constitutional democracy in 1992, Chávez supervised the drafting of a new constitution following his election as President in February 1999. Ratified the following December, Venezuela's new constitution concentrates more power in the presidency by abolishing the Senate (reducing the national legislature to a single chamber) and extending the President's term from five to six years. It created the Vice Presidency and devolved more power to the military. In 2006, Chávez was re-elected, and in the ensuing years he has nationalized many industries, withdrawn Venezuela from the International Monetary Fund, and generally attempted to become the chief spokesman and mover behind anti-U.S. sentiment in Latin America. In 2007, Venezuelan voters rejected changes to the constitution that would have further empowered the presidency and removed term limits. In February 2009, he tried again and succeeded.[25]

Chávez has inspired leftists in Latin America and beyond and is clearly attempting to nurture and harness a transnational socialist movement. As one journalist has put it, "Caracas in the early 2000s has become what Petrograd was under Lenin in the early 1900s." Leftists from around the world have gathered there to "soak up" the Bolivarist "revolution."[26] A group of progressives from Spain, headed by constitutional scholar Roberto Viciano Pastor, played a significant role in drafting Venezuela's constitution.[27] Most significant has been the mobilization of socialists in other Latin American countries and their networking with Chávez and his Venezuelan party, the Fifth Republic Movement (MVR). Chávez has built ties with the Castros in Cuba. Friends and enemies of the movement have claimed that a wave of socialism has rolled over Latin America since the 1990s, with the election of Luiz Inácio Lula da Silva in Brazil, Néstor Kirchner and then Cristina Fernández de Kirchner in Argentina, Tabaré Vázquez in Uruguay, Daniel Ortega Saavedra in Nicaragua, Manuel Zeyala in Honduras, Evo Morales in Bolivia, and Rafael Correa in Ecuador. (The center-right government of Álvaro Uribe in Colombia has accused Chávez of subsidizing the Marxist-Leninist guerrilla group, the Revolutionary Armed Forces of Colombia or FARC; Chávez has denied this and has since publicly called on the FARC to renounce violent revolution.)[28]

Clearly, a transnational ideological movement is at work, linked to the ideology and interests of the government of Venezuela and propelled by its successes in generating and redistributing wealth (successes themselves propelled by high oil prices). This ideology opposes the interests of many other elites, particularly exporters of industrial and agricultural goods, and the ideology of the center-right coalitions that governed most Latin American states in the 1990s. Bolivarism also explicitly opposes the interests of the government of the United States. For a genuine transnational ideological struggle of the sort I have examined in this book—and hence the threat of forcible regime change—to take hold, the ideologies must implicate the fundamental institutions or *regimes* of countries, and not simply their policies. In Europe, governments regularly move from center-right to center-left, sometimes in multinational waves; changes in law and policy typically follow these changes of government. But constitutional or regime changes do not follow.

The question concerning Latin America, then, reduces to one of whether Bolivarism is not simply an alternative set of policies within the liberal-democratic regimes of Latin America, but an alternative regime. If the latter, then ruling and other elites who adhere to the latter will find Bolivarism sufficiently threatening that they will suppress its adherents, and Bolivarists will do likewise to liberal democrats. At the time of this writing it is too early to tell whether Bolivarism and liberal democracy are alternative and opposing regimes. It is significant that Chávez has gained approval of a new constitution increasing the powers of the presidency. Of the new wave of socialist heads of government, Morales of Bolivia and Correa of Ecuador have followed Chávez in hiring Viciano, the Spanish professor, to help draft a constitution centralizing more power in the executive.[29] Ecuador's voters approved Correa's charter in September 2008;[30] Bolivia's approved Morales's constitution in January 2009.[31] Each President may serve for an unlimited number of terms, but each must run for re-election each time—just as America's own Franklin Roosevelt had to do—and each country retains robust opposition parties. As for Chávez himself, he submitted to his electoral setback in 2007 and has also renounced violent revolution. It is fair to say, however, that Bolivarists and liberal-democrats have been polarizing across states and that their competition could eventually spiral into a full-blown regime contest. A great deal rides on whether Chávez continues to amass power to the point of eliminating competitive elections. Much also depends on the continuing success of the Bolivarist model, which in turn depends on continuing high global energy prices which fuel its success in Venezuela.

Should such a contest emerge, then regime instability in particular states will tempt foreign governments of both regime types to intervene. U.S. administrations will likewise be tempted to intervene to defeat or contain Bolivarism, by force if necessary, to maintain American influence in the region.[32]

*Authoritarian Capitalism*

The thesis is also abroad that a global ideological contest is taking shape between liberal democracy and a new form of authoritarianism, more robust than communism owing to its acceptance of and even intimacy with capitalism and capitalists. The two states exemplary of this type of authoritarianism are China and Russia. Robert Kagan argues that Chinese and Russian successes are returning the world to grand ideological conflict between political liberty and authoritarianism. "Ideologically, it is a time not of convergence but of divergence. The competition between liberalism and absolutism has reemerged, with the nations of the world increasingly lining up, as in the past, along ideological lines."[33] The China of today is not that of 1956 or 1966. The ruling Communist Party permits greater individual freedom, particularly in commerce. China's economy is heavily capitalist, and the country is vastly more open to foreign influence than during the rule of Mao Zedong. But the Party retains the monopoly on political power it has held by force since 1949. Although the Party has begun to allow greater citizen influence locally, Chinese elections are not competitive, dissenters are frequently arrested, and the Internet is censored.[34] Russia has been changing since the 1990s from a liberal democracy to a soft but increasingly hard authoritarian regime under Vladimir Putin. As President from 2000 until 2008, Putin concentrated more and more power in the executive by weakening the independent press, regional governments, opposition political parties, and both houses of the Russian parliament. He has also cracked down on foreign nongovernmental organizations in the country.[35]

Both countries have enjoyed impressive economic success in recent years, in contrast to their performance in the 1970s as Marxist-Leninist states. China's export-led economic growth since the early 1980s has been spectacular, its economy routinely achieving double-digit economic growth until the global economic recession that began in 2008. Should current trends continue, at some point in the second quarter of the century the Chinese economy should surpass the American as the world's largest.[36] Russia's economy shrank year after year during its liberal-democratic decade of the 1990s, but in the Putin years Russia has averaged between 5 percent and 10 percent growth per annum. But the source of Russian success is that of Venezuela rather than that of China: high global energy prices.[37]

Kagan argues that the leaders of both states fully intend to mount an ideological challenge to liberal democracy. Sergei Lavrov, Russia's Foreign Minister, announced in April 2007 that "for the first time in the last decade and a half a real competitive environment has formed in the market for ideas," particularly regarding "value [systems] and development models."[38] Is Lavrov correct? Michael McFaul and Kathryn Stoner-Weiss argue that authoritarianism actually hindered Russian growth in the 2000s,[39] and it is not clear that Russian or Chinese successes have stimulated transnational ideological networks. There is as yet no unifying authoritarian-capitalist ideology comparable to Marxism or fascism; for all their surface similarities, the Chinese and Russian regimes have significant differences.[40] But perhaps it is best to look at the question from the other side. Perhaps it is liberal democracy that has transnational momentum and a unifying ideology, at least in the eastern European and central Asian states formerly in the Soviet Union, and perhaps the authoritarians are reacting to that momentum. If so, and if the anti-liberals are going so far as to reject liberal democracy as a regime, then we indeed have a real transnational ideological struggle in that region. A historical analogy, one weighted with irony, would be the struggle between communists and authoritarians in the Third World during the Cold War (chapter 6). Authoritarians had no unifying ideology; that belonged to the communists.

So our focus should be on liberal democracy and its advocacy networks. Liberal democracies take different forms—some are presidential,

others parliamentary; some are republics, others constitutional monarchies—but they have in common the attempt to marry majority rule with
individual civil rights. Like republicanism, they locate sovereignty in the
people; like constitutionalism, they feature various institutions designed
to inhibit the concentration of power in a single person or institution. It
is clear that liberal elites form transnational networks today. Liberal governmental organizations, linked to the European Union and United States,
and nongovernmental organizations (NGOs), constitute one of the most
robust and well-funded sets of TINs in history. These groups push for human rights and competitive elections and build ties with elites in Ukraine,
Georgia, Kyrgyzstan, Belarus, and Russia itself. Their members do not
think of themselves as belonging to ideological groups—they are simply
helping people, effecting justice, participating in human progress[41]—but
they fit the definition of TIN: they are working across national borders
for the spread and consolidation of a particular type of political regime.

Indeed, the wave of "color revolutions" of the early 2000s—the Bulldozer Revolution in Serbia in 2000, the Rose Revolution in Georgia in
2003, the Orange Revolution in Ukraine in 2004–5, and the Tulip Revolution in Kyrgyzstan in 2005—appear much like waves of unrest and
revolution so typical in chapters 4 through 7. Adherents of one ideology,
liberal democracy, drew inspiration from foreign confreres and agitated
to achieve serious change in their own countries. Mark Beissinger notes
that the work of peace scholar Gene Sharp has been influential among
liberal activists in this region, and argues that interactions among liberals across these countries and beyond them were crucial to the "revolutions." NGOs have been heavily involved; in the spring of 2003, the Soros
Foundation paid for a trip by Georgian liberal students to Belgrade to
meet members of Otpor, the Serbian student group who played a large
role in the Bulldozer Revolution; within a few months the Georgians
had formed their own group, Kmara, with several thousand members.
Kmara played a large role in the Rose Revolution. Equally significant is
the financial, logistical, and diplomatic support provided liberal groups
in these countries by U.S. government-funded entities, including the International Republican Institute and the National Democratic Institute
for International Affairs.[42]

In contrast to the falling dominoes in late 1989 in Central Europe, the
"color revolutions" have not produced permanent change. Far from defecting to liberal democracy, authoritarian elites have stood fast against
it, perhaps because of the support they receive from the Putin government in Russia. Indeed, the Russian invasion of the Georgian province of
South Ossetia in August 2008 may be interpreted as a forcible attempt
to topple the pro-Western government of Mikhail Saakashvili. Russia's
invasion was triggered by Saakashvili's dispatching of troops to South

Ossetia to bring to heel the rebellious province. During the crisis, Russian President Dmitri Medvedev called Saakashvili a "lunatic," and Foreign Minister Lavrov called on him to resign. One U.S. military analyst writes: "Russia's strategic goal is for Georgia to renounce its intention to integrate into Euro-Atlantic structures, primarily NATO, and to return to a Russian sphere of influence—giving Russia a voice in Georgian foreign and security policy. Achieving that outcome requires the departure of the Saakashvili government and its replacement by a more compliant, Russia-friendly regime." Russia's rulers also wished to signal Ukraine and Azerbaijan, two other former Soviet republics with strong liberal networks, to abandon any plans to join NATO.[43]

In this region, then, many of the processes and events common in chapters 4 through 7 are clearly present. Is this a full-blown contest over regimes? At the time of this writing it does not completely qualify, because the anti-liberals have not completely renounced democracy. The Putin-Medvedev government of Russia has not explicitly done so. The "color revolutions" were not true regime changes, but were rather responses to fraudulent elections in each country that, if left unchallenged, could well have led to the abandonment of liberal democracy in these countries.[44] The "revolutions," in other words, preserved or restored rather than overturned the regimes in Serbia, Georgia, Ukraine, and Kyrgyzstan. This distinction may be a quibble at this point, however, as liberals and anti-liberals in this region continue to polarize and the latter do appear to be articulating an alternative regime, exemplified by Russia.[45]

In sum, it is distinctly possible that forcible regime promotion will be a fairly common event in the coming decades in Eastern Europe and Central Asia and somewhat less likely that it will do so in Latin America. The interests of outside states, especially the United States, are at stake in both regions, so U.S. leaders will find themselves with incentives to intervene so as to preserve or extend American influence. Insofar as Washington does intervene, particularly by force, it may serve short-term U.S. interests but also will exacerbate transnational ideological polarization and prolong the macro-struggle. Indeed, it is possible that anti-liberals in Eastern Europe, Asia, and Latin America could attempt to coalesce if the threat from U.S.-propelled liberalism becomes sufficiently dire. Signs have appeared that anti-liberal leaders are contemplating such a coalition, as Chávez has offered the Russians an island for a military base.[46]

In any event, if the cases in chapters 4 through 7 are analogous, then it is not U.S. promotion of liberal democracy that will end these struggles, but rather the fate of exemplary regimes in Russia (and perhaps China), in Eastern Europe and Central Asia, and of Venezuela in Latin America. The example and material support of these regimes to anti-liberals is crucial to the transnational struggle.

## Islamism and Secularism: How Might the Struggle End?

I return, at the end, to the problem with which I began this book, the struggle within the Muslim world among various types of secularist and various types of Islamist and that struggle's relation to the non-Muslim world. In its nearly nine decades, the intra-Muslim struggle has produced relatively little forcible regime promotion. But what it has produced in recent years—U.S.-led interventions in Afghanistan and Iraq—is important enough, and it may well produce more in the coming years. In Pakistan, in Iran, in Lebanon, potentially in Jordan or Syria or Egypt or Saudi Arabia, regime instability could tempt intervention by outside states, complicating international relations beyond their already bewildering situation. If I am correct that this ideational structure, this transnational competition over the best regime, so heavily conditions domestic and foreign policy, then how might the struggle end? What would produce a change in structure and a consensus among Muslim elites over the best regime?

### More Forcible Regime Promotion by the United States

The hawkish position is that the United States can simply eliminate Islamism, or at least tame it, by using overwhelming force. The most notorious popular statement of hawkishness comes from the journalist Ann Coulter, who declared shortly after 9/11: "We should invade their countries, kill their leaders, and convert them to Christianity."[47] Hawkishness tends to follow the proposition that the West is in a zero-sum clash with Islamism if not Islam itself. Islamism is always and everywhere an extreme ideology better called jihadism or Islamo-fascism. It is our mortal enemy and must be fought always and everywhere. Hawks backed regime change in Iraq and attribute American setbacks to incompetence and a failure of nerve concerning Shia Iran and, for some, Sunni Pakistan and Saudi Arabia. They push for regime change in Iran, perhaps by force. Hawks tend to downplay rifts between Sunnis and Shii and hence the possibility of playing one off against the other.[48] No compromise or tactical cooperation with Islamists can work; one does not bargain with the devil. Attempts at tactical cooperation will only be taken as weakness and invite further aggression. Daniel Pipes argues that there are no moderate Islamists: even those who work for change by constitutional means intend to pursue extreme, intolerant policies once they hold power, so dealing with such people is laying a bad bet.[49]

One difficulty with the hawkish position is that tactical cooperation among ideological foes is often possible and fruitful, as when the Iranian government of Mohammed Khatami cooperated with the United States in Afghanistan in the autumn of 2001.[50] More pertinent to our question is that although forcible regime promotion can accomplish certain important short-term goals, it does not end transnational ideological struggles. The cases in chapters 4 through 7 show that forcible regime promotion can often enhance the promoting government's internal and external security. But promotion is a strategy for navigating a long ideological contest, not for bringing one to a close. Indeed, promotion typically intensifies transnational ideological polarization and hence prolongs the struggle. One promotion sometimes has such strong feedback effects that it leads to a wave of counter-promotion in other states, which further prolongs the struggle. Positive feedback is no mere academic observation: it means that a government that believes it is ending a transnational contest over the best regime is actually entering that contest. Great-power rulers learned this the hard way. Charles V believed he was eliminating Lutheranism in the Schmalkaldic War of 1546, but he was instead setting up conditions for a second religious war in 1553 and aiding in the spread of Calvinism, a more militant form of Protestantism (chapter 4). In suppressing liberal revolutions in the early 1820s, the Austrian government was further motivating liberal networks, who broke out with more revolutions in the early 1830s (chapter 5).

The U.S.-led invasion of Iraq in 2003 may yet redound to America's benefit if Iraq becomes a stable constitutional democracy. As countless critics have observed, however, the short-term consequences have included further inflammation of Muslim opinion against the United States and thousands more young Sunni and Shia men joining the jihadists' ranks. Notwithstanding Bush's intentions and the obvious fact that the United States is not a Muslim country, America cannot transcend the struggle between Islamism and secularism. Islamist ideology depicts America as the Great Satan, the Far Enemy, the chief engine of secularization. When it attacks Muslim countries, it is fulfilling Islamists' prophecies and enhancing the jihadists' credibility. It is becoming a full co-belligerent in an ongoing ideological struggle, and is helping to perpetuate that struggle. That does not mean that the United States should never use force in the Muslim world; sometimes force will be the best option. It does mean that using force alone will not destroy the social structure, the agonizing intra-Islamic contest over the best regime.

### Virtuous Interaction, Gradual Change?

An alternative is the dovish position of those who stop at that last insight and conclude that the solution must be to break the cycle of vicious interaction between the West and the Muslim world and replace it with a virtuous cycle of interaction. Interaction comprises not only war and peace but economic transactions, citizen-to-citizen contacts, and discourse or speech-acts. For these doves, Islamist terrorism and extremism, and their appeal to the masses, are reactions to the acts and speech-acts of the powerful, chiefly the United States. For years America has offered unstinting support to Israeli hawks and Arab tyrants, so long as they follow the imperial script by maintaining stable oil prices and suppressing anti-American actors. More recently, Bush administration policies, especially the war in Iraq, have aggravated the situation. Edward Said, the late Palestinian-American literary critic, held that Western discourse about Islam, specifically the tendency to make Muslims into an oriental "other," was the root of the problem. Said sharply criticized the "clash of civilizations" thesis of Bernard Lewis and Samuel Huntington as essentializing and homogenizing Muslims.[51]

For doves, innovative leaders (often nonstate actors) can, over time, alter discourses and speech-acts and set off interactions that can bring about a convergence of identities. Muslims and Christians or secularists are not necessarily mortal enemies, but only become so when agents construct them as such. Writes Fred Halliday: "'Muslims,' like non-Muslims, have multiple identities, the relative balance and character of which change over time."[52] For John Esposito, the fault lies not with the stars or the crescent moon but with ourselves: "At times it seems the West's attitude toward communism is being transferred to or replicated in the elevation of a new threat, 'Islamic fundamentalism.' "[53] Through collective action, say doves, we can reverse course and pull the world toward a shared progressive purpose. Thus do foreign policy experts call for Western negotiations with the Muslim Brotherhood,[54] with Hamas, and with the government of Iran.[55]

No doubt taking risks for peace can sometimes pay dividends and reconcile ideological enemies. One encouraging story comes from Tajikistan, which in the 1990s was torn by a complex civil war. Sharif Himmatzoda, a former rebel Islamist commander who joined the government after the 1997 cease-fire, concluded:

> The peace process in Tajikistan can be a model for Central Asia if all parties are willing to build peace just as we were. But governments in the region have to change their attitudes toward Islamic movements to give them a legal, constitutional way to express themselves and play a role in state building. If they don't do so, people will join the extremists.[56]

President Bush himself appealed to a form of this thesis at a United Nations conference on development in 2002: "We fight against poverty because hope is an answer to terror." Bush promised to increase U.S. aid to poor countries by 50 percent, or $5 billion, over the following few years.[57]

But here again, the cases in chapters 4 through 7 encourage little hope that attempts to transform vicious social interaction into virtuous can end a prolonged transnational contest over the best regime. In general, those who argue for this kind of solution appeal to some sort of social-interactionist model that falls under the constructivist heading in IR theory. I have already argued that that model, whatever its validity in some realms, by itself cannot account for the end of past grand ideological struggles. Most striking are the attempts to argue for and implement religious toleration, and hence to transcend the Catholic-Protestant ideological divide, in early modern Europe (chapter4). Sebastian Castellio published arguments for toleration in 1553, sixty-five years before the outbreak of the Thirty Years' War. Princes in the Empire, France, and elsewhere tried toleration as a *modus vivendi* for many decades. For all their compelling logic—compelling at least to today's liberal reader—their arguments did not stick. Protestant and Catholic elites continued to fall periodically into zero-sum competition that produced waves of forcible regime promotion, including the horrors that nearly destroyed German society in the 1620s and 1630s.

The same dreary story emerges from other ideological contests. Cooperation between the British, who were constitutional monarchists, and the Austrians, Prussians, and Russians, who were absolute monarchists, deteriorated when regimes began to change in the early 1820s and again in the early 1830s (chapter 5). The collapse of cooperation between communists and liberal democrats after the Second World War is well known. Changes in domestic regimes in Europe and elsewhere polarized governments and other actors according to ideology, and trust shriveled, to the surprise of many (chapter 6). Historians often lament "lost chances" for peace and cooperation, but that such chances are so often lost suggests that they may not have been realistic to begin with. In the late 1940s Henry Wallace, a former U.S. Vice President, advocated friendly relations with the Soviet Union and called on his country to be more understanding of Soviet insecurities. In the State Department were China experts who made and responded to overtures from Chou Enlai's moderate wing of the Chinese Communist Party. These all failed in the face of strong constraints on U.S. policy, domestic and foreign. In the late 1940s, communists and liberals really did have deep conflicts of interest owing to the generally held conviction that their regimes were in a zero-sum game.

The problem in all of these cases was that the structure—a transnational contest over the best regime—remained in place, perpetuated by TINs and governments. And simply offering a "third way" could not destroy that structure. In the early nineteenth century, constitutional monarchy on the British model seemed—certainly to the British—a third way between absolute monarchy and republicanism (chapter 5). Other European elites did not adopt constitutionalism in the 1810s or 1820s. When the French adopted it in 1830, other absolutist and republican elites still refused to do so do. In the twentieth century, fascists proposed their system as a third way between execrable Bolshevism and pathetic, exhausted constitutional democracy (chapter 6). Fascists were certainly agents of change who proposed ideas and practices that excited many, including the young who were impatient with creaky liberal regimes. But happily, not all elites gave up on liberal democracy. Transnational ideological contests lasted far longer than observers in the middle of them tended to think they would.

Of course, one never knows whether one is nearer the beginning or the end of such a struggle. But what is clear is that, in the current case of Islamism *versus* secularism, attempts to transcend the divide have failed thus far. Ironically, many in the West who seek to overcome this deep ideological divide are duplicating the Bush administration's actions by unwittingly entering the lists on the side of secularism—a softer-edged version, to be sure, but secularism nonetheless. Fred Halliday's policy suggestions are illustrative:

> To evolve a policy to solve or reduce what is presented as the conflict between the "West" and the Islamic world requires a dual programme: first, separate the real, material, specific and secular difficulties from their confused religious expression; then address these difficulties themselves. To sum it up, such a policy would have to be underpinned by a concept of universalism, *which would include secularism*, plus development.[58]

Edward Said's advice is similar:

> These are tense times, but it is better to think in terms of powerful and powerless communities, the *secular politics of reason and ignorance*, and universal principles of justice and injustice, than to wander off in search of vast abstractions that may give momentary satisfaction but little self-knowledge or informed analysis.[59]

By now the difficulty with this type of advice should be clear: Halliday and Said are secularists who consider the material real, and the religious merely imaginary. Their beliefs directly contradict those that devout Muslims hold dear, and in so doing they make Islamism more appealing to the devout. Western secularist intellectuals use word processors rather than aerial drones, but to Islamists they are still aggressors, not peacemakers. If there is a myth here, it is that secularism is above the fray.

*Islamism Fails, or Secularism, or Both*

My explanation for forcible regime promotion, and the cases in chapters 4 through 7, imply that the death-struggle between Islamism and secularism can end only in death—the death of one regime, or the other, or both. The account I advance for the emergence, persistence, and demise of this type of social structure is ecological, locating the causes of change in the environment itself rather than solely in agents and their ideas. An ideological macro-struggle fades when one or more of the contending ideologies are manifestly failing on their own terms. That happens when states that exemplify the regime are obviously failing on their own terms, while states that exemplify an opposing regime are succeeding. Without manifest failure and success of contending regime types, agents may formulate and propagate ideas to end or transcend the contest, but will gain few adherents. Eventually, permanent structural change does take place, and agency and interaction are essential to that process. But the ideas that shape identities themselves must have exhausted their credibility.

The end of the current macro-struggle in the Muslim world will involve either the collapse of Islamism or secularism, or some form of convergence in which the two not only agree to compete within the same constitutional order but have overlapping ends. The end of Islamism or secularism can only follow from the failure of states that exemplify it to achieve the goals their rulers set themselves. The leading Islamist exemplar remains Iran. Should Iran descend into deep poverty owing to a sustained fall in oil prices, or should its own people throw off its *faqih* regime—as appeared possible in June 2009—Islamism's prestige would degrade sharply, particularly among the Shii in Iraq, Lebanon, Bahrain, and elsewhere. The Iranian government's nuclear program is relevant to Islamism's prestige. Should Iran gain nuclear weapons, it would not only be secure from U.S. or Israeli attack and be freer to promote Shia Islamism abroad. It would also rise in the estimation of Muslims, even Arab and Sunni Muslims. As Mohammed El Baradei, head of the International Atomic Energy Agency, has said of Iran's nuclear quest: "But the ultimate aim of Iran, as I understand it, is that they want to be recognized as a major power in the Middle East and they are. This is to them the road to get that recognition to power and prestige and …an insurance policy against what they heard in the past about regime change, axis of evil."[60]

The case of Sunni Islamism is more complex. The Sunni-Islamist regime in Afghanistan fell in 2001, and that in Sudan has been sharing power since 2005. Sunni Islamists are fighting for control of Pakistan, Afghanistan, and Somalia but, at the time of this writing, have not succeeded.

The chief exemplar of Sunni Islamism remains Saudi Arabia, whose King is the "Custodian of the Two Holy Mosques," whose laws are a strict form of *Shariah*. As discussed in chapter 7, since 1964 the Saudis have used their wealth to propagate all over the world their Wahhabist form of Islam. Secularist Muslims have seen the Muslim Brotherhood as a carrier of Saudi influence. But Saudi relations with foreign Sunni Islamists are complex. The Saudis' pro-Western foreign policy has alienated radicals and contributed to the formation and expansion of al-Qaeda. Still, historical analogues suggest that a failure of Wahhabism on the Arabian Peninsula would inflict deep damage on the credibility of Sunni Islamism. The 1991 collapse of the Soviet Union damaged the global prestige of communism in general, including of the Eurocommunists who had been alienated from the Soviet regime since the 1960s.

Should Islamism's exemplars fail vis-à-vis their secularist rivals, then the counsel of Halliday, Said, and other secularists will begin to make sense to more and more Muslim elites. A cascade of defections from Islamism to secularism would take place. Of course, it might be secularism that ends up failing and Islamism triumphing. Leading secularist states in North Africa and southwest Asia are Egypt, Syria, and the non-Arab states of Pakistan and Turkey. These states have not enjoyed high prestige among foreign elites in recent decades, and all have significant Islamist movements. (It also should be noted that Egypt and Syria have authoritarian regimes that ruthlessly suppress Islamism, while both Pakistan and Turkey are semi-democratic.) Should these states manifestly perform poorly compared to Iran or perhaps Saudi Arabia, an elite cascade toward Islamism could take place.

It would be foolish to offer a firm prediction, but thus far neither secularism nor Islamism inspires confidence that it has a significant reproductive advantage in the Muslim world today. The social and material environment has not been kind to either model. Thus another possible end to the grand Islamist-secularist struggle is some kind of convergence, analogous to the conservative-liberal hybrid that emerged in state after state in Europe in the 1870s. In the European case (chapter 5), the revolutions of 1848 frightened absolutists, constitutionalists, and moderate republicans into striking a new bargain in the form of a reforming conservative regime on roughly the British constitutionalist model. That is, absolute monarchy had failed but its competitors had not fully triumphed; instead, a new shared threat, radical socialism and anarchism, had appeared in transnational strength. Could something similar happen in the Muslim world? Some analysts submit that a hybrid political party—Islamist yet liberal—already exists and has been governing Turkey since 2002. The Justice and Development Party (AKP) has Islamist roots, but its leaders claim to have abandoned the goal of imposing *Shariah* on Turkey. AK

Party leaders present themselves as a Muslim version of the Christian Democratic parties of Europe and Latin America.[61] The AK Party favors Turkish membership in the European Union and has passed a number of liberalizing reforms to that end.[62] Turkey's economy has grown impressively under its governance, averaging 6.5 percent annually between 2002 and 2008, compared to 2.5 percent in the preceding six-year period.[63]

Secularists in Turkey suspect the AK Party of harboring a secret Islamist agenda.[64] Regardless of how developments unfold in Turkey, it is clear that some Muslim writers are grappling with how to maintain a society shaped by the religion yet also respectful of human rights as modern liberals understand them. The works of such scholars as Adbdulaziz Sachedina,[65] Abdolkarim Soroush,[66] Khaled Abou El Fadl,[67] Sohail Hashmi,[68] and others are retrieving from Islamic theology and jurisprudence norms and practices more consistent with constitutional democracy and human rights than either Islamists or Muslim secularists have recognized and observed. Just as Castellio and other European Christians in the sixteenth and seventeenth centuries laid the intellectual groundwork for religious toleration in devoutly Christian societies, these Muslim writers could be doing the same for Muslim societies. Transnational networks already disseminate their ideas.[69]

It is worth recalling that Western liberal democracies too contain competing ideologies with opposing visions of the good society. Most relevant to the problem at hand, liberal democracies contain people and groups with different views on how far laws and policies ought to reflect moral norms that derive from religion. Although extremists in both groups portray the other as dangerous, the vast majority of religious and non-religious people in a country such as the United States uphold the liberal-democratic regime, and each side normally acknowledges the other's acceptance. Indeed, perhaps for all its problems the American polity is a type of loose model for the reconciliation of Islamists and secularists.[70] I have termed the American regime secular; it is a secularism tolerant of certain public expressions of religion and that allows religious groups autonomy.

For these arguments to win and some kind of secularist-Islamist hybrid to take shape in concrete form in real Muslim countries, an ecological change must occur to bring enough Islamist and secularist elites together to strike a bargain. If nineteenth-century Europe is instructive, then that shock could be overreaching by radical Islamists. Islamist violence in Algeria in the 1990s discredited the movement there. There is evidence that jihadists' killing of Muslims in Iraq and Taliban extremism in Pakistan has hurt their cause. Should radical Islamists—al-Qaeda and affiliate groups—carry out coordinated violent attacks across the Muslim world, devout Muslims who do not want their societies to imitate the West yet recoil from suicide bombing and ritual stoning could come to terms with secularists alarmed at the violence and weary of the struggle. Or should the rulers of Iran resort to savagery in suppressing reformist dissent, Islamism may lose such elite support in other states as to trigger a cascade away from it.

In any event, the cases in this book do suggest that transnational ideological struggles can last much longer than seems possible in the middle of them, and require patience across generations. There are indeed rifts among Islamists just as there are among secularists. Gilles Kepel is surely correct that Islamists are "[t]orn between those favoring rapprochement with democrats and those intoxicated by the mystique of jihad." More questionable is his conclusion that "the [9/11] attack on the United States was a desperate symbol of the isolation, fragmentation, and decline of the Islamist movement, not a sign of its strength and irrepressible might."[71] Catholic theocracy was desperate in 1546 and 1618; absolute monarchism, in 1793; liberal democracy, in the 1930s. All recovered and fought on for many decades. Experts have forecast the imminent demise of Islamism ever since the movement's emergence. Indeed, one source of its success has been the tendency of its secularist enemies to underestimate the appeal of such a seemingly atavistic movement. The continuing popularity of Islamism from England to Algeria to Malaysia suggests that journalist Rami Khouri is correct: "The winds of change in this region are blowing into the sails of a continuing Islamist revival that has now moved into the next stage, wherein Islamist parties exploit local and national grievances to gain power through elections. ...The wind will continue to blow in the same direction, as it has for thirty years now."[72]

Were there no Islamism or no secularism, or were the two to converge, the Muslim world would still have conflicts and power struggles. States would have conflicting interests and the same commitment problems stemming from international anarchy. Tensions between Muslims and Jews, Arabs and Persians, Sunnis and Shii, Pashtuns and Tajiks, Pakistanis and Indians, and oil-rich and poor countries would be present and doubtless lead to conflict. The United States would still be striving to maintain hegemony over the Middle East owing to the need of the U.S. economy—and the global economy upon whose health it increasingly depends—for cheap energy. America would still provide strong support for Israel. But the contest in the Muslim world over the best regime makes certain types and lines of conflict more likely by introducing a distinctive source of threat and opportunity to actors, including governments. Were it to end, fewer Muslims and fewer Americans would die.

And end it will, as at least some of the ideas that fuel it become discredited and no longer command the support of significant numbers of elites. We may be confident that the struggle will end because previous such struggles ended. We must be careful about teleological history, but it is striking that each of the three large ideological struggles chronicled and analyzed in this book ended with the triumph of a moderate constitutional regime. The religiously tolerant system pioneered by the Dutch; constitutionalism, exemplified by the British; liberal capitalist democracy, modeled by the United States and its allies: these were neither radical nor reactionary, but accommodated the social and material realities of their time. Although ideologies such as absolute monarchy or communism can endure for decades under the sponsorship of powerful states, the environment eventually pushes back. At a time we cannot predict, in ways we cannot control, it will push back and calm the agonies that have for so long convulsed the Muslim world.

## Appendix Concerning Data on
## Forcible Regime Promotion, 1510–2010

THE DATA COMPRISE ATTEMPTS by any state to use direct force with the object of constructing, preserving, or altering one or more political institutions in another state.[1] A *state* is a sovereign territorial unit. To qualify, a target state must retain legal sovereignty after the promotion. I limit targets to sovereign states because such cases are most relevant to IR theory. Through the centuries, imperial powers have likewise sought to impose their institutions upon conquered territories, but since the age of formal empires is ended it is more relevant to current events to limit analysis to cases in which targets were nominally sovereign. By *sovereignty* I mean a combination of what Stephen Krasner[2] calls Westphalian sovereignty and international-legal sovereignty. Westphalian sovereignty is "political organization based on the exclusion of external actors from authority structures within a given territory"; international-legal sovereignty relates to "the practices associated with mutual recognition, usually between territorial entities that have formal juridical independence." The line between a sovereign and a non-sovereign target is not always clear. I do include cases that many scholars would classify under informal imperialism, for example, U.S. promotions in Latin America and the Caribbean in the twentieth century or Soviet promotions in Central Europe in the late 1940s. It is certainly the case that the promoter had extensive influence in such target states, but influence is one of the purposes of regime promotion. Non-sovereign targets (excluded from the data) include states upon which annexation attempts are made, such as Germany in Austria in 1938 or North Korea in South Korea in 1950. Non-sovereign targets also include those that retain some of the nominal trappings of sovereignty but are ultimately ruled by an intervening state, for example, through a viceroy or governor general, such as Norway by Germany during the Second World War.

Those estates in the Holy Roman Empire not directly ruled by the Emperor, including most of the German-speaking estates, do qualify as sovereign targets for the Emperor as well as any other ruler. Daniel Nexon argues that in previously published work I am wrong to treat the estates of the Empire as sovereign.[3] The Empire had a bewilderingly complex constitution in which estates were formally loyal to the Emperor, Imperial diets were regularly convened to deal with political problems and set rules, and standing Imperial tribunals attempted to resolve disputes. Emperors, including Charles V (see chapter 4), had ambitions to gain the high degree of control over Germany that he had over Spain, or that his rival Francis I had over France. Yet, already in the fourteenth century the jurist Bartolus of Sassoferrato had noted that the rule *rex in regno suo est imperator regni sui* (the king in his domain is as the emperor in his) was emerging.[4] James Tracy refers to the "vast and ramshackle Holy Roman Empire, where each prince and city-state ruled more or less without interference from the emperor";[5] M. J. Rodríguez-Salgado, to the recognition of "the essential independence of each state."[6] Because emperors were elected by seven princes, the Empire had an intrinsic tendency to decentralize as candidates granted privileges to electors in exchange for their votes. Crucial moments in the empowerment of the imperial estates at the expense of the emperors include the "double election" of 1198, imperial cessions of various privileges to territorial princes in 1220 and 1231, and the *Interregnum* of 1256–73, which forced towns to transfer their loyalty from the emperor to local lords.[7] Another came in 1356 when Emperor Charles IV issued the Golden Bull, which eliminated Imperial jurisdiction in the territories of the electors and facilitated its erosion throughout the Empire.[8] Imperial German estates were independent enough that we may treat them as separate units. But the so-called Habsburg hereditary lands such as Bohemia do not qualify as targets when the promoter is the Empire (i.e., the Emperor and the Habsburg armies, sometimes from Spain or Flanders); they are targets, however, for outside powers such as Sweden or Transylvania, because the rulers of the latter do not seem to have intended to annex the targets.

Among Napoleon's conquests (chapter 5), I exclude those that he ruled directly, such as in Flanders, the Balkans, or north central Italy. I include territories ruled by others, including Napoleon's relatives, even though the Emperor exerted influence in such areas.[9] I exclude states the Soviet Union annexed, such as the Baltic States (chapter 6). Among Hitler's conquests, I exclude those ruled by a military commander or governor general, such as Poland and Norway. I include those ruled by a (nominally) sovereign government, such as Vichy France or Denmark (until 1943, when Berlin took direct control). Being militarily occupied per se does not disqualify a state from sovereign status; such occupations are traditionally treated in international law as temporary situations to be resolved at a subsequent peace conference.[10]

By *internal political regime* is meant any set of norms, or predominant rules, governing the relation of rulers to ruled within a given state's borders, that is, governing the administration of the state's coercive power over its own subjects and their property. Examples include liberal democracy, state socialism, Islamism, absolute monarchy, Bonapartism, and established Calvinism. Not included are interventions to replace one ruler or government with another under the same regime. Thus, wars over monarchical succession do not qualify unless a regime change (e.g., from absolute to constitutional monarchy) is at stake. Consequently, the War of the Spanish Succession (1701–14) does not qualify. Neither do U.S. interventions that were intended simply to save or overthrow one leader or faction within a regime, such as in Cuba 1906–1909. Interventions in civil wars in which no ideological differences among factions are evident do not qualify as cases. Thus, French and Libyan interventions in Chad in the 1980s are not included.

*Uses of force* are direct applications of violence, such as invasions, sieges, military occupations, naval attacks or blockades, and aerial bombardments by the assets of the intervening state (as distinguished from those of allies or nationals in the target state, or mercenaries from a third state). A state may use any amount of its own forces. I employ no threshold for numbers of troops or battle deaths. Interventions may succeed or fail, as long as the intervener understood that one object of the intervention was to promote institutions in the target.

The primary motive of the intervener need not have been to alter or preserve particular institutions in the target; I do not claim that all, or indeed any, of these interventions were motivated by a commitment to principle, although neither do I rule that out. The intervener need only have clearly intended to promote a particular regime (its own or another) in the target. Evidence of this intent is found in statements before or during the intervention, in actual behavior following the application of force, or both. Concerning the intent of the promoting state, cases come in two types. Ex post promotions are those in which the promoting government attacked the target during wartime, at least in part for strategic or tactical reasons, and upon conquering the target sets up a new regime. Typical examples are the uses of force by the French Republic in the 1790s and the Americans and Soviets in Europe in the late 1940s. Ex ante promotions are those in which the promoting state attacks the target in peacetime but during a civil conflict in the target, and among its stated reasons is that the side it favors would set up or preserve a certain regime. Typical examples are the waves of interventions by European great powers in smaller European states in the 1820s, 1830s, and 1840s.

I do not include implicit or explicit threats to use force, such as military, naval, or aerial exercises. Neither do covert actions such as material or intelligence support for coups d'états or revolutions qualify, unless those actions also involved application of the intervener's own military assets. U.S. covert interventions in Iran in 1953 and Guatemala in 1954 do not qualify. A state that sends military advisers, subsidies, or matériel for use in a target is not applying force directly; thus, FDR's use of lend-lease prior to its joining the Second World War does not count as forc-ible regime promotion on Germany and Italy. The main justification for these criteria is ease of application. Doubtless unexecuted threats, covert actions, subsidies, and other means of institutional promotion would en-hance our understanding of foreign regime promotion. But identifying the universe of cases of these events, particularly covert action, is pro-hibitively difficult.[11] I do note in chapters 4 through 7 some covert regime promotions and discuss the significance of their covertness.

I count as a single case any intervention in which multiple states in-tervened on the same side simultaneously. I count as two cases those in which one state intervened and a second state later intervened on the same side. I count interventions as two cases in which two or more states intervened on opposite sides.

Any event may be categorized in any number of ways. Depending on the purpose of analysis, the Second World War may be classified as a war, a hegemonic war, a global war, an ideological war, an imperialistic war, a war for civilization, or a tragedy. Many of the cases in the dataset could be (and have been) classified as wars, interventions in civil wars, aid to secessionists, or instances of informal imperialism. What they have in common are the features described above.

# Notes

CHAPTER I
FORCIBLE REGIME PROMOTION, THEN AND NOW

1. See the evolution of the term as tracked by the *Oxford English Dictionary*: http://www.oed.com/bbcwords/regime-new.html, accessed on June 28, 2009.

2. The graph, tables, and much of the discussion of it later in this chapter are modified from John M. Owen, IV, "The Foreign Imposition of Domestic Institutions," *International Organization* 56 (2002), 375–409.

3. David Easton, John G. Gunnell, and Michael Stein, "Introduction: Democracy as a Regime Type and the Development of Political Science," in idem, ed., *Regime and Discipline: Democracy and the Development of Political Science* (Ann Arbor: University of Michigan Press, 1995), 8–9.

4. Stephen D. Krasner, *Sovereignty: Organized Hypocrisy* (Princeton, NJ: Princeton University Press, 1999).

5. G. John Ikenberry and Charles A. Kupchan, "Socialization and Hegemonic Power," *International Organization* 44 (1990), 283–315.

6. Nigel Lo, Barry Hashimoto, and Dan Reiter, "Ensuring Peace: Foreign-Imposed Regime Change and Postwar Peace Duration, 1914–2001," *International Organization* 62 (2008), 717–36.

7. Jon Elster, "A Plea for Mechanisms," in Peter Hedström and Richard Swedberg, eds., *Social Mechanisms: An Analytical Approach to Social Theory* (New York: Cambridge University Press, 1998), 45–73.

8. Martin Wight, *Power Politics* (Harmondsworth, UK: Penguin, 1978), 81–94. I thank Andrew Hurrell for calling my attention to Wight's essay.

9. Raymond Aron, *Peace and War: A Theory of International Relations* (1966; new ed., New Brunswick, NJ: Transaction Publishers, 2003), 99–101.

10. K. J. Holsti, *Peace and War: Armed Conflicts and International Order 1648–1989* (New York: Cambridge University Press, 1991).

11. Mark N. Katz, *Revolutions and Revolutionary Waves* (New York: Palgrave Macmillan, 1999).

12. David Skidmore, ed., *Contested Social Orders and International Politics* (Nashville, TN: Vanderbilt University Press, 1997).

13. J. H. Leurdijk, *Intervention in International Politics* (Leeuwarden, The Netherlands: Eisma B.V., 1986); idem, *Armed Intervention in International Politics: A Historical and Comparative Analysis* (Nijmegen, The Netherlands: Wolf Legal Publishers, 2006).

14. Richard N. Rosecrance, *Action and Reaction in World Politics: International Systems in Perspective* (Boston: Little, Brown, 1963).

15. George Liska, "Alignments and Realignments," in Julian R. Friedman, Christopher Bladen, and Steven Rosen, eds., *Alliance in International Politics* (Boston: Allyn and Bacon, 1970), 104–20.

16. Stephen M. Walt, *Revolution and War* (Ithaca, NY: Cornell University Press, 1996).

17. Mark L. Haas, *The Ideological Origins of Great Power Politics, 1789–1989* (Ithaca, NY: Cornell University Press, 2005).

18. F. Gregory Gause III, "Balancing What? Threat Perception and Alliance Choice in the Gulf," *Security Studies* 13: 2 (Winter 2003/04), 273–305.

19. Realists could object that forcible regime promotion is not very costly; in that case it would be irrelevant to state power and uninteresting to realism. I address this objection below.

20. Paul Kowert and Jeffrey Legro, "Norms, Identity, and Their Limits: A Theoretical Reprise," in Peter J. Katzenstein, ed., *The Culture of National Security* (New York: Columbia University Press, 1996), 451–97.

21. Martha Finnemore and Kathryn Sikkink, "International Norm Dynamics and Political Change," *International Organization* 52 (1998), 916.

22. See Jeffrey T. Checkel, "The Constructivist Turn in International Relations Theory," *World Politics* 50 (1998), 332.

23. Thucydides, *History of the Peloponnesian War*, trans. C. W. Crawley (New York: Modern Library, 1982), 193–202.

24. Strictly speaking, Guelphs and Ghibellines were identified according to whether they backed the papacy (Guelph) or empire (Ghibellines) in the great struggle for political authority in Western medieval Christendom. See Edmund Garner, "Guelphs and Ghibellines," *Catholic Encyclopedia*, vol. 7 (New York: Robert Appleton, 1910), http://www.newadvent.org/cathen/07056c.htm, accessed on November 10, 2009.

25. Suzanne Werner, "Absolute and Limited War: The Possibility of Foreign-Imposed Regime Change," *International Interactions* 22 (1996), 67–88.

26. David Maland, *Europe at War 1600–1650* (Totowa, NJ: Rowman and Littlefield, 1980), 107.

27. Paul W. Schroeder, *The Transformation of European Politics, 1763–1848* (New York: Oxford University Press, 1994), 62.

28. Here great power status is based on statistics on military manpower in Paul Kennedy, *The Rise and Fall of the Great Powers: Economic Change and Military Conflict from 1500 to 2000* (New York: Random House, 1987), 56. In this book's appendix, I justify the classification of Imperial estates as sovereign states.

29. Werner, "Absolute and Limited War," finds that regime imposition increases with the power differential between victor and vanquished.

30. Civil unrest may be under-reported in table 1.1. In general, all of central Europe was in political ferment between 1618 and 1648, but only when the evidence was clear did I record a target as undergoing political unrest immediately before an intervention.

31. N. M. Sutherland, *Princes, Politics, and Religion, 1574–1589* (London: Hambledon, 1984), 74–80.

32. Maland, *Europe at War*, 15.

33. Niccolò Machiavelli, *The Prince*, trans. Harvey C. Mansfield, Jr. (Chicago: University of Chicago Press, 1998), chap. 5, 20–21. Machiavelli does not mention Athens's promotions of democracy in other Greek cities.

34. Thomas Schelling, *Arms and Influence* (New Haven, CT: Yale University Press, 1966), chap. 2.

35. Paul Pierson, *Politics in Time: History, Institutions, and Social Analysis* (Princeton, NJ: Princeton University Press, 2004).

CHAPTER 2
THE AGENTS: TRANSNATIONAL NETWORKS AND GOVERNMENTS

1. Thomas Risse-Kappen, "Ideas Do Not Float Freely: Transnational Coalitions, Domestic Structures, and the End of the Cold War," *International Organization* 48 (1994), 185–214.

2. Walter W. Powell, "Neither Market nor Hierarchy: Network Forms of Organization," *Research in Organizational Behavior* 12 (1990), 295–336.

3. Robert O. Keohane and Joseph S. Nye, Jr., *Power and Interdependence*, 3rd ed. (New York: Longman, 2001), 20–32.

4. Peter M. Haas, "Introduction: Epistemic Communities and International Policy Coordination," *International Organization* 46 (1992), 1–35.

5. Thomas Risse-Kappen, ed., *Bringing Transnational Relations Back In: Nonstate Actors, Domestic Structures, and International Institutions* (New York: Cambridge University Press, 1995).

6. Matthew Evangelista, *Unarmed Forces: The Transnational Movement to End the Cold War* (Ithaca, NY: Cornell University Press, 1999).

7. Daniel Thomas, *The Helsinki Effect: International Norms, Human Rights, and the Demise of Communism* (Princeton, NJ: Princeton University Press, 2001).

8. Margaret Keck and Kathryn Sikkink, *Activists beyond Borders: Advocacy Networks in International Politics* (Ithaca, NY: Cornell University Press, 1998), 8–9.

9. E.g., Ethan A. Nadelmann, "Global Prohibition Regimes: The Evolution of Norms in International Society," *International Organization* 44 (1990), 479–526; Thomas Risse and Kathryn Sikkink, "The Socialization of International Human Rights Norms into Domestic Practices: Introduction," in Thomas Risse, Stephen C. Ropp, and Kathryn Sikkink, eds., *The Power of Human Rights: International Norms and Domestic Change* (New York: Cambridge University Press, 1999), 1–38; Jacqui True and Michael Mintrom, "Transnational Networks and Policy Diffusion: The Case of Gender Mainstreaming," *International Studies Quarterly* 45 (2001), 27–57.

10. See http://www.socialistinternational.org/.

11. These include institutes in Australia, Greece, Guatemala, and the United States. See http://www.fraserinstitute.org/aboutus/Other_Info_Sources.htm.

12. David Easton, John G. Gunnell, and Michael Stein, "Introduction: Democracy as a Regime Type and the Development of Political Science," in idem, ed., *Regime and Discipline: Democracy and the Development of Political Science* (Ann Arbor: University of Michigan Press, 1995), 8–9.

13. Douglas McAdam, Sidney Tarrow, and Charles Tilly, *Dynamics of Contention* (New York: Cambridge University Press, 2001).

14. On early modern religio-political networks and their effects on international politics, see Daniel Nexon, *The Struggle for Power in Early Modern Europe: Religious Conflict, Dynastic Empires, and Political Change* (Princeton, NJ: Princeton University Press, 2009).

15. For a contemporary example of the latter, see Chetan Kumar, "Transnational Networks and Campaigns for Democracy," in Ann M. Florini, ed., *The Third Force: The Rise of Transnational Civil Society* (Washington, DC: Carnegie Endowment for International Peace, 2000), 115–42.

16. Anthony Downs, *An Economic Theory of Democracy* (New York: Harper & Row, 1957).

17. Sidney Tarrow, "Transnational Politics: Contention and Institutions in International Politics," *Annual Review of Political Science*, 4 (2001), 1–20. The Communist International and its successor the Comecon might better be seen as hierarchies than as networks; see Powell, "Neither Market nor Hierarchy."

18. David Skidmore, ed., *Contested Social Orders and International Politics* (Nashville, TN: Vanderbilt University Press, 1997), 3; John M. Owen, IV, *Liberal Peace, Liberal War: American Politics and International Security* (Ithaca, NY: Cornell University Press, 1997); idem, "Transnational Liberalism and U.S. Primacy," *International Security* 26:3 (2001/2002), 124; Mark L. Haas, "Ideology and Alliances: British and French External Balancing Decisions in the 1930s," *Security Studies* 12:4 (2003); idem, *The Ideological Origins of Great Power Politics, 1789–1989* (Ithaca, NY: Cornell University Press, 2005); Kevin Narizny, "The Political Economy of Alignment: Great Britain's Commitments to Europe, 1905–39," *International Security* 27:4 (2003), 184–219.

19. Nigel Gould-Davies, "Rethinking the Role of Ideology in International Politics during the Cold War," *Journal of Cold War Studies* 1 (Winter 1999), 98.

20. For a survey of literature on revolutions, see Jack A. Goldstone, "Toward a Fourth Generation of Revolutionary Theory," *Annual Review of Political Science* 4 (2001), 139–87.

21. For a general analysis of the effects of a revolution on the internal and external security of foreign states, see Stephen M. Walt, *Revolution and War* (Ithaca, NY: Cornell University Press, 1996), esp. 39–43. I corroborate many of Walt's findings; at the end of chapter 3, I distinguish my claims from his.

22. On the tendency for revolutions to inspire imitations, see Mark Katz, *Revolutions and Revolutionary Waves* (New York: Macmillan, 1997), esp. 39–40, 118–19. On the related phenomenon of "norm cascading," see Finnemore and Sikkink, "International Norm Dynamics."

23. Mark R. Beissinger calls the pooling equilibrium "elite defection" and the separating equilibrium "elite learning." Beissinger, "Structure and Example in Modular Political Phenomena: The Diffusion of Bulldozer/ Rose/Orange/Tulip Revolutions," *Perspectives on Politics* 5 (2007), 259–76.

24. Peter L. Berger and Thomas Luckmann, *The Social Construction of Reality* (Garden City, NY: Anchor Books, 1966), 157–63; Finnemore and Sikkink, "International Norm Dynamics," 903–4; Sheldon Stryker, Timothy J. Owens, and Robert W. White, eds., *Self, Identity, and Social Movements* (Minneapolis: University of Minnesota Press, 2000).

25. Timur Kuran, "Sparks and Prairie Fires: A Theory of Unanticipated Political Revolution," *Public Choice* 61 (1989), 41–74; W. H. Kaempfer and A. D. Loewenberg, "Using Threshold Models to Explain International Relations," *Public Choice* 73 (1992), 419–33.

26. Georg Simmel, "The Web of Group Affiliations" ("Die Kreuzung sozialer Kreise," *Soziologie* [Muenchen: Duncker & Humblot, 1922], 305–44), trans. Reinhard Bendix, in Simmel, *Conflict and the Web of Group-Affiliations* (Glencoe, IL: Free Press, 1955), 133–73.

27. Charles Tilly, *Identities, Boundaries, and Social Ties* (Boulder, CO: Paradigm, 2005), esp. 143–4.

28. In the language of a recent influential article, identity grounded in ideology combines a "social purpose" with a "relational" aspect. See Rawi Abdelal, Yoshiko M. Herrera, Alastair Iain Johnston, and Rose McDermott, "Identity as a Variable," *Perspectives on Political Science* 4 (2006), 695–711.

29. See Paul Pierson, *Politics in Time: History, Institutions, and Social Analysis* (Princeton, NJ: Princeton University Press, 2004).

30. Robert Jervis, *System Effects: Complexity in Political and Social Life* (Princeton, NJ: Princeton University Press, 1997), 125.

31. Christopher Hitchens, "God-Fearing People: Why Are We So Afraid of Offending Muslims?" *Slate* (July 30, 2007), http://www.slate.com/id/2171371/.

32. For a good summary, see Cass Sunstein, "The Law of Group Polarization," *Journal of Political Philosophy* 10 (2002), 175–95.

33. David Stasavage, "Polarization and Publicity: Rethinking the Benefits of Deliberative Democracy," *Journal of Politics* 69 (2007), 59–72.

34. Benjamin A. Most and Harvey Starr, "Theoretical and Logical Issues in the Study of International Diffusion," *Journal of Theoretical Politics* 2 (1990), 391–412; Harvey Starr, "Diffusion Approaches to the Spread of Democracy in the International System," *Journal of Conflict Resolution* 35 (1991), 356–81; Susanne Lohmann, "The Dynamics of Informational Cascades: The Monday Demonstrations in Leipzig, East Germany, 1989–91," *World Politics* 47 (1994), 42–101; Haas, *Ideological Origins;* Kristian Skrede Gleditsch, *All International Politics Is Local: The Diffusion of Conflict, Integration, and Democratization* (Ann Arbor: University of Michigan Press, 2005), esp. 50–54.

35. Beissinger, "Modular Political Phenomena."

36. Haas, *Ideological Origins.*

37. Dale C. Copeland, *The Origins of Major War* (Ithaca, NY: Cornell University Press, 2000).

38. James Davison Hunter, "The Enduring Culture War," in idem and Alan Wolfe, *Is There a Culture War? A Dialogue on Values and American Public Life* (Washington, DC: Brookings, 2006), 10–40.

39. They may also convert to democracy and try a moderate policy toward oligarchs. Either type of conversion to democracy—hard- or soft-line—would give the rulers of B and C the opposite incentives, namely to promote democracy and combat oligarchy in other states.

40. Morton A. Kaplan, "Intervention in Internal War: Some Systemic Sources," in James N. Rosenau, ed., *Inernational Aspects of Civil Strife* (Princeton, NJ:

Princeton University Press, 1964), 92–121; John Vasquez, *The War Puzzle* (New York: Cambridge University Press, 1993), 57.

41. Karl W. Deutsch, "External Involvement in Internal War," in *Internal War: Problems and Approaches*, ed. Harry Eckstein (New York: Free Press, 1964), 100–10. See also Steven David, *Choosing Sides: Alignment and Realignment in the Third World* (Baltimore, MD: Johns Hopkins University Press, 1991). David's concept of omnibalancing, wherein a government balances between domestic and foreign threats to its rule, is fruitful. But he does not consider threats to be a function of ideology, and indeed dismisses a causal role for ideology in alignment.

42. Benjamin E. Goldsmith, Stephan K. Chalup, and Michael J. Quinlan, "Regime Type and International Conflict: Towards a General Model," *Journal of Peace Research* 45 (2008), 743–63; Stanley Hoffman, "The Problem of Intervention," ed., *Intervention in World Politics* (Oxford: Clarendon Press, 1984), 11.

43. G. John Ikenberry and Charles A. Kupchan, "Socialization and Hegemonic Power," *International Organization* 44 (1990), 283–315.

44. Randolph Siverson and Harvey Starr have found states likely to change alliance portfolios following domestic regime change. Siverson and Starr, "Regime Change and the Restructuring of Alliances," *American Journal of Political Science* 38 (1994), 145–61.

45. Regime promotion my be an exercise in what Michael Barnett and Raymond Duvall call a state's or ruler's structural power and its productive power. See Barnett and Duvall, "Power in International Politics," International Organization 59 (2005), 39–75.

46. See the agrument of Tanisha Faizal that great power rivals will be tempted to attack "buffer states," i.e., states that lie between them, because a buffer state offers a large advantage to the rival that conquers it and a large disadvantage to the rival that does not. Faizal, *State Death: The Politics and Geography of Conquest, Occupation, and Annexation* (Princeton: Princeton University Press, 2007), 38–40.

47. Thus Hedley Bull asserts that in ideolically heterongeneous international systems (cf. Raymond Aron) "the wars themselves tend to accentuate ideological conflict, as each warring state allies itself with domestic factions within the enemy state," Bull, *The Anarchical Society* (New York: Columbia University Press, 1977), 247.

48. Cf. Katz, *Revolutionary Waves*, 65.

49. Niccolò Machiavelli, *The Prince*, trans. Harvey C. Mansfield, Jr. (Chicago: University of Chicago Press, 1995), chap. 18. Machiavelli himself rejects that possibility as too risky: should the enemies actually win power, the prince would be worse off than before.

50. John M. Owen, IV, "When Do Ideologies Produce Alliances? The Holy Roman Empire, 1517–55," *International Studies Quarterly* 49 (2005), 73–99.

51. Alastair Smith argues that "reliable" alliances are more likely to deter war, and in some of the historical chapters below ideological wars are consistent with that claim. Smith, "Alliance Formation and War," *International Studies Quarterly* 39 (1995), 405–25.

52. See Ido Oren, "The War Proneness of Alliances," *Journal of Conflict Resolution* 34 (1990), 208–33.

53. For similar arguments see Haas, *Ideological Origins*; F. Gregory Gause, III, "Balancing What? Threat Perception and Alliance Choice in the Gulf," *Secu-*

*rity Studies* 13:2 (Winter 2003/04); Richard N. Rosecrance, *Action and Reaction in World Politics: International Systems in Perspective* (Boston: Little, Brown, 1963); and George Liska, "Alignments and Realignments," in Julian R. Friedman, Christopher Bladen, and Steven Rosen, eds., *Alliance in International Politics* (Boston: Allyn and Bacon, 1970), 104–20.

54. See Walt, *Revolution and War*, 33–5, which discusses spirals of hostility between revolutionary and normal states. Walt does not take demonstration effects as seriously as I (ibid., 40–42), and hence he ascribes a greater role to misperceptions of spreading ideologies, and less to actual common interests among adherents of an ideology.

55. Tilly, *Identities*.

56. For a pioneering treatment of such contests and their consequences for international relations, see Skidmore, *Contested Social Orders*.

57. George Eliot, *Middlemarch* (New York: Modern Library, 2000), 799.


CHAPTER 3
THE STRUCTURES: TRANSNATIONAL IDEOLOGICAL CONTESTS

1. Alexander L. Wendt, "The Agent-Structure Problem in International Relations," *International Organization* 41, no. 3 (Summer 1987), 335–70.

2. Arthur L. Stinchcombe, *Constructing Social Theories* (Chicago: University of Chicago Press, 1968), 103.

3. Paul Pierson, *Politics in Time: History, Institutions, and Social Analysis* (Princeton, NJ: Princeton University Press, 2004).

4. Paul Kowert and Jeffrey Legro, "Norms, Identity, and Their Limits: A Theoretical Reprise," in Peter J. Katzenstein, ed., *The Culture of National Security* (New York: Columbia University Press, 1996), 451–97.

5. Ann Florini, "The Evolution of International Norms," *International Studies Quarterly* 40 (1996), 363–89; Emanuel Adler, "Seizing the Middle Ground: Constructivism in World Politics," *European Journal of International Relations* 3 (1997), 319–63; Alexander L. Wendt, *Social Theory of International Politics* (New York: Cambridge University Press, 1999), 318–36.

6. Peter J. Katzenstein, *A World of Regions: Asia and Europe in the American Imperium* (Ithaca, NY: Cornell University Press, 2005), 4–12.

7. What follows is from Thomas Kuhn, *The Structure of Scientific Revolutions* (Chicago: University of Chicago Press, 1962), passim.

8. Aristotle, *The Politics*, trans. Carnes Lord (Chicago: University of Chicago Press, 1984), book 3, chap. 6, 94–5.

9. Kuhn, *Scientific Revolutions*, 92.

10. See Raymond Aron's notion of a heterogeneous international system in his *Peace and War: A Theory of International Relations* (Garden City, NY: Doubleday, 1966), 99–104.

11. My argument is similar to that of Jack A. Goldstone: revolutions have an early phase when ideas are forming and subsequent phases, "when the institutional constraints of the Old Regime have collapsed, ideology and culture develop a momentum of their own. In fact, in the second and third phases, ideology and culture play the leading, rather than a following, role." Goldstone, *Revolution*

*and Rebellion in the Early Modern World* (Berkeley: University of California Press, 1991), 418.

12. See especially Hedley Bull, *The Anarchical Society* (New York: Columbia University Press, 1977).

13. On elites and new ideas, see Martha Finnemore and Kathryn Sikkink, "International Norm Dynamics and Policy Change," *International Organization* 52, (1998), 887–917.

14. On new ideas and their effects on policy, see Sheri Berman, "Ideas, Norms, and Culture in Political Analysis," *Comparative Politics* 33 (January 2001), 231–50, and the books Berman reviews: Ronald Inglehart, *Modernization and Postmodernization: Cultural, Economic, and Political Change in 43 Societies* (Princeton, NJ: Princeton University Press, 1997); Katzenstein, *Culture of National Security*, passim; David D. Laitin, *Identity in Formation: The Russian-Speaking Populations in the Near Abroad* (Ithaca, NY: Cornell University Press, 1998); and Kathleen R. McNamara, *The Currency of Ideas: Monetary Politics in the European Union* (Ithaca, NY: Cornell University Press, 1998).

15. Max Weber, "Politics as a Vocation," in Weber, *From Max Weber: Essays in Sociology*, ed. H. H. Gerth and C. Wright Mills (New York: Routledge, 1948), 77–128. Following Weber, I use "legitimacy" in the empirical rather than the normative sense, mindful of the normative critiques of that usage.

16. Peter A. Hall, ed., *The Political Power of Economic Ideas: Keynesianism across Nations* (Princeton, NJ: Princeton University Press, 1989).

17. John Maynard Keynes, *The General Theory of Employment, Interest and Money* (London: Macmillan, 1936), 351.

18. Charles Tilly, *The Politics of Collective Violence* (New York: Cambridge University Press, 2003), 8–9.

19. Cf. Richard Price, *The Chemical Weapons Taboo* (Ithaca, NY: Cornell University Press, 1997).

20. See http://www.monarchy.net/, home page of the International Monarchist League.

21. For a survey, see Robert J. Alexander, *International Maoism in the Developing World* (Westport, CT: Praeger, 1999).

22. See, e.g., Richard Pipes, "Can the Soviet Union Reform?" *Foreign Affairs* (Fall 1984), 47–61.

23. Thomas Risse-Kappen, "Ideas Do Not Float Freely: Transnational Coalitions, Domestic Structures, and the End of the Cold War," *International Organization* 48 (1994), 185–214.

24. Charles Tilly, however, argues that socioeconomic structures—how urbanized was an area—helped determine its residents' attitudes toward the revolution. Tilly, *The Vendée* (Cambridge, MA: Harvard University Press, 1976).

25. Niccolò Machiavelli, *The Prince* (1532), trans. Harvey C. Mansfield, Jr., 2nd ed. (Chicago: University of Chicago Press, 1998), chap. 18.

26. Daniel Philpott, *Revolutions in Sovereignty: How Ideas Shaped Modern International Relations* (Princeton, NJ: Princeton University Press, 2001), 52–4.

27. Jeffrey W. Legro, *Rethinking the World: Great Power Strategies and International Order* (Ithaca, NY: Cornell University Press, 2005), 28–35; see also Kowert and Legro on ecological "shocks" such as Japan's losing the

Second World War and becoming a pacific nation. Kowert and Legro, "Norms, Identity."

28. Kuhn, *Scientific Revolutions*, 92. For an early, pre-scientific exposition, see the biblical book of Deuteronomy, where God tells the Hebrews how to distinguish a true from a false prophet: "And if thou say in thine heart, How shall we know the word which the LORD hath not spoken? When a prophet speaketh in the name of the LORD, if the thing follow not, nor come to pass, that is the thing which the LORD hath not spoken, but the prophet hath spoken it presumptuously: thou shalt not be afraid of him." Deut. 18:21f.

29. Jack A. Goldstone, "Toward a Fourth Generation of Revolutionary Theory," *Annual Review of Political Science* 4 (2001), 148–52.

30. Legro, *Rethinking*, 34.

31. David Dessler, "Beyond Correlations: Toward a Causal Theory of War," *International Studies Quarterly* 35 (1991), 337–55, esp. 349–51.

32. Charles Tilly, *Identities, Boundaries, and Social Ties* (Boulder, CO: Paradigm, 2005).

33. Tilly, *Identities*, 143–4.

34. As with international norms; cf. Peter Katzenstein, ed., *Between Power and Plenty: Foreign Economic Policies of Advanced Industrial States* (Madison: University of Wisconsin Press, 1978).

35. Charles Pouthas, "The Revolutions of 1848," in J.P.T. Bury, ed., *The New Cambridge Modern History*, vol. 10, *The Zenith of European Power 1830–1870* (Cambridge: Cambridge University Press, 1960), 389.

36. Gilles Fauconnier and Mark Turner, *The Way We Think: Conceptual Blending and the Mind's Hidden Complexities* (New York: Basic Books, 2002); Ernst B. Haas, *Nationalism, Liberalism, and Progress*, vol. 1, *The Rise and Decline of Nationalism*, (Ithaca, NY: Cornell University Press, 2000), 22–61.

37. Cf. Legro, who argues that "consolidation," or the emergence of sufficient social support, is necessary for a new set of ideas to replace an old. An exogenous shock alone will not suffice. Legro, *Rethinking*, 35.

38. Katz, *Revolutionary Waves*, 83–9.

39. A different type of evolutionary argument is the famous one of Francis Fukuyama, *The End of History and the Last Man* (New York: Free Press, 1992). Fukuyama's Hegelian argument is that liberal democracy finally won not simply because it best handles environmental shocks but because it is the regime best suited to human nature, in particular man's need for recognition.

40. Mario Bunge, "Systemism: The Alternative to Individualism and Holism," *Journal of Socio-Economics* 29 (2000), 147–57. I thank Jarrod Haayes for introducing me to Bunge's work.

41. James G. March and Johan P. Olsen, "The Institutional Dynamics of International-Political Orders," *International Organization* 52 (1998), 943–69. See also Stephen D. Krasner, *Sovereignty: Organized Hypocrisy* (Princeton, NJ: Princeton University Press, 1999). Rejecting the centrality of this distinction are James D. Fearon and Alexander Wendt, "Rationalism *v.* Constructivism: A Skeptical View," in Walter Carlsnaes et al., eds., *Handbook of International Relations* (Beverly Hills, CA: SAGE, 2002), 52–72.

42. An outstanding example of this type of argument is by Odd Arne Westad, *The Global Cold War: Third World Interventions and the Making of Our Times* (New York: Cambridge University Press, 2005). Westad argues that each super-power was motivated to intervene in Third World politics by the belief that its system was best.

43. On the conceptual transition from Machiavelli's prince—an individual—to the modern unitary state, see Harvey C. Mansfield, Jr., "On the Impersonality of the Modern State: A Comment on Machiavelli's Use of *Stato*," *American Political Science Review* 77, no. 4 (December 1983), 849–57.

44. Kenneth N. Waltz, "Globalization and Governance," *PS: Political Science and Politics* 32 (1999), 693–700.

45. Kenneth N. Waltz, *Man, the State, and War* (New York: Columbia University Press, 1959), 174–6.

46. Stephen M. Walt, *Revolution and War* (Ithaca, NY: Cornell University Press, 1996), 41–2.

47. Walt, *Revolution and War*, 32.

48. Put another way, this argument is non-realist because it appeals to what James Fearon calls domestic audience costs: once a government has declared its support for the promotion of democracy, it is bound to honor that declaration, else it risks losing power. Fearon, "Domestic Political Audiences and the Escalation of International Disputes," *American Political Science Review* 88 (1994), 577–92.

49. Leonard Schoppa, "The Social Context in International Coercive Bargaining," *International Organization* 53 (Spring 1999), 307–42.

50. Martha Finnemore an[46]d Kathryn Sikkink, "International Norm Dynamics and Political Change," *International Organization* 52 (1998), 887–917. For an application see Finnemore, *The Purpose of Intervention: Changing Beliefs about the Use of Force* (Ithaca, NY: Cornell University Press, 2004).

51. Neta C. Crawford, *Argument and Change in World Politics: Ethics, Decolonization, and Humanitarian Intervention* (New York: Cambridge University Press, 2002).

52. Thomas Risse, "'Let's Argue!' Communicative Action in World Politics," *International Organization* 54 (2000), 1–40.

53. Jon Elster, "A Plea for Mechanisms," in Peter Hedstrøm and Richard Swedberg, eds., *Social Mechanisms: An Analytical Approach to Social Theory* (New York: Cambridge University Press, 1998), 45–73; Dessler, "Beyond Correlations."

CHAPTER 4
CHURCH AND STATE, 1510–1700

1. Quoted in Martin Wight, *Power Politics* (London: Continuum, 2002), 87.

2. Jane E. A. Dawson, *The Politics of Religion in the Age of Mary, Queen of Scots: The Earl of Argyll and the Struggle for Britain and Ireland* (New York: Cambridge University Press, 2002), 1–2.

3. R. B. Wernham, *Before the Armada: The Emergence of the English Nation, 1485–1588* (New York: Norton, 1966), 245–6.

4. Rosalind K. Marshall, *Mary of Guise* (Edinburgh: NMS Publishing, 2001), 86.

5. Geoffrey Parker, *The Grand Strategy of Philip II* (New Haven, CT: Yale University Press, 1998), 148.

6. Frederic J. Baumgartner, *Henry II, King of France 1547–1559* (Durham, NC: Duke University Press, 1988), 231; F. C. Spooner, "The Reformation in Difficulties: France, 1519–59," in Geoffrey Elton, ed., *The New Cambridge Modern History*, vol. 2, *The Reformation 1520–59* (New York: Cambridge University Press, 1959), 225.

7. Wernham, *Before the Armada*, 250.

8. Wernham, *Before the Armada*, 244–6, 248.

9. Stephen Alford, "Knox, Cecil and the British Dimension of the Scottish Reformation," in Roger A. Mason, ed., *John Knox and the British Reformations* (Aldershot, UK: Ashgate), 201.

10. Alford, "Knox," 205.

11. E. I. Kouri, "For True Faith or National Interest?" in Tom Scott and E. I. Kouri, eds., *Politics and Society in Reformation Europe: Essays on Behalf of Sir Geoffrey Elton on His Sixty-fifth Birthday* (London: Macmillan, 1987), 413; Wernham, *Before the Armada*, 250–51.

12. Parker, *Strategy of Philip II*, 152.

13. Evan Luard, *War in International Society* (London: I. B. Tauris, 1986), 149–50.

14. The medieval political system was even more complex than I can describe here; for a fuller treatment that concerns many of the questions in this chapter, see Daniel Nexon, *The Struggle for Power in Early Modern Europe: Religious Conflict, Dynastic Empires, and Political Change* (Princeton, NJ: Princeton University Press, 2009), esp. chap. 3.

15. Philip S. Gorski, *The Disciplinary Revolution: Calvinism and the Rise of the State in Early Modern Europe* (Chicago: University of Chicago Press, 2001), 18.

16. M. Searle Bates, *Religious Liberty: An Inquiry* (New York: International Missionary Council, 1945), 148.

17. Rodney Bruce Hall, "Moral Authority as a Power Resource," *International Organization* 51 (1997), 591–622.

18. Thomas Oestereich, "Pope Boniface VIII," *The Catholic Encyclopedia*, vol. 2 (New York: Robert Appleton, 1907); http://www.newadvent.org/cathen/02662a.htm, accessed May 15, 2008.

19. Dante, *Monarchy* (1313; New York: Cambridge University Press, 1996).

20. Arthur O. Lovejoy, *The Great Chain of Being: A Study in the History of an Idea* (Cambridge, MA: Harvard University Press, 1936).

21. A general treatment is William Dallman, *John Hus: A Brief Story of the Life of a Martyr* (1915; reprint, Whitefish, MT: Kessenger, 2006).

22. G. R. Elton, "Introduction: The Age of the Reformation," in idem, ed., *Reformation*, 5.

23. Alister McGrath, *The Intellectual Origins of the European Reformation* (Oxford: Basil Blackwell, 1987), chap. 2. The reformers Huldrych Zwingli and John Calvin are typically categorized as humanists, and Desiderius Erasmus was for a time an ally of Luther.

24. Steven Ozment, *Protestants: The Birth of a Revolution* (New York: Doubleday, 1991). Ultimately, the Reformation may best be seen as linked to other changes in Europe in these centuries, e.g., the replacement of feudalism by capitalism (see, e.g., Maarten Prak, ed., *Early Modern Capitalism: Economic and Social Change in Europe 1400–1800* [New York: Routledge, 2001]), and the rise of nationalism (see, e.g., Liah Greenfeld, *Nationalism: Five Roads to Modernity* [Cambridge, MA: Harvard University Press, 1992]), and the states system (see Daniel Philpott, *Revolutions in Sovereignty* [Princeton, NJ: Princeton University Press, 2000].)

25. For the text in English, see http://www.iclnet.org/pub/resources/text/wittenberg/luther/web/ninetyfive.html.

26. Philip Schaff, *History of the Christian Church*, vol. 7, *The German Reformation* (Oak Harbor, WA: Logos Research Systems, 1997; reprinted from New York: Scribner's Sons, 1910), §33, "The Theses-Controversy"; http://www.ccel.org/ccel/schaff/hcc7.ii.iii.iv.html.

27. G. W. Bromiley, "General Introduction," in idem, ed., *Zwingli and Bullinger* (Philadelphia: Westminster Press, 1953), 19–21.

28. Schaff, *German Reformation*, §34, "Rome's Interposition. Luther and Prierias"; http://www.ccel.org/ccel/schaff/hcc7.ii.iii.v.html.

29. For a full treatment of this question, and a sampling of the passions it inspired, see the polemical exchange between Erasmus, who argued that man can choose salvation, and Luther, who argued rather that God chooses man. Desiderius Erasmus and Martin Luther, *Discourse on Free Will* (New York: Ungar, 1961).

30. http://www.papalencyclicals.net/Leo10/l10exdom.htm.

31. E. G. Rupp, "Luther and the German Reformation to 1529," in Elton, ed., *Reformation*, 80; Schaff, *History*, §§37–43. The official name of the empire was the Holy Roman Empire of the German Nation (*Heiliges römisches Reich deutscher Nation*).

32. Schaff, *German Reformation*, §§ 47–8; http://www.ccel.org/ccel/schaff/hcc7.ii.iii.xviii.html.

33. Hajo Holborn, *A History of Modern Germany*, vol. 1, *The Reformation* (London: Eyre & Spottiswoode, 1965), 137. Luther's pamphlets were a boon to the new printing industry, as the publication of books in Germany increased sixfold between 1518 and 1524. Benedict Anderson argues that "print capitalism" not only spread Luther's movement but created the conditions for early modern nationalism by building a new "imagined community" of people who spoke the same language. Anderson, *Imagined Communities: Reflections on the Origin and Spread of Nationalism* (London: Verso, 1991). See also Anne Hudson, *The Premature Reformation: Wycliffite Texts and Lollard History* (New York: Oxford University Press, 1988).

34. Text at: http://www.ctsfw.edu/etext/luther/babylonian/babylonian.htm#9.

35. The political ramifications of Protestantism are pushed past their logical conclusions by Thomas Hobbes in his *Leviathan*, roughly one-half of which defends naming the sovereign, rather than a foreign potentate, head of the Church.

36. Schaff, *German Reformation*, §34.

37. T. Kolde, "John the Steadfast," in Samuel Macauley Jackson et al., eds., *The New Schaff-Herzog Encyclopedia of Religious Knowledge* (Grand Rapids, MI: Baker, 1958), 218<n-<19; http://www.ccel.org/ccel/schaff/encyc06.j.vi.html.

38. T. Kolde, "Philip of Hesse," in Jackson et al., eds., *Schaff-Herzog*, vol. 9, 25; http://www.ccel.org/ccel/schaff/encyc09.html?term=Philip%20of%20Hesse.

39. Rupp, "Luther and the Reformation," 86; Philpott, *Revolutions in Sovereignty*, 123–5.

40. Peter Blickle, *The Revolution of 1525: The German Peasants' War from a New Perspective*, trans. Thomas A. Brady, Jr., and H. C. Erik Midelfort (Baltimore, MD: Johns Hopkins University Press, 1981). The text of the Twelve Articles is available at http://personal.ashland.edu/~jmoser1/peasantarticles.htm (accessed on April 13, 2009).

41. Holborn, *Modern Germany*, 173.

42. James M. Stayer, *The German Peasants' War and Anabaptist Community of Goods* (Montreal: McGill-Queen's University Press, 1991), 38–9.

43. Stayer, *Peasants' War*, 40–44.

44. Blickle, *Revolution of 1525*, 185.

45. Holborn, "Modern Germany," 201–4; Leopold von Ranke, *History of the Reformation in Germany*, trans. Sarah Austin, ed. Robert A. Johnson (London: George Routledge and Sons, 1905), 360–61.

46. Holborn, *Modern Germany*, 201–4.

47. Richard Andrew Cahill, *Philipp of Hesse and the Reformation* (Mainz: Verlag Philipp von Zabern, 2001), 151–80.

48. Holborn, *Modern Germany*, 204–6.

49. Gorski, *Disciplinary Revolution*, 13–14.

50. Holborn, *Modern Germany*, 183–94.

51. For polemicizing of a high order, see the fourteenth-century exchange between Pope Boniface VIII, *Unam Sanctum* (1302), http://www.fordham.edu/halsall/source/b8-unam.html, and Dante Alighieri, *Monarchy* (1313), ed. Prue Shaw (New York: Cambridge University Press, 1996).

52. Manuel Fernández Alvarez, *Charles V: Elected Emperor and Hereditary Ruler* (London: Thames and Hudson, 1975), 43.

53. Rupp, "Luther and the Reformation," 81–84. The immortal reply attributed to Luther, "Hier stehe ich und kann nicht anders," or "Here I stand, I can do no other," does not appear in the original transcript. Imperial diets were occasional congresses held among the princes of the Empire.

54. Holborn, *Modern Germany*, 144–52.

55. G. Schwaiger, "Katholische Kirche und evangelisches Christentum in Bayern: Ein geschichtischer Überblick," *Stimmen der Zeit* 167 (1960/61), 369; Ranke, *Reformation*, 320–22. I thank Patricia Owen for helping me to translate Schwaiger's article.

56. Ranke, *Reformation*, 365–8; Rupp, "Luther," 91–2.

57. Ranke, *Reformation*, 417–20. For an examination of the waxing and waning of Catholic and Protestant alliances during this period, see John M. Owen, IV, "When Do Ideologies Produce Alliances? The Holy Roman Empire, 1517–55," *International Studies Quarterly* 49 (2005), 73–99.

58. In the appendix to this book, I justify my treatment of most Imperial estates as sovereign, notwithstanding the Emperor's hegemony.

59. Karl Brandi, *The Emperor Charles V: The Growth and Destiny of a Man and of a World-Empire*, trans. by C. V. Wedgwood (London: Jonathan Cape, 1939), 239–47.

60. Brandi, *Charles V*, 251–3.

61. Brandi, *Charles V*, 297; Holborn, *Modern Germany*, 205–8.

62. P. S. Fichtner, *Ferdinand I of Austria: The Politics of Dynasticism in the Age of the Reformation* (New York: Columbia University Press, 1982), 80–82; C. C. Christensen, "John of Saxony's Diplomacy, 1529–1530: Reformation or Realpolitik?" *Sixteenth Century Journal* 15 (1984), 420–21.

63. Christensen, "John of Saxony," 422–3; Holborn, *Modern Germany*, 208–10.

64. Ranke, *Reformation*, 630–36; T. A. Brady, "Phases and Strategies of the Schmalkaldic League: A Perspective after 450 Years," *Archiv für Reformationsgeshichte* 74 (1983), 163.

65. Brandi, *Charles V*, 328–32; Holborn, *Modern Germany*, 217–20; R. J. Knecht, *Francis I* (New York: Cambridge University Press, 1984), 232–3.

66. Holborn, *Modern Germany*, 180, 221.

67. Brandi, *Charles V*, 450–51; Holborn, *Modern Germany*, 222–4.

68. Brandi, *Charles V*, 501–3; Holborn, *Modern Germany*, 223.

69. D. L. Potter, "Foreign Policy in the Age of the Reformation: French Involvement in the Schmalkaldic War," *Historical Journal* 20 (1977), 525–44.

70. Brandi, *Charles V*, 540–46.

71. Holborn, *Modern Germany*, 227–31; Spooner, "Reformation in Difficulties," 353–6.

72. Quoted in Alvarez, *Charles V*, 131.

73. Potter, "French Involvement."

74. Brandi, *Charles V*, 576–9; Holborn, *Modern Germany*, 231–3.

75. Brandi, *Charles V*, 603–6.

76. Natalie Zemon Davis, "Missed Connections: Religion and Regime," *Journal of Interdisciplinary History* 1 (1971), 381–94.

77. Philip S. Gorski (*Disciplinary Revolution*) sees in Calvinism's discipline the origins of the modern state.

78. John Witte, Jr., *The Reformation of Rights: Law, Religion, and Human Rights in Early Modern Calvinism* (New York: Cambridge University Press, 2007), 3–10. For a superb exploration of the political and social implications of early Calvinism, see Michael Walzer, *The Revolution of the Saints: A Study in the Origin of Radical Politics* (Cambridge, MA: Harvard University Press, 1965).

79. Holborn, *Modern Germany*, 249–52.

80. Holborn, *Modern Germany*, 258. See also T. M. Parker, "The Papacy, Catholic Reform, and Christian Missions," in Wernham, ed., *Reformation*, 58–9.

81. Alastair Duke, "The Ambivalent Face of Calvinism in the Netherlands 1561–1618," in Menna Prestwich, ed., *International Calvinism 1541–1715* (New York: Oxford University Press, 1985), 109–34.

82. Menna Prestwich, "Calvinism in France, 1555–1629," in idem, ed., *International Calvinism*, 73.

83. Patrick Collinson, "England and International Calvinism, 1558–1640," in Prestwich, ed., *International Calvinism*, 198–99.

84. Michael Lynch, "Calvinism in Scotland, 1559–1638," in Prestwich, ed., *International Calvinism*, 225–55.

85. Henry J. Cohn, "The Territorial Princes in Germany's Second Reformation, 1559–1622," in Prestwich, ed., *International Calvinism*, 138–39 (chapter is 135–65); Claus-Peter Clasen, *The Palatinate in European History 1555–1618* (Oxford: Basil Blackwell, 1966).

86. R.J.W. Evans, "Calvinism in East Central Europe: Hungary and Her Neighbours, 1540–1700," in Prestwich, ed., *International Calvinism*, 170–73.

87. Collinson, "England," 200.

88. Gillian Lewis, "Calvinism in Geneva in the Time of Calvin and Beza (1541–1605)," in Prestwich, ed., *International Calvinism*, 40–41.

89. Prestwich, "Changing Face," 2, 5.

90. Collinson, "England and International Calvinism," 208–11.

91. Andrew Pettegree, "Religion and the Revolt," in Graham Darby, ed., *The Origins and Development of the Dutch Revolt* (New York: Routledge, 2001), 72.

92. Garrett Mattingly, "International Diplomacy and International Law," in R. B. Wernham, ed., *New Cambridge Modern History*, vol. 3, *The Counter-Reformation and Price Revolution 1559–1610* (Cambridge: Cambridge University Press, 1968), 155–6.

93. Gorski, *Disciplinary Revolution*.

94. Holborn, *Modern Germany*, 270–74.

95. Wernham, *Before the Armada*, 337–38.

96. Geoffrey Parker, ed., *The Thirty Years' War*, 2nd ed. (New York: Routledge, 1997), 20.

97. Jasper Godwin Ridley, *Elizabeth I* (New York: Viking, 1987), 117.

98. Prestwich, "Calvinism in France," 71–73.

99. H. G. Koenigsberger, "The Organization of Revolutionary Parties in France and the Netherlands in the Sixteenth Century," *Journal of Modern History* 27 (1955), 335–51.

100. Ridley, *Elizabeth I*, 118.

101. Prestwich, "Calvinism in France," 88; Mack P. Holt, *The French Wars of Religion, 1562–1629* (New York: Cambridge University Press, 1995), 47.

102. R. J. Knecht, *The French Civil Wars, 1562–1598* (New York: Longman, 2000), 85–7.

103. Wernham, *Before the Armada*, 265.

104. James Westfall Thompson, *The Wars of Religion in France 1559–1576: The Huguenots, Catherine de Medici, Philip II* (New York: Frederick Ungar, 1957), 95–6.

105. Geoffrey Parker, *Strategy of Philip II*, 118–21.

106. Ridley, *Elizabeth I*, 121; Wernham, *Before the Armada*, 266.

107. Wernham, *Before the Armada*, 264–7; Ridley, *Elizabeth I*, 121–6.

108. Andrew Pettegree, "Religion and the Revolt," in Graham Darby, ed., *The Origins and Development of the Dutch Revolt* (New York: Routledge, 2001), 71–2.

109. Koenigsberger, "Revolutionary Parties," 340.

110. Charles Wilson, *Queen Elizabeth and the Revolt of the Netherlands* (Berkeley: University of California Press, 1970), 30–31.

111. Knecht, *French Civil Wars*, 134.

112. Ridley, *Elizabeth I*, 121.

113. Knecht, *French Civil Wars*, 135–7.

114. Knecht, *French Civil Wars*, 155–6.

115. Thompson, *Wars of Religion*, 442–5.

116. Knecht, *French Civil Wars*, 159–60; Thompson, *Wars of Religion*, 446–8.

117. Thompson, *Wars of Religion*, 437–9.

118. H. G. Koenigsberger, "Western Europe and the Power of Spain," in R. B. Wernham, ed., *The New Cambridge Modern History*, vol. 3, *The Counter-Reformation and Price Revolution 1559–1610* (Cambridge: Cambridge University Press, 1968), 290; Leonie Frieda, *Catherine de Medici* (London: Weidenfeld & Nicolson, 2003), 276.

119. Wallace T. MacCaffrey, *Queen Elizabeth and the Making of Policy, 1572–1588* (Princeton, NJ: Princeton University Press, 1981), 171.

120. Frieda, *Catherine de Medici*, 278.

121. Ridley, *Elizabeth I*, 183.

122. MacCaffrey, *Making of Policy*, 171–2; Wernham, *Before the Armada*, 325. The continuing symbolic potency of the slaughter in France is seen in the fact that seventeen years later, Christopher Marlowe wrote *The Massacre at Paris* about the event. Also see Thompson, *Wars of Religion*, 467–8.

123. MacCaffrey, *Making of Policy*, 173–6.

124. Thompson, *Wars of Religion*, 457–60.

125. Thompson, *Wars of Religion*, 473–5.

126. Thompson, *Wars of Religion*, 462–8.

127. Holt, *French Wars*, 122–3.

128. Parker, *Strategy of Philip II*, 171–2.

129. Holt, *French Wars*, 1995, 124; Wernham, *Before the Armada*, 366–8.

130. Wernham, *Before the Armada*, 369–70.

131. Werhnam, *Before the Armada*, 370–71.

132. Geoffrey Parker, *Spain and the Netherlands, 1559–1659: Ten Studies* (London: Collins, 1979), 70–71; MacCaffrey, *Making of Policy*, 338–9; on the Irish expedition, 293–4.

133. Parker, *Spain and the Netherlands*, 70–71.

134. MacCaffrey, *Elizabeth and the Making of Policy*, 340–43.

135. Wernham, *Before the Armada*, 378–3.

136. Holt, *French Wars*, 125–7.

137. Parker, *Strategy of Philip II*, 179–80.

138. J. H. Elliott, *Imperial Spain 1469–1716* (London: Penguin, 2002), 282; Andrew Pettegree, *Europe in the Sixteenth Century* (Oxford: Blackwell, 2002), 223.

139. Elliott, *Imperial Spain*, 283.

140. Elliott, *Imperial Spain*, 284.

141. MacCaffrey, *Elizabeth I*, 138.

142. Parker, *Strategy of Philip II*, 273.

143. MacCaffrey, *Elizabeth I*, 140–41; Wernham, *After the Armada*, 154–7.

144. Parker, *Strategy of Philip II*, 274–5.

145. Howell A. Lloyd, *The Rouen Campaign 1590–1592: Politics, Warfare and the Early Modern States* (Oxford: Clarendon Press, 1973), 46–8.

146. Holborn, *Modern Germany*, 249–52.

147. The Lutherans understood the Peace to allow a ruler who converted to change his estate's regime accordingly; the Emperor, however, secretly inserted an "Ecclesiastical Reservation" (*reservatio ecclesiastica*) that prohibited such changes. Holborn, *Modern Germany*, 244–5.

148. Holborn, *Modern Germany*, 288.

149. Holborn, *Modern Germany*, 289; A. W. Ward, "The Empire under Rudolf II," in A. W. Ward, G. W. Prothero, and Stanley Leathes, eds., *The Cambridge Modern History*, vol. 3, *The Wars of Religion* (Cambridge: Cambridge University Press, 1907), 707–9.

150. Holborn, *Modern Germany*, 295.

151. Holborn, *Modern Germany*, 296–302.

152. Robert A. Kann, *A History of the Habsburg Empire 1526–1918* (Berkeley: University of California Press, 1974), 48.

153. Clasen, *Palatinate*, 23.

154. Holborn, *Modern Germany*, 296–302.

155. David Maland, *Europe at War 1600–1650* (London: Macmillan, 1980), 49–50. Oldenbarneveldt's intervention outraged Dutch Calvinists and led to his ouster and execution.

156. Pettegree, *Europe in the Sixteenth Century*, 258.

157. R.J.W. Evans, *Rudolph II and His World: A Study in Intellectual History 1576–1612* (Oxford: Clarendon Press, 1984), 68–82.

158. Asch, *Thirty Years' War*, 54–66.

159. Marc R. Forster, "The Thirty Years' War and the Failure of Catholicization," in David Luebke, ed., *The Counter-reformation: Essential Readings* (Malden, MA: Blackwell, 1999), 165.

160. Parker, *Thirty Years' War*, 65.

161. Maland, *Europe at War*, 89.

162. Ronald Asch, *The Thirty Years' War: The Holy Roman Empire and Europe* (New York: Macmillan, 1997), 84–6; Parker, *Thirty Years' War*, 68.

163. Gábor Barta et al., *History of Transylvania* (Budapest: Akademiai Kiado, 1989), 323.

164. Parker, *Thirty Years' War*, 68–70.

165. Parker, *Thirty Years' War*, 68–70; Clasen, *Palatinate*, 26–30.

166. Asch, *Thirty Years' War*, 101–34.

167. Stephen D. Krasner, "Westphalia and All That," in Goldstein and Keohane, eds., *Ideas and Foreign Policy* (Ithaca, NY: Cornell University Press, 1993), 240–44. For the text of the two treaties in English, see http://law-ref.org/WESTPHALIA/index.html.

168. C. V. Wedgwood, *The Thirty Years' War* (New York: New York Review of Books, 2005; reprinted from London: Jonathan Cape, 1938), 506.

169. John Miller, *James II* (New Haven, CT: Yale University Press, 2000), 66.

170. Anthony Levi, *Louis XIV* (New York: Carroll and Graf, 2004), 247.

171. David Ogg, "Britain after the Restoration," in F. L. Carsten, ed., *The New Cambridge Modern History*, vol. 5, *The Ascendancy of France 1648–88*, 301–12; J. R. Jones, *The Revolution of 1688 in England* (London: Weidenfeld and Nicolson, 1972), esp. 189–210. It is striking that, notwithstanding the struggles between Louis and the papacy, in the minds of the English, Scottish, and Dutch, Catholicism was a carrier of absolutism.

172. J. H. Shennan, *Louis XIV* (London: Routledge, 1986), 36–7.

173. See the document at http://www.yale.edu/lawweb/avalon/england.htm.

174. Miller, *James II*, 233–4.

175. Roland H. Bainton, *The Travail of Religious Liberty* (Philadelphia: Westminster Press, 1951), 29.

176. Perez Zagorin, *How the Idea of Religious Toleration Came to the West* (Princeton, NJ: Princeton University Press, 2003), 93–5.

177. Bainton, *Religious Liberty*, 152.

178. John Owen, *Indulgence and Toleration Considered: In a Letter unto a Person of Honour* (London: n.p., 1667).

179. John Locke, *A Letter Concerning Toleration*, ed. James H. Tully (Indianapolis, IN: Hackett Press, 1983).

180. R. Po Hsia-Chia and H.F.K. van Nierop, eds., *Calvinism and Religious Toleration in the Dutch Golden Age* (New York: Cambridge University Press, 2002). The quotation is from p. 1.

181. Maarten Prak, *The Dutch Republic in the Seventeenth Century* (New York: Cambridge University Press, 2005), 46–7.

182. Willem Frijhoff, "Religious Toleration in the United Provinces: From 'Case' to 'Model,' " in Hsia-Chia and van Nierop, eds., *Calvinism and Religious Toleration*, 31.

183. Frijhoff, "Religious Toleration," 33–4.

184. For the full text, see http://en.wikisource.org/wiki/Observations_upon_the_United_Provinces_of_the_Netherlands.

185. Bainton, *Religious Liberty*, 185–6.

186. Bates, *Religious Liberty*, 186; Bainton, *Religious Liberty*, 193, 206, 186.

187. Richard Cawardine, *Transatlantic Revivalism: Popular Evangelicalism in Britain and America, 1790–1865* (Carlisle, UK: Paternoster, 2007).

CHAPTER 5
CROWN, NOBILITY, AND PEOPLE, 1770–1870

1. William E. Echard, *Napoleon III and the Concert of Europe* (Baton Rouge: Louisiana State University Press, 1983), 5–7.

2. A.J.P. Taylor, *The Italian Problem in European Diplomacy 1847–1849* (New York: Barnes & Noble, 1970), 197–8.

3. Frank J. Coppa, *Pope Pius IX: Crusader in a Secular Age* (Boston: Twayne Publishers, 1979), 14–15, 90–93.

4. William L. Langer, *Political and Social Upheaval 1832–1852* (New York: Harper & Row, 1969), 441–2.

5. Langer, *Political and Social Upheaval*, 442.

6. Coppa, *Pius IX*, 119–21.

7. Echard, *Napoleon III*, 5.

8. John Bierman, *Napoleon III and His Carnival Empire* (New York: St. Martin's Press, 1988), 79–81.

9. Taylor, *Italian Problem*, 231–2.

10. K. J. Holsti, *Peace and War: Armed Conflicts and International Order 1648–1989* (New York: Cambridge University Press, 1991).

11. Alexis de Tocqueville, *The Old Regime and the Revolution*, trans. Alan Kahan (Chicago: University of Chicago Press, 1998). Tocqueville's book was originally published in 1853, as the long ideological contest finally began to wane.

12. Francis Bacon, *The Advancement of Learning* (1605; reprinted London: J. M. Dent and Sons, 1915), 72.

13. Thomas A. Spragens, Jr., *The Politics of Motion: The World of Thomas Hobbes* (Lexington: University of Kentucky Press, 1973).

14. John M. Owen, IV, and J. Judd Owen, "Introduction," in idem, eds., *Religion, the Enlightenment, and the New Global Order* (New York: Columbia University Press, 2010).

15. See Hobbes's *Leviathan* (1651), ed. C. B. Macpherson (Harmondsworth, UK: Penguin, 1982). Hobbes was a royalist during the English civil wars of the seventeenth century and was a favorite of Charles II after the restoration (see below).

16. See Locke's *Second Treatise on Government* (1689), in idem, *Political Essays*, ed. Mark Goldie (New York: Cambridge University Press, 1997). Locke was on the side of Parliament during the Glorious Revolution of 1688 (see below). It is evident that by "subjects" Locke meant not the people as a whole but the aristocracy or landed class. See the *Fundamental Constitutions of Carolina* (1669), which Locke co-authored with the Earl of Shaftesbury: http://www.yale.edu/lawweb/avalon/states/nc05.htm.

17. See Rousseau, *On the Social Contract* (1762), trans. Maurice Cranston (Harmondsworth, UK: Penguin, 1968).

18. Bossuet, *Politics*, from J. H. Robinson, ed., *Readings in European History* (Boston: Ginn, 1906), vol. 2, 274–5; http://history.hanover.edu/texts/bossuet.html. Note that for Bossuet, as for other absolutists, absolutism was not despotism, for the monarch was constrained by God: "Kings should tremble then as they use the power God has granted them; and let them think how horrible is the sacrilege if they use for evil a power which comes from God."

19. C.B.A. Behrens, *The Ancien Régime* (London: Thames and Hudson, 1967), 87–95; J. Lough, "France under Louis XIV," *The New Cambridge Modern History*, vol. 5, *The Ascendancy of France 1648–88*, ed. F. L. Carsten (New York: Cambridge University Press, 1957), 238–9.

20. Sir George Clark, "The Social Foundations of States," in Carsten, ed., *Ascendancy of France*, 188; François Furet, *Revolutionary France 1770–1880* (Cambridge, MA: Blackwell, 1992), 7–9.

21. Clark, "Social Foundations," 192.

22. Behrens, Ancien Régime, 88.

23. Behrens, Ancien Régime, 102.

24. In his novel *L'ingénu*. Behrens, Ancien Régime, 104–5.

25. Steven Pressman, review of Werner Stark, *History and Historians of Political Economy* (1994), in *Journal of Economic Literature* 33, no. 2 (June 1995), 819.

26. R. R. Palmer, *The Age of the Democratic Revolution: A Political History of Europe and America, 1760–1800*, vol. 1, *The Challenge* (Princeton, NJ: Princeton University Press, 1959), 85–98.

27. Palmer, *Challenge*, 99–103.

28. Palmer, *Challenge*, 103–8.

29. See Edmund Burke's *Thoughts on the Cause of the Present Discontents*, in Burke, *Pre-revolutionary Writings*, ed. Ian Harris (New York: Cambridge University Press, 1993), 103–92. Burke was secretary to Rockingham.

30. Palmer, *Challenge*, 103.

31. Palmer, *Challenge*, 71.

32. Republicans and constitutional monarchists had in common what came to be called liberalism, by which I mean a commitment to the equal autonomy of each adult male (later, each adult). In the remainder of this chapter I sometimes use *liberal* to refer to republicans and constitutional monarchists, owing to their incipient liberal commitments. In the twentieth century, as seen in chapter 6, liberalism came to be associated with democracy; hence *liberal democracy*, a regime that attempts to unite equal individual autonomy with majority rule. I also use *constitutional democracy* to denote this regime.

33. Palmer, *Challenge*, 106.

34. See Rousseau, *Social Contract*.

35. For an argument that the American and French revolutions were caused by contradictions in the old regime and ushered in a new basis of sovereignty in international affairs, see Mlada Bukovansky, *Legitimacy and Power Politics: The American and French Revolutions in International Political Culture* (Princeton, NJ: Princeton University Press, 2002).

36. Samuel P. Huntington, "Political Modernization: America *vs.* Europe," *World Politics* 18 (1966), 378–414.

37. Palmer, *Challenge*, 153–9, 171–81.

38. E. Wood, "Locke against Democracy: Consent, Representation and Suffrage in the *Two Treatises*," *History of Political Thought* 13 (1992), 657–89.

39. Orville Theodore Murphy, *Charles Gravier, Comte de Vergennes: French Diplomacy in the Age of Revolution, 1715–1787* (Albany: SUNY Press, 1982), 252–60.

40. Palmer, *Challenge*, 239–52.

41. Richard J. Walter, "Revolution, Independence, and Liberty in Latin America," in Isser Woloch, ed., *Revolution and the Meaning of Freedom in the Nineteenth Century* (Stanford: Stanford University Press, 1996), 114–15.

42. J. P. Brissot de Warville, *New Travels in the United States of America, 1788*, ed. Durand Echeverria (Cambridge, MA: Belknap/Harvard University Press, 1964).

43. Palmer, *Challenge*, 261–3.

44. Palmer, *Challenge*, 325–34.

45. Iain McLean, "Thomas Jefferson, John Adams, and the *Déclaration des Droits de l'Homme et du Citoyen*," in Robert Fatton and R. K. Ramazani, eds.,

*The Future of Liberal Democracy: Thomas Jefferson and the Contemporary World* (New York: Palgrave Macmillan, 2004), 13–30.

46. Behrens, Ancien Régime, 119; Furet, *Revolutionary France*, 45–56.

47. Furet, *Revolutionary France*, 63–70.

48. T.C.W. Blanning, *The Origins of the French Revolutionary Wars* (New York: Longman, 1986), 73–4.

49. Palmer, *Challenge*, 424.

50. Palmer, *Challenge*, 412–33.

51. Richard Price, *A Discourse on the Love of Our Country* (London: T. Cadell, 1790), available at http://books.google.com.

52. Jennifer Welsh, *Edmund Burke and International Relations* (New York: St. Martin's, 1995), 102–3.

53. Charles W. Ingrao, *The Habsburg Monarchy 1618–1815* (Cambridge: Cambridge University Press, 1994), 220–21; Blanning, *Origins*, 72.

54. Palmer, *Challenge*, 400–401.

55. Ernst Wangermann, *From Joseph II to the Jacobin Trials: Government Policy and Public Opinion in the Habsburg Dominions in the Period of the French Revolution* (New York: Oxford University Press, 1959), 62–7; Stephen Walt, *Revolution and War* (Ithaca, NY: Cornell University Press, 1996), 64–5. For an argument that the Flight to Varennes was crucial to the eventual outbreak of European war, see Mark L. Haas, *The Ideological Origins of Great Power Politics* (Ithaca, NY: Cornell University Press, 2003), 47–50

56. Blanning, *Origins*, 96–121.

57. T.C.W. Blanning, *The French Revolutionary Wars* (New York: Arnold, 1996), 88–93; Emma Vincent MacLeod, *A War of Ideas: British Attitudes to the Wars against Revolutionary France 1792–1802* (Aldershot, UK: Ashgate, 1998), 1–10.

58. E. J. Hobsbawm, *The Age of Revolution* (New York: New American Library, 1962), 80–81; R. R. Palmer, *The Age of the Democratic Revolution: A Political History of Europe and America 1760–1800*, vol. 2, *The Struggle* (Princeton, NJ: Princeton University Press, 1962), 50–52. Edmond-Charles "Citizen" Genêt came to the United States in April 1793 to try to persuade the country to join the war on the side of France.

59. Johann Amadeus Baron von Thugut, note to Austrian ambassador in St. Petersburg, May 29, 1794, quoted in Blanning, *French Revolutionary Wars*, 130.

60. Blanning, *French Revolutionary Wars*, 128–32.

61. Palmer, *Struggle*, 150–51.

62. Palmer, *Struggle*, 146–55.

63. Paul W. Schroeder, *The Transformation of European Politics, 1763–1848* (New York: Oxford University Press, 1994), 123–4.

64. Walter, "Revolution, Independence," 115–16.

65. John M. Owen, IV, *Liberal Peace, Liberal War: American Politics and International Security* (Ithaca, NY: Cornell University Press, 1997), chap. 3.

66. Desmond Gregory, *The Ungovernable Rock: A History of the Anglo-Corsican Kingdom and Its Role in Britain's Mediterranean Strategy during the*

*Revolutionary War (1793–1797)* (Cranbury, NJ: Associated University Presses, 1985), 38–40.

67. Blanning, *French Revolutionary Wars*, 170.

68. Blanning, *French Revolutionary Wars*, 174.

69. Blanning, *French Revolutionary Wars*, 178.

70. Blanning, *French Revolutionary Wars*, 228; Schroeder, *Transformation*, 183.

71. Schroeder, *Transformation*, 195.

72. Blanning, *French Revolutionary Wars*, 169.

73. R. A. Humphries, "The Emancipation of Latin America," in *The New Cambridge Modern History*, vol. 9, *War and Peace in an Age of Upheaval 1793–1830*, ed. C. W. Crawley, 624.

74. Felix Markham, "The Napoleonic Adventure," in Crawley, ed., *War and Peace*, 321.

75. See also Furet, *Revolutionary France*, 248–52.

76. Stuart Semmel, "British Radicals and 'Legitimacy': Napoleon in the Mirror of History," *Past and Present* 167 (May 2000), 140–75.

77. Owen, *Liberal Peace*, quoting Robert W. Tucker and David Hendrickson, *Empire of Liberty: The Statecraft of Thomas Jefferson* (New York: Oxford University Press, 1990).

78. For the British situation, see J. Ann Hone, *For the Cause of Truth: Radicalism in London, 1796–1821* (Oxford: Clarendon Press, 1982), compare 97–8 with 137–8.

79. Michael Broers, *Europe under Napoleon 1799–1815* (London: Arnold, 1996), 9.

80. Broers, *Europe under Napoleon*, 62.

81. Charles Esdaile, *The Wars of Napoleon* (London: Longman, 1995), 8, 34.

82. Esdaile, *Wars of Napoleon*, 13, 74; Schroeder, *Transformation*, 239.

83. Alexander Grab, *Napoleon and the Transformation of Europe* (New York: Macmillan, 2003), 97–9; Esdaile, *Wars of Napoleon*, 73.

84. John Anthony Davis, *Naples and Napoleon: Southern Italy and the European Revolutions 1780–1860* (New York: Oxford University Press, 2006), 187–208; Esdaile, *Wars of Napoleon*, 26, 72–3.

85. Esdaile, *Wars of Napoleon*, 73, 90.

86. Grab, *Napoleon and the Transformation*, 99–103; Esdaile, *Wars of Napoleon*, 73, 81.

87. Grab, *Napoleon and the Transformation*, 103.

88. Charles Esdaile, *The French Wars 1792–1815* (New York: Routledge, 2001), 23.

89. Esdaile, *Wars of Napoleon*, 90.

90. Michael Broers, *Europe under Napoleon 1799–1815* (New York: Arnold, 1996), 61-63.

91. Schroeder, *Transformation*, 431–4; Grab, *Napoleon and the Transformation*, 134–6.

92. Richard Herr, "The Gospel according to 1812," in Woloch, *Revolution and the Meanings*, 93.

93. R. A. Humphries, "The Emancipation of Latin America," in Crawley, ed., *War and Peace*, 624.

94. Esdaile, *Wars of Napoleon*, 239–41.

95. G. John Ikenberry, *After Victory* (Princeton, NJ: Princeton University Press, 2001).

96. Henry A. Kissinger, *A World Restored: The Politics of Conservatism in a Revolutionary Age* (New York: Grosset & Dunlop, 1964), 124–5.

97. Kissinger, *World Restored*, 178–9.

98. G. de Bertier de Sauvigny, "French Politics, 1814–47," in Crawley, ed., *War and Peace*, 337–9 (chapter is 337–94).

99. Schroeder, *Transformation*, 571–2.

100. Schroeder, *Transformation*, 596. To be precise, the powers did to varying degrees allow some features of the Napoleonic system to remain in France and elsewhere. In France, the restored Louis XVIII had to agree to a constitution limiting his powers; in Spain, Italy, Germany, Poland, the Netherlands, certain features of the Napoleonic model were retained by princes impressed by its efficiency. In some states the *gendarmerie* were kept; in some, the non-noble bureaucracy. For more, see David Laven and Lucy Riall, "Restoration Government and the Legacy of Napoleon," in idem, eds., *Napoleon's Legacy: Problems of Government in Restoration Europe* (Oxford: Berg, 2000), 1–26, esp. 11.

101. Kissinger, *World Restored*.

102. Broers, *Europe after Napoleon*, 13–14.

103. Laven and Riall, *Napoleon's Legacy*, 11–12.

104. Crawley, "Introduction," in idem, ed., *War and Peace*, 23.

105. Geoffrey Best, *War and Society in Revolutionary Europe 1770–1870* (Leicester, UK: Leicester University Press, 1982), 257–60.

106. Frederick B. Artz, *Reaction and Revolution 1814–1832* (New York: Harper & Brothers, 1934), 3.

107. Edward Vose Gulick, *Europe's Classical Balance of Power* (Ithaca, NY: Cornell University Press, 1955).

108. For a full treatment see Bruce Cronin, *Community under Anarchy: Transnational Identity and the Evolution of Cooperation* (New York: Columbia University Press, 1998), esp. chap. 3.

109. Hobsbawm, *Age of Revolution*, 112–13.

110. Artz, *Reaction and Revolution*, 160–62; Crawley, "International Relations, 1815–30," in idem, ed., *War and Peace*, 669.

111. Herr, "Constitution of 1812," 93–94.

112. Thomas G. Otte, "Of Congresses and Gunboats: Military Intervention in the Nineteenth Century," in Andrew M. Dorman and Thomas G. Otte, eds., *Military Intervention: From Gunboat Diplomacy to Humanitarian Intervention* (Aldershot, UK: Dartmouth, 1995), 24–7; J. H. Leurdijk, *Intervention in International Politics* (Leeuwarden, The Netherlands: B.V. Eisma, 1986), 238.

113. C. W. Crawley, "International Relations, 1815–30," in idem, ed., *War and Peace*, 679–81; G. de Bertrand de Sauvigny, "French Politics, 1814–47," in *War and Peace* , 349; Leurdijk, *Intervention*, 238.

114. Artz, *Reaction and Revolution*, 149–52, 163–5.

115. Crawley, "International Relations," in idem, ed., *War and Peace*, 674.

116. See, e.g., Carsten Holbraad, *The Concert of Europe: A Study in German and British International Theory, 1815–1914* (Harlow, UK: Longmans, 1970).

117. De Sauvigny, "French Politics," 349–52.

118. Leurdijk, *Intervention*, 239; Crawley, "International Politics," 684; Raymond Carr, "Spain and Portugal, 1793 to c. 1840," in Crawley, ed., *War and Peace*, 452–3.

119. David Thomson, *Europe since Napoleon* (Harmondsworth, UK: Penguin, 1966), 165–6; de Sauvigny, "French Politics," 349–56.

120. Schroeder, *Transformation*, 670–91.

121. Schroeder, *Transformation*, 697.

122. Schroeder, *Transformation*, 699–705; James Joll, "Prussia and the German Problem, 1830–66," in *The New Cambridge Modern History*, vol. 10, *The Zenith of European Power 1830–1870*, ed. J.P.T. Bury (New York: Cambridge University Press, 1960), 493–4.

123. Schroeder, *Transformation*, 705–9.

124. Gordon Craig, "The System of Alliances and the Balance of Power," in Bury, ed., *Zenith*, 248–53; Philip Guedalla, *Palmerston* (London: Ernest Benn, 1926), 196–7. It is interesting that, as Craig notes (253–4), Louis-Philippe, who was by now growing more conservative, did not like the new Quadruple Alliance, and initiated secret conversations with the Austrians for a permanent Franco-Austrian alliance.

125. Schroeder, *Transformation*, 720–26.

126. Thomson, *Europe since Napoleon*, 175.

127. James Maxwell Anderson, *The History of Portugal* (Westport, CT: Greenwood Press, 2000), 135–6.

128. Hobsbawm, *Age of Capital*, 10.

129. Frank G. Weber, "Palmerston and Prussian Liberalism, 1848," *Journal of Modern History* 35, no. 2 (June 1963), 128.

130. Weber, "Palmerston," 127–9.

131. Leurdijk, *Intervention*, 240–42.

132. Charles Pouthas, "The Revolutions of 1848," in Bury, ed., *Zenith*, 407.

133. Roland Quinault, "1848 and Parliamentary Reform," *Historical Journal* 31, no. 4 (1988), 831–51.

134. Weber, "Palmerston," 134–5.

135 Robert C. Binkley, *Realism and Nationalism 1852–1871* (New York: Harper & Brothers, 1935), 134–5.

136. J.A.S. Grenville, *Europe Reshaped 1848–1878* (Hassocks, UK: Harvester, 1976), 229–60.

137. Broers, *Europe after Napoleon*, 118.

138. Grenville, *Europe Reshaped*, 274–5; 316–19.

139. Grenville, *Europe Reshaped*, 305–6.

140. Grenville, *Europe Reshaped*, 350–51.

141. Grenville, *Europe Reshaped*, 334–6.

142. Grenville, *Europe Reshaped*, 261–71.

143. Grenville, *Europe Reshaped*, 9–10.

144. Quoted in E. J. Hobsbawm, *The Age of Capital, 1848–1875* (London: Weidenfeld and Nicolson, 1975), 15.

145. Broers, *Europe after Napoleon*, 117–18.

146. Paul Kennedy, *The Rise and Fall of the Great Powers: Economic Change and Military Conflict from 1500 to 2000* (New York: Random House, 1987), 171.

147. Hobsbawm, *Age of Revolution*, 91.

148. Broers, *Europe after Napoleon*, 110.

CHAPTER 6
INDIVIDUAL, CLASS, AND STATE, 1910–1990

1. Carl C. Hodge and Cathal J. Nolan, "'As Powerful as We Are': From the Morgenthau Plan to Marshall Aid," in idem, ed., *Shepherd of Democracy? America and Germany in the Twentieth Century* (Westport, CT: Greenwood Press, 1992), 55–9.

2. Having by far the most money, the United States set the agenda in the western zones, and until the middle of 1946 the blueprint was laid out in Joint Chiefs of Staff (JCS) memorandum 1067.

3. Jean Edward Smith, *Lucius D. Clay: An American Life* (New York: Henry Holt, 1990), 368–78.

4. Smith, *Clay*, 367.

5. Smith, *Clay*, 381.

6. Smith, *Clay*, 378–89; Richard L. Merritt, *Democracy Imposed: U.S. Occupation Policy and the German Public, 1945–1949* (New Haven, CT: Yale University Press, 1995), 64–8. Byrnes's speech built upon a draft by Clay; the final version was drafted by John Kenneth Galbraith and Charles Kindleberger.

7. "Joint Statement by James F. Byrnes and Ernest Bevin (3 December 1946)," http://www.ena.lu/mce.cfm.

8. Charles Williams, *Adenauer: The Father of the New Germany* (Boston: Little, Brown, 2000), 327.

9. Willie Thompson, *The Communist Movement since 1945* (Oxford: Blackwell, 1998), 35–8.

10. Williams, *Adenauer*, 315–16.

11. E. J. Hobsbawm, *The Age of Extremes: A History of the World 1914–1991* (New York: Vintage, 1996).

12. Theodore Roosevelt, "State of the Union Message, December 6, 1904," http://www.theodore-roosevelt.com/sotu4.html, accessed on May 11, 2009.

13. Serge Ricard, "The Roosevelt Corollary," *Presidential Studies Quarterly* 36 (2006), 17–26.

14. Kris James Mitchener and Marc Weidenmier, "Empire, Public Goods, and the Roosevelt Corollary," *Journal of Economic History* 65 (2005), 658–92.

15. David P. Forsythe, "Democracy, War, and Covert Action," *Journal of Peace Research* 29 (1992), 385–95.

16. See Douglas J. Macdonald, *Adventures in Chaos: American Intervention for Reform in the Third World* (Cambridge, MA: Harvard University Press, 1992); Fred Halliday, *Cold War, Third World: An Essay on US-Soviet Relations*

(London: Hutchinson Radius, 1989); Tarak Barkawi and Mark Laffey, "The Imperial Peace: Democracy, Force, and Globalization," *European Journal of International Relations* 5 (1999), 403–34; David F. Schmitz, *Thank God They're on Our Side: The United States & Right-Wing Dictatorships, 1921–1965* (Chapel Hill: University of North Carolina Press, 1999).

17. Forsythe, "Covert Action," 393–4.

18. E. J. Hobsbawm, *The Age of Capital, 1848–1875* (London: Weidenfeld and Nicolson, 1975), 166–7.

19. A.J.P. Taylor, *The Struggle for Mastery in Europe 1848–1918* (Oxford: Clarendon Press, 1954), 219.

20. David Thomson, *Europe since Napoleon* (Harmondsworth, UK: Penguin, 1966), 528–9.

21. John M. Owen, "How Liberalism Produces Democratic Peace," *International Security* 19, no. 4 (Fall 1994), 121–2.

22. Jack A. Goldstone, *Revolution and Rebellion in the Early Modern World* (Berkeley: University of California Press, 1993).

23. Albert S. Lindemann, *A History of European Socialism* (New Haven, CT: Yale University Press, 1983), 2–25.

24. Lindemann, *European Socialism*, xv–xvii; 158–60.

25. Hobsbawm, *Age of Capital*, 17–20.

26. Hobsbawm, *Age of Capital*, 109–15.

27. Hobsbawm, *Age of Capital*, 115.

28. Lindemann, *European Socialism*, 135–7.

29. Thomson, *Europe since Napoleon*, 405–13.

30. Zeev Sternhell, *The Birth of Fascist Ideology*, trans. David Maisel (Princeton, NJ: Princeton University Press, 1995), 13–27.

31. Thomson, *Europe since Napoleon*, 402–5. *Bolsheviki* is Russian for "majority-men," denoting that Lenin won a majority of party delegates. The *Mensheviki* or "minority-men" favored opening decision making to all party members. Bolsheviks and Mensheviks worked together until 1912.

32. Thomson, *Europe since Napoleon*, 418–22; Lindemann, *European Socialism*, 147–58.

33. Lindemann, *European Socialism*, 185–90. Michael Doyle argues that the SPD's decision was consistent with the writings of Friedrich Engels, who had died in 1895. Doyle, *Ways of War and Peace: Realism, Liberalism, Socialism* (New York: Norton, 1997).

34. Lenin, "Imperialism, the Highest Stage of Capitalism" (1916); for text, see http://www.fordham.edu/halsall/mod/1916lenin-imperialism.html.

35. V. I. Lenin, "The Proletarian Revolution and the Renegade Kautsky" (1918), available at http://www.marxists.org/archive/lenin/works/1918/prrk/equality.htm, accessed on May 11, 2009.

36. Kenneth N. Waltz, *Man, the State, and War* (New York: Columbia University Press, 1959), 138–41.

37. George F. Kennan, *Soviet-American Relations 1917–1920* (Princeton, NJ: Princeton University Press, 1956), 18–20.

38. Thomson, *Europe since Napoleon*, 565; George F. Kennan, *Russia and the West under Lenin and Stalin* (Boston: Little, Brown, 1961), 29.

39. Kennan, *Russia and the West*, 23–6; Richard K. Debo, *Revolution and Survival: The Foreign Policy of Soviet Russia, 1917–18* (Liverpool, UK: Liverpool University Press, 1979), 3–4.

40. Text available at http://www.historyguide.org/europe/decree.html.

41. Kennan, *Russia and the West*, 54–9.

42. Kennan, *Soviet-American Relations*, 74–5, 151.

43. Debo, *Revolution and Survival*, 28–9; Kennan, *Russia and the West*, 64.

44. Kennan, *Soviet-American Relations*, 156–7.

45. Peter G. Filene, *Americans and the Soviet Experiment, 1917–1933* (Cambridge, MA: Harvard University Press, 1967), 24.

46. Kennan, *Russia and the West*, 67–108.

47. John Lewis Gaddis, *Russia, the Soviet Union, and the United States: An Interpretive History* (New York: Wiley, 1978), 72.

48. Lenin, from August 1918 and November 1918, respectively, quoted in Debo, *Revolution and Survival*, 356.

49. Lindemann, *European Socialism*, 206.

50. Lindemann, *European Socialism*, 211.

51. Ken Post, *Communists and National Socialists* (Houndsmills, UK: Macmillan, 1997), 79–81.

52. Kennan, *Russia and the West*, 157–9.

53. Kennan, *Russia and the West*, 159–61.

54. J. Hampden Jackson, "German Intervention in Finland, 1918," *Slavonic and East European Review* 18 (1939), 93–101.

55. See Witold S. Sworakowski, ed., *World Communism: A Handbook 1918–1965* (Stanford, CA: Hoover Institution Press, 1973), passim.

56. Lindemann, *European Socialism*, 214–16.

57. Stephen Blank, "Soviet Politics and the Iranian Revolution of 1919–1921," *Cahiers du monde russe et soviétique* 21 (1980), 173–94.

58. Thomson, *Europe since Napoleon*, 588–600.

59. Post, *Communists and National Socialists*, 84.

60. Jon Jacobson, *When the Soviet Union Entered World Politics* (Berkeley: University of California Press, 1994), 33–78.

61. Thomson, *Europe since Napoleon*, 636; Kyle Lascurettes, "Cooperation after War: Explaining Trade between Great Power Potential Adversaries after Major Wars" (M.A. thesis, University of Virginia, 2006).

62. Thomson, *Europe since Napoleon*, 669–73.

63. Juan Linz, "Fascism," in Roger Griffin, ed., *International Fascism: Theories, Causes and the New Consensus* (London: Arnold, 1998), 178–9.

64. Eugen Weber, *Varieties of Fascism: Doctrines of Revolution in the Twentieth Century* (Princeton, NJ: D. Van Nostrand, 1964), 28–43.

65. Stanley G. Payne, "A Form of Revolutionary Ultra-nationalism," in Roger Griffin, ed., *International Fascism: Theories, Causes and the New Consensus* (London: Arnold, 1998), 149. Zeev Sternhell regards rejection of Marxian and liberal materialism as the root of fascism; Sternhell, *Fascist Ideology*.

66. Weber, *Varieties of Fascism*, 26–8.

67. Roger Griffin, "Fascism," in Griffin, ed., *International Fascism*, 36.

68. Alistair Hennessy, "Fascism and Populism in Latin America," in Walter Laqueur, ed., *Fascism: A Reader's Guide* (Berkeley: University of California Press, 1976), 255–7.

69. Sternhell, *Fascist Ideology*.

70. Linz, "Fascism," 175–80.

71. Alan Cassels, *Mussolini's Early Diplomacy* (Princeton, NJ: Princeton University Press, 1970), 168–74.

72. Post, *Communists and National Socialists*, 99–103.

73. Stanley G. Payne, *The Spanish Civil War, the Soviet Union, and Communism* (New Haven, CT: Yale University Press, 2004), 22.

74. Thompson, *Communist Movement*, 16–17.

75. Thomson, *Europe since Napoleon*, 726–7.

76. Philip Morgan, *Fascism in Europe, 1919–1945* (New York: Routledge, 2003), xiii–xx.

77. H. James Burgwyn, *Italian Foreign Policy in the Interwar Period 1918–1940* (Westport, CT: Greenwood, 1997), 75–82.

78. Morgan, *Fascism in Europe*, 168–70.

79. Andrew Gordon, *A Modern History of Japan: From Tokugawa Times to the Present* (New York: Oxford University Press, 2002), 195–6.

80. Thomson, *Europe since Napoleon*, 702–3.

81. Lindemann, *European Socialism*, 257, 301–11.

82. Payne, *Spanish Civil War*, 60–141; Morten Heiberg, "Mussolini, Franco and the Spanish Civil War: An Afterthought," in Gert Sørensen and Robert Mallett, eds., *International Fascism 1919–45* (London: Frank Cass, 2002), 56–8.

83. Frederick M. Watkins, "Military Occupation Policy of the Axis Powers," in Carl J. Friedrich, ed., *American Experiences in Military Government in World War II* (New York: Rinehart & Co., 1948), 86–107.

84. Raphaël Lemkin, *Axis Rule in Occupied Europe* (Washington, DC: Carnegie Endowment for International Peace, 1944), 178–80.

85. Lemkin, *Axis Rule*, 141–3.

86. Lemkin, *Axis Rule*, 252–5.

87. Lemkin, *Axis Rule*, 159–64.

88. Randall L. Schweller, *Unanswered Threats: Political Constraints on the Balance of Power* (Princeton, NJ: Princeton University Press, 2006), 118–25.

89. Propaganda posters are instructive in this regard; see, e.g., Peter Paret, Beth Irwin Lewis, and Paul Paret, *Persuasive Images: Posters of War and Revolution* (Princeton, NJ: Princeton University Press, 1992), esp. 170–81.

90. John Lamberton Harper, *American Visions of Europe: Franklin D. Roosevelt, George F. Kennan, and Dean G. Acheson* (New York: Cambridge University Press, 1995), 78–90. William Bullitt, the first U.S. ambassador to the USSR, urged FDR during the war to join with Britain to contain Soviet power, arguing that Stalin aimed at world domination but was more patient than Hitler. Roosevelt ignored the advice. See ibid., 93–4.

91. Thompson, *Communist Movement*, 30–34.

92. David S. Painter and Melvyn P. Leffler, "Introduction: The International System and the Origins of the Cold War," in Leffler and Painter, eds., *Origins of the Cold War: An International History* (New York: Routledge, 1994), 7.

93. James Edward Miller, *The United States and Italy, 1940–1950: The Politics of Diplomacy and Stabilization* (Chapel Hill: University of North Carolina Press, 1986), 131–2.

94. E.g., *Foreign Relations of the United States 1943*, vol. 2, *Europe* (Washington, DC: Government Printing Office, 1964), 367–9. The following month the British embassy informed the U.S. State Department that the Soviets wanted "a satisfactory position on the Control Commission for Italy or whatever authority was set up to ensure the carrying out of the surrender terms." Ibid., 408–9.

95. Thompson, *Communist Movement*, 22.

96. Harper, *American Visions*, 97.

97. Gaddis, *Russia, the Soviet Union, and the United States*, 164–71.

98. Donald Sassoon, "Italian Images of Russia, 1945–56," in Christopher Duggan and Christopher Wagstaff , eds., *Italy in the Cold War: Politics, Culture and Society 1948–58* (Oxford: Berg, 1995), 194–7.

99. Miller, *United States and Italy*, 155–8.

100. Sassoon, "Italian Images," 198; Miller, *United States and Italy*, 147–50.

101. Miller, *United States and Italy*, 155–8; Michael Ledeen, *West European Communism and American Foreign Policy* (New Brunswick, NJ: Transaction Books, 1987), 29–49.

102. Anton W. DePorte, *Europe between the Superpowers: The Enduring Balance*, 2nd ed. (New Haven, CT: Yale University Press, 1986), 118–20.

103. DePorte, *Europe between the Superpowers*, 120–21.

104. Jeronim Perovic, "The Tito-Stalin Split: A Reassessment in Light of the Evidence," *Journal of Cold War Studies* 9, no. 2 (Spring 2007), 32–63.

105. Gaddis, *Russia, the Soviet Union*, 171.

106. Michael Schaller, *The American Occupation of Japan: The Origins of the Cold War in Asia* (New York: Oxford University Press, 1987), 21–45.

107. William W. Stueck, *The Korean War: An International History* (Princeton, NJ: Princeton University Press, 1995), 29.

108. Douglas J. Macdonald, "Communist Bloc Expansion in the Early Cold War: Challenging Realism, Refuting Revisionism," *International Security* 20:3 (1995–96), 166–79.

109. Stueck, *Korean War*, 28–30; Michael Yahuda, *The International Politics of the Asia-Pacific, 1945–1995* (New York: Routledge, 1995), 167.

110. Stueck, *Korean War*, 53.

111. Spencer D. Bakich, "Information, Diplomacy, and Strategy: Balancing Avoidance in Limited Warfare," Ph.D. Dissertation, University of Virginia, 2006, chap. 3.

112. Melvyn P. Leffler, *For the Soul of Mankind: The United States, the Soviet Union, and the Cold War* (New York: Hill and Wang, 2007), 80.

113. For similar arguments about the importance of ideology to the Cold War, see Macdonald, "Communist Bloc Expansion"; and Nigel Gould-Davies, "Rethinking the Role of Ideology in International Politics during the Cold War," *Journal of Cold War Studies* 1 (1999), 90–109.

114. Martin McCauley, *The Khrushchev Era, 1953–1964* (New York: Longman, 1995), 20–22.

115. On the flowering of "new thinking" in the Soviet Union during the Khrushchev Thaw, see Robert D. English, *Russia and the Idea of the West: Gorbachev, Intellectuals, and the End of the Cold War* (New York: Columbia University Press, 2000), 49–80.

116. McCauley, *Khrushchev Era*, 46–7.

117. Karl P. Benziger, *Imre Nagy, Martyr of the Nation: Contested History, Legitimacy, and Popular Memory in Hungary* (Lanham, MD: Lexington Books, 2008), 46–8.

118. Miklós Molnár, *A Concise History of Hungary*, trans. Anna Magyar (New York: Cambridge University Press, 2001), 307–19.

119. Gaddis, *Russia, the Soviet Union*, 266.

120. David Lane, *The Rise and Fall of State Socialism* (London: Polity Press 1996), 42.

121. Lane, *State Socialism*, 153.

122. Thompson, *Communist Movement*, 27–8; 46–8.

123. Odd Arne Westad, *The Global Cold War: Third World Interventions and the Making of Our Times* (New York: Cambridge University Press, 2005), 73–109.

124. John Lewis Gaddis, *We Now Know: Rethinking Cold War History* (New York: Oxford University Press), 155–6.

125. Gaddis, *We Now Know*, 158–63.

126. George C. Herring, *America's Longest War: The United States and Vietnam, 1950–1975*, 2nd ed. (New York: Alfred A. Knopf, 1986), 43–108.

127. Leurdijk, *Intervention*, 248.

128. Herring, *America's Longest War*, 234–7, 260–71.

129. A strong case is made in Robert Jervis and Jack Snyder, eds., *Dominoes and Bandwagons: Strategic Beliefs and Great Power Competition in the Eurasian Rimland* (New York: Oxford University Press, 1991).

130. Amitav Acharya, "Regionalism and Regime Security in the Third World: Comparing the Origins of the ASEAN and the GCC," in Brian Job, ed., *The Insecurity Dilemma: National, Regime, and State Securities in the Third World* (Boulder, CO: Lynne Rienner, 1992), 143–64.

131. Westad, *Global Cold War*, 66–72.

132. Christopher Andrew and Vasili Mitrokhin, *The World Was Going Our Way: The KGB and the Battle for the Third World* (New York: Basic Books, 2005), 4–7.

133. Don Munton and David A. Welch, *The Cuban Missile Crisis: A Concise History* (New York: Oxford University Press), 76–80.

134. Walter LaFeber, *Inevitable Revolutions: The United States in Central America* (New York: Norton, 1984), 156–8.

135. Ronald E. Powaski, *The Cold War: The United States and the Soviet Union, 1917–1991* (New York: Oxford University Press, 1998), 154–5; LaFeber, *Inevitable Revolutions*, 157.

136. Powaski, *Cold War*, 234.

137. Tony Hodges, *Angola: From Afro-Stalinism to Petro-Diamond Capitalism* (Bloomington: Indiana University Press, 2001), 10–11.

138. "Dhofar Rebellion in Oman 1964–75," On War website, http://www .onwar.com/aced/data/oscar/oman1964.htm.

139. Jimmy Carter, "Human Rights and Foreign Policy," *Public Papers of the Presidents of the United States: Jimmy Carter, vol. 1* (1977), 954; available at http://usinfo.state.gov/usa/infousa/facts/democrac/55.htm.

140. James Chace, "Foreign Policy and the Democratic Process: Is a Foreign Policy Consensus Possible?" *Foreign Affairs* 57, no. 1 (Fall 1978) (italics mine).

141. Thompson, *Communist Movement*, 183.

142. Moynihan, *Pandaemonium: Ethnicity in International Politics* (New York: Oxford University Press, 1992), 8–40. Moynihan adds, however: "It would take time for this news to reach the Vietnamese jungle, Angolan bush, or Nicaraguan mountains."

143. Lane, *State Socialism*, 176.

144. Fred Halliday, *Revolution and World Politics: The Rise and Fall of the Sixth Great Power* (London: Macmillan, 1999), 217.

145. Zbigniew Brzezinski, *The Grand Failure: The Birth and Death of Communism in the Twentieth Century* (New York: Charles Scribner's Sons, 1989), 213.

146. Brzezinski, *Grand Failure*, 215; Thompson, *Communist Movement*, 193.

147. Brzezinski, *Grand Failure*, 215.

148. Erica Gould attributes the more monetarist conditions to pressure from private lenders, who began to provide a higher proportion of loans in the 1980s. Gould, *Money Talks: The International Monetary Fund, Conditionality, and Supplementary Financiers* (Stanford: Stanford University Press, 2006).

149. Anne Morrow Lindbergh, *The Wave of the Future: A Confession of Faith* (New York: Morrow, 1940).

150. See Hannah Arendt, *The Origins of Totalitarianism* (New York: Harcourt, Brace, 1951); Jeanne Kirkpatrick, "Dictatorships and Double Standards," *Commentary* (November 1979). These and others are cited in Timur Kuran, "Now out of Never: The Element of Surprise in the East European Revolutions of 1989," *World Politics* 44:1 (October 1991), 7–8.

CHAPTER 7
MOSQUE AND STATE, 1923–

1. Dilip Hiro, *The Longest War: The Iran-Iraq Military Conflict* (New York: Routledge, 1990), 32–3.

2. Hiro, *Longest War*, 28.

3. Philip Robins, "Iraq: Revolutionary Threats and Regime Reponses," in John Esposito, ed., *The Iranian Revolution: Its Global Impact* (Miami: Florida International University Press, 1990), 86–7.

4. Hiro, *Longest War*, 28.

5. Ephraim Karsh and Inari Rautsi, *Saddam Hussein: A Political Biography*, rev. ed. (New York: Grove Press, 2002), 107–9; Robins, "Iraq: Revolutionary Threats and Regime Reponses,", 87–8.

6. Hiro, *Longest War*, 35–6.

7. David E. Long, "The Impact of the Iranian Revolution on the Arabian Peninsula and the Gulf States," in Esposito, ed., *Iranian Revolution:*, 106. The official

name of the Saudi King is "Custodian of the Two Holy Mosques," viz. those in Mecca and Medina.

8. R. K. Ramazani, *Revolutionary Iran: Challenge and Response in the Middle East* (Baltimore, MD: Johns Hopkins University Press, 1986), 58–60. Ramazani concludes that these were probably Khomeini's forces trying to help Iraqi Shii.

9. For a similar explanation of the Iran-Iraq War, see Stephen M. Walt, *Revolution and War* (Ithaca, NY: Cornell University Press, 1996), 238–40.

10. Islamists are in Indonesia and other Southeast Asian countries but thus far have not sufficiently threatened regimes to warrant inclusion in this chapter. See John Gershman, "Is Southeast Asia the Second Front?" *Foreign Affairs* 81 (July/ August 2002), 60–74.

11. "Islamic Law," in John L. Esposito, ed., *Oxford Dictionary of Islam* (New York: Oxford University Press, 2003), via *Oxford Reference Online,* http:// www.oxfordreference.com/views/ENTRY.html?subview=Main&entry=t125. e1107, accessed December 12, 2007.

12. The Afghan constitution of 2004 is available at http://www.jemb.org/eng/ legislation.html.

13. Gilles Kepel, *The Revenge of God: The Resurgence of Islam, Christianity, and Judaism in the Modern World,* trans. Alan Braley (University Park: Pennsylvania State University Press, 1994); Peter L. Berger, "Secularism in Retreat," in John L. Esposito and Azzam Tamimi, eds., *Islam and Secularism in the Middle East* (New York: NYU Press, 2000), 38–51.

14. Dinesh D'Souza, *The Enemy at Home: The Cultural Left and Its Responsibility for 9/11* (New York: Broadway, 2007).

15. Andrew Sullivan, *The Conservative Soul: Fundamentalism, Freedom, and the Future of the Right* (New York: Harper Perennial, 2006).

16. Mohammed Ayoob, *The Many Faces of Political Islam* (Ann Arbor: University of Michigan Press, 2008), 42–63.

17. Cf. Mark Juergensmeyer, *The New Cold War? Religious Nationalism Confronts the Secular State* (Berkeley: University of California Press, 1993).

18. Albert Hourani, *Arabic Thought in the Liberal Age, 1789–1939* (New York: Cambridge University Press, 1983), 4–8.

19. Hourani, *Arabic Thought,* 20–30.

20. Hourani, *Arabic Thought,* 40–44.

21. Azzam Tamimi, "The Origins of Arab Secularism," in John L. Esposito and Azzam Tamimi, eds., *Islam and Secularism in the Middle East* (New York: NYU Press, 2000), 13–28.

22. William L. Cleveland, *A History of the Modern Middle East,* 3rd ed. (Boulder, CO: Westview Press, 2004), 119–20.

23. Hasan Kayali, *Arabs and Young Turks: Ottomanism, Arabism, and Islamism in the Ottoman Empire, 1908–1918* (Berkeley: University of California Press, 1997), 30–2.

24. Cleveland, *History of the Middle East,* 181.

25. Kayali, *Arabs and Young Turks,* 40; David Fromkin, *A Peace to End All Peace: The Fall of the Ottoman Empire and the Creation of the Modern Middle East* (New York: Avon Books, 1989), 34–8.

26. Fromkin, *Peace,* 39–40.

27. Cleveland, *History of the Middle East*, 119.

28. Fromkin, *Peace*, 40–44.

29. Fromkin, *Peace*, passim.

30. Cleveland, *History of the Middle East*, 180–82.

31. Serif A. Mardin, "Ideology and Religion in the Turkish Revolution," *International Journal of Middle East Studies* 2 (1971), 197–211; Mehran Kamrava, *The Modern Middle East: A Political History since the First World War* (Berkeley: University of California Press, 2005), 54.

32. Kamrava, *Modern Middle East*, 57–61; Cleveland, *History of the Middle East*, 183–5.

33. Cleveland, *History of the Middle East*, 222–4.

34. Cleveland, *History of the Middle East*, 195–6.

35. For a comprehensive treatment, see David Dean Commins, *The Wahhabi Mission and Saudi Arabia* (London: I. B. Tauris, 2006).

36. Cleveland, *History of the Middle East*, 225–6.

37. Cleveland, *History of the Middle East*, 230–31.

38. Baqer Moin, *Khomeini: Life of the Ayatollah* (London: Tauris, 1999), 54–6.

39. Moin, *Khomeini*, 56.

40. M. Naeem Qureshi, "Muslims of British India and the Kemalist Reform in Turkey, Iqbal, Jinnah and Atatürk," *Atatürk Arastirma Merkezi Dergisi*, Sayi 35, Cilt XII, Temmuz 1996; http://www.atam.gov.tr/index.php?Page=DergiIcerik &IcerikNo=719.

41. Cf. Bassam Tibi, "Islam and Modern European Ideologies," *International Journal of Middle East Studies* 18 (1986), 23.

42. For an account of the alienation of the Muslim Brotherhood from Nasser's new regime, see Richard P. Mitchell, *The Society of Muslim Brothers* (New York: Oxford University Press, 1969), 105–62. I thank Audrey Kurth Cronin for alerting me to this source.

43. Talal Asad, "Thinking about Secularism and Law in Egypt" (Leiden, Netherlands: ISIM, 2001), 3; https://www.openaccess.leidenuniv.nl/bitstream/1887/10066/1/paper_asad.pdf.

44. Ibrahim Abu-Lughod, "Retreat from Secularism? Islamic Dilemmas of Arab Politics," *Review of Politics* 28 (1966), 466.

45. Barnett Rubin, *Islamic Fundamentalism in Egyptian Politics*, updated ed. (New York: Palgrave, 2002), 13.

46. Saïd K. Aburish, *Nasser: The Last Arab* (New York: St. Martin's Press, 2004), 76–83.

47. Kamrava, *Modern Middle East*, 95–6.

48. Maridi Nahas, "State Systems and Revolutionary Challenge: Nasser, Khomeini, and the Middle East," *International Journal of Middle East Studies* 17 (November 1985), 514; Paul Dresch, *A History of Modern Yemen* (New York: Cambridge University Press, 2000), 79.

49. Kamrava, *Modern Middle East*, 108–11.

50. Aburish, *Nasser*, 168–70. In 1956, Nasser had rejected a request by Iraqi army officers to help them overthrow the monarchy for fear of alarming the Eisenhower administration. Ibid., 149.

310 • Notes to Chapter Seven

51. Kamrava, *Modern Middle East*, 109–10.

52. Guy Arnold, *Wars in the Third World since 1945* (New York: Cassell, 1991), 439–40.

53. Tom Cooper with Ray Kolakowski, "Lebanon and Jordan 1958," Air Combat Infantry Group Middle East Database (September 24, 2003); http://www.acig.org/artman/publish/article_259.shtml, accessed on May 22, 2009.

54. Aburish, *Nasser*, 170.

55. Madawi al-Rasheed, *A History of Saudi Arabia* (New York: Cambridge University Press, 2002), 110–12.

56. Al-Rasheed, *Saudi Arabia*, 116–17.

57. Nahas, "States Systems," 515–16.

58. Commins, *The Wahhabi Mission*, 152–4; Dale F. Eickelman, "Transstate Islam and Security," in Susanne Hoeber Rudolph and James Piscatori, eds., *Transnational Religion and Fading States* (Boulder, CO: Westview Press, 1997), 31; Cary Fraser, "In Defense of Allah's Realm: Religion and Statecraft in Saudi Foreign Policy Strategy," in Rudolph and Piscatori, eds., *Transnational Religion*, 219–20.

59. On Qutb's enduring influence upon and inspiration of jihadis—both his ideas and the suffering he endured at the hands of the Nasser regime—see Fawaz A. Gerges, *The Far Enemy: Why Jihad Went Global* (New York: Cambridge University Press, 2005), 4–9.

60. Quoted in Ibrahim M. Abu-Rabi, *Intellectual Origins of Islamic Resurgence in the Modern Arab World* (Albany: State University of New York Press, 1996), 180.

61. Bruce Lincoln, "Mr. Atta's Meditations, September 10, 2001: A Close Reading of the Text," *The Religion and Culture Web Forum*, December 2002: http://marty-center.uchicago.edu/webforum/122002/commentary.shtml, quoting from Qutb, *Milestones* (Mumbai: Bilal Books, 1998).

62. Kepel, *Revenge of God*, 19–21.

63. Arnold, Wars in the Third World, 456–7.

64. Dresch, *Modern Yemen*, 89–91.

65. Kepel, *Revenge of God*, 14–17.

66. Kepel, *Revenge of God*, 21.

67. James P. Piscatori, *Islam in a World of Nation-States* (New York: Cambridge University Press, 1996), 26–8. See also Bassam Tibi, *The Challenge of Fundamentalism: Political Islam and the New World Disorder*, updated ed. (Berkeley: University of California Press, 2002); Fouad Ajami, *The Dream Palace of the Arabs* (New York: Vintage, 1998).

68. See text of the Khartoum Resolutions at http://www.yale.edu/lawweb/avalon/mideast/khartoum.htm.

69. Nahas, "State Systems and Revolutionary Challenge," 517–18.

70. Mark Juergensmeyer, "The New Religious State," *Comparative Politics* 27 (1995), 385 [379–91].

71. Kepel, *Revenge of God*, 23.

72. Fraser, "Allah's Realm," 222.

73. Commins, *Wahhabi Mission*, 152–4. Faysal was assassinated by his nephew to avenge the execution of Faysal's brother (the assassin's father).

74. Olivier Roy, *Globalised Islam: The Search for a New Ummah* (London: Hurst & Co., 2002), 236–7.

75. Mark Tessler, *A History of the Israeli-Palestinian Conflict* (Bloomington: Indiana University Press, 1994), 435–6.

76. Kamrava, *Modern Middle East*, 225–6.

77. Tessler, *Israeli-Palestinian Conflict*, 437–40.

78. Aryeh Y. Yodfat and Yuval Arnon-Ohanna, *PLO Strategy and Tactics* (London: Croon Helm, 1981), 55–6.

79. Arnold, *Wars in the Third World*, 440–42.

80. Arnold, *Wars in the Third World*, 310–14.

81. "Islamic Law," *Oxford Dictionary of Islam*. John L. Esposito, ed., Oxford University Press Inc. 2003. *Oxford Reference Online*. Oxford University Press. University of Virginia Library. 9 November 2009, http://www.oxfordreference.com/views/ENTRY.html?subview=Main&entry=t125.e1107.

82. John L. Esposito and James P. Piscatori, "Introduction," in Esposito, ed., *Iranian Revolution*, 18.

83. Moin, *Khomeini*, 246.

84. Moin, *Khomeini*, 64–95; Nikki R. Keddie, *Roots of Revolution: An Interpretive History of Modern Iran* (New Haven, CT: Yale University Press, 1981), 154–9.

85. John L. Esposito, "The Iranian Revolution: A Ten-Year Perspective," in idem, ed., *Iranian Revolution*, 22.

86. Esposito, "Iranian Revolution," 31.

87. R. K. Ramazani, "Iran's Export of the Revolution: Politics, Ends, and Means," in Esposito, ed., *Iranian Revolution*, 48.

88. Vali Nasr, *The Shia Revival: How Conflicts within Islam Will Shape the Future* (New York: W. W. Norton, 2006), 137–8; Esposito, "Iranian Revolution," 31.

89. Ramazani, "Iran's Export," 106.

90. David E. Long, "The Impact of the Iranian Revolution on the Arabian Peninsula and the Gulf States," in Esposito, ed., *Iranian Revolution*, 106.

91. Augustus Richard Norton, "Lebanon: The Internal Conflict and the Iranian Connection," in Esposito, ed., *Iranian Revolution*, 122–31.

92. Shahrough Akhavi, "The Impact of the Iranian Revolution in Egypt," in Esposito, ed., *Iranian Revolution*, 144.

93. Akhavi, "Egypt," 141.

94. Ramazani, *Revolutionary Iran*, 164–73.

95. Gerges, *Far Enemy*, 44–6. Here again, it is unclear how far, if at all, the Khomeini movement influenced Faraj.

96. Gilles Kepel, *Jihad: The Trail of Political Islam* (Cambridge, MA: Harvard University Press, 2002), 131–3.

97. Lisa Anderson, "Tunisia and Libya: Responses to the Islamic Impulse," in Esposito, ed., *Iranian Revolution*, 158.

98. Fraser, "Allah's Realm," 212.

99. Fraser, "Allah's Realm," 216.

100. Ramazani, *Revolutionary Iran*, 92.

101. Esposito, "Iranian Revolution," 33–4.

102. Fraser, "Allah's Realm," 212.

103. Esposito, "Iranian Revolution," 32–4.

104. David E. Long, "The Impact of the Iranian Revolution on the Arabian Peninsula and the Gulf States," in Esposito, ed., *Iranian Revolution*, 107; Akhavi, "Egypt," 141.

105. Nasr, *Shia Revival*, 147–53.

106. Ramazani, *Revolutionary Iran*, 119–20, 131–2.

107. Barbara D. Metcalf, "'Traditionalist' Islamic Activism: Deoband, Tablighis, and Talibs" (Leiden, Netherlands: International Institute for the Study of Islam in the Modern World, 2002); https://openaccess.leidenuniv.nl/bitstream/1887/10068/1/paper_metcalf.pdf.

108. One such group is the Jami'at-ul-Ulama-i-Islam or JUI; another is the Jama'at-i Islami or JI, founded in 1941 by Abul Ala Maududi, one of Islamism's most influential thinkers. The JI favor a confessional state from the start, but work through existing Pakistani institutions, whereas the JUI are more militant. See Roy, *Globalised Islam*, 5; also Commins, *Wahhabi Mission*, 145–6.

109. Olivier Roy, "Islamic Radicalism in Afghanistan and Pakistan," UNHCR Emergency and Security Service Writenet Paper No. 06/2001 (January 2002), available at http://www.ecoi.net/file_upload/470_1162819345_3c6a3f7d2.pdf.

110. Henry A. Bradsher, *Afghanistan and the Soviet Union* (Durham, NC: Duke University Press, 1983), 91.

111. Anthony Arnold, *Afghanistan: The Soviet Invasion in Perspective* (Stanford, CA: Hoover Institution Press, 1985), 77.

112. Shirin Tahir-Kheli, "The Soviet Union in Afghanistan: Benefits and Costs," in Robert H. Donaldson, ed., *The Soviet Union in the Third World: Successes and Failures* (Boulder, CO: Westview Press, 1981), 219–25.

113. Westad, *Global Cold War*, 300–310.

114. Bradsher, *Afghanistan and the Soviet Union*, 157.

115. Bradsher, *Afghanistan and the Soviet Union*, 100–101.

116. Nasr, "International Politics," 171–90; Olivier Roy, "The Mujahidin and the Future of Afghanistan," in Esposito, *Iranian Revolution*, 179–202. Shii compose roughly 20 percent of the populations of Pakistan and Afghanistan; *CIA World Factbook*, https://www.cia.gov/library/publications/the-world-factbook/index.html.

117. Fraser, "Allah's Realm," 213.

118. Olivier Roy, "Mujahidin and Afghanistan," 194–7.

119. Rubin, *Fragmentation of Afghanistan*, 248–9.

120. Rubin, *Fragmentation of Afghanistan*, 196–9.

121. Vali R. Nasr, "International Politics, Domestic Imperatives, and Identity Mobilization: Sectarianism in Pakistan, 1979–1998," *Comparative Politics* 32 (2000), 178.

122. Roy, *Globalised Islam*, 13.

123. Robert M. Gates, *From the Shadows: The Ultimate Insider's Story of Five Presidents and How They Won the Cold War* (New York: Touchstone, 1996), 143–4.

124. Kepel, *Jihad*, 255–6.

125. Kepel, *Jihad*, 159–76, 254–75.

126. "Sudan," *World Factbook* (Washington, DC: Central Intelligence Agency); https://www.cia.gov/library/pulications/the-world-factbook/geos/su.html #People.

127. Kepel, *Jihad*, 176–84.

128. Millard Burr and Robert O. Collins, *Revolutionary Sudan: Hasan al-Turabi and the Islamist State, 1989–2000* (Boston: Brill, 2003), 57–63.

129. Esposito, "Iranian Revolution," 36–8.

130. John F. Burns, "Islamic Rebels Renew a Siege to Win Kabul," *New York Times* (October 16, 1995), A11.

131. Ahmed Rashid, *Jihad: The Rise of Militant Islam in Central Asia* (New Haven, CT: Yale University Press, 2002), 5–10.

132. Rashid, *Jihad*, 102.

133. Rashid, *Jihad*, 91; idem, "Austere Beginning: Taliban's Fundamentalist Crackdown Endangers Aid," *Far Eastern Economic Review* (October 17, 1996), 19.

134. John F. Burns, "Afghanistan's New Rulers Soft-Pedal Their Hard Line," *New York Times* (October 2, 1996), A3.

135. Rashid, *Jihad*, 19.

136. John F. Burns, "2 Afghan Factions Sign Pact to Fight New Kabul Rulers," *New York Times* (October 11, 1996), A1.

137. Kamal Matinuddin, *The Taliban Phenomenon: Afghanistan 1994–1997* (Karachi: Oxford University Press, 1999), 154.

138. John F. Burns, "Pakistan Shifting Stance on Hard-Line Afghans," *New York Times* (March 27, 1996), A11.

139. Nasr, "International Politics," 179.

140. Islamists often refer to Westerners as polytheists owing to the Christian doctrine of the Trinity, which asserts that God exists in three equal persons—Father, Son, and Holy Spirit.

141. Lawrence Wright, *The Looming Tower: Al-Qaeda and the Road to 9/11* (New York: Knopf, 2006), 156–8.

142. Gerges, *Far Enemy*, 30–31.

143. Burr and Collins, *Revolutionary Sudan*, 69–71; Wright, *Looming Tower*, 164–5.

144. Wright, *Looming Tower*, 220–21.

145. Burr and Collins, *Revolutionary Sudan*, 216–18.

146. "Bin Laden's Fatwa," Online Newshour, Public Broadcasting Network; http://www.pbs.org/newshour/terrorism/international/fatwa_1996.html.

147. Wright, *Looming Tower*, 287–9.

148. Gerges, *Far Enemy*, 119–77.

149. David Thaler, "The Middle East: The Cradle of the Muslim World," in Angel M. Rabasa et al., eds., *The Muslim World after 9/11* (Santa Monica, CA: RAND, 2004), 125–7.

150. "Afghan on Trial for Christianity," BBC News (March 20, 2006); http://news.bbc.co.uk/2/hi/south_asia/4823874.stm, accessed on June 28, 2009.

151. The Afghan Constitution is available at http://www.jemb.org/eng/legislation.html. On the difficulty of promoting liberal regimes in certain countries, see Valerie Bunce, "Promoting Democracy in Divided Societies," *Review of International Affairs* (Serbia) 61/62, no. 1120 (October 2005/March 2006), 32–8.

152. Full text at http://thomas.loc.gov/cgi-bin/query/z?c105:H.R.4655.ENR:.

153. Peter J. Boyer, "The Believer," *New Yorker* (November 1, 2004); http://www.newyorker.com/archive/2004/11/01/041101fa_fact?currentPage=all.

154. The letter was from the Project for a New American Century. Full text is available at http://www.newamericancentury.org/iraqclintonletter.htm.

155. Cf. Nasr, *Shia Revival*, 85–6.

156. Jane Mayer, "The Manipulator," *New Yorker* (June 7, 2004); http://www.newyorker.com/archive/2004/06/07/040607fa_fact1.

157. Thaler, "Middle East," 131–5.

CHAPTER 8
THE FUTURE OF FORCIBLE REGIME PROMOTION

1. For a similar stance toward the "logics" question as it applies to early modern Europe, see Daniel Nexon, *The Struggle for Power in Early Modern Europe: Religious Conflict, Dynastic Empires, and Political Change* (Princeton, NJ: Princeton University Press, 2009). To reiterate: many constructivists do not insist that agents act according to a logic of appropriateness.

2. Karl Brandi, *The Emperor Charles V: The Growth and Destiny of a Man and of a World-Empire*, trans. C. V. Wedgwood (London: Jonathan Cape, 1939), 501.

3. For a justification of U.S. support for anti-communist authoritarians, see Jeanne Kirkpatrick, "Dictatorships and Double Standards," *Commentary* 68:5 (November 1979) 34–45.

4. Claus-Peter Clausen, *The Palatinate in European History 1555–1618* (Oxford: Basil Blackwell, 1963).

5. Stephen Jay Gould, *Punctuated Equilibrium* (Cambridge: Belknap Press, 2007). For another application to international relations, see J. Samuel Barkin and Bruce Cronin, "The State and the Nation: Changing Norms and the Rules of Sovereignty in International Relations," *International Organization* 48 (1994), 107–30.

6. James D. Fearon and Alexander Wendt, "Rationalism *v.* Constructivism: A Skeptical View," in Walter Carlsnaes et al., eds., *Handbook of International Relations* (Beverly Hills, CA: SAGE, 2002), 52–72.

7. James D. Fearon, "Rationalist Explanations for War," *International Organization* 49, no. 3 (Summer 1995), 379–414.

8. James D. Fearon, "Domestic Political Audiences and the Escalation of Disputes," *American Political Science Review* 88, no. 3 (September 1994), 577–92.

9. Alexander Wendt, *Social Theory of International Politics* (New York: Cambridge University Press, 1999), esp. chap. 4.

10. Randolph M. Siverson and Julian Emmons, "Birds of a Feather: Democratic Political Systems and Alliance Choices in the Twentieth Century," *Journal of Conflict Resolution* 35 (1991), 285–306; William R. Thompson and Richard Tucker, "A Tale of Two Democratic Peace Critiques," *Journal of Conflict Resolution* 41 (1997), 428–54.

11. Brian Lai and Dan Reiter, "Democracy, Political Similarity, and International Alliances, 1816–1992," *Journal of Conflict Resolution* 44 (2000), 203–27.

12. Suzanne Werner and Douglas Lemke, "Opposites Do Not Attract: The Impact of Domestic Institutions, Power, and Prior Commitments on Alignment Choices," *International Studies Quarterly* 41 (1997), 529–46.

13. Randolph M. Siverson and Harvey Starr, "Regime Change and the Restructuring of Alliances," *American Journal of Political Science* 38 (1994), 145–61.

14. E.g., Michael W. Simon and Eric Gartzke, "Political System Similarity and the Choice of Allies: Do Democracies Flock Together, or Do Opposites Attract?" *Journal of Conflict Resolution* 40 (1996), 617–35.

15. Stephen Walt, *The Origins of Alliances* (Ithaca, NY: Cornell University Press, 1987); Steven David, *Choosing Sides: Alignment and Realignment in the Third World* (Baltimore, MD: Johns Hopkins University Press, 1991).

16. Mark L. Haas, *The Ideological Origins of Great Power Politics, 1789–1989* (Ithaca, NY: Cornell University Press, 2005); F. Gregory Gause, III, "Balancing What? Threat Perception and Alliance Choice in the Gulf," *Security Studies* 13 (2003/04), 273–305.

17. For more, see John M. Owen, IV, "When Do Ideologies Produce Alliances? The Holy Roman Empire, 1517–55," *International Studies Quarterly* 49 (2005), 73–99.

18. Demonstration effects are one of Haas's three mechanisms by which ideologies can cause alliances. Haas, *Ideological Origins*.

19. Stephen M. Walt ascribes more importance to ideology as a cause of war in *Revolution and War* (Ithaca, NY: Cornell University Press, 1996). I am extending some of the dynamics Walt identifies—fears of revolutionary contagion and temptations to spread ideology, both of which make war more likely—over many decades. Walt confines these dynamics to periods of major revolution (the French or Russian revolution), but does not compare these periods to more "normal" periods. By selecting on the independent variable, Walt misses that these revolutions inaugurated a long transnational struggle over the best regime, such that the dynamics reappeared time and again.

20. Sidney Tarrow, "Transnational Politics: Contention and Institutions in International Politics," *Annual Review of Political Science*, vol. 4 (2001), 1–20.

21. John Herz, "Idealist Internationalism and the Security Dilemma," *World Politics* 2 (1950), 157–80; Robert Jervis, "Cooperation under the Security Dilemma," *World Politics* 30 (1978), 167–214.

22. Robert Jervis, *System Effects* (Ithaca, NY: Cornell University Press, 1997).

23. G. John Ikenberry, *After Victory: Institutions, Strategic Restraint, and the Rebuilding of Order after Major Wars* (Princeton, NJ: Princeton University Press, 2001).

24. Francis Fukuyama, *The End of History and the Last Man* (New York: Free Press, 1992).

25. "Hugo Chávez," *Times Topics* (*New York Times*), updated March 17, 2009 http://topics.nytimes.com/top/reference/timestopics/people/c/hugo_Chávez/index .html, accessed on June 13, 2009.

26. Sara Miller Llana, "Leftwing Activists Flock to Venezuela to Soak Up the Socialist 'Revolution'," *Christian Science Monitor* (March 25, 2008), p. 20.

27. Joshua Partlow, "Latin America's Document-Driven Revolutions," *Washington Post* (February 17, 2009), p. A1. Viciano is at the Centro de Estudios Políticos y Sociales (http://www.ceps.es/).

28. David Usborne, "Armed Revolution in Latin America Is Over, Says Chávez," *Independent* (London) (June 10, 2008), p. 18.

29. Partlow, "Document-Driven Revolutions."

30. Simon Romero, "President Wins Support for Charter in Ecuador," *New York Times* (September 28, 2008); http://www.nytimes.com/2008/09/29/world/americas/29ecuador.html?_r=3, accessed on June 12, 2009.

31. Matthew Taylor, "Evo Morales Hails 'New Bolivia' as Constitution Is Approved," *Guardian* (Manchester, England) (January 26, 2009); http://www.guardian.co.uk/world/2009/jan/26/bolivia, accessed on June 12, 2009.

32. In 2002, Chávez blamed the Bush administration for a failed coup d'état against his government. "Hugo Chávez," *Times Topics.*

33. Robert Kagan, "End of Dreams, Return of History," *Policy Review* (August–September 2007); idem, *The Return of History and the End of Dreams* (New York: Knopf, 2008).

34. "China 2008," Freedom House, http://www.freedomhouse.org/template.cfm?page=363&year=2008, accessed on June 15, 2009.

35. Michael A. McFaul and Kathryn Stoner-Weiss, "The Myth of the Authoritarian Model: How Putin's Crackdown Holds Russia Back," *Foreign Affairs* (January-February 2008), 68–84.

36. Many projections have been done, with widely varying results under widely varying assumptions, but the consensus seems to converge around the second quarter of the twenty-first century; see, e.g., Albert Keidel, "China's Economic Rise—Fact and Fiction," *Policy Brief* 61 (July 2008), Carnegie Endowment for International Peace, http://www.carnegieendowment.org/files/pb61_keidel_final.pdf.

37. McFaul and Stoner-Weiss, "Myth of the Authoritarian Model."

38. Thomas Ambrosio, *Authoritarian Backlash: Russian Resistance to Democratization in the Former Soviet Union* (Burlington, VT: Ashgate, 2009), 3.

39. McFaul and Stoner-Weiss, "Myth of the Authoritarian Model."

40. But there is evidence that some Russian elites view China's as a model regime. See Clifford J. Levy, "Russia's Leaders See China as Template for Ruling," *New York Times* (October 17, 2009), p. A8, http://www.nytimes.com/2009/10/18/world/europe/18russia.html?_r=1.

41. James Davison Hunter and Joshua Yates, "In the Vanguard of Globalization: The World of American Globalizers," in Peter L. Berger and Samuel P. Huntington, eds., *Many Globalizations: Cultural Diversity in the Contemporary World* (New York: Oxford University Press, 2007), 323–58.

42. Mark R. Beissinger, "Structure and Example in Modular Political Phenomena: The Diffusion of Bulldozer/Rose/Orange/Tulip Revolutions," *Perspectives on Politics* 5 (2007), 259–76. On Ukraine in particular, see Michael McFaul, "Ukraine Imports Democracy: External Influences on the Orange Revolution," *International Security* 32:2 (2007), 45–83; and Oleksandr Sushko

and Olena Prystayko, "Western Influence," in Anders Åslund and Michael Mc-Faul, eds., *Revolution in Orange: The Origins of Ukraine's Democratic Breakthrough* (Washington, DC: Carnegie Endowment for International Peace, 2006), 125–44.

43. Robert E. Hamilton, "Russia's Strategy in the War against Georgia," *Strategic Questions*, Center for Strategic and International Studies, August 14, 2008, http://www.csis.org/media/csis/pubs/080814_cq_hamilton_russia.pdf.

44. Joshua A. Tucker, "Enough! Electoral Fraud, Collective Action Problems, and Post-Communist Colored Revolutions," *Perspectives on Politics* 5 (September 2007), 535–51.

45. The same might be said of the unrest in Iran following the elections in June 2009. At the time of this writing, the dispute was over voting fraud within the extant regime rather than regime change.

46. Ellen Barry, "Russia Is Weighing 2 Latin Bases, General Says," *New York Times* (March 15, 2009), p. 12.

47. Ann Coulter, "This Is War," *National Review Online* (September 13, 2001), http://www.nationalreview.com/coulter/coulter.shtml.

48. E.g., Norman Podhoretz, *World War IV: The Long Struggle against Islamofascism* (New York: Doubleday, 2007); and Michael A. Ledeen, *The Iranian Time Bomb: The Mullah Zealots' Quest for Destruction* (New York: St. Martin's Press, 2007). Ledeen argues that Iran's Islamist regime can be ousted without the use of force.

49. Daniel Pipes, *Militant Islam Reaches America* (New York: W. W. Norton, 2003), esp. 38–51.

50. Robin Wright, "Iran's President Foresees 'Long Warfare' Next Door," *Los Angeles Times* (November 13, 2001); http://articles.latimes.com/2001/nov/13/news/mn-3573, accessed June 16, 2009. Iran, Russia, and India had helped create the Northern Alliance that U.S. forces later aided.

51. Edward W. Said, "The Clash of Ignorance," *The Nation* (October 22, 2001); http://www.thenation.com/doc/20011022/said. See also idem, *Covering Islam: How the Media and the Experts Determine How We See the Rest of the World* (New York: Vintage, 1997).

52. Fred Halliday, *Islam and the Myth of Confrontation*, 2nd ed. (London: I. B. Tauris, 2003), 124. Note the quotation marks around "Muslim' but not around "non-Muslim."

53. John Esposito, *The Islamic Threat: Myth or Reality?* 3rd ed. (New York: Oxford University Press, 1999), 218.

54. Robert S. Leiken and Steven Brooke, "The Moderate Muslim Brotherhood," *Foreign Affairs* (March / April 2007), 107–21.

55. Ray Takeyh, "Time for Détente with Iran," *Foreign Affairs* (March / April 2007), 17–32.

56. Quoted in Ahmed Rashid, *Jihad: The Rise of Militant Islam in Central Asia* (New Haven, CT: Yale University Press, 2002), 109.

57. David Corn, "Finally, a Not-so-bad Bush Doctrine: Poverty Breeds Terrorism," *The Nation* Blog (March 25, 2002); http://www.thenation.com/blogs/capitalgames?pid=39.

58. Halliday, *Myth*, 128, italics mine.

59. Said, "Clash of Ignorance," italics mine.

60. "Iran Seeking Nuclear Weapons Technology: El Baradei," Reuters (June 16, 2009); http://www.reuters.com/article/email/idUSTRE55G21V20090617, accessed on June 16, 2009.

61. E.g., Olivier Roy, ed., *Turkey Today: A Modern European Nation?* (London: Anthem Press, 2005). The same may be true of Islamists in Indonesia; see "Where 'Soft Islam' Is on the March," *Economist* (January 10, 2008).

62. Beken Saatcioglu, "How Does the European Union's Political Conditionality Induce Compliance? Insights from Turkey and Romania," Ph.D. Dissertation, University of Virginia, June 2009.

63. Andrew Higgins and Farnaz Fassihi, "Muslim Land Joins Rank of Tigers," *Wall Street Journal* (August 6, 2008); http://online.wsj.com/article/SB12 1798369220315407.html, accessed on June 17, 2009.

64. Saatcioglu, "European Union's Political Conditionality," chap. 5.

65. Abdulaziz Sachedina, *The Islamic Roots of Democratic Pluralism* (New York: Oxford University Press, 2001); idem, "Reason and Revelation in Islamic Political Ethics," in John M. Owen, IV, and J. Judd Owen, eds., *Religion, the Enlightenment, and the New Global Order* (New York: Columbia University Press, 2010).

66. Abdolkarim Soroush, *Reason, Freedom, and Democracy in Islam: Essential Writings of Abdolkarim Soroush*, ed. and trans. Mahmoud Sadri and Ahmad Sadri (New York: Oxford University Press, 2000).

67. Khaled Abou El Fadl, *The Place of Tolerance in Islam* (Boston: Beacon, 2002); idem, *Islam and the Challenge of Democracy* (Princeton, NJ: Princeton University Press, 2004).

68. Sohail H. Hashmi, "Islam, Constitutionalism, and Liberal Democracy," in Owen and Owen, eds., *Religion, the Enlightenment*.

69. See, e.g., http://www.drsoroush.com/index.htm.

70. Marc Hujer and Daniel Steinvorth, "A Lesson for Europe: American Muslims Strive to Become Model Citizens," *Spiegel Online International* (September 13, 2007); http://www.spiegel.de/international/world/0,1518,505573,00.html.

71. Kepel, *Jihad*, 375–76.

72. Rami G. Khouri, "Islamist Wind Blows Ever Stronger in Middle East," *Daily Star* (Beirut), July 23, 2005.

Appendix

1. This is a modified version of the data appendix in John M. Owen, IV, "The Foreign Imposition of Domestic Institutions," *International Organization* (Spring 2002), 375–410.

2. Stephen D. Krasner, *Sovereignty: Organized Hypocrisy* (Princeton, NJ: Princeton University Press, 1999).

3. Daniel Nexon, *The Struggle for Power in Early Modern Europe: Religious Conflict, Dynastic Empires, and Political Change* (Princeton, NJ: Princeton University Press, 2009), 55, 82. Nexon refers to my "When Do Ideologies Produce

Alliances? The Holy Roman Empire, 1517–55," *International Studies Quarterly* 49 (2005), 73–99.

4. Martin Wight, *Power Politics* (London: Continuum, 1977), 130.

5. James Tracy, *Emperor Charles V, Impresario of War* (New York: Cambridge University Press, 2002), 22.

6. M. J. Rodríguez-Salgado, *The Changing Face of Empire: Charles V, Philip II and Habsburg Authority, 1551–1559* (New York: Cambridge University Press, 1988), 20.

7. F.R.H. Du Boulay, *Germany in the Later Middle Ages* (London: Athlone Press, 1983), 23–4, 125; Joachim Leuschner, *Germany in the Late Middle Ages*, trans. Sabine MacCormack (New York: North-Holland, 1980), 29–34, 56–7.

8. William Stubbs, *Germany in the Later Middle Ages, 1200–1500*, vol. 2 (New York: Howard Fertig [1908/1969]), 130–32.

9. Michael Broers, *Europe under Napoleon 1799–1815* (London: Arnold, 1996).

10. Raphäel Lemkin, *Axis Rule in Occupied Europe* (Washington, DC: Carnegie Endowment for International Peace, 1944), 12–13.

11. Krasner, *Sovereignty*, chapters 6 and 7, analyzes a number of cases in which great powers coerced new states in the nineteenth and twentieth centuries to adopt particular institutions without directly applying violence.

# Index

PRINCETON STUDIES IN INTERNATIONAL
HISTORY AND POLITICS

SERIES EDITORS

G. John Ikenberry and Marc Trachtenberg

RECENT TITLES

*Driving the Soviets up the Wall: Soviet-East German Relations, 1953–1961*
by Hope M. Harrison

*Legitimacy and Power Politics: The American and French Revolutions in International Political Culture*
by Mlada Bukovansky

*Rhetoric and Reality in Air Warfare: The Evolution of British and American Ideas about Strategic Bombing, 1914-1945*
by Tami Davis Biddle

*Revolutions in Sovereignty: How Ideas Shaped Modern International Relations*
by Daniel Philpott

*After Victory: Institutions, Strategic Restraint, and the Rebuilding of Order after Major Wars*
by G. John Ikenberry

*Stay the Hand of Vengeance: The Politics of War Crimes Tribunals*
by Gary Jonathan Bass

*War and Punishment: The Causes of War Termination and the First World War*
by H. E. Goemans

*In the Shadow of the Garrison State: America's Anti-Statism and Its Cold War Grand Strategy*
by Aaron L. Friedberg

*States and Power in Africa: Comparative Lessons in Authority and Control*
by Jeffrey Herbst

*The Moral Purpose of the State: Culture, Social Identity, and Institutional Rationality in International Relations*
by Christian Reus-Smit